AFRICA IN THE CONTEMPORARY INTERNATIONAL DISORDER

Crises and Possibilities

Mulugeta Agonafer

University Press of America, Inc.
Lanham • New York • London

Copyright © 1996 by
University Press of America,® Inc.
4720 Boston Way
Lanham, Maryland 20706

3 Henrietta Street
London, WC2E 8LU England

Library of Congress Cataloging-in-Publication Data

Agonafer, Mulugeta
Africa in the contemporary international disorder : crises and
possibilities / Mulugeta Agonafer.
p.   cm.
Includes bibliographical references and index.
1. Africa, Sub-Saharan--Politics and government--1960- 2. Africa,
Sub-Saharan--Economic conditions--1960- 3. Africa, Sub-Saharan--
Foreign relations--1960- I. Title.
DT30.5.A376   1996   967.03'29--dc20   95-26706 CIP

ISBN 0-7618-0252-5 (cloth: alk. ppr.)

DEDICATION

**To the millions of innocent Africans who
have fallen victims of ethnic cleansing!**

CONTENTS

PART I. AFRICA IN THE NEW INTERNATIONAL ORDER/DISORDER

PART II. HUMAN RIGHTS AND U.S. FOREIGN POLICY TOWARDS
     AFRICA

PART V. POLITICAL DEVELOPMENT OR MALDEVELOPMENT?

FOREWORD*

Guests and Springfield College colleagues attending this conference today, I bring you greetings from the entire Springfield College family. The topic you have chosen to address is of special interest to me. Starting nearly 30 years ago, each summer for about 15 years, I would catch the 7 p.m. Pan Am flight from Kennedy Airport in New York and land early the next morning at the airport located near Dakar, Senegal. My assignment was to meet with both government officials and, where applicable, private industry parties to discuss the exploration for and development of ferrous and non-ferrous mineral deposits. A few days later, I would continue traveling along the West African coastline spending several days each in Freetown, Sierra Leone; Monrovia, Liberia; Abijdian, Ivory coast; Accra, Ghana; Lagos, Nigeria; Douala, Republic of the Cameroons; Kinshasa, Zaire; and finally, Luanda, Republic of Angola. I planned and supervised airborne magnetometer and radiometric surveys in Liberia and assisted in interpreting similar surveys in Sierra Leone and Nigeria. I have examined nickel deposits near Sassandra in the Ivory Coast; quartz reef gold deposits near Kumasi, Ghana; tin deposits on the Jos Plateau in Nigeria; and the huge copper carbonate deposits in Zaire and iron ore in Liberia. I have studied the potentially economic copper and cobalt deposits in southeastern Sudan, southwestern Ethiopia and in the Eritrea Province along the Red Sea in northern Ethiopia. In South Africa, I have visited the diamond fields in Namibia Desert, the western deep gold mines near Johannesburg, the platinum deposits associated with the Bushveld Complex at Rustenburg, and a potential uranium deposit on the vast Karoo Plateau near Beaufort West. I am currently advising a U. S. petroleum company on oil prospects in the Chad basin and offshore Angola. A few years ago, I was a consultant on hydrocarbon deposits in Algeria, Lybia, Egypt, Saudi Arabia and Yemen. Finally, I assisted in re-organizing the university geology and mining programs at Bukavu, Lumbumbashi, and Kinshasa, Zaire, and helped develop ground-water programs in Syria, Jordan, and Mauritania.

While traveling to and from these areas, I visited several other African countries including Mali, Niger, Uganda, Kenya, Somalia, Zambia, Zimbabwe, Botswana, Mozambique, and Malawi.

Please allow me to digress slightly here at Malawi since, while somewhat amusing, it reveals a serious problem still existing in many areas of the African continent. President Banda of Malawi had invited me to provide advice to him and his government on a possible copper deposit in Malawi. Although my general knowledge of African geology and the known lack of infra-structure support suggested to me that the likelihood of an economically viable copper deposit in Malawi was very doubtful, I agreed to go, since at the time President Banda and the Malawi Embassy in Washington were very insistent. To make me feel slightly better, I combined my visit with a couple of lectures at the Geological Survey located at Zomba. I then left my wife and two younger children in Nairobi and flew to Blantyre. Following a visit with President Banda, my lectures at the geological survey in Zomba, and two very pleasant days on the lovely sand beach at Lake Malawi, I gathered up my aerial photographs and my stereo plotter and I was flown east to where we landed on the top of a flat-topped mountain near the Malawi border with Mozambique. My visual inspection of the rocks verified that it was what is referred to in the profession as a moderate size porphry-copper deposit, however, it was located in difficult mountainous terrain without access roads, located more than 200 miles west of the shoreline of the Indian Ocean in Mozambique and three hundred miles across undeveloped country east of the southwest to Harare, Zimbabwe. Knowing that this would be a very disappointing message to relate to President Banda, although it was not disappointing to the Malawi geologist at Zomba, I decided I would provide the President with a preliminary geological map outlining the copper deposit. So, using the aerial photographs and the stereo plotter, I began constructing a schematic topographic base map and, finally, in order to place the map into a rough geographical coordinate system, I sketched the border between Malawi and Mozambique. Much to my surprise, based on my calculations, President Banda's non-economic copper deposit was a few miles inside Mozambique. Although the incident was amusing, due to inadequate geographic data bases, it is still a rather prevalent occurrence throughout many parts of the African continent.

The primary reason that I traced my personal and professional experiences on the African continent to you today was not simply to provide you with a travelogue, but to indicate to you the extremely complex, vast, and relatively unmapped and untapped mineral and hydrocarbon resources of this very large continent. I also advised you that despite years of exploitive efforts by the European colonialists, much remains to be explored, discovered, and exploited using new and sophisticated exploration technology and long-term systematic geological mapping programs. These programs could be initiated by first returning to the African countries, the extensive geological and mining data-bases now located in many European countries namely Brussels, Belgium; London, England; and Lisbon, Portugal. Using recent and current satellite data, a systematic topographic mapping program at a usable geographic base map scale should be planned and implemented. Resource deposits are useless if you do not know precisely where they are geographically located.

A continent-wide comprehensive road, railroad, and pipeline transportation infrastructure within and between countries should be carefully planned and built over the next century. Again, resource deposits are useless if you cannot transport them from mines or well-heads to the mills, refineries, or the shipping ports. A broad regional surface and groundwater mapping program is of critical importance and should be very quickly developed across country boundaries in order to greatly expand farming and cattle-raising and to, most importantly, mitigate the devastating effects of the cyclical droughts and desertification very common to the African continent and, for that matter, parts of most other continents.

Finally, an international technology transfer program should be developed as rapidly as possible to address the requirements of all of the previously described economic resource and infrastructure programs. I know that to plan and develop these constructive programs will cost a considerable amount of money; however, the billions of dollars worth of destructive armament, tanks, war planes, guns, and ammunition that has been poured into Africa over the last three decades would have constituted a substantial down payment on these proposed constructive programs. In fact, the other nations of the world will, in the longer term, also reap the benefits of a modern, productive, and economically sound African continent.

Three decades ago, President Kwame Nkrumah of the Republic of Ghana said, "If Africa's multiple resources were used in her own development, they could place her among the modernized continents of the world. But, her resources have been, and still are, being used for the greater development of overseas interests" and "Africa is still paramountly an uncharted continent economically."

Twenty years earlier, nearly a half century ago, at the end of World War II, Dr. W. E. B. Du Bois proposed a book entitled "The Africas." In his letter to the publisher, Dr. Du Bois wrote:

Gentlemen:

I have in mind a book along the following lines: title to be "The Africa" emphasizing the fact that Africa is not one country, one group or one race but a conglomerate of peoples with various degrees of importance and possibilities who are going to play roles in the post-war world.

The book will be a study of the condition of the various African nations, colonies and groups at the time of the first World War, since that war, during the present war, with a forecast of what is going to happen in Africa after the war.

I want to emphasize that fact merely because news from Africa is not broadcast, this does not mean that important developments are not taking place. The people of Africa are normal human beings with all possibilities for development. Their country is extraordinary for its climate and possibilities and the geography of Africa places it today in the midst of world events.

I think that a small book of one hundred and fifty or two hundred pages on this subject might attract readers. I should be glad to know what you think of the proposition.

Signed,
W. E. B. Du Bois

Both of these world giants were well aware of the crisis and possibilities of the African continent and chose to focus their attention on the possibilities, although fully cognizant of the disorder and crisis. Finally, President Julius K. Nyerere, over three decades ago, in his independence message to the Tangyanika African National Union (TANU) said: "We have been talking for a long time about what sort of house we want to build on this land. Now we have the chance to do it. We have agreed on certain basic principles; now is the time to put these principles into operation. We have based our struggle on our belief in the equality and dignity of all mankind and on the Declaration of Human Rights. We have agreed that out nation shall be a nation of free and equal citizens, each person having equal right and opportunity to develop himself, and contribute to the maximum of his capabilities to the development of our society. We have said that neither race nor tribe nor religion nor cleverness, nor anything else, could take away from a man his own rights as an equal member of society. This is what we have now to put into practice."

I hope the efforts of this conference would focus on the possibilities for the combined countries, the United Republics of Africa, the theme that I hope

I have conveyed to you in my remarks today. Good luck, and thanks for bringing these critically important issues to Springfield College, a campus that for more than a century has followed its mission of "humanitarian service to others" on an international scale.

NOTE*

Keynote speech presented by Dr. Randolph W. Bromery, President of Springfield College at the First Annual Conference, organized by African, African-American, Development, Education, Research, and Training Institute (AADERT), at Springfield College on 3 December, 1993.

PREFACE

The purpose of this volume is to publish within a single set of covers recent analyses of major political and economic developments in the continent's domestic and international operation. As Africa moves into the 21st century, it is imperative that information about the continent's political economic condition be presented to students of Africa in the developed world in a fair and objective fashion. A comprehensive and objective understanding and discussion of the successes and failures is the only way that an appropriate African-oriented American foreign policy can emerge. Despite the ending of the Cold War and the breaking up of the Soviet Union, such discussions are not taking place today.

Still, the day-to-day quality of life experienced by Africans is directly affected by domestic problems such as poverty, crime, homelessness, inadequate health care, discrimination against women and ethnic minorities, and the many facets of deterioration in African cities. These problems are still pressing.

Most of the articles in this collection have been compiled from papers presented during the first and second Conferences on Africa held at Springfield College, in the falls of 1993 and 1994, as they were originally presented. I hope that this publication will enlighten the ongoing debate on African development policy problems and solutions. The high level of analysis is typical of the articles appearing in the various African Journals, both on a wide range of domestic political processes and policy problems, and on subjects of foreign and military policy. In addition to policy makers, this volume will be very useful for Africanists teaching graduate courses in African studies.

This book is published by the University Press of America. Since its inception, the University Press of America, to my knowledge, has endeavored to make the knowledge of experts available to policy makers and to the wide audience among the general public who are interested in serious discussion of the most significant issues facing our plant. I thank them for that.

I wish to thank the authors of the articles in this collection for giving me permission to print them in this volume. I am especially grateful to Dr. Randolph W. Bromery, President of Springfield College, for allowing us to include his keynote speech as the Foreword to the volume. My special thanks also goes to my good friend and colleague, Dr. Dan Russel, Professor of Political Science, for his collaboration in putting the 1993 and 1994 Conferences together. Whether they realize it or not, the following people have also contributed immensely t the success of the two Conferences: John Wilson, Ken Wall, Verne McArthur, Bobbie Harro, JoAnne Jones, Joe Wronka, Ann Roy, Dan Nussbam, Clifton Bush, Wosene Yefru, Frank Holmquist, Pat True, and Rene Newkirk. Rene did a superb job of putting together the brochures for the two conferences. I am grateful to Ms. Susan Engelbrecht, who prepared the draft of the manuscript to be camera-ready with her customary efficiency. I cannot begin to explain how amazed I am that she was able to work on this manuscript in the face of tragedy after tragedy. She is indeed a courageous woman. Finally, I wish to express my thanks to all my colleagues, faculty, staff, and administrators for making the environment in the School of Human Services conducive to work. I want to especially thank the School of Human Services for partially funding the project.

The opinions expressed in this volume are those of the individual authors and not necessarily those of the sponsors, nor of the African and African-American Development, Education, Research, and Training Institute (AADERT), which takes no position on subjects it presents for public discussion.

Mulugeta Agonafer
Springfield, MA
September, 1995

PART I

AFRICA IN THE NEW INTERNATIONAL ORDER/DISORDER

"...the ideas of economists and political philosophers, both when they are right and when they are wrong, are more powerful than is commonly understood. Indeed, the world is ruled by little else. Practical men, who believe themselves to be quite exempt from any intellectual influences, are usually the slaves of some defunct economist. Madmen in authority, who hear voices in the air, are distilling their frenzy from some academic scribbler of a few years back. I am sure that the power of vested interests is vastly exaggerated compared with the gradual encroachment of ideas."

JOHN MAYNARD KEYNES

INTRODUCTION

AFRICA IN THE CONTEMPORARY WORLD ORDER:
CRISES AND POSSIBILITIES

Mulugeta Agonafer

The demise of the cold war was so dramatic, so sudden, so unexpected that it left many African Countries groping in the dark for economic development and democratic guidance. We decided to hold a conference and publish the proceedings in an attempt to seek explanation for the current economic and political chaos in Africa, and to seek relief from the sense of anger, impotence, and frustration caused by what some of us call "maldevelopment". For years, a thread of optimism -- even wishful thinking - has run through much of western writings and thinking about development in Africa. Suddenly the demise of the cold war snapped the thread and it became clear that the dissenting minority, those who had doubted the reality and durability of Africa's supposed development and political reforms, had possessed the clearer vision. Some of those dissenters are among the contributors to this volume. The currenthunger, civil (ethnic) war that is sweeping Africa made it vital that this Post-Cold war thinking should be quickly brought together in a wide-ranging assessment of how matters now stand with Africa.

The title of this book was inspired by the Reagan-Bush administration's claim to having initiated the "New World Order". Africans have been calling for a "New International Order" long before their presidency and for at least two decades now. With the demise of the Soviet system a new "Theater of Operation" had to be invented and Africa seemed to provide that fertile ground, in contradistinction to what Lt. Commander Finn's piece seem to imply.

It is tempting to believe that all problems have a solution and that in the long run, things will get better. This deeply rooted idea of the inevitability of continuous progress stands as a barrier to understanding Africa. Another barrier is the related assumption that as Africa progresses it will become more like the West. The west looks at Africa and sees not what is but a mirror image of its own hopes, dreams and nightmares as it reflects back and relates its own relations with its own diverse population of various descent.

Ever since the demise of the communist system and with it the end of support for many communist African countries by the former Soviet Union, Africa has played unerringly to this western weakness. The West had high hopes, failing to realize that any system (communist or capitalist) that fails to take the indigenous societies culture into account is inherently incapable of reform. International experience suggests that overcoming economic problems must start with the institutionalization of the rule of law, and the respect for human rights -- a necessary but far from sufficient condition for economic progress.

What emerges from this collection of papers is a broadly shared "optimistic skepticism" about many of the "democratic achievements" of Africa's recent past and a deep pessimism for some, and a serious concern coupled with guarded optimism for many, about its future. (There are, of course different shades of light to both pessimism and optimism.) Foreign imposed "isms" in Africa may be doomed from the start, but its legacy of ruin and social dislocation will remain for a generation to come. The present civil and political disorder in numerous African countries may be inevitable, but after three decades of economic mismanagement, poverty, and a population brutalized by three decades of relentless political terror, in most cases by some muddle headed mainly military and sometimes civilian dictators, worse horrors may follow. Indeed the recent political turmoil in Rwanda and the consequent tragic loss of over 200,000 innocent lives indicate, unless African leaders are careful, how all of Africa is on the brink of disaster.

One common illusion of the current political reform in Africa, including South Africa, is that Africa is not only successfully modernizing but that it is also going capitalist, democratic, and pluralist. As Mangaliso's piece on South Africa illustrates, the motives behind political reforms in Africa are incongruent to what the west claims. Consider also the case of Ethiopia. The state department's notion that Ethiopia is going our way, that the current leaders of Ethiopia believe in economic liberalization which in turn will necessarily lead to a democratized political system, reflected Western wishful thinking, not Ethiopia's reality. As the recent proliferation of opposition groups and fragmentation of the Ethiopian nation-state into various ethnic groups demonstrated, when the West is determined on a romantic view of Africa there is no limit to the amount of barbarism and anarchy that can be rationalized.

Africa's inability to live with the modern world is its enduring problem. This was as true in the 1960s -- the heyday of optimism -- as it is today. For the last three decades, Africa has sought (and imposed upon itself) Western technology without taking its own culture into consideration and failing to realize that societies which innovate and generate wealth do so mainly because they have rule of law, property rights, civil freedoms and the respect for human rights among others. In other words, I don't believe that modernization (where the basic needs of life for every citizen are taken care of) will ever come to Africa without a shift toward the universal values -- primarily, the respect for human rights -- which alone free the creative spirit. As intimated in Wronka's and Levi's paper, the validity of human rights does not depend on the particular culture involved. Every person on the surface of the earth should have these rights, regardless of where they live.

As an African who lives outside the African Continent, I find myself puzzled by this lack, since (unlike what others think of Africans) our sophistication, learning, and advancement in so many other areas is impressive. I sometimes ask myself whether the present moment will one day be characterized as a period when, as a society, (or as an intellectual project) we have preferred to avoid rather than to confront ourselves. Have we spent too much time defending against outsiders and not enough time examining our own reality? Have we accepted invented traditions and false portrayals of ourselves in preference to greater approximations to our complex but nevertheless fascinatingly problematic actuality? And, as supporters of both Pan Africanism and of African liberation have we simply failed to take advantage of the real historical opportunity to develop our continent, to free ourselves from the myths of the past, to take our place fully as a great nation among the other nations of the world? I hope not, but as time hurtles forward I wonder why we are still waiting to accept the cultural, economic political and moral challenge before us. My very limited point of view has not given me the answer to this question, so I ask it with anticipation and interest.

The authors in this volume recognize this and realize that without accepting those challenges any attempt at political and economic reform is meaningless. Readers should feel free to read the chapters in any order, although there is a loose logic to the arrangement. I hope this book will transmit the subject's inherent excitement and challenge.

Africa in The Contemporary International Disorder is divided in to five parts. In part I, I offer readings which examines pressing issues that confront Africa in the contemporary international order/disorder. In Chapter One, Mulugeta Agonafer highlights some of the economic problems Africa faces in the post-cold war era. He states, as Russia and its erstwhile East European allies abandon collectivist certitudes and slowly join the world market system, the prognosis for Africa is not encouraging. He argues that if the example of the current state of Eastern Europe is any yardstick to go by, then African countries will have to get used to stiff political conditions being imposed before they are able to attract foreign capital to flow, if at all. He asks, "what hope is there for African countries' future development in the emerging so called new International Order?"

In Chapter Two, James Mitchell asserts that the viability of the present new world order, providing a mandate for the expansion of pluralism globally, will be threatened if democracy appears to fall short of expectations. His inquiry starts with regime theory and its relationship to assertions of a new world order. Mitchell first considers African debt and the dilemma it poses for sustaining democracy in Africa. He then introduces, the task of answering the recent call for achieving sustainable development, as an additional obstacle to economic development. Examining the impact of these developments on sustaining democracy will be the final ingredient in the chapter. He argues that citizens, the final arbiters of this latest wave of democracy are looking to it to deliver them to a better quality of life. Among the standards that they will use when assessing government performance will be economic well being. The prevalence of debt, domestic as well as foreign, will mitigate the ability of these nations to achieve the self-sustained growth that will cement their legitimacy. The collapse of democracy in a few of these new nations can have a snowball effect imperiling pluralist movements elsewhere. The aggregate effect of these challenges to democracy, he concludes, might be the collapse of the entirety of the new world order.

In Chapter Three, Aloy Chife focuses on the changes that have taken place in the African economic arena and how this has improved the attractiveness of these economies. The specific emphasis is on emerging trends and prospects in its manifold political economy dynamics, namely, credit expansion, the creation of overhead capital, resource management and foreign private investments. At issue, according to Chife, is the continent's position and subsequent role in the contemporary international economic order. To that extent, our preoccupation with these issues, though not exclusive, is to allow us to determine how Africa can properly articulate its interests in a global context and fulfill its growth potentials and, subsequently, its development aspirations. To carry out these stated objectives properly, Chife isolates the economic changes that will largely define the nature of Africa's response to the challenge of competing in the international market economy and as such will constitute a dynamic force towards the growth of output and the realization of a beneficial interchange in its international economic relations.

In Chapter Four, Simeon Ilesanmi argues that many African countries are today stifled by a mixture of democratic political instability and pluralistic religious cosmologies. He argues that recent scholarly efforts to explore the basic theoretical grounding for an understanding of the relation of religion to political life have prescribed two contradictory solutions. On the one hand, there are those who predicate a sustainable economic development and political stability in Africa upon the withdrawal of religion from public life. Opposing this seemingly "neutral" conception of politics, others call for a complete sacralization of the polity with the fundamentalist precepts of religious ideologies. Finding both of these positions inadequate, Ilesanmi proposes the concept of dialogic politics which strips the state of hegemonic pretensions and limits religious institutions to mediating role within the public life. He concludes by saying that this position offers a corrective to those who deny any positive public role to religious values.

Part Two, provides with readings that revolve around general issues on Human Rights and U.S. foreign Policy Towards Africa. In Chapter Five, George White argues that American diplomacy toward Africa has deep roots which extend for at least a century and a half. Traditionally, U.S. diplomacy towards Africa reflects American treatment of its African population. Thus, the pertinent issue is not whether the U.S. has a policy toward Africa, but how such a policy, or for much of the time, non-policy, evolved in overlapping conjoining phases which are best understood in the context of American race relations. In Chapter Six, Joseph Wronka states that the United States has officially stated that invasion of a foreign land does not constitute a human rights violation. Given the changing dimension of human rights from the more commonly understood civil and political rights, like freedoms of speech, the press and religion, to the lesser understood economic, social and solidarity rights, like rights to shelter, health care, and international cooperation, Wronka questions the validity of that official posture. He argues that a human rights culture, which recognizes, among other things, the interdependency of all rights, the intimate relation between duties and a just social and international order, and the problem of "hidden agenda" in human rights work, may be a strategy to expand people's consciousness in regard to U.S. foreign policy, in particular toward Africa.

In Chapter Seven, Ojo Bamidele examines the historical contradictions in the United States foreign policy in Africa and the uncertainties of the New World Order impact on the attainment of the U.S. foreign policy goal -- Exporting Democracy therein. Using Africa as an example because of the euphoria surrounding the increased democratic activities on the continent on one hand and the preeminence of the promotion of human rights and democracy on the foreign policy agenda of the United States on the other, Ojo examines the implementation of such foreign policy goals in light of the uncertainties of the present international system.

In Chapter Eight, Antonia Levi presents a comparative historical analysis of how the current campaign against genital surgeries in Africa and the Middle East mirrors earlier Western campaigns against <u>Sati</u> (widow burning) in India and footbinding in China. It begins with an Orientalist analysis of why western cultures focus on such issues and then considers the impact, or lack of impact, such campaigns have on actual practices.

Part III looks at issues that concern U.S. and Russian Policy Towards Africa. In Chapter Nine, Yury Polsky examines Russia's foreign policy including an account of the Yeltsin administration's course toward Africa since January 1992 until the present time. Included in this chapter are: the Soviet Legacy in Africa, the differences between the current (Yeltsin's) course and the former Soviet stand, relations with radical and conservative African nations, Russia's positions in the current conflicts in Africa, and an emphasis on economic factors.

In Chapter Ten, LCDR Richard Finn reports on the process and product of Global War Game-93's Regional Action Plan for Africa. Finn states during Global War Game-1993 at the U.S Naval War College, the challenges presented by contemporary Africa to the security and economic well-being of the United States and its allies were explored. He describes how a working group composed of civilian and military personnel met to formulate a possible interagency approach to prevent and resolve potential crises within Africa and to define a coherent role for U.S Policy.

In Chapter Eleven, Donald Williams examines the recent development in Nigeria, where the process of political liberalization has not been consistantly supported by the international community. This can be attributed largely to the fact that agitation directed by elements in the indigenous democratic movement posed a threat to international economic interests present in the country. To be more specific, the multinational oil companies doing business in Nigeria were faced with losses attributable to unauthorized labor strikes designed to force the military government to accede to the demands of the pro-democracy forces.

Part IV examines issues that concern U.S.-South African relations. In Chapter Twelve, James Hentz suggests a comprhensive United States' foreign policy in the post-cold war era for southern Africa. He contends that current United State's Foreign policy is adrift, and its Africa policy, in particular, lacks direction. Consequently, the old foreign policy, which, for a long time was informed by a strategy of containment, should be replaced.

In Chapter Thirteen, Richard Cummings, makes an incisive and interesting analysis of the current South African behind the scene political manuevering and power politics. He explains, in some detail, "the survival of Chief Mangosuthu Buthelezi and F.W. deKlerk and how the African National Congress ended up on the United States payroll." Cummings uncovers, behind the veneer of ANC's ideological purity, corruption and who really controls the African National Congress. In Chapter Fourteen, Mzamo Mangaliso discusses the issue of concentration of ownership and control of large corporations in South Africa. He argues that the newly found political democracy is jeopardized by this concentration, and suggests that the private sector must be proactive in addressing this problem before the government takes the initiative. Mzamo proposes several practical ways by which this can be accomplished.

Part V examines issues of political and economic development in Africa. In Chapter Fifteen, Mulugeta Agonafer shows that Africa's economic and political reforms are largely illusionary. He states the internal reform of a communist or a capitalist system of development has never been achieved because such a change requires simultaneous changes in institution, poverty rights, economic policies, politics, culture, technology, the rule of law, and education among others. Agonafer calls for deconstructing and re-examining the existing development paradigms prior to implementing development policies.

In Chapter Sixteen, Ladun Anice identifies the critical legacies of sociopolitical maldevelopment in Africa following three decades of political independence. He suggests an explanatory reformulation of the process of maldevelopment and sociopolitical decay as a domestically, internally induced and institutionalized process of governance with a rational calculus of its own. He contends that the consolidation of this process of maldevelopment has been reinforced by the geopolitical and strategic imperatives of post world war II superpower rivalries, and Cold War ideological manipulations of African rulers by external interests. This perspective suggests a need for extending the framework of analysis of African contemporary problems beyond traditional explanations based on the theories of underdevelopment and neocolonialism to include new insights gained from the accumulated studies of the behaviors of African rulers over three decades of intentional and personalized misrule.

In Chapter Seventeen, Julius Ihonvbere, examines the origins of African crisis, its present manifestations, regional and international responses, and discusses the limitations of these responses. He concludes by making projections and prescriptions for Africa's future in the emerging (old) new world order.

In Chapter Eighteen, Kelechi Kalu does the following: (a) explores a definition of "development" as it applies to Africa using three works that provide insights into African development; (b) examines what appears to be the pricipal obstacles to development in Africa; and, (c) articulates the framework of Domestic Development Emphasis (DDE) as an alternative research focus for studying and evaluating research and development policies in African countries. The book ends with some concluding remarks by the editor.

CHAPTER 1

THE NEW INTERNATIONAL ORDER/DISORDER:

IMPLICATIONS FOR AFRICAN DEVELOPMENT*

What informs the meaning of international order? This question demands a revisit to definitions advanced by European scholars of **Realpolitick**. One such scholar, Hedley Bull, defines it as "those patterns or dispositions of human activity that sustain the elementary or primary goals of social life among mankind as a whole."[1] Such a definition supports the primacy of the "ordered" nation-state in relation to individuals and the state system in relation to collectives.

Bull regards "order" as "the condition of the realization of other values," including the pursuit of justice..[2] He admits, however, that the demands for justice relate, in a profound way, to the search for acceptable forms of order. Yet, only if the party can agree on just results, or if a consensus on an international level can be achieved, can order and justice be reconciled. If not, the state accords priority to considerations of order as against the claims of justice.[3] Bull's system-maintenance image of world order is implied by his preference for order over justice.[4]

Another scholar, Morton Kaplan, from kindred school, defined the system as a "very loose bipolar system" categorized by the uncommitted NICs playing an important and noticeably independent role in world politics.[5] The word "order," where used in this sense, implies purposeful arrangement, which in international affairs in turn implies understood relationships, an observable pattern of repetitive behavior, and the satisfaction of needs or the achievement of goals by the actors concerned.

The international order conceived as a system of state relations, as the definitions thus far suggested, presupposes that the conscious mind is detached from the world and that the subject transcends objectivity. Such a metaphysical assumption leads to policies of social control that seek to apply "rational" models of homogeneity, stability and order to the world, often with force, and without justice.

Since World War II the structure and context of the international political and economic order has changed markedly. It has moved from a loose bipolar system with the nation-state dominant to a "bipolar-multipolar" system with the nation-state dominated by the U.S. and the USSR with an increasing number of non western nation-state actors, which joined the international system as a result of the breakdown of colonial empires and the struggles waged by emerging nation-states in Africa and elsewhere, competing in the economic and political spheres.[6] And now, thanks to Gorbachev's Perestroika and Glasnost, a new Unipolar security and Tripolar economic global order under the hegemony of the United States is emerging.

Despite this, however, as Robert O. Keohane observed, the international order still remains a function of superpower Realpolitik.[7] Moreover, the ideological divide (realist-capitalist versus realist-communist) which informs the superpowers' competition and the nuclear context in which the competition takes place, compels the superpowers to view other non-European actors in the international system as peripheral to their national security concerns. This is still true even after Gorbachev's Glasnost and Perestroika that has changed both the internal and external political behavior of nation-states so significantly.

The ideological divide and the nuclear context also shaped Africa's perception of the two superpowers in relation to its national security within the prevailing international order. For Africa, the security concerns of the superpowers has a detrimental effect on its development strategy since the strategy must be carried out within the rules created by these powers and their allies. The rules often reflect the security concerns of the superpowers without regard to the security and developmental concerns of Africa. In other words, for the superpowers, the stability of the prevailing order takes precedence over any individual weak state's security concerns.

A brief review of the writings of Henry Kissinger on American foreign policy reflect this tendency. Kissinger writes, "The West is deeply committed to the notion that the real world is external to the observer, that knowledge consists of recording and classifying data."[8] This metaphysical hypothesis, which dichotomizes subject and object, means that the differences between East and West, and North and South, in their perceptions of the international order are not the result of complex and dynamic processes, including class and non-class processes, but, according to Kissinger, of different mind-sets. He writes, "The instability of the current world order may thus have at its core a philosophical schism which makes the issues producing most political debates seem tangential."[9]

To regard the political issues as tangential is to call them epiphenomenal, derivative, and accidental vis-a-vis the question of the mindset, considered the essence. If the mind is the standard of measure, then it follows that rationality is the norm. Once this is asserted, in a blatantly ethnocentric (even racist) way, the norm attaches to the Western Industrialized Countries (ICs) mind. "Empirical reality," Kissinger states, "has a much different significance for many of the new countries than for the West because in a certain sense they never went through the process of discovering it."[10]

Thus, it is the ICs as political actors who think of empirical reality as separate from mind, who "manipulate reality" in order to attain "equilibrium," which is the principle of rational balance in the world. Kissinger writes, "we must construct an international order before a crisis imposes it as a necessity."[11]

This tendency in the discourse (and practice) of international relations can also be found in the speeches and writings of Zbigniev Brzezinski, former National Security Adviser to the Carter administration. For him, the ICs prove that "people can cooperate on behalf of central ideas."[12] In other words, Africa, for example, is disorderly not because of material needs, the needs for principles of distributive justice, or decentralized and equal distribution of wealth and resources, but because of a lack of central ideas.

Such a philosophy also guides Russia's foreign policy as it frantically attempts to join the western dominated contemporary international order and seek to be seen as 'normal' by the West. In general, the "East" (now increasingly becoming western) and the West believe that the world is to be ordered, managed, and shaped from a detached subjective position and according to their perspective and respective national security needs.

Such a realist informed preCold War International Order arrangement suddenly finds itself, in the post Cold War era, under stress.[13] The former Soviet Union, which traditionally associated itself with the oppressed, suddenly abandoned them, leaving the West to define the "New World Order" unchallenged. As the West maneuvers to define the "New World Order" in its own image, it found itself in a costly interventionist policy in a largely complex, unequal, and interdependent World Order.[14] The policy implications of such a practice is, in light of the continuing crises, in the Gulf, Somalia, Sudan, Angola, Ethiopia among others, will prove to be adversarial to the development efforts of Africa and, in the long run, to the national interests of the Western ICs as well.

The corollary of this is that the post Cold War contemporary International Order has created a disjunction, in the perception of countries, between the ICs and the African Countries. From the perspective of Africa, the impact of the basic rules of the contemporary order is perceived as detrimental to their development efforts, whereas the opposite view is held by the ICs.[15] Such dichotomous views suggest that, unless there is a fundamental change in the order which could accommodate the Africans, the Asians, the

Arabs among others, the system will remain crisis-ridden, under stress, and unresponsive to Africa's development needs. Eventually it will affect the national security of the ICs and African Countries and, by implication, will trigger a world-wide crisis which, in my opinion, is already underway.

The Security Dilemma

The concept of security is rooted in the Latin term "sinecura-securitas," meaning "lack of absence of care, of toil and anxiety."[16] The contemporary Great Power security system finds its origin in Europe during the classical era, and has since gradually evolved to incorporate the entire globe.[17]

Since the end of World War II, the concept of security has come to be identified with the global policy formulated by the major powers to stabilize the international system as they saw fit and to avert any new causes of disorder and war.[18] The basic charters of the UN Security Council, the US National Security Act of 1947, and the Convocation of the European Conference of Security and Cooperation in the 1970s, along with many other regional alliances for security purposes, exemplify the superpowers quest for national security.[19]

Security also serves to define and delimit the term of "peace" itself. It is not just any kind of peace, but rather one based on national security considerations. It is international peace which prevents violent disturbances and guarantees the conservation of the dominant systems.[20] In this sense, from the perspective of the Realists, the term "security" has always seemed to imply the maintenance of the status quo favoring the superior power.[21] But it has often been seen by African Countries as impediments to their development aspirations as well as to their special security concerns.[22] On the one hand, the recent U.S. intervention in Granada, Nicaragua, Panama, Ethiopia, Somalia, among others; the Iraqi invasion of Kuwait and the subsequent U.S. and Allied response by a massive military mobilization in the region; and on the other, the former USSR's invasion of Afghanistan, intervention in Angola, Ethiopia, and Somalia accentuates this point.

Given the absence of a world government, as envisioned by the idealists, to guarantee international peace and security by monitoring each state's behavior, proponents of a realist theory advocate that each state must in the end look out for its own security, protection, and survival and that nation-states have to learn from the past, especially from the statesmen who were responsible for maintaining peace via the "balance of power" in Europe in previous centuries.[23] Thus, as long as nation-states, individually or in alliance with others, do not allow adversaries to gain military superiority, national security will be served and peace will be maintained.[24]

The corollary of this is that any major threats to the security of the dominant powers and their allies takes the character of a crisis for the whole system, thus calling for immediate action.[25] Put differently, a threat to the Western or Eastern alliance-system is viewed by the major powers as destabilizing the global balance of power between them, a balance which, in their view, forms the underpinning of the stability and security of the contemporary international order.[26]

From this realist school perspective, regional wars involving, for example, Ethiopia, are viewed as less threatening, unless they become big enough to threaten the existing balance of power, or the Western IC's "way of life", in which case the superpowers will intervene to contain them.[27] Witness the massive military mobilization by the U.S. to dislodge the Iraqis from Kuwait, the invasion of Grenada, and Panama, (both of which were against the international law) with impunity.

On the other hand, as noted, the international system viewed from the perspective of the NICs is disorderly, chaotic, and insecure.[28] This is because, what the ICs consider international peace and security, for the NICs means not only war, but also the presence of structural violence resulting from lop-sided international political and economic relationships.[29] Most African Countries continue to suffer from direct military conflict and structural violence.[30] The hardest hit by such international disorder arrangement are weak states like Ethiopia.

Africa's (in concert with other NICs) repeated attempt to improve its economic and political condition by making such proposals as the New International Economic Order (NIEO), and support of the reforms suggested by the Brandt Commission report,[31] continue to be frustrated by the ICs. The latter view the proposals as destabilizing and a threat to their primary pursuit of the maintenance of the status quo. The ICs fail to see (or choose to ignore) that the debate among those visions will help create a new order beneficial for all sides concerned.[32]

For the ICs, the system is in order and, with the exception of minor reforms, they are quite content to live with it. But, from the perception of many African States, the order as it relates to them is often what the superpowers want it to be, and is, therefore, necessarily unresponsive to their urgent needs and priorities.[33] This perception is further complicated by Africa's poor political and economic conditions as well as by its internal ethnic, class and non-class processes -- which is further complicated by historically produced weak state structures. This is a condition whose source, in part, can be traced back to the colonial era and often leads to a condition that invites superpower intervention.[34]

Several reasons account for the historically produced weak state structure in Africa.[35] These include the following:

(i) the boundaries of most African states, were arbitrarily drawn by Europeans in 1884-1885 at the Berlin Conference, resulting in the forcible incorporation of ethnic groups who do not identify with the artificially created state structures,[36]

(ii) as a result of Africa's instability and the leaders' political insecurity, many leaders spend their time and the countries' meager resources in shoring up their own security rather than planning the countries' long-term development programs.[37]

Consequently, the quality of governance found in Africa is often indistinguishable from simple looting. Many so-called sovereignties in Africa (and elsewhere as in Bosnia) are slipping into indistinct chaos. Revenge-minded and ethnically based liberation fronts, as in Angola (and in a less violent way in Ethiopia), settle their vendettas by gunfire -- not through ballot boxes. Many African territories have already become the preserve of Bandits or gruesome insurgencies, as in some parts of Ethiopia where the non-ruling ethnic people get barbaric treatment.

This does not imply that there exists a strong relationship between the internal disorder of Africa and the order and stability of the international system. It does, however, imply that a strong link exists between the security of the illegitimate "leaders" in Africa (and other NICs), on the one hand, and the international order and stability, on the other. For example, while economic problems and political conflicts in Africa create internal disorder, this disorder provides the leaders the opportunity and the excuse to accumulate weapons in order to forcibly control their own people for the mere purpose of strengthening their political power position.[38] This, in turn, contributes in some small way to the enhancement of the economic and political stability of the ICs.

In this respect, the interests of the ruling elites in Africa (i.e., to remain in power for life) and the interests of the ICs (i.e., to sell arms and prevent Africa from aligning with the real or imaginary enemy) coincide, since both have vested interests in the security of the contemporary international order, though for different reasons.[39] Seen in this light, it is no wonder that internal or intra-regional conflicts within and among the African Countries are viewed by the ICs as non-threatening (or, peripheral) to the prevailing order (balance of power), and therefore tolerable.[40] The recent regional conflicts in the Horn of Africa, the Iran-Iraq war, the crisis in Latin America, and the struggle for liberation in South Africa, the Lebanon civil war, and the ongoing Liberian, Sudan, and Angolan civil war testify to this view. But when Iraq invaded Kuwait, it was regarded as a threat to the economic security of the ICs and thus swift action was taken to bring back the status quo ante bellum.

One can argue that the congruence of the interests of the power elites in the ICs and the power elites in the African Countries, to some extent, as responsible to the continuing internal political disorder in Africa.[41]   This helps the political elites in Africa, as mentioned earlier, to secure their political power position, and allows the ICs to advance their economic and geopolitical interests.[42]

Some of the interests of the ICs include the following:[43]

a) keeping the arms industry and the Research and Development (R&D) in the ICs functioning (witness the crisis in the Gulf and the Bush administrations attempt to sell $20 billions worth of military hardware to Saudi Arabia);

b) enabling the ICs to test their latest weapons (witness the first use of the stealth bomber in Panama); and

c) providing the ICs the opportunity to demonstrate their reliability in times of crisis to those allies they consider vital to their security and worldwide geopolitical strategy.

In the processes of advancing these interests, the ICs often impinge upon the already internally weak state structures of African States in a way seriously exacerbating the existing political, economic, and ethnic problems in those countries.[44]   Already, the people in Africa suffer from a variety of problems such as state legitimation crisis, identity crisis, disarticulated economic development, economic exploitation, political repression, outside intervention, and natural disasters to name a few.[45]   In light of this reality, what are the implications of the New International order for Africa's development?

The Implication for Africa

The elimination of the Iron Curtain which divided the Post-world war II, as a result of Perestroika and Glasnost, has the potential to further a free and democratic development in Africa as well.   Witness Ethiopia, Haiti, Angola, Mozambique, Namibia and even Zambia, who have recently responded positively to the multiparty system. This is possible more than ever because of the experience and lessons learned in the era of the Cold War and, even more, because -- at the present time of vigorous economic and technological development -- no ideology, no weapons and no sphere of interest can have the same importance as they had before.   Moreover, the processes of negotiation and agreement between the superpowers, the crumbling of ideologies in the intellectual sphere and demilitarization of geopolitical areas are not a temporary truce and respite but -- with all possible and inevitable oscillations -- a long-term trend in the world.

However, for all these to have a positive and lasting impact on the development of Africa, I believe, a simultaneous change in three important and intertwined dimensions must take place. The first change must be in the current realist informed international order. The realist form(s) of order still dominates discussions of international relations. Its key theme of "national interest" understood in terms of power is omnipresent in everyday international political discourse.

For realists, interests are intimately related to security, understood in the sense of preventing a potential adversary invading one's territorially understood space which, in turn, relates to physical protection and political alliances at, in the U.S. case, the global scale. This concept of interest and security and its related discourse premised their analysis on the eternal enmity of the Communist system. In light of this, that interest and security continue being military-political concepts in the West even with a cessation of the Cold War and mutual rapproachment between the major powers, should not be surprising.

The same is true with the East in general and the USSR in particular. The motive that drives the West to protect its interest has become the same in Russia and the former Warsaw pact countries. Todays Russia, driven by overwhelming internal problems, have abandoned its commitment to the creation of an international Communist society. Not more than a decade ago Soviet Russia hoped that Communism would constitute an alternative to the realist informed international order. Instead, its leaders have opted to become part of it. This means, given the dominance of the realist international order, putting the clock back to the pre-World War I international system.

Thus, as Russia abandons collectivist certitudes and edges itself nervously into the world market system, and becomes "normal," some of the tension of the last 40 years will take the form of traditional Great Power rivalry, as reflected in the then balance of power system, rather than ideological competition. That is to say, the post Cold War alliances will end wars motivated by doctrinal rectitude but not wars motivated by sheer greed. Russia may continue to be aggressive and dangerous, even after it relinquishes its role as the custodian of international Marxist revolution. But it will speak a language that is rational and the same with the West. The West, in turn, will abandon its criticism of Russia so long as the latter remain "normalized" and passive in the future direction of the prevailing international order.

This does not bode well for the future development of Africa -- indeed for all NICs. We must not forget that it was such a European order that led to the scramble for Africa in the 19th century. Given the current social disorder in Africa (and elsewhere in NICs) who can predict what the future holds for them? Now that the West has won its ideological battle with the Soviet Union, how will it use its new-won victory in its relations with Africa? How will Africa figure in this calculation?

At the height of the Cold War, it was easy for Africa and other NIC's leaders to play off one side against the other and to extract extra amounts of aid in this way. Such aids sustained many African dictators to hold on to their power. Those days are yet to be over. Donor countries continue to gain and maintain spheres of influence, increase military and strategic interests, and spread ideological models of development. In doing so, they continue to sustain dictators much like the Cold War era.

Thus, the end of the Cold War means uncertain future for the people of Africa and other NICs. The portents of 1993 and beyond for peace, stability and development in Africa and elsewhere look bleak. Already six out of seven wars since 1976 have erupted in those countries. Many of the most volatile subwar disputes in the past few years have occurred there. Even as I write this, thirty-two civil wars, the most destructive wars since the second World War, are taking place in the world. Many others including Africa are poised to host large numbers of intra- and interstate disputes.

The second change must take place in the dominant models of development: the neoclassical, the dependency and orthodox Marxism. These paradigms are inadequate in charting the development strategies of the African countries. The neoclassical strategy has been premised, since Adam Smith, on human preferences, on the given endowments of productive resources that human beings privately own, and on the productive capabilities (the available technology) that enable humans to produce what they desire in an environment of political stability [See dec.dev. from dev. to maldev. M.A.,1). Human nature is, therefore, the theoretical entry point around which the argument of this school revolves.

The dependency strategy views power as its theoretical point of entry and essence, and constructs its theoretical argument on that basis. It is diametrically opposed to the prescriptions, tactics, and strategies of neoclassical theorists. It suggests for NICs to opt for an autarky by delinking with what it calls exploitative international trade.

The Orthodox Marxist strategy uses either class, power, or consciousness as its point of entry and essence. Orthodox Marxists base their production of knowledge about a particular society on one or more of these three aspects. Paradoxically, this school bears striking resemblance to the neoclassical approach in that it affirms the determining influence of the human being's power (God given power) on economic events.

Thus, each is different in its focus, or organizing idea, and each is similar in its reductionist logic. Consequently, the implementation of economic and political development policies in Africa (and elsewhere in the NICs) based on and guided by any one of these paradigms will lead, even if economic growth and political stability is registered by this means, to maldevelopment rather than to "sustainable development."

The third change must take place in the political system of Africa. What I mean by political system is a set of institutions and activities that link together people, politics, and policy. To change it one needs to know and change three basic political processes in Africa. First, we need to know how policy issues get on the policy agenda; second, we need to know how policymakers make policy; and third, we need to know what impacts policies have on the African people.

First, political issues should begin with people, since a political issue arises when people disagree about a problem and public policy choice. There is never any shortage of political issues in Africa or any other African countries. Many African regimes never act upon any issue that originate from the people even when it gets their attention. Often, in African political system, most issues that concern the people never catch government's eye. The government and the society have no linkage -- unlike the West where linkage is possible through a variety of institutions. For example, in the U.S. this is possible through at least three major linkage institutions: political parties, interest groups, and elections. Such linkage institutions are the channels or access points through which issues get on the government's policy agenda. Africa must somehow find a way to build comparable institutions that link the citizens with the government.

Second, there are no developed institutions for effective policy making. Almost all policies in Africa are made by a single policymaking institution acting often on behalf of a dictator -- be it military or civilian. Africans must design policy making institutions comparable to that of the Executive, the Legislature, the Judiciary and the Federal structure found in the West. Under no circumstances should policies be left to one man or one institution.

Third, there are no freedoms of speech, press or assembly in Africa. If these are granted, then people will feel free to voice the positive or negative impacts policies might have on their lives. People will begin to advocate policies that they think will benefit them. News media should remain free so they may educate the public in making political choices. Ignorance has condemned the African people to sway with the most available rhetoric or demagoguery be it from the left or right.

The upshot of all this is that Africa should not expect much from the post Cold War international order. Indeed, compared with the preCold War period, economic aid and foreign investment will decline, and secessionist wars will increase significantly. At the height of the cold war and the U.S. and the USSR rivalry, it was easy for Africa and other NICs to play off one side against the other and to extract extra amounts of aid in this way. Those days are over.

It should also not expect significant investment and trade from the west as a result of U.S./USSR cooperation. First, the markets in Eastern Europe and the developmental potential of their economies are more attractive for Western entrepreneurs and bankers than markets in Africa. Second, East Europeans are geographically close to the production centers in the West, and infrastructure is comparatively well developed. Third, there are plenty of skilled and educated people and the wage level is lower than in the West. Fourth, the East Europeans bonds of a common history, culture, race, and sometimes even language which make them a natural place for Western economic investment and expansion.

The final point in terms of our discussion, the impact of the new International Order/Disorder on African Development, is that it will have no positive impact unless Africans change in the three dimensions mentioned above. To do that, African leaders should avoid adhering rigidly to any one of the models of development and avoid engaging in the politics of hate and personal vendetta. Rather, they must deconstruct and hold multiple theoretical positions in order to search for workable solutions to their country's particular development problems. They must also be able to accommodate other political persuasions.

In addition, Africa, along with other NICs, must simultaneously struggle to have a substantive say in the emerging international order. To have any effect, this must be done before superpower's security discourse establishes an ideological space from which to dominate, exclude and delegitimize discourses from Africa, and before the new international order constructs Africa and other NICs as a threatening "Other" that must be permanently suppressed, its speech drowned out, and its people's genuine democratic struggle nipped in the bud.

CHAPTER 1

ENDNOTES

* Unless otherwise noted, most of the information presented in this chapter is taken from *Contending Theories of Development in the Contemporary International Order/Disorder*, Mulugeta Agonafer, University Press of America, 1994.

1. Ibid, 96-7.

2. Ibid.

3. Hedley Bull, <u>The Anarchical Society: A Study of Order in World Politics</u> (New York: Columbia University Press, 1977), pp. 86, 96-97.

4. Morton Kaplan, "Variants of six models of the international system," in <u>International Political and Foreign Policy</u>, ed. by James N. Rosenau (New York: The Free Press, 1969), pp. 300-301.

5. Richard K. Ashley, "The Poverty of Neo-Realism," <u>International Organization</u>, 38, No. 2 (Spring, 1984), 227.

6. This should not be surprising since the contemporary international system is a function not only of the states but also of numerous other governmental and nongovernmental agencies.

7. Robert O. Keohane and Joseph S. Nye, <u>Power and Interdependence: World Politics in Transition</u> (Boston: Little, Brown, 1977), see especially chapter two.

8. Henry Kissinger, <u>American Foreign Policy</u>, (3rd ed.; New York: Norton, 1977), p. 48.

9. Ibid.

10. Ibid.

11. Ibid.

12. "The World According to Brzezinski," <u>New York Times Magazine</u>, 31 December 1978, pp. 9-11.

13.   Robert W. Tucker, The Inequality of Nations (New York: Basic Books, 1977).

14.   James Der Derian and Michael J. Shapiro, eds., International/Intertextual Relations: A Postmodern Reading of World Politics (Lexington, MA and Toronto: Lexington Books, 1989), p. 100.

15.   Robert W. Tucker, The Inequality of Nations (New York: Basic Books, 1977).

16.   Furio Cerutti, "Political Rationality and Security in the Nuclear Age," in Philosophy and Social Criticism, Vol. 13, No. 1, (1987), p. 69.

17.   A.B. Bozeman, Politics and Culture in International History (Princeton, NJ; Princeton University Press, 1960).

18.   The search for international order by the superpowers often creates insecurity for others, particularly small nation-states. See Charles W. Kegley, Jr. and Eugene R. Wittkopf, World Politics: Trend and Transformation (2nd ed.; New York: St. Martin's Press, 1985), pp. 371-72.

19.   Fuiro Cerutti, "Political Rationality and Security in the Nuclear Age," in Philosophy and Social Criticism, 13, No. 1(1987), p. 70.

20.   Bruck Russett, Harvey Starr, and Richard J. Stoll, eds., Choices in World Politics: Sovereignty and Interdependence (New York: W.H. Freeman, 1989), pp. 288-93.

21.   Richard J. Barnet, Real Security: Restoring American Power in a Dangerous Decade (New York: Simon and Schuster, 1981), ch. 3.

22.   Ibid., 114.

23.   See, Henry A. Kissinger, Nuclear Weapons and Foreign Policy (New York: Harper, 1957), pp. 316-20; A World Restored (New York: Grosset and Dunlap, 1964), pp. 106, 145-47; and "The White Revolutionary: Reflections on Bismarck," in Daedalus, 97, No. 3 (Summer, 1968(pp. 888-924.

24.   Department of State Bulletin, Vols. 66, 67 (1972).

25.   The current structure is much more ambiguous than stated here. For extended discussion, see Joseph L. Nogee, "Polarity: An Ambiguous Concept," in Orbis, 28 (Winter, 1975), pp. 1193-1224.

26.   Morton A. Kaplan, "Models of International Systems," in Analyzing International Relations, ed., by William D. Coplin and Charles W. Kegley, Jr. (New York: Praeger, 1975), pp. 257-69.

27.   Raymond Aron, "Macht, Power, Puissance: Democratic Prose or Demoniacal Poetry?" in Power, ed. by Steven Lukes (New York: New York University Press, 1986), ch. 13.

28.   Among 116 conflicts (crises, interstate military intervention, international wars) between 1946-77, a total of 99 or 85.34% of all international conflicts occurred in the NICs. For details and extensive data, see Mark Zacker, International Conflict and Collective Security, 1946-1977 (New York: Praeger, 1979), pp. 222-82.

29.   Johan Galtung, The True Worlds (New York: The Free Press, 1980).

30.   Stephen D. Krasner, Structural Conflict: The Third World Against Global Liberalism (Berkeley: University of California Press, 1985), ch. 2.

31.   The Lagos Plan of Action and the Special Memorandum make explicit recommendations how this (the NIEO...) should be implemented in Africa in the short, medium and long run. See, "Economic Commission for Africa," Special Memorandum by the ECA Conference of Ministers on Africa's Economic and Social Crisis, (E/ECA/CM. 10/3/Rev.1).

32.   Robert Cox, "Ideologies and the NIEO: Reflection on Some Recent Literature," International Organization, 33, No. 2 (Spring, 1979), pp. 257-302.

33.   One only needs to witness the resistance NICs like Nicaragua or Afghanistan are facing in attempting to determine their own destiny.

34.   For a discussion, see Ekkart Zimmermann, et al., Political Science, Crises and Revolutions (Cambridge, MA: Schenkman Publishing, 1983).

35.   See, Special Memorandum by the ECA Conference of Ministers on Africa's Economic and Social Crisis, (E/ECA/CM. 10/37Rev.1), May 1984, p. 5, para. 12.

36.   Bahgat Korany, "Strategic Studies and the Third World: A Critical Evaluation," in International Social Science Journal, No. 110 (1986), p. 550.

37.   Ibid., 551.

38.   Atul Kohli, A World Politics Reader: The State and Development in the Third World (Princeton, NJ: Princeton University Press, 1986), pp. 274-79.

39.   A.M. Babu, African Socialism or Socialist Africa? (London: Zed Press, 1981), ch. 6.

40.   The war between Ethiopia and Somalia, and Iran and Iraq are some of the examples considered non-threatening to the existing international order since their contribution to the balance of power is negligent. On the other hand, the Arab-Israeli war, or a war between a NATO member country and a Warsaw member country, will be taken seriously, and both superpowers will work hard to bring the war to an end, as was true in the 1973 Arab-Israeli war. For further understanding of the danger of such selective concern for international order, see Noam Chomsky and Edward S. Herman, "The Washington Connection and Third World Fascism," The Political Economy of Human Rights, Vol. I (Boston: South Bend Press, 1979), ch. 1.

41.   This is, of course, a highly controversial position to hold. But once we are clear that we live in an era where superpowers' relations with their client states are based on a simple Manichean view of the forces of evil (communism or capitalism, depending on which superpower we are referring to) versus the forces of good, then it becomes much easier to understand why this is so.

42.   John Herz, "Political Realism Revisited," in International Studies Quarterly, 25, No. 2 (June), pp. 182-97.

43.   For data supporting these, see Mohamed Ayoob, ed., Conflict and Intervention in the Third World (London: Croom Helm, 1980).

44.   See Noam Chomsky and Edward S. Herman, "The Washington Connection and Third World Fascism," The Political Economy of Human Rights, Vol. I (Boston: South End Press, 1979).

45.   Adedeji Adebayo, "Introduction," ECA and Africa's Development, 1983-2008, p. 94, para. 242.

CHAPTER 2

AFRICAN DEBT AND THE NEW WORLD ORDER: PUTTING THE REGIME AT RISK

On September 11, 1990, before a joint session of Congress, former President George Bush introduced the phrase "new world order"[1] into the parlance of global politics. In uttering those words, President Bush was taking note of the dismantling of the Soviet Union and the end of the cold war. While clear on the nature of the era that had drawn to a close, Bush said less about what should ensue. Scant reference was made to new world order during the balance of the Bush Administration.[2]

While President Bush might have been become disenchanted with the new world order reference, scholars in the area of international politics seized upon the phrase recognizing it as an apt description of the prevailing international regime. The current U.S. president, Bill Clinton, has articulated a post-containment foreign policy that emphasizes an "enlargement" of democratic market societies globally. For the scholarly community, the end of the cold war ushered in a new world order where liberalism, free market economics, and the rule of international law would reign supreme[3]. The fact that none of the foregoing are standards to which nations are formally obliged to adhere does not obviate their saliency. Regime theory was first articulated by Stephen Krasner in his seminal article on the subject.[4] It accounts for the phenomenon of nations complying with standards of behavior that are implicit and unwritten as well as those that are formally agreed upon.

The task of democratization is among those that nations must undertake in the contemporary era of new world order. Domestic and international actors today regard a state as legitimate only insofar as its governors enjoy the mandate of the governed. The establishment of a democratic polity is essential to the efforts of any nation to be found in compliance with the imperatives of the new world order.

The onslaught of democracy has lain siege upon all of the world's regions. At the end of 1991, Freedom House rated as "politically free" 75 nations, nearly 15% more than the figure of just a year before.[5] In its most recent incarnation, it was spawned in the decade of the 1980s in Latin

27

America. Authoritarians in the Middle East and Asia have similarly been under pressure to liberalize their polities. The pluralist emergence in Eastern Europe in the last half decade has commanded the attention of the world. The democratic wave has hit the shores of the African continent. The Nigerian elections of 1992 have attracted the most attention in the region. Not to be ignored, however are the democratic transitions in Zambia, Mozambique, Ivory Coast, Angola and Ghana, among other locales on the continent. For the nations of Africa to be able to buy into the democratic premise of the new international regime they must concomitantly achieve levels of economic development that will enable to their leadership to deliver the goods to salient groups among the citizenry. Failing to do so, in a way that appears to be at least fair if not in fact egalitarian, will undermine the tenuous legitimacy that typifies the governments of new nations. The political instability that can result from the incidence of these developments can torpedo embryonic democracy. This study asserts that the viability of the present new world order, providing a mandate for the expansion of pluralism globally, will be threatened if democracy appears to fall short of expectations. Regime theory and its relationship to assertions of a new world order will be the starting point of the inquiry. African debt and the dilemma it poses for sustaining democracy will then be considered. The task of answering the recent call for achieving sustainable development will be introduced as an additional obstacle to economic development. The impact of these developments on sustaining democracy will be the final ingredient in the essay. Citizens, the final arbiters of this latest wave of democracy are looking to it to deliver them to a better quality of life. Among the standards that they will use when assessing government performance will be economic well being. The prevalence of debt, domestic as well as foreign, will mitigate the ability of these nations to achieve the self-sustained growth that will cement their legitimacy. The collapse of democracy in a few of these new nations can have a snowball effect imperiling pluralist movements elsewhere. The aggregate effect of these challenges to democracy might be the collapse of the entirety of the new world order.

REGIME THEORY AND NEW WORLD ORDER

While the tenets of new world order are perhaps uncomfortably ambiguous for a statesman to espouse, they fit snugly into rubric of an international regime. Regimes are, "implicit or explicit principles, norms, rules, and decision-making procedures around which actors expectations converge in a given area of international relations."[6] Krasner devised regime theory to account for instances in the post-war era when explicit arrangements for the maintenance of global stability were found to be ineffectual, yet order persisted. The United Nations was the principal institution constituted for the maintenance of collective security. The U.N. Security Council, the organ with collective security responsibility, was hopelessly deadlocked throughout much of the post-war era. This was because of the U.S.-Soviet rivalry of that period and the veto power that each had over resolutions on international conflict brought before the body. This development marginalized the U.N. as a instrument for keeping peace among the major powers.

Peace persisted between the two superpowers, nonetheless. The only war they waged with one another was of the "cold" variety despite the incidence of the kind of disputes between them that heated conflict between states in earlier eras. For this particular rivalry MAD or, mutually assured destruction governing the strategic relationship between the two sides,kept them apart. The presence of nuclear deterrence between the superpowers kept them from either employing weapons of mass destruction against one another or even engaging their conventional forces directly on the battlefield. There was nothing about the imperatives emanating from MAD that were formally agreed upon. Nonetheless, MAD and deterrence served as a regime governing superpower relations and keeping World War III at bay.

Regime theory accounts for more than absence of warfare between erstwhile adversaries. It also accounts for instances where nations violate conventional conceptions of realpolitik and adhere to norms or standards of behavior that they are not by treaty, or by force, obliged to meet. The logic of contemporary neorealism makes norms of behavior such as respecting international law, embracing free market economic principles, and democratization, behavior that is in the national interest. These norms of behavior, while implicitly held, are standards against which nations are judged in the present day. They are standards that nations must strive to meet in order to regarded as legitimate actors in the international community.

There is perhaps no more elemental a feature of the new world order regime than the democratization imperative. The fact that so many nations are either in the process of making the transition to democracy, or at least pledging to do so, is emblematic of this development. Francis Fukuyama presaged this outcome in his sensational 1989 essay, "The End of History". In it Fukuyama forecasted the triumph of liberal democracy. He saw it as an inevitable outcome of the clash between communism and capitalism. As capitalism proved triumphant, the inheritors of its laurels would demand a recognition of their status, in a word, democracy.

Fukuyama appears incredibly prescient today. Certainly liberal democracy has proven triumphant. There is no guarantee, however, of its resiliency. There is no assurance that the end of history is upon us. For democratization to continue to prevail it must be buttressed by its delivery to its supporters of economic prosperity. For much of the third world, and Africa in particular, prosperity remains a pipedream. The obstacle of debt resolution must first be surmounted before prosperity can even be considered.

THE DEMOCRATIC RENEWAL IN AFRICA

As of 1992 twelve African nations were in the process of transitioning to democratic systems of the multiparty variety.[7] In 1991 alone five nations held multiparty elections for the first time in their histories.[8] The list of African nations in some stage of the transition to democracy spans the African continent. Included among the nations in the process of transition have been such notoriously nondemocratic polities as Benin, the Central African Republic, and Ethiopia.[9]

This is not the maiden voyage of democracy in Africa. Beginning with Ghana in 1957, nearly all of the nations of the continent that were part of the first wave of independence experimented with multiparty democracy. Most of them had been obliged by colonial powers to hold democratic elections as a condition for gaining independence. In the preponderance of these cases the democratic experiment was short-lived. The challenge of maintaining order in these rapidly changing culturally plural societies proved too great for these fledgling states. Newly elected regimes were under pressure to deliver the goods to their core constituency, groups clustered around such primordial identities as race, ethnicity, and religion, which were locked in a zero-sum struggle with others. The potential bounty was relatively considerable given that virtually all of the economic assets of the nation were relinquished to the new governments by the colonial powers. The fact that societal cleavages were mirrored in divisions in these governments and exacerbated by their policies served to undermine their viability. The failure of these new governments to achieve a sufficient degree of institutionalization to ensure their legitimacy compelled many of them to stage executive coups, eliminating political opposition.Others found themselves ousted by military coup d'etats that brought a swift end to democracy.

The African nations currently immersed in the transition to democracy have gone to great lengths to diffuse the divisive power of the zero-sum struggle among competing groups. In the case of Nigeria, for example, the primordial divisions were diffused by the breakup of the nation's formerly monolithic regions into a multiplicity of states. This along with a change in electoral rules requiring that a candidate for the presidency attract nationwide support, served to pit members of the same group against one another in some instances. It also compelled them to form inter-group coalitions diminishing primordial conflict as a source of political instability.

The foregoing maneuvers notwithstanding, these democratic aspirants are not without challenges. Their principal challenge at this juncture is one of achieving self-sustained economic growth. The story of their sluggish growth has been told exhaustively elsewhere. Suffice it to say that the economic performance of developing nation regimes has lagged behind that of the rest of the world. The onerous debt burden that saddles many of these nations must be resolved before there is any realistic chance of realizing self-sustained growth. The prospects of that occurring in time to sustain the democratic effort appear dim.

THIRD WORLD DEBT

In the post-war period, the independent nations of the third world have been faced with the challenge of achieving economic development in a system that is largely inhospitable to their efforts. The multilateral development banking system placed a premium on lending to governments in the process of reconstructing their economies rather than those that were newly emergent. For the period from 1946-1955, the World Bank placed a low priority on project lending to developing nations. Chile, in 1948, was the recipient of the first World Bank development loan although the financing that it received fell far short of its request.[10]   The first Asian nations to receive development finance were India and Thailand in 1950.[11]   World Bank development assistance was infrequently granted and far less than requested in every instance. Consequently Latin American and Asian governments were compelled to turn to commercial banks for development finance.

After 1955, a change in multilateral development bank philosophy made loans more available to third world states. In the 1960s, financial assistance from official and bilateral sources increased. The United States government, through the Agency for International Development increased its profile as a donor.[12]   The strict requirements of economic reform contained in bank conditionality, combined with the unacceptable strings that were often tied to U.S. assistance, compelled less developed countries to continue their dependence on private bank finance.

Third World indebtedness climbed incrementally in the 1960s. By 1970, the debt figure had reached $70 billion.[13]   By 1984, that figure had grown more than ten-fold to $800 billion.[14] In 1991 alone, developing nation indebtedness increased 5 1/4% to $1.348 trillion.[15]

The distribution of that debt between public and private sources shifted from 44% public in 1970 to 30% by the end of the decade.[16]   The acceleration of indebtedness in the 1970s owes itself largely to the dramatic rise in energy prices during that decade. Oil price shocks occurred during the 1973-74 period and again in 1979.[17] Borrowing to finance oil imports during that period was often done in anticipation of future revenue. The global recession of 1981-82 resulted in a diminution of developing nation exports.[18] Inflationary pressures of the period, exemplified by the appreciating dollar, raised the prices of essential factors of production for third world economies. Anticipated revenues fell far short of projections. Petrodollar recycling, the commercial bank lending of the deposits of oil producers, kept liquidity at a level that continued to make loan funds available to the less developed countries.

THE UNIQUENESS OF AFRICAN DEBT

The magnitude and nature of African indebtedness stands in contrast to that found elsewhere in the developing world. As African nations gradually gained their independence in the 1960s, they found themselves confronted by capital requirements similar to those faced by the nations of Latin America and Asia in the preceding decade. With the World Bank shifting the emphasis of its lending priorities by the 1960s, developing countries seeking finance for infrastructure development found funds available. As mentioned above, the earlier emphasis on reconstruction in the World Bank compelled Latin American and Asian economies to turn to private commercial banks as sources of development lending. Latin American and East Asian debtors owed 70.2% and 51.8% respectively to commercial banks as of 1991.[19] Less than 5% of African debt is owed to commercial banks. By the end of 1990 Africans debtors owed $161 billion to bilateral and multilateral lenders.[20] African access to World Bank funds were further enhanced by the Bank's change in emphasis to the basic needs or "social investment" approach in 1968.[21]

Easy access to World Bank funds expanded with the establishment of the International Development Association (IDA) in 1960.[22] The IDA was devised as a "soft-loan" window providing concessional funding to the low income countries typically found in Africa. In 1979, the World Bank inaugurated a program of Structural Adjustment Lending (SAL) aimed at further increasing the volume of funds available to low income nations.[23] Unlike the more orthodox World Bank project loans, SALs would be "quick dispersing" in a fashion similar to IMF funding. By 1982, of the thirteen nations that availed themselves of SALs, the majority were African.[24] The IMF also increased the reservoir of funds it made available to low income nations at the sam time that African nations were increasing their borrowing. Among the programs created under its sponsorship were the Enhanced Financing Facility (EFF) in 1974, the Supplemental Financing Facility (SFF) in 1979, and the Enlarged Access Policy in 1981.[25] Among the more recent IMF innovations has been the Enhanced Structural Adjustment Facility (ESAF), established in 1987.[26]

The G-7 group of advanced industrialized countries expressed their agreement that the African debt problem is indeed unique among the ranks of the LDCs, and one that requires and extraordinary response. At the economic summit of industrialized nations held in Vienna in June 1987, the decline in African fortunes was a principal topic.[27] The summit communique devoted two of its eight pages to the African economic malaise. The inability of Ivory Coast and Zambia to meet their debt obligations was raised by President Mitterand and Prime Minister Mulroney, of France and Canada, respectively.[28] The signatories to the summit communique agreed to a debt relief package of between $20-25 billion for twelve debt-distressed African nations. Gambia, Madagascar, Mali, Mauritania, Niger, Senegal, Sierre Leone, Somalia, Tanzania, Togo, Zaire, and Zambia are the nations that were identified as particularly in need of debt relief.[29] By 1989, six more nations were added, swelling their ranks to eighteen.

A plethora of statistical data can be cited to illustrate the depth of the African predicament. Per capita income levels for the region declined from $630 in 1981 to $200 by 1987.[30] Inflation rose from 21% to 61% over the same period.[31] From 1980-89 those economies experienced a 20% drop in their standard of living.[32] Of the 41 nations represented at the 1990 Conference of Least Developed Countries, 28 were African.[33]

THE CONDITIONALITY TRAP

The dilemma of developing nation indebtedness has not suffered from a dearth of attention. The deleterious effects that chronic LDC debt can have on the health of the global economy have been universally acknowledged. The volume of international trade will remain well below its potential as long as developing economies are unable to simultaneously finance their import needs and service their foreign debt. Commercial and multilateral development banks continue to be dangerously exposed because of loans outstanding and the ever present specter of third world debt repudiation. Mexico and Peru both confronted creditors in the 1980s with threats of reneging on their debt obligations. The fear on the part of the lenders was that other nations might become similarly disposed. Ivory Coast, despite its effort to implement the structural adjustment program tailor-made for its economy, was compelled to suspend repayment of its external debt in 1987.[34]

Traditionally, IMF/World Bank financing has been available to borrowers on the condition that they agree to implement a prescribed "stabilization" program. By 1992, over half of the 46 states in Sub-Saharan

Africa had submitted to structural adjustment programs, with decidedly mixed results.[35] The mission of the IMF is to provide funds to its members to assist them in reducing short-term balance of payments deficits. The IMF is responsible for assuring that the policies pursued by the borrowing nations are consistent with the expectations detailed   in the Fund's articles and decisions.[36] The policy demands made by the IMF on behalf the borrowing countries comprise what is known as "conditionality". Continued access to not only multilateral bank money, but international credit in general, is contingent upon the successful implementation of policy remedies prescribed by the Fund. Conditionality provisions are ostensibly designed to enable the borrower to return to balance of payments equilibrium in the short-term. The long-term goal is one of achieving sustainable economic growth.

IMF operations are fairly standardized. The financial contribution of the member constitutes its quota. The amount of that quota is determined as a result of aggregating the national income, export dependence, gold and foreign exchange reserves, and fluctuation in foreign trade of the members.[37] Borrowing limits are linked to the credit tranches of the Fund. The first 25% is the known as the Gold or Reserve Credit tranche. Three more tranches exist that provide the members with access to Fund resources exhausting the remaining 75% of the After   drawing upon the funds available in the First Credit Tranche, gaining further access to resources is will be dependent upon compliance with a stabilization program prescribed by the Fund as detailed in a stand-by agreement.[38]

The stabilization program has a dual intent. On the one hand, its aim is to improve the economic prospects of the borrower. On the other, it places a high priority on safeguarding viability of the international economic system. The program is particularized in that it is crafted jointly by representatives of the Fund and the borrowing nation. Program design follows a comprehensive analysis of the borrowing nation's economy in order to determine the causes of the balance of payments disequilibrium.[39]   The program is more generalized in that it prescribes deflationary measures and a contraction of demand in the domestic economy of the borrower, combined with trade liberalization measures.[40]   The particulars of the stabilization program vary according to the specific needs of the borrower. In general, the stabilization program calls for a combination of:(a) currency devaluation, (b) a reduction in public expenditures along with increased taxation for revenue generation and, (c) the dismantling of any and all import controls and subsidies to domestic exporters in order to enhance medium and long-term efficiency of the economy.[41]

The rationale underlying the IMF adjustment prescription is that currency devaluation and anti-inflationary measures will raise the prices of imports, while reducing those of exports. The net result of this should be more export demand. This development, combined with a decline in spending on the part of the borrower, should result in an increase in the income of the borrower. Consequently debt repayment should be possible while economic growth continues

Conditionality requirements were advanced solely by the IMF until 1979 when the World Bank launched a program of policy-based lending.[42] The Bank's sectoral (SECAL) and structural adjustment (SAL) loans tied the provision of funds to IMF-type conditions.[43]   Conditionality is a useful device. Its imposition of monetary and fiscal discipline on borrower is an important first step toward the achievement of economic viability. It is also designed to safeguard the interests of the international economic system. Its record in accomplishing the latter objective has been reasonably successful. For the former, it has been far less promising. The empirical evidence overwhelmingly indicates that orthodox structural adjustment requirements have been ill-suited to lead less developed countries out of the mire of external debt.

The austerity requirements of the macroeconomic reform programs appear sound. Reducing public spending, holding down inflation, and increasing investment, can work together in the aggregate to enhance the competitiveness of LDC exports, enabling their governments to generate necessary foreign exchange. The trade liberalization aspect of the stabilization programs appear to be directed more at the international economy than the domestic economies of the debtors. The effect of the requirements for trade liberalization serve to reverse all of the potential gains made toward economic growth by successful adherence to the rest of the adjustment program. Several of the erstwhile supporters of IMF/World Bank conditionality have been similarly critical of the trade liberalization plank of the stabilization program. Participants in an IMF-sponsored seminar on Fund-supported adjustment programs in Africa offered an assessment of trade liberalization in a their final report.

> While not rejecting the principle of trade liberalization, participants expressed reservations regarding the timing of such measures. Their concerns focused on the impact of liberalization on the existing industrial structure and on the ability of key sectors to withstand international competition in the short-run without some temporary protection.[44]

In a similar vein, Ian Golden Head of Program for the OECD Development Center, cast aspersion on the timing of trade liberalization requirements, "The...increasing openness of those (developing) countries to world markets is being frustrated by the failure of the industrialized countries to level the playing field and provide stable perspectives regarding the future."[45] The newly industrialized countries (NICs) that have been regarded as the economic miracles of the post-war era, all enjoyed a period of protecting their industries and providing incentives to producers. Japan, Korea, Taiwan, and Singapore are foremost among those nations that found a positive correlation between the provision of incentives to their exporters and their export volume.

The embryonic industries of the LDCs have by and large failed to gain a niche in the international marketplace. Left to compete with producers of longstanding with no assistance, the LDC producers are seriously inhibited in their efforts to grab a substantial market share. This phenomenon diminishes LDC economic growth potential. In fact, the process of currency devaluation raises the costs of the factors of production that the LDCs need to import, thus raising the price of their products. Cheryl Payer in the Debt Trap cites case studies that reveal that IMF stabilization programs often led to foreign take-overs of domestic industries because of their inability to compete without incentives.[46]

What appears increasingly evident is that the requirement of trade liberalization for developing economies works at cross purposes with their effort to achieve sustained growth. Robert Girling in Multinational Institutions and the Third World, argues that the prevailing World Bank's "...free-trade theology should be replaced by a more objective diverse appraisal of economic prospects and recommendation that improve trade that respects the need of the third world to protect fledgling industries. Economic difficulties stem, not only from poor government policies, but also from inequities--including trade barriers to Third World goods in the advanced industrial countries--in international markets."[47]

This is not a clarion call for a sweeping policy that will reverse the entire evolution of trade liberalization that has developed over the course of the last four decades. Instead it is a suggestion that some formula be devised to enable selective debt-distressed nations to protect targeted sectors and industries that might be generators of foreign exchange.

The hardship posed by the task of debt resolution and the adherence to conditionality is not solely an economic one with indirect political implications. Stabilization conditionality also poses immediate political pitfalls for responsible regimes.

CONDITIONALITY DEPENDENCY

The attendant conditions of developing nation indebtedness have placed these nations in a new and perhaps more insidiously dependent state than ever before. The phrase that has been used elsewhere to capture this phenomena is "conditionality dependency."[48] The prerequisite for considering a nation as having taken on the conditionality dependent condition is that it first has reached a level of borrowing and indebtedness obliging it to acquiesce to an IMF-type standby agreement for continued access to international financial resources. That status alone is a necessary condition for conditionality dependence but not a sufficient one. Many nations have been compelled to adhere to conditionality dependency without experiencing adverse effects. A debtor nation will have to continue to follow the policy prescriptions of conditionality even when they appear to run counter to the economic policy choices it would have made independent of external influence. This circumstance, while also an essential ingredient of falls short of consigning debtors to the condition of acute dependency.

If a nation continues to implement conditionality provisions when they have proven to be detrimental to development efforts, it can be regarded as being conditionality dependent. The contention that a nation implementing policies not of its making and contrary to its interests has effectively relinquished its sovereignty, seems unassailable. This loss of policy-making prerogative places the debtor nations in a state that in fundamental ways echoes their colonial past. Debtor regimes responsible for this loss of sovereignty are undermining their own legitimacy. In the absence of legitimacy they will be increasingly compelled to use force in order to maintain domestic stability. This does not bode well for the prospect of a democratic future.

THE ACCOMMODATION

"The Debt Crisis RIP" was the title of a recent article typifying a view advanced by many in the North regarding the current state of the debt situation.[49] That sentiment fairly accurately captures the position of most commercial bank lenders. By increasing their loan-loss reserves and implementing other debt reduction techniques, private banks have to regard the debt crisis as one has receded into the past.[50] This fact has diminished the sense of urgency previously felt by rich nations in devising effective strategies for third world debt resolution. The debt crisis remains a reality for many third world debtors, particularly those in Africa. The debt resolution instruments that rescued states such as Mexico remain out of the reach of African debtors. There is virtually no secondary market in existence for the discounted sale of their debt. Debt swaps are also rarely implemented in debt-distressed African states. African nations also fall beyond the geopolitical perimeter that makes their rescue a strategic priority for the major powers. In a report published by the IMF on the occasion of the tenth anniversary of the debt crisis the continuing problems of the third world were noted.

..the debt crisis is far from over for more than 40 developing countries, which continue to have difficulties in servicing their debt originally contracted. In particular, much remains to be done for the poorest developing countries, 26 of which are classified as severely indebted. For these countries -- mostly in Sub-Sahara Africa -- official support has been strong through the 1980s, in terms of the provision of both new money and progressively more concessional debt relief.[51]

This essay has suggested a linkage between economic development and democratization in the developing world. Until debt resolution becomes a reality for third world states generally, and Africans in particular, the level of economic development that will support democracy will prove elusive. If the pluralist experiment falters in the fledgling democracies in Africa, the continent could potentially become rife with instability. There is no guarantee that the ramifications of that will be contained in Africa. Political instability in the former Yugoslav Republic and stark poverty in Somalia drew in external actors in 1992. Turmoil among African polities might appear to warrant similar attention should it occur in future. Delegitimizing democracy in the developing world, more tellingly, instigate a reappraisal of the viability of pluralism, the foundation of the new world order regime.

The newly-installed government of President Bill Clinton of the United States can make an important contribution to the prospect of achieving sustained economic growth in Africa. The Clinton group can readdress the viability of prevailing economic reform strategies and conditionality requirements when considering the plight of the debt-distressed. Targeted protection, selective import substitution, and trade preferences are among the measures that might facilitate an increase in LDC export volume. Only the United States has sufficient clout to have these suggestions included on the agenda of MDB deliberations. MDB decisions are made on the basis of the consensus raised among its leading contributors. The United States has developed strategies that have enabled it to have been successful influencing MDB policy.[52]   A United States Treasury study that subjected decisions of the MDBs to empirical investigation, found that for 70 issues over a ten-year period, the United States has been able to successfully advance its position 85% of the time.[53]

The most severely debt-distressed nations of Africa might be the ones initially subjected to a newly-devised formula for debt relief and sustained growth. If an improvement in their economic wellbeing is in the offing, a similar course might be prescribed for African economies that have even better prospects of responding favorably to those remedies at this stage in their development process. The stakes are high. World order could be among them.

CHAPTER 2

ENDNOTES

1. Adam Roberts, "A New Age in International Relations," International Affairs, July 1991, p. 519.

2. Joseph Nye, "What New World Order, Foreign Affairs, Spring 1992.

3. Lawrence Freedman, "Order and Disorder in the New World," Foreign Affairs, American and the World 1991/92, p. 27.

4. Stephen Krasner, "Structural Causes and Regime Consequences: Regimes as Intervening Variables," International Relations (Ithaca: Cornell University Press, 1983), p. 2.

5. Larry Diamond, "Promoting Democracy," Foreign Policy, January 1992, p. 25.

6. James F. Keeley, "Toward A Foucaldian Analysis of International Regimes", International Organization, Winter 1990, p. 83.

7. Michael Chege, "Remembering Africa", Foreign Affairs, America and the World 1991/92, p. 148.

8. Ibid.

9. Ibid.

10. Edward S. Mason and Robert E. Asher, The World Bank Since Bretton Woods (Washington: The Brookings Institution, 1973), p. 157.

11. Ibid., p. 159.

12. Roger S. Leeds, "External Financing of Development: Challenges and Concerns," in John Stremlau, The Foreign Policy Priorities of Third World States (Boulder: Westview Press, 1982), p. 97.

13. Robert Girling, Multinational Institutions and the Third World, (New York: Praeger, 1985), p. xix.

14. Ibid.

15. International Monetary Fund, World Economic Outlook, (Washington, D.C.: IMF, 1992), p. 29.

16. Leeds, Roger S., op. cit., p. 97.

17. Collen McGuiness and Patricia Russette, U.S. Foreign Policy: The Reagan Imprint (Washington, D.C.: Congressional Quarterly, 1986), p. 126.

18. Patricia Wertman, The International Debt Problem: Options for Solution (Washington, D.C.: Congressional Research Service, October 17, 1989), p. 1.

19. York W. Bradshaw and Ana-Maria Wahl, "Foreign Debt Expansion, the International Monetary Fund, and Regional Variation in Third World Poverty," International Studies Quarterly, September 1991, p. 252.

20. Girling, Robert, Op. cit., p. 65.

21. Ibid.

22. Detlev Dicke, Foreign Debts in the Present and a New International Economic Order (Boulder: Westview Press, 1986), p. 44.

23. Girling, Robert, op. cit., p. 69.

24. Ibid., p. 71.

25. "Economic Groupings: ECOWAS," Africa Research Bulletin, December 31, 1988, p. 9348.

26. Ibid.

27. Rosalind Racid, "Reagan Urged to Initiate Multinational Debt Summit," Journal of Commerce, June 16, 1987, pp. 1A, 5A.

28. Barry Wood, "Africa and the Venice Summit," Journal of Commerce, June 15, 1987, p. 12A.

29. "Economic Commission for Africa (ECA)," Africa Research Bulletin, January 31, 1989, p. 9384.

30. Blair Harden, "Africa's Poor on the Brink," Washington Post, June 7, 1987, pp. A1, A25.

31. Ibid.

32. "Economic Commission for Africa (ECA)," op. cit., p. 9384.

33. Steven Greenhouse, "Richer Nations Are Asked to Double Their Aid to Poor," New York Times, September 4, 1990, p. D10.

34. Paul Bluestein, "Treasury Developing Plan to Address Third World Debt," Washington Post, March 7, 1989, p. C1.

35. Chege, Michael, op. cit., p. 153.

36. "Financial Support for Member Countries Works in Tandem With Policy Reforms," IMF Survey, August 1990, p. 9.

37. Kjell J. Havnevik, The IMF and the World Bank in Africa (Upsalla: SLAS, 1987), p. 10.

38. Ibid., p. 11.

39. IMF Survey, op. cit., p. 9.

40. Girling, Robert, op. cit., p. 87.

41. Havnevik, Kjell J., op. cit., p. 13.

42. Girling, Robert, op. cit., p. 15.

43. Havnevik, Kjell J., op. cit., p. 13.

44. IMF Survey, op. cit., p. 27.

45. "Structural Adjustment and Developing Countries," IMF Survey, June 22, 1992, p. 198.

46. Cheryl Payer, The Debt Trap (Washington, D.C., IMF, 1986), . 28.

47. Girling, Robert, op. cit., p. 80.

48. James A. Mitchell, "IMF Conditions and Dependence: The Case of Nigeria," World Review, September 1991, p. 23.

49. "The Debt Crisis RIP," The Economist, September 12-18, 1992, p. 15.

50. Ibid.

51. Masood Ahmed and Lawrence Summers, "A Tenth Anniversary Report on the Debt Crisis," Finance and Development, Summer 1992, p. 5.

52. Robert Girling, op. cit., p. 80.

53. Ibid.

CHAPTER 3

AFRICA IN THE UNFOLDING INTERNATIONAL SYSTEM: PRELIMINARY NOTES ON THE RENEWED DRIVE FOR GROWTH AND DEVELOPMENT, 1989-1993

The collapse of communism, forcefully projected by the fall of the Berlin Wall, seemed to have initiated a renewed drive for development in the continent of Africa. Four years after this new dawn seemed to have been proclaimed, this paper examines the difficult questions and the problems of development that have faced Africa and how they have been managed. The discussion is located within the context of international capital movements in the ever changing international economic environment. By looking at the institutional frameworks supporting growth and development, the attempt is to isolate emerging economic trends and determine the degree of useful attachment in the international system as these constitute a dynamic force towards the growth of output and the realization of a beneficial interchange in Africa's international economic relations.

The paper further analyzes the support or obstacles to development which has resulted from the application of the prevailing model of the Breton Woods, and studies, in general, the lack of articulation of overall national interests and other internal political contradictions. It hopes to determine, by gauging the residual strength of the economy, whether there has been provided, a solid foundation for a real "drive to take-off."

INTRODUCTION

Independence for the continent of Africa in the 1960s invited an enormous optimism concerning the prospects for sustained growth. This hope was, however, not realized because a myriad of internal problems set severe limits on development as a corollary of both domestic and external activity. Subsequently, this situation   vastly diminished confidence in the economies of the continent. Foreign investment dried up and with it the level of income

45

and activity. Many economies went into deep recession. The period following the decade, 1980, thus became one of profound and traumatic dislocation for many economies in Africa. It was a period that witnessed a further deterioration in the economic fortunes of the continent. That these problems were ineluctable given the state of the world economy at this period was of no consolation, for this process seemed to have ushered in a period signifying the collapse of many economies already tottering on the brink of disaster. Seen in terms of a continuum of international development, this seemed to actualize the perception already established in many places -- the line of thinking that Africa's underdevelopment was the inexorable decree of fate and that their economies were caught in a web of inherent disability in their participation in the international economy. The link between the causes of underdevelopment and the relationship between the North and the South which was first forged by Dr Raul Prebisch in *The Economic Development of Latin America and its Principal Problems* (1949)- which sustained the argument that structural variations in the conditions of demand and supply between developed and developing countries placed the latter at a disadvantage in the international system -- and later by dependency theorists, was now seemingly true. This pattern was characterized by asymmetrical interdependence and was, therefore, inherently biased, precluding any potential for growth and development in Africa.

This line of thinking, as a causal explanation of Africa's lack of development, however, was not altogether tenable given the structural distortions in the domestic economy. Distortions that owed largely to internal political and social contradictions. Thus, the theory would seem to have described the historical process of development, not explain it. Nonetheless, this theory of underdevelopment that was formulated, in line with the prevailing ideological chasm, was seized by some of Africa's leadership to justify a most negligent inactivity, constituting local overlordship and building graves and private bank accounts instead of the nation. This was mainly because this was not an ideological schemata to which they were welded. There is no basis to think that this kind of conceptualization clarity marked the African leadership approach because in Africa at this time, political systems were not so persuasively definitive but remained amorphous or simply depended upon vapid sentimentality. The impetus was however to encourage certain groups acting on erratic whims and selfish caprices or simply those whose cupidity were excited by the national treasury some of which, like in Nigeria, now held loot beyond the dreams of avarice, to seek to overthrow their systems. This was one result of the ideological cleavage. On the other side were those states brazenly cultivated as client states. Regimes were not accountable to the people and dictatorships thrived largely because within each prevailing dogma was imbedded an element of expediency manifested in the sacrifice of the universal principles allocating responsibilities to governments, for camp membership. Seen either from one perspective or another, the cumulative effect was stagnation. While other economies with identical colonial heritage elsewhere in South-east Asia tackled the practical problems of development with increasing success, Africa languished.

As these economies failed, submerged as they were in that veritable labyrinth of inertia which characterized the growth and development process in Africa, on the one hand, and on the other assaulted by the bankruptcy of obligatory intellectual diagnosis and the weakness of domestic structures, another dominant model was developed and has since become dominant. This paradigm was that which the Breton Woods institutions constructed. A prognosis that without the benefit of success anywhere, was hailed as a panacea. The cornerstone of this approach was the application of a rigid set of models depending on a strictly monetary approach to balance of payments difficulties which overlooked the fact that development involved both social, economic and political factors. Since according to this position, the problem of underdevelopment was essentially one of mismanagement of domestic and international returns, the African states with largely underutilized factors and undercapitalized private sectors were encouraged to adopt a less *dirigiste* approach. The lack of success of the IMF/IBRD prescriptions notwithstanding, it has since become the new orthodoxy.

The strength with which the IMF/IBRD has enclosed Africa is that of the octopus. This position is amply illustrated by the number of loan agreements involving structural reforms (popularly known as Structural Adjustment Programs, [SAP]) which the Breton Wood institutions maintain with several African countries. In the period, 1980-88 for instance, 33 African countries borrowed from the IMF and 15 had structural adjustment loans from the IBRD. In some countries, this financing accounted for a disproportionate amount of available capital. For instance, between April 1983 to March 1992, IMF financing available to Ghana amounted to a total of $1,640 million. The World Bank supported this, between 1984 and 1989, with $400 million in credit-based financing and with conventional lending of $268 million.

Through this extension of much needed financial facilities, the Breton Wood's influence in running the economy in Africa has become all encompassing. These capital transfers have enabled them not only to dictate policy options but to influence local politics. Their inextricable binding with the developed Western economies have further allowed them to increase the dimensions of this dominance. Since it is able to influence bilateral lending, a leverage which it has not hesitated to use, it has been able to threaten countries with sanctions which involves cutting-off all external sources of funds. Many African countries have capitulated and pursued these policies even when they were inimical to the peoples social welfare and had amounted to committing political suicide on the part of the leadership.

From the standpoint of the African economies, however, the tendency may have been towards the distortion, not stimulation, of growth. In many places, the complications arising from this program have inimically affected the political process and this dislocation has translated into the rapid deterioration of the economy since political instability willy-nilly counterbalances economic growth.

Since the triumph of this new approach, a circumstance dictated by its being the only viable model that by necessity and by the absence of alternatives and supporting institutions, must be adopted, there has emerged, in some countries in Africa, a perceptible shift in economic policy. Consequently, there has been a redefinition and sorting out of priorities to allow for growth and development. Their readiness to adapt to this development may be traced to the monumental changes in the international order brought on by the fall of the Berlin wall and the collapse of the Soviet Empire. Africa has not been left out in this general expectation of many peoples optimistic for some kind of progression in the growth and development process. Coinciding with this period of rapid changes in the international system in terms of alignments and the collapse of old systems, there seemed to be proclaimed a willingness to tackle old problems with renewed vigor. Economic structure reforms in concert with limited political reforms were undertaken as governments seemed to find a new convergence between private and public interests in states and societies that were not necessarily congruent. A flurry of other activities have followed and partnerships with foreign investors have been sought within the framework of a new philosophy that views foreign partnerships as additives and not substitutes for local initiative.

Provided below is an account of the renewed efforts to activate growth in Africa. In sum, the changes that have taken place in the economic arena and how this has improved the attractiveness of these economies. The emphasis is on emerging trends and prospects in its manifold political economy dynamics, namely, credit expansion, the creation of overhead capital, resource management and foreign private investment. At issue is the continent's position and subsequent role in the contemporary international economic order. To that extent the preoccupation with these issues is to allow the determination whether Africa has properly articulated its economic interests in a global context and fulfilled its growth potentials and subsequently, its development aspirations.

CREDIT BASE EXPANSION

African economies seek the path to sustainable growth, consequently they are seeking to establish the necessary frameworks to sustain it. To this extent, they have sought to expand their credit base and to deepen their financial facilities. The process of economic modernization must include the widening of capacity of financial markets which underpin it. The necessity of revamping financial services to bring it to a level where credit was managed in such a way that ready access to capital was provided could never be more urgent than in Africa where, prior to this period, these facilities have been almost nonexistent with grave repercussions for the development of an indigenous enterpreneural class capable of moving the states towards economic viability. An application of the Wai model[1] of measurement of growth in this market may help reveal the extent to which business activity was greatly incapacitated because of inadequate financial facilities. Given the dictates of the new open market approach -- the necessary changes called for by the market place -- the existence of such institutions have become non-negotiable factors. Many African economies perceiving this need have sought to modernize their financial markets. This approach has taken two forms; introducing foreign exchange markets and in line with the prevailing ideology dictating a *laissez-faire* economy, deregulating them where they have existed. And, the creation of capital markets (mainly a stock exchange). By seeking to bring their stock markets on par with this modernizing trend, and where they have not existed, to create them, what may have become evident is a great scope for expansion and increasing market activity. Although these exchanges are still rudimentary, being as they are in most places still infant, this inherent propelling factor cannot be discounted in any determination as to the prospects for growth. The trend is widespread in the "new" Africa.

In Nigeria, financial markets have been deregulated and finance houses have mushroomed. Although many of these finance houses are small business operations (some no more than glorified *bureau du change*), the need to widen financial facilities has been attacked with robust enthusiasm. Although there is, potentially, great room for the use of finance capital and for capital expansion here given the large population and vast resources of the country, the low level of manufacturing activity, the country's endemic political instability and the style of management of the existing market[2] may put question marks on the capability to realize the intended outcome. Botswana, the fastest growing economy in Africa, created a stock exchange in 1989 and already boast a sizable capital market. In Ghana, the creation of a stock exchange in 1992 was the counterpart of an adopted pragmatic ideology which has allowed Ghana to attract the interest of foreign financial institutions on a scale not rivalled elsewhere in Africa.

In some African states, gradualism has marked this approach to deregulation and deepening of financial facilities. First, government controls imposed on foreign exchange transactions is lifted and a stock exchange is created with limited government control. This pattern is clearly evident in Zambia, Sudan and Kenya.

In Zambia, it was required by law for commercial banks to secure the approval of the Central Bank before releasing customer requests for hard currency. This was a cumbersome and troublesome administrative procedure and widespread state corruption made it all but impossible to procure required sums and at the appropriate time. The same was true of Kenya where it was a major offense to trade in or possess foreign currency. In both places, these laws have been rescinded (Kenya in 1992 and Zambia in 1993) and it has become possible to acquire foreign exchange through privately organized foreign exchange markets. This measured approach is also evident in the Sudan where the government has created stock and money markets but is pursuing the liberalization of the market for foreign exchange as a limited objective. It must be noted that the stock market is not an alien concept in Sudan but it had existed without activation. A stock and securities department had been created by the Bank of Sudan in 1973 but licenses were not granted to stock brokers. The 1993 initiative was, therefore, an attempt at a resuscitation, albeit circumspectly.

In many respects, these changes have been quite revolutionary for the continent. Like the Marketing Boards which controlled and afforded buffer to producer prices, the practice of tightly controlling the foreign exchange market was widely diffused in Africa. It was a means through which government regulated scarce foreign exchange by monitoring its movements. Allocation depended on the fulfillment of a rigid criteria which made hard currency available for only capital expenditure and not for expenditure on luxury items. It was an objective designed for efficient allocation of limited resources, but the element of corruption robbed this of its ideological purity with the result that it became a means to state social control. Although financial markets have been introduced, their base broadened and public access to foreign currencies have been guaranteed, real growth in this sector has been difficult to achieve as an objective in one respect. The low average propensity to save and invest (in part, due to the fossilization of incomes in its pre-independence levels) has the tendency to ensure that the intended objective of propelling the economy may not be achieved without commensurate transformation in wages and in the income earning capacities of labor. This and the lack of required management and manpower capability which has obliged some states to use imported human and material resources (in Zambia, the US investment bank of Pangaea and Partners of Madison,

Wisconsin was contracted to manage the program of creating a stock exchange and a government securities regulating agency) may mean that the intended dynamic effect may flow largely to foreigners leaving local capacities largely unaffected and thereby continuing the old dominance of the modern sector by foreign interests.

The setting up of capital and money markets have not been the only means through which the expansion of credit base was pursued. In line with this trend of deregulation, the banking sector has been opened up. Libya, which had banned private commercial banking, has liberalized its financial laws to accommodate private ownership of commercial banks. With a capitalization of $37 million, enterpreneural interests would be free to collect deposits. Designed in the same manner to encourage the flow of private capital, Tanzania has authorized the re-establishment of foreign banks, an activity that was banned in the 1960s as a vital consequence of its adopted Africanist-Marxist philosophy. (The legislation which is now in effect overturned the nationalization of private banks that followed the Arusha Declaration of 1967). This same line was also adopted in Uganda where deregulation of commercial banking has enabled United Kingdom bankers to return. Multilateral credit organizations have helped this effort by providing assistance for capital growth through the creation of new debt instruments. ECOBANK, for instance, has provided venture capital for investment in high-growth-high-risk activities (targeted $20 million) covering Nigeria, Ghana, Benin, Cote D'Ivorie and Togo[3]. To further increase the availability of capital and hence the opportunity for capital growth, Western finance houses especially those whose services were indispensable in the capital base expansion program of the Asian Development Bank, are currently exploring the possibilities to institute the same measure for the African Development Bank.

The principle guiding these attempts may be the high marginal productivity of capital that can be realized through an overall expansion of the market.[4] The prospects of rising marginal efficiency schedule of capital investment is easily perceptible in an African economy that offers different returns for identical factors employed in different sectors of the economy, i.e., a dual economy. With the weighted average rate of interest in Africa between 26-30 per cent, embodied in the integrative process that is likely to take place may be a tremendous opportunity for enterprenueral profit.

THE CREATION OF OVERHEAD CAPITAL

Here, the African attempts tie very closely to the programs for capital expansion discussed above. However, since government expenditure is the leading source of development capital in Africa, investment to create public goods deserves special treatment. The creation of an infrastructural base through adequate investment in social and public overheads has been, in conventional terms, the preoccupation of government development planning at the initial phase of the nation building process. The provision of infrastructure is critical, for it is the factor that underpins and thus propels any growth economy. In the path of development of Africa, such an investment did not take place at the required level. One reason for this was the disconnected pace which attended the process of transforming society in Africa. The result of disarticulation of national interests which precluded either the emergence of long-term policy objectives or a systematic and gradualistic approach. The inadequate attention paid to this indispensable factor subsequently helped to produce internal discontinuities that gradually emerged as a major bottleneck to development. To illustrate the paucity of this investment, it may be necessary to draw an analogy as a comparative basis of support. In the African colonial economy, investment in infrastructure was designed to fit perfectly into the structures of extraction so defined as the *raison d'etre* of imperialism. In building railways, for instance, the tracks were constructed to take produce from production areas directly to the coast without connecting contiguous or outlying areas.[5] This attempt, albeit for a purpose not pertinent to domestic improvement, allowed the newly independent African states to inherit some rudimentary infrastructure. Undoubtedly, this was grossly insufficient. Nonetheless, on average, it was more than post-independent African states accomplished. To continue with this railway construction, it is of interest to note that one of the few major addition to the rolling stock in Africa were EXIM Bank of Japan- supported expansion projects in Nigeria and Zambia - - both in the 1970s. This neglect was most extraordinary in many places. The republic of Chad, which has less than 500 miles of paved roads, and Mozambique, with very little or no infrastructure, may represent the extremes, but theirs is not an exclusive phenomenon. For instance, telecommunications infrastructure is so underdeveloped in Africa that the chances of completing an intra-city telephone call depends on fortune. To connect one African country to another by telephone becomes almost impossible. As a result, African states, in attempting to redefine their development goals, have been forced to go back to the basics. Although they have been constrained by the Breton Woods obligational constructs which severely restricts infrastructure creating expenditure, many have proclaimed a desire to embark on ambitious infrastructure development programs. The types of programs pursued have included housing, the construction of roads and bridges, energy development and the establishment and upgrading of modern telecommunications systems. A few of these attempts are worth mentioning.

Coinciding with the robust passion with which Tanzania is renewing its developmental goals, many notable investments in infrastructure have been undertaken. Energy development has taken the priority, requiring an investment of $28 million by the Tanzania Electric Supply Company, TANESCO, in an electricity generating power plant project. This plant which is expected to go into operation in February 1994, is part of a sustained infrastructure improvement program in pursuit of which it has been assisted by foreign countries, among them the Swedish International Development Agency which has provided it with a disbursement of $40 million for manpower training and improvement of its telecommunications system. A similar telecommunications improvement effort in Zambia is also funded by a foreign agency, the Japan Overseas Economic Cooperation Fund. In that link between Japanese aid and private capital pointed out by Andrew Spindler[6] and Rothacher[7] and empirically demonstrated by Chife in Africa[8], and like in an earlier Japanese effort in Nigeria, this $173 million worth of assistance would be run by Marubeni Corporation.

Other significant attempts have also been made in other states. Algeria is embarking on a 3,7000 unit housing project which it is expecting to complete with significant support from Saudi Arabia. That kind of external input has generally been the factor that has enabled these developments (investment in infrastructure) to take place thus helping the African states to achieve sectoral linkages. Both the Arab Bank for Economic Development in Africa and the OPEC Special Fund have played a major role in that respect. Although the extension of aid from these bodies to Africa have been generally skewed in favor of Arab states in Africa and as such have met with criticism in the continent[9], both funds established in the 1970s to help African states alleviate severe development difficulties arising from the oil crisis of 1973, have been most invaluable to development efforts in the continent. It is in that frame of reference that their recent assistance to Cape Verde islands, Madagascar and Burkina Faso, were extended -- all for the development of infrastructure.[10]

It is thus obvious that many African states have become aware of infrastructure's overriding necessity and thus are attempting to correct that structural malignancy and lay the groundwork for growth. The desire is to provide the framework necessary for increased income and activity. The tempo of this approach is striking, the tendency diffused as widely as possible. Even states lacking immediate resources have declared an interest in setting out to accomplish this. There are plans in poverty stricken Mozambique to make huge outlays for the replacement of war damaged infrastructure and the creation of new ones required to sustain a modern economy. The desire of

African states to accomplish infrastructure growth have however, been debilitated by their being enclosed in an ideological straitjacket: within the conditionalities of Breton Woods, such capital outlay is outside the bound of sanctionable activity. Their desires have thus largely become pious hopes and may remain so for a long time to come. So far, the only notable exception to this rule has been Lesotho where provisions for social infrastructure -- education and health -- have been rising steadily.[11]

NATURAL RESOURCE DEVELOPMENT

At the end of a 9-nation tour of Africa by a Japanese mission in February 1970, it referred to Africa as "a treasure house of natural resources" stating that with the Japanese dependence on overseas resources, it was imperative that an active cooperation with Africa be developed.[12] A similar report to the Committee on Foreign Relations, United States Senate, had also reached the same conclusions.[13] These observations underscore two major facts for the purpose of this discussion. First, the contention still holds true that Africa is a "treasure house" of the world's natural resources despite its enormous problems. Of the world's top twenty oil exporters, Africa occupies four places.[14] It is also an important producer of other strategic minerals like uranium. The developed countries' dependence ratio on its mineral resource is quite significant. Japan very adequately illustrates this point. It depends entirely on South Africa for many of its raw material needs. Nigeria is the USA's second largest supplier of oil. This natural disposition has, however, constrained the continent to a huge dependance ratio on exports of primary resources, a fact underlined in Belinda Coote's recent study, *The Trade Trap*. Thus, in 48 out of the 55 countries in Africa, tea, coffee and cocoa account for more than 50 per cent of total foreign exchange earnings.[15] Some states, like Chad, are entirely dependent on products with exceedingly low elasticities of foreign demand, namely, cotton and cattle. In the light of their renewed attempts at development, many African countries have embarked on resource diversification programs.

Second, the critical role of the primary product sector would indicate the concentration of foreign investment and major development activity. This is the case. The existence of these vast resources in Africa and the ever declining prices of these products in the world market, has meant that these states, starved of foreign exchange, have had to rely almost exclusively on foreign investment and grant assistance for project development.

The overwhelming importance of this specialization on raw materials production can be gauged therefore from the fact that it has been to the development of these resources, propelled by the pull of external economic needs and the push of the necessity for economic growth, that a disproportionate attention in the renewed drive for development has been focused.[16] In this dynamic, the development of energy resources has taken the lion's share of all foreign investment, business activity and other inputs. It is not difficult to see why. Oil continues to maintain a relatively high price with traditional markets (stable demand) which would readily provide the needed funds for development. The preponderance of investment in the energy sector also follows closely the fact that many large states in the continent depend on it entirely for sustenance. And large economic units are the ones more likely to sustain a demand for consumer products. Since most African countries rely on the marketing of a single commodity, mainly oil, for their export earnings, (in Nigeria, for instance, oil accounts for about 98 per cent of total foreign exchange earnings. Oil exports occupy the same position in Angola's exports [about half of this production, 300,000 b/pd, owes to the US oil companies, Chevron and Texaco and is concentrated in the Cabinda region] accounting for 90 per cent of its foreign earnings), it is not surprising to find that oil production intensification attempts in the form of new rights of exploration, product base expansion, diversification arrangements and marketing deals constitute, as a percentage of these efforts, almost the totality.[17]

In Nigeria (OPEC's sixth largest exporter of oil) this has taken the form mainly of providing financial incentives, namely, production sharing agreements with foreign firms. As part of the overall strategy, a gas processing contract aimed at increasing its gas sales and worth $450 million with Chevron and Bechtel Limited has been signed. (Prior to this arrangement, much of its natural gas was flared). It is also vigorously pursuing a petro-chemical expansion program. In Algeria, a comprehensive gas production and marketing program has taken off. Here, a 20-year export agreement was recently signed with the Italian company, Sonatrach, to deliver 4 billion cubic meters of gas annually to the Italian state electricity company, ENEL. In terms of monetary value, the contract is valued at $6 billion. Apart from this major deal, it has also signed new joint venture agreements with French, Spanish, British, Japanese and US firms. It has, further, reached an agreement with Spain and Morocco on the details of the first phase of its $1.5 billion pipeline designed to carry its gas to demand centers in Spain and Western Europe. New rights of exploration and production have also been granted. As in Algeria, new avenues exist for venture capital in Angola's petroleum production, potentially one of Africa's largest. As a prelude to what it envisages as a sustained program of petroleum resources development, its state company, Sonangalp, has concluded an arrangement with the Portuguese company, Petroeleos de Portugal (in a joint venture agreement between Angola and Portugal completed in April, 1992), to distribute petroleum products in both countries. A similar development has also taken place in Egypt. According to a speech given by the oil minister in Abu Dhabi in September, 1992, Egypt projects (for a 5-year period), that investment in oil production activity would exceed $9 billion.[18]

This increased attempt at oil production is not restricted to these large states but have, albeit to a smaller extent, been reproduced in many other places in the continent. While Ranger oil of Canada has been granted an exploratory license by Namibia, Cameroun's SNH has signed a new drilling contract with Pecten (a subsidiary of Shell petroleum). Shell and Elf Aquitane have both returned to Congo in the wake of new legislation allowing such participation. (Shell had withdrawn from here in the 1970s when all oil companies were nationalized). In Gabon, an important producer country, a new round of bidding for exploration license in an attempt at diversification and increased productivity held between September 1992 and June, 1993 resulted in the 11th exploration concession which has been granted to foreign oil companies. New oil fields have been opened here. In Zaire, the Belgian oil company, Petrofina, has resumed production counteracting its withdrawal when riots erupted in the country. In strife-torn Somalia, American oil companies, namely Comoco, Amoco, Chevron and Philips have indicated their willingness to exercise exploration concessions granted before the civil strife in 1991. This promises a huge source of development capital for the country since large deposits of oil have been discovered here. Shell, Chevron and Exxon have formed a joint venture to exercise the rights to petroleum exploration which Chad had granted them in 1969. The World Bank International Development Agency, IDA, is sponsoring this venture for the Chadian government.[19]

Although the lion share of foreign investment have been taken by the petroleum sector, the development of other mineral resources has not lagged very far behind. Mining activity, mainly of gold, have also been renewed. The World Bank's Multilateral Investment Guarantee Agency, MIGA, has provided the insurance for these foreign ventures mainly Australian concerns, as well as for two other mining projects including Uganda's Cobalt extraction project. This represents the largest investment ever made by the agency since it was formed in 1988 to encourage foreign investment in developing countries by providing investment guarantees. In Ghana, the privatization of the Ashanti Gold Fields by the government allowed the World Bank's International Finance Agency, IFC, to offer a syndicated loan of $140 million to enable the Ashanti Goldfields Corporation to develop this major foreign exchange earner for the country. The Australian Golden Shamrock Mines, the principal foreign partner in this venture, has also helped Guinea to re-open its Siguiri gold mines. Another Australian company, Australian Delta Gold, is the largest in the consortium of business interests helping to develop Zimbabwe's newly discovered platinum resources. With commercial activity anticipated to take off in 1996, this reserve, the second largest in the world, may serve to help Zimbabwe realize in full its growth potential. Botswana "The African tiger", has reopened its Tati Gold Fields. Dating from 1869, this field has not been worked for 45 years and this serves adequately to illustrate the vigor with which the new drive for development in Africa is being pursued. There is also increased activity in other areas of mineral resource extraction. In Zambia, the government privatization efforts has allowed the Anglo-American Corporation to take over the Zambia Consolidated Copper Mines, ZCCM. In both Burkina Faso and Namibia, plans are underway for the development of new manganese mines.

At first glance, the outlook for development given the possession of these resources appear to be very promising. From the trend in international resource related investments, the prospects can be gleaned. A study carried out by Salomon Brothers, the US investment house, relates this experience. After a survey of 247 American companies, it forecast a drop of nearly 20 per cent in 1992 spending on North American exploration and production. Spending by these same companies outside the USA was projected to rise by 9.5 per cent.[20] This net leakage has affected Africa as we have seen from the increasing and projected activities of US oil companies. Such economic optimism may need to be qualified however. Recent developments in the international system, as far as the marketing of these commodities is concerned, seems to point to a completely different expectation. These indicators are highly relevant for Africa given the continent's lack of export diversification. That determination is highly significant in that it will help us gauge whether the enumerated developments, the sum of Africa's renewed drive for growth, has provided the economy with residual strength capable of becoming the dynamic force towards the growth of output. Let us examine the emerging trends in the relevant world markets.

THE COMMODITIES MARKET

Inherent in the picture painted by the study by Salomon Brothers above, is an increase overall in world energy production. The increase in outside North American activity has been due largely to more lucrative ventures in many parts of the world where new sources have been discovered or known reserves activated. The old Soviet Union illustrates to the fullest the extent of this development.

Long known to hold the world's largest reserves, the latent power of production of the old Soviet Union is now on the way to being fully realized with new investments. Partnerships between Western investors and Russian state companies have been very crucial to this development. A noticeable example is the agreement between a Houston based firm, Hytexplor, and the Crimea Krymgeologia (state geological production association) to form a joint venture to develop and operate fields in the Crimea and four neighboring states in the Ukraine.[21] Exploratory and production activities in the Russian Arctic Tundra are now at full pace. This increased activity among states in the old Soviet Union accounted for the rise in 1992 of their oil exports by 22 per cent. There have also been new discoveries and increased exploration and production activities in Eastern Europe and other parts of the world, as well as among OPEC member states. Among OPEC member states, some developments are very relevant to this analysis.

Having rejected an OPEC decision at a meeting in September 1992 to set a market share for member countries, Iran has embarked on a massive increase in production output (partly to support the increasing budget for its resurgent defense program). Its neighbor, Iraq has accepted the long term monitoring of its program of nuclear energy development by the UN, and sanctions imposed on the marketing of its oil is bound to be lifted. When this is done, the necessity of repairing a war ravaged economy and fulfilling defense needs may also oblige it to increase its production output irrespective of OPEC's quota. Other developments in consumer nations may also be as important as the above in glutting the market. For instance, a recent report released by the US Energy Department indicates a big increase in US oil reserves.[22]

This constellation of events betrays what is readily apparent -- the volatility of oil prizes. There has been a steady decline in the index of oil prizes in the commodity markets since the end of the Gulf War from a record high of about $41 per barrel to the current level of about $15. Given the conditions obtainable in the market, it is difficult to see realistically, the possibility that this commodity will sustain the drive for the growth of these African economies. Although despite the developments in the energy market, the prospects for African economies emphasizing oil as a growth catalyst may still be considered with guarded optimism, the situation in the market for other commodities on which African economies depend is not very encouraging. Here, the worsening terms of trade for primary commodities have not boded well for Africa's attempt at a redefinition of economic growth.

There has been a 17 per cent drop in the contract prices (to March 1994) of manganese despite the fact that the prevailing market prices have remained at their base in the mid-1980s. For Burkina Faso and Namibia with new plans above, this slump may be adverse to growth projections. Although with Brazil reviewing the financing for its stock under the Producers Retention Scheme, it is anticipated that world prices of coffee will rise, the pattern, since the collapse of the International Coffee Agreement in 1989, is that of rapidly declining producer prices. This has adversely affected the producer countries in Africa. In Rwanda, for instance, earnings from coffee which accounts for over 50 per cent of foreign exchange, had declined from $90 million in 1988 to $36 million in 1992 (In Uganda, the decline in revenue was from $400 million in 1987 to $123 million in 1990). Since the civil war which erupted here in October 1990 ended with the August 1993 peace accord, there has been renewed attempt to restore and increase post-war production levels. The decline in world prices have had such a profound impact on local cultivation based on the system of *Umuganda* (collectives) that deprivation fostered desperation facilitating the rise of extreme religious groups. Major disturbances in the Kibuye and Bugesa regions which destroyed several tree crops have been witnessed.

The prospects for cocoa producers appear slightly better with the Geneva Agreement signed by 44 producer countries under the auspices of UNCTAD on the 16th of July 1993. An emphasis on supply side management, the agreement is designed to achieve price equilibrium in the medium and long term through adjustments in production. That is, that member states would agree to restrict their production. Higher prices for this commodity is yet to be achieved however, and this agreement may not affect the level of prices, given that necessity has always overcome ideals in such arrangements and that two of the largest producers, Malaysia and Indonesia were not part of this agreement. Even if this is achieved, the restrictions imposed by the necessity of participating within the paradigm of the Breton Woods is such that major producers will continue to face the prospects of declining income. The case of Ivorien cocoa production is illustrative. The required liberalization of the market which has obliged the government to remove its producer subsidies has contributed to a crisis in the industry. Many farms have closed and the government has had to accommodate the wrath of farmers with little or no income. Hitherto, government succor, like the US or EEC subsidies to agriculture, had served to cushion producers against adverse fluctuations in the world price of cocoa.

The increasing availability of substitutes, ever rising environmental standards, the lack of industrial transformation of the primary products sector and the homogeneity of their products continue to set blocks against the ability of the agricultural exports sector in Africa to help bring about economic transformation. Even the prevailing state organization of the sector has not allowed it to achieve its natural spread effect on the economy. Realized sales figures often mask the fact that the spread has not been as diffuse among farmers to allow for growth in income. This is an especially disturbing development considering the benefits of three decades of engagement. Governments may point to the beneficial effects of production but new scholarship with different perspective is increasingly emerging in Africa. A recent study of the tobacco industry in Uganda provides an account that can hardly be ignored.[23]

THE INVESTMENT CLIMATE

Foreign investment has, for a very long time, been the leading source of investment capital in Africa. As a result of the negative trend of growth in Africa, the inimical political milieux and the policies of some multinational corporations however, foreign direct investment, both portfolio and greenfield, were either positively discouraged or ceased of its own accord. African states had instituted indegenization programs (nationalizations and stock redistribution) to complete the import-substitution-industrialization phase that was part of the departure point of their industrialization process.[24] Subsequent upon this, the demand for foreign exchange pushed many towards what is partly an export-production-oriented (export-led) growth, and the need to accommodate an open economy as dictated by external management forces. No matter the predisposition, the participation of foreign private capital has remained a critical and compelling need. It was therefore important, in the renewed drive for growth, that a conducive business environment be established by granting concessions to these interests.

A high growth orientation of industrial policy may have allowed African states naturally to provide a favorable investment environment as Southern states have been inclined to do.[25] In the new dispensation enthroned by the prevailing Breton Woods ideology under which they have had to function, this requirement became non-negotiable. In fact, if ever one aspect of a region's economy has indicated the type of market philosophy pursued, deregulation in Africa would have been its large neon sign. Nowhere has the total dominance of the Breton Woods ideology been more manifest as in the privatization and liberalization initiatives which are being pursued in the continent of Africa.[26]

As we indicated earlier in the discussion, the old climate of the African economy was one in which the newly independent states used the management prerogative to arrange the combination of production factors and determine sectoral distribution of resources in the economy. This reinforced their political autonomy. In many places, the exercise of this hand of authority over investors was not an arbitrary interjection but one which helped to define the kind of progress by determining how and in which direction domestic growth was projected. This was an authority many did not hesitate to use to secure a measure of economic independence that by necessity must follow political autonomy. Albeit limited, the indegenization and nationalization programs and allied investment laws often succeeded in giving Africans the much needed foothold in the new economies providing opportunities for the revolutionary transformation of domestic factors of production. In the current climate that the African economies have been forced to operate, what has disappeared is this power of determining economic destiny.

As we have mentioned, the role of foreign investment in the African economy has been very important. Even during the sometimes turbulent period of indegenization, which was an attempt to accommodate foreign venture capital by seeking a viable synthesis between domestic and external resource inputs, inward investments had remained crucial to economic growth. In fact, excluding infrastructure and capital associated with small-scale activity, the ratio of this capital to the GDP of the continent generally remained at 40 per cent of medium to large scale productive activity. This trend may continue for in the new world order of economic importance, as indicated by some emerging trends and developments in the international system, the equation for growth may just be right for Africa. The on-going recessionary difficulties in the economies of the developed systems is likely to result to industrial restructuring and relocation away from low to medium scale specialization to higher value added specialization. This may lead to the relocation of limited sophistication technology oriented industries. Given traditional relationships and other factors such as low labor costs, it may be assumed that there would be a net leakage of investible resources into Africa. This kind of international division of labor, a trend already set by the relationship between Japan and Southeast Asia,[27] is likely to characterize future Africa/West relationship. For one thing, the options may not be many in the industrial North -- these kinds of industries increasingly cannot compete with the East Asian NICs. The NAFTA agreement between Canada, the USA and Mexico serves significantly to highlight this trend. Indeed, if the pronouncement of some of the G7 Finance ministers is anything to go by, respective Western governments are trying to incorporate this as part of industrial policy. Also, states like Israel, with whom African relations have recently been revitalized, would be looking for joint ventures. This is especially important given Africa's specialization in agricultural production. In this sector, Israel had maintained a leading influence with phenomenal investments before the unfortunate break in diplomatic relations.[28] The increasing globalization of the trading empires, and this increasing willingness in the developed economies to achieve more international division of labor by relinquishing small to medium scale industrial activities to the developing states may mean that this form of capital transfer will become very important to growth of output calculations in Africa.

Many states in Africa, having seemingly contributed to a new economic philosophy, namely, that foreign investments should be complementary to, not substitutes for local capital, are trying to accommodate this kind of transition and increase their ability to take a respectable share of participation in the international economy. The need for external resources is of course more urgent than it has ever been in the continent's history. Various African states are in dire need of investments (For the fourth year, even the relatively mighty South African economy has recorded negative growth and unemployment is rising in its dominant mining sector). Because of the African states' unparalleled decline, many domestic investors have been holding negative equities and desperately need the opportunity for additional inputs which would reinvigorate the market. Even in states where followership of an ideological schemata or a reactionary predisposition would have precluded such an attempt, structural impediments such as the 'facilitating fee' which has obstructed the movement of this capital in the past, are increasingly being removed. Although it may not be possible here to give a country by country account of the complete reversal in policy, since almost all African economies have adopted this position, a cursory look at the process in a few states will highlight the trend.

In Nigeria, foreign investment laws had previously limited the sectors to which access is allowed to foreign capital while restricting the ratio of investment capitalization (usually between 40-60 per cent). These laws further regulated the composition of the management of these firms.[29] In the new dispensation, these kinds of legislation have been repealed and foreigners are now allowed, if they so choose, both a 100 per cent capital ratio investment and management freedom. In Zambia, the economic philosophy leading to the policy of nationalizations of foreign interests which took place in 1968 was reversed in June 1993. In the old system, the remittance of dividend to home countries by foreign firms had been limited to 20 per cent of profits (subject to 50 per cent of after-tax profits). Under the new arrangement, no limit is imposed on foreign remittances of profit so long as enough replacement capital has been provided in order to avoid malinvestment. This same approach is now being followed in Zimbabwe where a comprehensive new policy, with respect to foreign participation, has been developed under a five year plan of economic reform and trade liberalization. As part of the new attitude, Zimbabwe has relaxed its strict exchange controls and opened its stock markets to foreign capital. Foreign firms are now allowed to retain 50 per cent of foreign exchange earned from exports. All other remittance can be carried out without restriction and businesses no longer require direct foreign exchange allocation from the state, as had been previously the case. The only restriction now in place is on capital gains and this is a temporary measure to help address the country's balance-of-payments difficulties. In fact, an open door policy with respect to foreign private investment has been adopted in Ghana, Tanzania (abolished a number of restrictions, including the removal of price controls), Sudan (mainly through limited privatization of unprofitable government holdings), Uganda (divesting of government commercial sector share holdings), Mauritius (free port in the port Lonis harbor), Eritrea (an investment center created to aggressively campaign to attract capital from expatriate Eritreans and from other foreign sources), and Malawi (in the formation of the Malawi Export Development Finance Scheme financed with a World Bank Loan of $10 million) as well as in many other African states. The principle behind this approach can be related to the political economy of capital transfers in North-South relations.

Capital investment is an important measurement of the degree of economic cooperation in North-South relations and also of national transformation. These investments are indispensable to the capital accumulation process in Southern economies (since they involve the transfer of a package of resources, technology and managerial expertise, they exercise even greater impact on the country's productive capabilities.[30]) This input may be affected by development strategy and market philosophy, as Goldsbrough[31] and Ohlin[32] have shown. Even when these conditions are not favorable, they may be offset by other favorable conditions such as low labor costs. The resources available to the North for investment are not unlimited and because the investment climate often affects capital transfer decisions, Southern states generally need to pursue liberal economic policies in order to attract the needed capital from abroad. It is to provide the necessary environment that these developments have taken place in Africa.

The net effect of this new approach -- attracting foreign resources -- has been quite significant in many places. According to the IFC, private sector investment in sub-saharan Africa was highest in 1990. The amount of foreign direct investment in Africa in 1991, for instance, was $1.16 billion or 4.6 per cent of the world total.[33] Compared with previous levels, the changes have been quite revolutionary although they may seem striking since the base levels were so low. Countries like Zimbabwe experienced a 67 per cent growth in foreign investment in the period between 1985 and 1990, making it the fourth highest among the third world.[34] The story however, has not been the same in all states in Africa. Nigeria has witnessed a net loss of foreign investment. A hemorrhage of investments had resulted in the wake of that country's continuing political instability. The US oil company, Texaco, has, for instance, sold its 60 per cent holdings in Texaco Nigeria and, generally, other foreign businesses have discounted their long term investments in debt instruments before their maturity. Since the liabilities to foreigners account for a significant amount of assets in the modern sector, the calling in of these claims have led to disinvestment in an economy already performing very much below par.

It goes without saying that profitability is the underlying factor affecting Northern investment decisions. To this end, political stability is a major determinant of the level of investments and especially, the ability of this capital to produce the needed dynamic effect on the whole economy. This consideration is important in our analysis of the unfolding developments in Africa since it enables us to gauge the real impact of these investments.

Africa is viewed as a bad risk in the North.[35] This is partly because the political arena is one of recurrent instability. The threat of military *coup d'etat* and dictatorships has been an inherent almost endemic factor. In the 1960s, for instance, there were no less than 42 *coup d'etat*.[36] By 1976, according to Eric Nordlinger, "coups had occurred in more than half of the African countries, and in that year, the military occupied the seat of government in half of them."[37] Authoritarianism manifested by personal dictatorships which brutalized the people had become pervasive. A study by Jackson and Rosberg highlight this trend[38] which was continuous in the eighties and still marks African politics in the nineties (In 1993, there was yet another military takeover in Nigeria despite the fact that the country had all but finished its return to democracy). As a result of this political instability, there has been no easily discernible, sustainable or coherent economic policy in many African states, and development policies have ranged from left-of-center socialist models to the anarchic capitalism of the far right. Because the African governments are steeped in a tradition underpinned by an elaborate system of corruption and political racketeering, this produces a baneful effect on the business environment which cannot be overemphasized. Bertil Ohlin's point that "direct foreign investment in new facilities in a country with a relatively inefficient and not quite honest administration is less attractive than in a country where there is less risk of arbitrary or 'negative' intervention by the administration"[39] is of particular relevance in application to Africa. Even under the new dispensation, as so referred, the political arena is far from stable. The continent is engulfed in conflict, mostly internecine civil war fueled by ethnic and religious differences. The so called democratic elections where they have happened, have been a travesty of the process and very little, if anything at all, has changed in Africa.[40] Because fundamentally nothing has changed as far as the business environment was concerned, these investments have not necessarily become the systematic and calculated long-term capital outlays normally resulting from such activity. What was being taken advantage of was merely the open system being pursued under the Breton Woods dogma providing in effect, a *carte blanche* to these investors for the plunder of the African economies.

This possibility is not far fetched. The pattern of investment is most noticeable in the extractive industries where multilateral development agencies have provided insurance risks to cover investors and domestic governments have given huge concessions or have simply sold the businesses at bargain basement prices (this certainly was the case with the Anglo-American Corporation take-over of the Zambian consolidated copper mines where a British consulting company advised against the sale on account of what was on offer but government disposed of it because they needed money to repay debts). The African countries are usually not in any position to bargain. The increased incidence of foreign investment in Africa, to a large extent, therefore simply represent the opportunism of fly-by-night financial cowboys out to make a ready killing in the Breton Woods open system. These investments have not reflected positively on these countries' potential for growth and are harmful to these economies for the following reasons. The short-term export of capital (repatriation of profits) have served not only to affect the African balance-of-payments adversely, but will in the long run have the tendency to depress, not stimulate, their economies. Again, because of this short-termism of approach, depreciation provisions are inadequate to finance replacement. That is, profit is being repatriated without adequate provisions for replacement capital causing disinvestment. This is illustrated by the fact that whenever these businesses have met with difficulties, they have not hesitated but have easily wound up their operations. It is also particularly instructive that despite this renewed interest and the fact that the International Finance corporation has so far approved financing of $193 million for 45 projects in Africa (mainly through disbursements in two funds; the Mauritius Fund and the Fund for Investments in Africa), its 1993 report concludes that the "investment climate" in sub-saharan Africa remains difficult".[41] It is perhaps a telling point that these foreign investments have gone mostly into limited areas in Africa, namely, Ghana, Zimbabwe, Mauritius and Botswana, Africa's growth economies. They have not been as widespread and as diversified as a genuine renewed interest on the continent would dictate.

THE POLITICAL CLIMATE AND PREVAILING ECONOMIC DOGMA AND THE PROSPECTS OF REAL GROWTH FOR AFRICA

The economic outlook presented above however encouraging, must be viewed within the political context. This, in turn, provides the setting for a consideration of the ideology which underpins these attempts.

In much of the African continent there exists, no doubt, an unquestionable willingness and a yearning to change old ways. This disposition, however, obtains against a background of a political culture that is not as yet completely amenable to change. Despotic rulers and an entrenched repressive system act, very resolutely, as a bulwark against any democratic change. Undoubtedly, some very pronounced changes have taken place in some African countries, but this group remains the exception, and a very minute exception at that.   An almost complete abandonment of the principles defining and allocating responsibilities to institutions for the protection of the people on whose behalf governments exercise its power defines the political climate in Africa.   Since these changes have been undertaken under a system that has not redefined itself nor taken the peoples interests into consideration, the fundamental problem of lack of articulation of overall national interests facing Africa, has not been addressed.   The economic changes, such as they are, have been built upon the most ephemeral of foundations.   It is therefore highly doubtful that any long lasting change has taken place.   The new wine that has been put in an old bottle may simply burst the old bottle.   For Africa to undertake economic changes first without necessary adjustments in the political process, is analogous to putting the cart before the horse: an undertaking futile for the arranger and annoying to the horse.   Let us consider the economic philosophy that has provided this impetus.

The paradigm constructed by the Breton Woods institutions -- the open market system -- has not as yet met with any easily discernible success quantified in terms of expansionary tendencies, that is, sustained social and economic transformation.   This is because the cornerstone of this approach is that, once these states adopted realistic exchange rates, curbed the money supply, balanced their budgets and cut subsidies (the structural adjustment package usually include cuts in social spending, privatization of public companies, wage suppression, business deregulation, trade liberalization and tight restrictions on credits and interest rates), growth was all but assured. That is, these prescriptions were provided as a panacea.   This approach is however, as it has been observed elsewhere, a strictly monetary approach and a preoccupation with balance- of- payments analysis which generated too uniform and rigid conclusions on the required content of programs.[42]   In Africa, the gravitational tendency of this application has been towards the contractional, not the expansionary.   This is because most governmentt have been required to drastically cut their expenditure programs and government expenditure in Africa is the largest source of capital growth.   Two examples will illustrate the leading role played by the governments of Africa in their economies.   In Tanzania, 95 per cent of all credit extended between 1970 and 1980 went to the public sector,[43] and in Zambia, 80 per cent of the economy is under government control.   These two examples are not exclusive but illustrative of this major attribute of the African economy.   One major explanation for this is the existence of a large informal sector side by side with the modern economy.   While the subsistence sector may be, "in one sense a stabilizing influence on the economy, where expansion in output is a key objective, it clearly acts as a drag".[44]   This has precisely been the case in Africa. The lack of real growth in Africa has left capital ossified at the finite quantity of pre-capitalist production. The reason why these governments have been required to relinquish this leading role was the claim that the kind of expenditure, usually involving large deficit financing, which the African countries are wont to make is excessive and leads to inflationary pressures. But the zone in which a rise in demand will lead to significant price changes relates to the zone where unemployment is extremely low so that no significant rise in output from existing productive capacity is possible. It is difficult to envision the application of this Keynesian model of growth to Africa where capital is still the missing link in the development chain and as such its marginal productivity is still very high. In an economy with mass unemployment and underemployment (so called disguised unemployment in agriculture), and against a structural backdrop of undercapitalized private sector and underutilized factors, it is not so clear the relevance of such an advocacy. The reality is that the Breton Woods institutions have not taken cognizance of the structural differences[45] between the developed industrial North and the under-developed African economies. The emphasis on deregulation, especially on privatization seems to be culled directly from the economic principles obtainable in the United States which is welded to an ideological schemata that obliges it to seek to maintain a dichotomy between government and industrial/entrepreneurial capital. It also reflects the extremely short term approach to economic planning here marking a civilization, as Gunnar Mydral, has written, which interests is "focused upon the immediate, the concrete and the experimental"[46] with the result that there is an incredible "tendency to near sightedness among both politicians and experts".[47] The emphasis on the open market has excluded the need to lay a solid foundation for an economy and start it on a slow and even course of growth, which is after all what real development means. Because the African economies are not corporations which must show profits at the end of the year, such Margaret Thatcher- and Ronald Reagan-like artificially induced growths with predictable consequences, cannot be relevant for Africa. The approach to economic development in Japan and Southeast Asia where government and private business is not distinguishable is more instructive (Africa can identify with their experience of development). Harohiko Fukui for instance, has pointed out the immense importance of the tripodal nature of the Japanese economic decision making environment to Japan's international trade.[48]

If Western economic models must be transplanted, ideologues of the Breton Woods need to take a developmental historical reference point that is appropriate. The present production relations of Africa resemble an earlier industrial developmental stage in the West and it is from here that an appropriate inference must be drawn. Having made the point about historical process relevance, it is still compounding that Africa is called upon to maintain an ideological purity even when this has been greatly diluted in the West. The African economies, for instance, have been required to cut all subsidies and, as we have noted, these subsidies have been cut in almost all African states with disastrous social consequences (In Zimbabwe on bread, in Cote D'Ivoire to agriculture and in Nigeria on petroleum products, to mention a few cases). A major fallacy inherent in this approach is the presupposition that these subsidies are injurious to economic development. Even when contemporary Western economies continue to maintain huge subsidies (the current round of GATT talks was held up for a considerable number of years over European and American disagreements on agricultural subsidies), protectionist covers and other non-tariff barriers in place, the African countries have been required, as a condition of economic progress, to remove them. Cote D'Ivoire, for instance is required to cut all subsidies in support of its struggling agricultural sector, the mainstay of its export economy, yet the EEC and the USA continue to provide succor and extend extensive protectionist cover to their own non-infant sectors. There are also many other contradictions of particular relevance. For instance, Nigeria was required to cut petroleum subsidies on the assumption that the domestic price of this product was below its natural level. Subsequently, prices were hiked. But this hike in prices was the equivalent of the imposition of additional tax burden where income is stagnant which removes disposable incomes and depreciates little available savings. As with these kinds of assumptions, the premise is often false. Such a belief that domestic prices are below the market price often is a most horrific sacrifice of reason to profit making. To derive the local cost of petroleum from the price which consumers pay in the world market is to assume that the international market price is *the* natural level. Cartel and oligopolies may work in the politics of international economic relations to influence world commodity prices, but the local cost of any commodity must still follow the price mechanisms established by domestic relations of production. With local petroleum products, an abundant commodity, at their natural local prices, the Nigerian increment has been tantamount to an arbitrary hike unnecessarily burdening consumers when growth in consumption was what was needed. Even if there was a subsidy, there is a certain economic logic behind it which can hardly be faulted. This rationale may be related for this analysis by an appropriate comparison for that kind of subsidy, based on the critical role in the economy, and at the commensurate level of economic development. This is the controls imposed on the price of wheat in 18/19th century England and France when prices were held down by subsidy to allow for even growth in industrial activity. A full account is given by Kindleberger.[49] Since the economic model developed for Africa is one which is inappropriate, it is of little wonder that the resultant effect of this package has been to curb inflation in a few places (in Ghana from 123 per cent to 13 per cent in August, 1993 -although the African Development Bank puts this figure at 28 per cent) but overall, to produce little or no cumulative progression in the growth and development process (We conceive of development as "less dependency and self-sustained growth based on the local capital accumulation and on the dynamism of the industrial sector.")[50] Indeed, following these programs, some states are mired in worse economic situations than they could possibly ever be.

It is a fact that IMF/IBRD bashing has become as fashionable in Africa as Japan bashing has become in the USA. Often, this reflects more on emotional considerations than on economic reasoning. The effects of these policies on Africa have generally been ruinous, a fact that has been carefully documented.[51]   Our analysis is therefore not based on humbugging sentiments. It is for this reason that we have chosen Ghana, the country in which the IMF/IBRD involvement has been very pronounced, to illustrate the inadequacy of the normative principles being pursued.

Between April 1989 and March 1992, Ghana received funding to the tune of $1,640 million from the IMF, and between 1984 and 1989, it received about seven policy based credits worth $400 million supported with further conventional lending of about $269 million. With the strong recommendation of these institutions, funds from other bilateral sources were made readily available to the government which generally has received funds in excess of its requests. To follow the account provided by the *West Africa* magazine, in 1986, it was pledged $608 million, $108 million above the level suggested by the World Bank, by the Paris Club of donor nations. In 1987, it further received $800 million from the Paris Club. This was followed in 1989 by another $900 million grant (exceeding by $100 million the World Bank's suggested amount). In that same year, 1989, it secured funding to the value of over $500 million from bilateral sources plus $430 million received from the World Bank and its affiliates. It also received a further $120 million concessional credit from the International Development Association, IDA, in support of the second phase of its structural reform program. In 1991, it received additional support worth $970 million from the Consultative Group on Ghana (nine countries and the World Bank). About $2.1 billion was pledged in 1993.[52]   Despite the pliability of the Ghanaian leadership, the tremendous influence enjoyed by the Breton Woods institutions, and the readily available development funds, there has been very little noticeable impact on the Ghanaian economy with respect to certain conventional critical indices of economic measurement.

This program is yet to account for any satisfactory impact on the standard of living of the people of Ghana. The index of real per capita income for instance, was higher in 1980 than in 1991. Well aware of this situation, the Minister for Finance and Economic Planning was forced to conclude in a public statement[53] that it will take about 30 years for the people of Ghana to reap the benefit of this program. Despite the fact that the program was purchased with a loss of national dignity and a diminution in national prestige as Zaya Yeebo's study has shown,[54] the social costs have been quite profound. The adjustments called for by this orthodoxy obliged the government to make about 200,000 workers redundant and under the open economy many local businesses have been forced to close in the face of unfair competition with goods from the East-Asian NICs. Apart from these social and economic costs, there has been very little movement in the rate of economic growth. Ghana has maintained, over the period of the adjustment, a GDP growth of about-3 percent, a marginal improvement over the 1.3 per cent annual average of 1965-1980. The anticipated structural transformation of the economy is yet to take place. As percentages of GDP by sector, agriculture still accounts for 48 per cent of all activity, industry for 16 per cent and manufacturing for 9 per cent.[55] What has changed was Ghana's debt service ratio (as percentage of export earnings) from 13.1 per cent in 1980 to 34.9 in 1990 and to 36.7 in 1992. Ghana's debt which has steadily grown from about $1.4 billion to $3.5 billion in 1990 to the current level of $4.2 billion has resulted to place it in a position of chronic capital hemorrhage. With a total debt to the IMF of about $1.35 billion, Ghana for instance, has paid the organization since 1987, more than what it has received, as one carefully documented study has shown.[56] The case of Ghana clearly illustrates Carol Lancaster's point that economic reform in Africa is 'hampered by a large debt overhang which absorbs scarce foreign exchange.'[57]

For Ghana and for many other countries in Africa, it is a vicious cycle of debt, more capital to pay and more debt. Ghanaians in particular must be wondering, in the words of Albert Camus, why the doctrines that explain everything to them also debilitate them at the same time. The Breton Woods doctrine seems to have relieved them of the weight of their own lives, yet they have had to carry it alone.

Although Ghana provides an adequate example, it is not an isolated case. The social impact of these policies on Kenya have been quite as profound. Here, following the policy requirement, 26 per cent of the civil service population and 20 per cent of the teaching staff have lost their jobs. In Cote D'Ivoire, the government removal of its support to cocoa farmers has decimated the industry and has forced many small producers, the back bone of the African production system, out of the industry. An increase in the number of women dying in childbirth in Zimbabwe, in the wake of forced cutbacks in public health expenditure, has also been documented.[58] Still, nowhere in Africa has any transformation been produced following the adoption of these policies. It is also very difficult to see where any framework for sustainable growth has been laid. There can, therefore, hardly be any doubt that the application of these policies have been beneficial. Clearly, they have not. Like Sisyphus, whose "whole being is exerted toward accomplishing nothing", Africa's face is a face too close to stone and a "face that toils so close to stones is already stone itself"[59]

Although the financial discipline imposed by these programs, in addition to some limited internal political reorganizations within these economies, may have, to some extent, curbed the accumulated structural distortions in the domestic structure, the African states' lack of articulation of overall national interests and the incoherence of their policy objectives have not been the subject of any extensive re-examination. In fact, the necessity for the continuation of signed contracts have predisposed the organizations to support repressive regimes and compromise acceptable political values. When Jerry Rawlings rigged Ghanaian elections to his favor, it was to the unstated wish of the IMF/IBRD that he stay in power to pay his debts.

Reubens[60] has pointed out the entanglement of US foreign aid programs in schemes for 'resisting' and 'containing' the cold war and thus serving very little purpose for development in the recipient countries. Like this aid, the programs run by these organizations which the US controls,[61] is distorting development in Africa. This is being accomplished in a number of ways.

While the policy of trade liberalization is negating domestic industrial production in the failure to affect the growth of local capital, deregulation has allowed governments to lose control over fiscal and monetary policy. Based on the classical economics notion of the invisible hand, the policy of liberalization allows the economy to run entirely on the dictates of the market. That is, self correcting market forces would remedy imbalances in the market place. Additional resources will, for instance, be attracted to hitherto monopoly profit areas, the open market serving an equilibrating function. In that same vein, additional capital will be attracted to depressed areas. The goal is the efficient allocation of resources by the interplay of the forces of demand and supply. This is an imperative not different from Milton Friedman's. Indeed, Friedman became the "chief priest" of this orthodoxy by providing a dialectic that conceives of freedom in terms of the free market.[62] Although Friedman was not concerned with developing systems, this is the position from which much of the scholarship and rhetoric of the "supply siders" has drawn. It is the intellectual force behind the system devised by the IMF and the World Bank and extended to Africa.

What this kind of approach neglects is the low level of political development in the continent as well as the fact that capital is *the* scarce factor in Africa. Such an open system, rather than serve an equalization function, will merely serve to reinforce the level of existing market distortions. It is to foreigners who are more likely to possess the needed capital that the alleged benefits will accrue. This is because many of these foreign companies already enjoy large economies of scale attendant upon large scale industrial production. This enables them to corner the market and to reap monopoly rents. In the new environment underlined by relaxed foreign repatriation laws, this profit will easily be repatriated. In terms of the supply and the marketing of consumer products, local capital will easily be eased out by cheap sources from elsewhere (as happened in Ghana). In this kind of environment, foreign investment, rather than have a dynamic impact, will simply, as Hla Myint[63] has posited, "fossilize the efficiency and the earnings of the 'domestic factors' of production at their limited low level". As this happens, the foreigners 'become the managers as the indegenes wield shovels'. In the words of Kindleberger, the rich (North) gets richer while the poor(South) have children. The Japanese operate a largely regulated and tightly closed domestic market. In the USA and Europe high tariffs and other non-tariff barriers and large subsidies to private companies which give them a competitive edge in the market, have become *de rigueur*. What has been proposed and is already in place in Africa is not an approach to development that can be found in existence among the developed or the developing economies.

In terms of the effect of this approach on government capability in Africa, this cannot be better illustrated than by the remarks of the former head of the World Bank, Robert S. McNamara. As he phrased it;

> In Africa, entire ministries are no longer in adequate control of their budget and personnel, public officials have lost the capacity to carry out their proper tasks, state universities, scientific facilities, statistics offices that have seriously declined in the quality of their work, parastatal organizations and marketing boards that impede rather than promote productivity and critically important agricultural research institutions that are becoming increasingly ineffective".[64]

Indeed, the requirement restricting public goods expenditure is yet the most ominous development arising from this program. This is because no government initial development program has ever failed to recognize the centrality of the creation of public overhead facilities in forwarding growth and development. In that respect, all have given it priority and even when growth has taken place at a desirable level, improvement and replacement outlay still feature very prominently in the budgets of these nations. Bill Clinton, President of the USA, greatly emphasized this need during his 1992 campaign for the presidency and infrastructure building is one of the main bedrocks of the 1993 US budget. In the case of Africa, expenditure in non-self liquidating but absorptive capacity increasing infrastructure is critical to long-term growth. N. Kaldor puts the point about this need quite succinctly. According to him, "irrespective of the prevailing ideology, or the political color of particular governments, the economic and cultural development of a country requires the efficient and steadily expanding provision of a whole host of non-revenue-yielding services -- education, health, communication systems and so on -- commonly known as 'infrastructure'".[65] As important as this is to development, it is almost unacceptable within the confines of the Breton Woods dogma prevailing in Africa. It is, therefore, difficult to see where the residual strength have been built up for these economies and how the program is constructed to serve to optimize Africa's growth potential. Although scholarship in the West are wont to attribute every conceivable progress in these economies to this philosophy, it is not within the context of this paradigm that a renewed prospect for growth, much unlike the earlier post-independent optimism which was not accompanied by structural changes, can be realized. In adhering to this program and not fulfilling their social responsibilities, the gap between government and the governed in Africa have further widened.[66] While governments have danced to the tune of an imported piper, the people deafened by hunger and deprivation cannot enjoy the music. Communication continues to be lost and state and society remain incongruous.

The Breton Woods institutions cannot dismiss internally generated ideas and development inputs as the obscurantism of the past with respect to economic growth as they have done, for its own idea is not a panacea. Rather, a sustainable development -- one which must be predicated on the long run must involve a concert of efforts. A crucial partnership, an eclectic fusion of domestic and external variables, must be forged. Alone it cannot provide the necessary capital and, therefore, it must allow for the development of local capital, thus, it must make provisions for a partnership with domestic capital. As the Carnegie Endowment National Commission on America and the New World[67] study has shown, capital from abroad will increasingly be unavailable and "most developing countries will have to finance their domestic investment requirements largely from their own resources". This document goes on further to observe that "concessional aid for the world's poorer countries will remain extremely tight, partly because of new requirements of the states of Eastern Europe and the Former Soviet Union.[68]   For this reason, the growth of domestic capital must be encouraged. The realities of modern growth precludes an emphasis on rigid dogma. A Kindleberger has appropriately observed, it is simply "fatuous to be doctrinaire about development problems."[69]

It is a fact that the Breton Woods institutions are concerned to help the African economies curb accumulated structural distortions in their domestic structure and to that extent, they require that the transitional process of changing the base of growth be accomplished. This transitional process of building up and changing the economic base must take place for resisting the changes called for by the market place will put these economies at an even greater peril. That paradigm constructed by the Breton Woods institutions simply does not properly articulate this need for Africa.

CHAPTER 3

ENDNOTES

1. Namely, the ratio of deposit money to money supply and the ratio of the banking systems' claims on the private sector to national income. See U. Tun Wai "Interest rates in the organized money markets of underdeveloped countries" *International Monetary Fund Papers*, vol.5, no.2, August 1956.

2. The Nigerian Stock Exchange reacted to a dramatic downward swing in the economy during a sustained closure of businesses and run on banks precipitated by the political crisis of 1993, by placing an embargo on all trading. This position was however overturned by the Securities and Exchange Commission. It shows however the underdeveloped nature of these institutions.

3. A n account provided by the London, "Financial Times" March 16, 1992. Page vi (Survey on Nigeria).

4. Ragner Nurske, *The Problem of Capital Formation in Underdeveloped Countries* (Oxford: Basil Blackwell) 1953 page 28. As Adam Smith simply explains, 'whenever a great deal can be made by the use of money, a great deal will commonly be given for the use of it'. See, *An Inquiry into the Nature and Causes of the Wealth of Nations*, (eds.) R.H Campbell, A.S Skinner and, W.B Todd (Oxford: Clarendon Press) 1976. Page 105.

5. See, M. Crowder, *West Africa Under Colonial Rule* (London:Hutchinson Publishers) 1978.

6. To Spindler, "the links between Japanese commercial banking and foreign policy reflect both a natural extension of domestic economic and political relationships and an adaptive response to Japan's relative position of vulnerability in the world". Andrew J. Spindler, *The Politics of International Credit: Private Finance and Foreign Policy in Germany and Japan* (Washington D.C: The Brookings Institute) 1984. Page 114.

7. As Albretcht Rothacher puts it, "government and business are linked in every aspect of business abroad" See, "The Formulation of Japanese Foreign Policy" *Millenium, Journal of International Studies,* London School of Economics. Spring 1981, vol.10, no.1, 19 (pp1-13).

8.   Aloy Chife, "The Political Economy of North-South Relations:Japan's Relations with Nigeria, 1960-1985. Ph.D Thesis, London School of Economics. August 1992. Page 271.

9.   Maurice J. Williams, "The Aid Problems of the OPEC countries, *Foreign Affairs*, Vol 54, 1976 pp.309/315.

10.   To date, the OPEC fund has supported 14 developments in Burkina Faso with credit assistance totalling $58.38 million.

11.   As reflected in the country's budget for the 1992/93 fiscal year.

12.   Account provided by the "Nigerian Review" December, 1968 Page 25. To strengthen their position in Africa, the Federation of Economic Organizations, Japan's most powerful business organization, set up a special Africa commission while the Japanese diet (parliament) established the "Association for Economic cooperation and Development in Africa".

13.   "*US Corporate Interests in Africa*" Report to the Committee on Foreign Relations United States Senate by Senator Dick Clark, Iowa Chairman, Sub-Committee on African Affairs. January 1978 (Washington: US Government Printing Office) 1978.

14.   The Economist, *Book of Vital World Statistics* (Great Britain: Hutchinson Business Books) 1990.

15.   London, 1993. Quoted in "West Africa" 2-8 August 1993. Page 1343.

16.   A comprehensive account of these resource diversification attempts is provided by Paul Onya "Africa digs deep to tap plentiful ores and minerals" PP14-15, in "Africa business" April 1992.

17.   For a more elaborate account, see "The African Petroleum Monitor", Vol.1, No.2, Nov/Dec. 1992.

18.   *ibid*, page 13.

19.   The IDA provided the sum of $11 million in 1991 which enabled Chad to construct a refinery, an oil pipeline and a power plant.

20.   London "Financial Times", July 13, 1992.

21. "The Petroleum Monitor *ibid.*

22. *ibid*, Page 8.

23. Ogen Kevin Aliro, *Uganda: Paying the Price of Growing Tobacco* (London: The Panos Institute) 1993.

24. For a full account of this process, see, Adebayo Adedeji (ed.),*The Indegenization of African Economies* (London: Hutchinson University Library) 1981.

25. David Goldsbrough, 'Foreign Direct Investment in Developing Countries: Trends, Policy issues and Prospects' in Toivo Miljan (ed.), *The Political Economy of North-South Relations* (Peterborough, Canada: Broadview Press) 1987 Page 220, 224.

26. Despite the fact that one serious study evaluating the policy of privatization in Africa finds that this policy can only play a limited role in the economic future of the continent. See, William Cavendish, Percy S. Mistry and Christopher Adam *Adjusting Privatization* (London: James Curry) 1992.

27. For elaboration, See, Okumura Ariyoshi, 'Japan and East Asia' in Christopher Sanders (ed.), *The Political Economy of New and Old Industrial Countries* (London: Butterworth and Company), 1981.

28. Most African states had cut diplomatic relations with Israel in sympathy with the Arab members of the Organization for African Unity, OAU, following the Arab-Israeli war of 1973. Most of these states have since re-established these ties.

29. See, Emeka Ezeife, 'Nigeria' in Adebayo Adedeji (ed.) *ibid* PP164-186. Relevant laws on page 169/170, 173/174.

30. Goldsbrough 'Foreign direct investment...'in Miljan *ibid* Page 220. Further discussion of these benefits is provided by Kathryn Morton and Peter Tulloch, *Trade and Developing Countries* (London: Overseas Development Institute) 1977. Page 214ff.

31. Goldsbrough, *ibid* Page 220.

32. Bertil Ohlin, *Some Insufficiencies in the Theories of International Economic Relations* (Princeton University: International Finance Section) 1979 Page 5.

33.   International Finance Corporation, *Trends in Private Investments in Developing Countries* 1992.

34.   *ibid.*

35.   Especially in Japan. See, Hideo Oda and Kazuyoshi Aoki,'Japan and Africa: beyond the fragile partnership' in Robert S. Ozaki and Walter Arnold (eds.), *Japan's Foreign Relations: A Global Search For Economic Security* (Boulder: Westview Press), 1985. PP153-68.

36.   See, Dharam P. Ghai, 'Perspectives on future economic prospects and problems in Africa'in Jagdish N. Bhagwati, *Economics and World Order from the 1970s to the 1990s* (New York: Macmillan publishers) 1972. PP257-286.

37.   Eric Nordlinger, *Soldiers and Politics: Military Coups and Governments* (Englewood Cliffs, N.J.: Prentice Hall) 1977, page 6.

38.   Robert Jackson and Carl Rosberg, *Personal Rule in Black Africa: Princes, Autocrats, Prophets, Tyrants* (Berkeley: University of California Press) 1982.

39.   Ohlin *ibid* Page 7.

40.   As this author has shown in "Plus ca change, plus ca la meme chose: The Political Sociology of Change for Development in the 'new' Africa" Revised Paper Presented at the Annual Third World Studies Conference, University of Nebraska, Omaha, Nebraska October 1993.

41.   The International Finance Corporation *1993 Report* Quoted in "African Business" No 81, October 1993 Page 4.

42.   The conclusion of the study, *North-South: A Programme for Survival* Report of the Independent Commission on International Development Issues Under the Chairmanship of Willy Brandt (London: Pan Books), 1980 Page 215.

43.   Report of the Directorate of Economic Research and Policy Planning.

44.   The United Nations, *World Economic Survey, 1969-1970: The Developing Countries in the 1960s: The Problem of Appraising Progress* (New York) 1971 Page 15.

45. This point was made as early as 1981 by Graham Bird, in "Financial Flows to Developing Countries: The role of the International Monetary Fund" *Review of International Studies*, 7, 1981 Page 93.

46. Gunnar Myrdal *Challenge To Affluence* (New York: Vintage Books) 1965, page 86.

47. Gunnar Myrdal, *An American Dilemma* (New York: Harpers) 1944. Quoted in *Challenge to Affluence, ibid.*

48. Harohiko Fukui, 'Foreign Policy Making in Japan'. Paper Presented at the 1974 Annual Meeting of the Association of Asian Studies, Boston, 1-3 April, 1974.

49. Charles P. Kindleberger, *Foreign Trade and the National Economy* (New Haven: Yale University Press) 1962.

50. Fernando Henrigue Cardosso and Enzo Faletto, *Dependency and Development in Latin America* (Trans. Majory Mattingly Urquidi) (Berkeley: University of California Press) 1979 Page 10.

51. The Development Group of Alternative Policies, *The Other Side of the Story: The Real Impact of World Bank and IMF Structural Adjustment Programs* Washington 1993. OXFAM, *Africa: Make or Break* London 1993 (Advises these institutions to keep out of Africa if they cannot tailor policy prescriptions to domestic requirements reflecting Africa's situation. Notes that their activities have become 'increasingly damaging' to these economies). The British Overseas Development Institute, *Development Policy Review* 1993 (believes that these policies are moving African economies away from a satisfactory development path). The detrimental effects of these policies have further been documented in a "West Africa" magazine study titled the 'debt trap'. See edition of 2-8 August, 1993. PP1337-1339.

52. "West Africa" 26 July-1 August, 1993.

53. Interview given to the BBC. "West Africa" *ibid.*

54. Zaya Yeebo, *Ghana: The Struggle for Popular Power* (London: New Beacon Books), 1992.

55. Figures from World Bank *Report 1990*.

56. The Development Group of Alternative Policies *ibid.*

57.   Carol Lancaster, *African Economic Reform: The External Dimension* (Institute for International Economics), 1991.

58.   The Development Group of Alternative Policies, *ibid.*

59.   Albert Camus, *The Myth of Sisyphus and other Essays* (New York: Vintage Books) 1955 Page 89.

60.   Edwin P. Reubens,'An Overview of the NIEO' in Edwin P. Reubens (ed.), *The Challenge of the New International Economic Order* (Boulder: Westview Press), 1981 Page 31.

61.   The United States constantly uses its "influence to obtain or reject loans for countries based on how well it likes the policies of their governments... this influence is often decisive in the institutions because votes are weighted according to the size of the voting country's financial contribution and the US is the biggest contributor." Report of the Congressional Research Service authored by Caleb Rossiter of Cornell University. Quoted in "West Africa" *ibid.*

62.   As Friedman put it, "every act of government intervention limits the area of individual freedom directly and threatens the preservation of freedom indirectly." See, Milton Friedman, *Capitalism and Freedom* (Chicago: The University of Chicago Press) 1982. Passage quoted on page 32. .

63.   The gains from international trade and the Backward countries" *Review of Economic Studies* No 58, 1954-1955. PP129-142.

64.   Quoted in "West Africa" 2-8 August, 1993 Page 1338.

65.   N. Kaldor, "Taxation for economic development" *Journal of Modern African Studies* Vol 1, No 1, 1963. PP7-11,13.

66.   Closing this gap is very important because as Myron Weiner has written, "in modern societies, governments are so engaged in effecting the economy, social welfare, and defense that there must be a closer interaction between government and the governed". See, Myron Weiner, 'Political integration and political development' in *New Nations: The Problem of Political Development. The Annals of the American Academy of Political and Social Science.* March 1965 Page 61.

67.   *Changing Our Ways: America and the New World* 1993.

68. *ibid.*

69. Charles P. Kindleberger, *Economic Development* (New York: McGraw Hill) 1977, page 130.

CHAPTER 4

Religious Institutions as Mediating Structures: A Theological-Ethical Perspective on Political Reform in Africa

Introduction

In October 1990, as Iraq on one side and the United States and its allies on the other confronted one another in the Persian Gulf, President George Bush gave a speech at the United Nations on a theme that was meant to provide a new moral framework for world politics. The end of the Cold War, according to Mr. Bush, brought with it the opportunity to build a new world order. The key task of this world's moral renaissance, "now, first, and always," he further submitted, would "be to state that aggression will not be tolerated."[1] A year after President Bush delivered his speech, a former Nigerian Foreign Affairs minister, Professor Bolaji Akinyemi, attempted to provide an epistemological and sociological link between the theme of "New World Order" and the internal politics of post-colonial Africa. In a lecture given at the inaugural meeting of the Nigerian Society of International Affairs, Akinyemi argued that unless the nations of Africa contextualized this macrocosmic moral-political concern, the continent would be further marginalized in the emerging global race to establish a new political ethos. Included in the catalog of prevailing values and practices which Africa must rid herself of, he pointed out, are "a combination of one party rule or military rule and a government-owned economy," all of which have hitherto functioned as "a recipe for corruption and mismanagement."[2] In addition to Africa's unsavory political climate, the continent also faces innumerable social and cultural problems. Food scarcity, high unemployment and declining wages, human rights violations, ethnic violence, widening regional disparities, and an overemphasis on military spending are strong indicators of disintegration in several African countries today.

To be sure, each of these 'problem indicators' sufficiently qualifies as a subject of scholarly inquiry for the simple reason that all of them deserve urgent and very comprehensive solution. However, my focus in this paper is on Africa's political predicament, and more narrowly, on the religious dimension of this enigma. Many African countries are today held captive to divergent and conflictual religious theories of governance. For example, efforts to contrive and institutionalize civil unity in the Sudan and Nigeria, among others, have been paralyzed not only because a sustainable political vision is lacking but also because of cacophonous religious voices. A central question that I hope to address in this paper, therefore, is how the sociological fact of religious plurality in Africa can be transformed from being a cultural slander to a catalyst for political reform. More specifically, how may diverse communities of faith in Africa help supply a vision of a common political ground which can serve as a basis of deliberation and judgment in their respective social settings?

Admittedly, thrusting religion into the realm of politics presents a fundamental problem not only for Africa but for several parts of the world today. In fact, the conventional wisdom seems to be in favor of domesticating and privatizing religion as strictly as possible because, as one journalist put it, "religion is a slippery terrain, more slippery than a banana peel, and wisdom's path is to avoid that terrain."[3] In a similar vein, Don Ohadike was of the view that a society which

> draws its entire inspiration from religion, whether traditional or universalistic, lives in the past. Such a society progresses in a cyclical fashion, living under the same economic, legal, and political systems, and, in concrete terms, achieves nothing."[4]

Even more poignantly paradoxical is the structure of the emerging world order which is anything but stable and the aggressive contributions of religion to this frightening scene. As rightly noted in a recent illuminating study of this problem, "the new world order...is characterized not only by the rise of new economic forces, a crumbling of old empires, and the discrediting of communism, but also by the resurgence of parochial identities based on ethnic and religious allegiances."[5] Nowhere is the divisive potential of religion more pronounced than in Africa. The contiguity of Africa's religious diversity with its extraordinary ethnic and regional diffuseness has contributed immensely to the practice of politicizing communalistic identities. Given this reality, the onus of responsibility is on those who seek a more public role of religion in Africa, and this is precisely what I intend to demonstrate in this paper.

Towards this end, I shall begin with a methodological clarification. Students of religion generally disagree on which of religion's three variables, as identified by Max Weber--namely, theological doctrine, practical religion, and the practical religion of the converted--should receive primary attention.[6] The dominant theories of religion and politics in Africa have tended to emphasize one or the other of these aspects of religious culture, thereby circumscribing the true dynamics of interaction between religion and politics on the continent. In his contribution to this debate, David Laitin pointed out that "world religions constitute complex social realities; and adherents to these religions are not limited in their repertoires for action by a single system of symbols."[7] So understood, religion in Africa must be seen as constituting a confluence of significance in which theological doctrines, ethical prescriptions, and the organizational structures of religious communities impinge themselves on society. According to Sulayman Nyang, there is always a strikingly religious hermeneutic underpinning the daily rhythm of life in Africa:

> Social developments have always assumed a religious character. Each new development in the African social universe has been a lesson in religious understanding, and each social event carries religious meanings attached to it by the members of society.[8]

The discussion that follows in this paper presupposes all these aspects of religious culture. In the first part, I define the concept of mediating structures as it has arisen in social and political philosophy. The subsequent sections focus on two distinctive ways in which religious morality, despite and because of its diversity, can be responsibly mediated to society as an exercise in political rejuvenation. A topic of this kind also requires a contextual specificity, considering the fact that Africa is really a family name for a multitude of countries. I have chosen to focus on Nigeria as an illustration of the peculiar predicament facing post-colonial Africa. This should hardly sound pretentious. As the most populous country in Africa, it has faced more political crises in the religious domain than any other countries in that part of the world. Moreover, it has experimented with a variety of political systems, all proving culturally and prescriptively elusive. A theological and ethical exploration of the theme of mediating structures as applied to a study of religious temperament in Nigeria could thus justifiably serve as a basis for gaining a clearer perspective on the larger African reality. It is to this theme that I now turn.

Religions As Mediating Structures

In Nigeria, an accurate census has been a historical rarity. Consequently, there are no reliable data about the numbers of religious adherents in the country. However, over 80 million of the estimated 105 million Nigerians belong to the two dominant religions in the country, namely, Islam and Christianity. It has also been suggested that more than half of the rest of the population associate themselves with the indigenous religions.[9] Religious presence in Nigeria is thus a very formidable phenomenon. What is more unsettling, as Dr. Olukunle of the University of Ibadan has pointed out, is the disjunction between this high religiosity and a very arid moral life of the people. In his usual melancholic prognostication about Nigeria, he said,

> The future is not particularly bright for religious dispositions in this country, not because there are not enough copies of the Bible and the Koran and not because there are not enough religious leaders to preach but precisely because the grounds have been prepared to make religion (not God) a lame duck.[10]

While Olukunle's prophecy may be dismissed by some people as a rattle of an unrepentant Marxist, a religious insider's observation may serve to confirm the point that the ethical impact of religions in Nigeria has been microcosmic. Pastor Adebanjo Edema, of a Nigerian Pentecostal Church, said in a study paper presented to the Nigerian Fellowship of Graduate Christians, that the greatest malady which has infested the country is not really the absence of religious people in public service but the failure of those who have served to mediate the ethical meaning of their respective traditions to society *writ large*. In a tone reminiscent of the Old Testament prophets, he told his audience that:

> The indifference or short-sightedness of most Christians about national affairs [has] brought...the nation to her knees...The Christians who once participated in politics made little or no impact on our culture. Many were easily carried down the lane of moral bankruptcy having listened to and imitated those who have no regards for morals.[11]

Mutatis mutandis, what Edema said about the Christians is equally applicable to the Muslims, and certainly, to all Nigerian religious adherents who are concerned about making a positive public difference.

One way in which Nigeria's religious people and communities can mediate an appropriate ethical meaning to the society is by conceiving of themselves as "mediating structures." Peter Berger and Richard Neuhaus define mediating structures as "those institutions standing between the individual in his private life and the large institutions of public life."[12] Examples of these are the neighborhood, family, church, and voluntary associations. Mediating structures are those "little platoons [which] we belong to in society," and constitute "the first principle of public affections."[13] Alex de Tocqueville describes the science of mediating structures or independent associations as "the mother of science; the progress of all the rest depends upon the progress it has made."[14]

The concept of mediating structures is no doubt fraught with definitional imprecision. In many accounts of the concept, not only are the boundaries not clearly defined, the contours constantly shift and the landmarks change. By rejecting the commonplace description of mediating structures as nonprofit and nongovernmental, Franklin Gamwell prefers the term "independent associations" which, to him, "are the most important associations in the social order."[15] In political science literature, the concept of mediating structures has been somehow identified with the idea of "middle structures" existing in both the governmental and the private sector. Johannes Althusius was said to be the first to use the concept of "middle structures" to describe "the lower tiers of government, such as the provinces (or states) and the local governments, along with the family and other associations not under the direction of the central political order."[16] What now pass for "voluntary associations" in contemporary discourse are just a component of Althusius' idea of middle organizations.

James Luther Adams appropriates Althusius' insight to render "democratic society" or state as "an association of associations."[17] This is a more expansive definition of associational life, and certainly extends the scope of the concept beyond the early Tocquevillian approach or some contemporary discussions of the concept of mediating structures which tend to bracket out the governmental sector and large multinational corporations from this category. I shall be using "mediating structures" in this essay against the backdrop of the definition offered by Berger and Neuhaus. It is noteworthy that James Luther Adams himself believes that these structures, in the way being construed here, "function as wedges" that prevent "overweening powers from presenting a united front against criticism."[18]

The ethical understanding of mediating structures is that they are indispensable to the moral reconstruction of public life. The modern world, according to Berger and Neuhaus, is characterized by the crisis of "meaning, fulfillment, and personal identity."[19] This crisis is of a kind that no government can singularly alleviate it by imposing on life one comprehensive order of meaning. Antonio Gramsci, an Italian philosopher, once said that "society is a system of sectors which are partly autonomous, analytically distinct, but mutually influential."[20] Moreover, given the fact that "human needs are multiple and complex, diverse forms of social organizations are required to address them."[21] In this wise, politics assumes quite a different meaning than that which is usually ascribed to it. Contrary to a self-serving conception of politics as an enterprise for calculating "who gets what, when, and how" or simply "a game in which individuals or groups of individuals make moves,"[22] the idea of mediating structures relocates political life within its original Aristotelian context. The defining characteristic of politics, according to this tradition, is dialogue or deliberation oriented to the promotion of the common good. Not only do beliefs about human good play a vital role in defining the parameters of this public discourse, participants in it are bonded by a common normative concern to discover ways in which "human beings are meant to live and what they require from one another to flourish in a human society."[23]

For this purpose, Gramsci specifically pressed for an appreciation of the potentially reformist contributions of religion to public life. He rejected certain anti-intellectual and anti-religious implications of the Marxist dictum that it was not consciousness that determined existence, but existence that determined consciousness. He stressed the creative role of those who, like the Protestant Reformers or the *philosophes* of the French revolution, were clearly thinkers, but were "organically" related to decisive groups of society.[24] It is thus the case that the potential for political and cultural reform increases as mediating structures are able "to pose alternative visions of a better future, to provide citizen training, to foster community rebuilding, and to work for constructive public policy change."[25]

In the last two decades, African scholarship has been marked by a significant appreciation for the potential role of mediating structures to initiate political innovations on the continent. At the core of the arguments in this direction is that "the empowerment of groups in civil society and the enhancement of their capacity to serve as building blocks of the new order" is a fundamental requirement if Africa wants "to forge its own political renaissance."[26] This desired new political culture must be democratic in orientation, and the mediating structures, otherwise referred to in the literature as voluntary or independent associations, can advance it by helping to "give voice to popular demands" as well as encouraging the pluralization of "the institutional environment."[27]

Religious communities should be able to take a lead in this venture, but they will only succeed in doing so if they are willing to "accept and value diversity of membership in an increasingly pluralistic society," "restrain crusading habits of repressive moralism or tendencies to exclude people who are different," and "act in solidarity with the powerless to challenge unjust institutional practices and empower movements for change."[28] In this regard, two specific criteria become pertinent to measuring the effectiveness and relevance of religious contributions to political reform, namely, the prophetic-critical message of religion and the concrete structures of religious *praxis*. I shall now examine each of these areas in turn.

The Prophetic-Critical Functions of Religions

Bryan Hehir, an American Catholic theological ethicist, suggested that the success of the participation of religious bodies in the formation of public policy, will partly depend upon the availability of a strong intellectual leadership and of institutional vehicles of dissemination.[29] These two requirements have been met in Nigeria, not by separate denominational bodies, but mainly through the activities of ecumenically formed bodies within Islam as well as within Christianity.

As early as 1929, the Christian Council of Nigeria (CCN) was formed to provide a single theological-ethical voice for the mainstream Protestant Churches in the country at both the national and international levels.[30] But in post-independence Nigeria, the most unified voice for the Christian community in the country has been aired through the Christian Association of Nigeria (CAN), formed on the 27th of August, 1976. The members of CAN include the Catholic Church, all members of the CCN, and other Christian Churches that do not belong to the CCN.[31] The equivalent ecumenical body among the Muslims is the Nigerian Supreme Council for Islamic Affairs, founded in 1974.[32]

Most studies of the activities of religious bodies (mostly Christian Churches) during the Nigerian civil war (1967-1970) have emphasized their relief and philanthropic roles.[33] But by far their greatest contribution was their interpretation of the events of that period which made it possible to anticipate the war and to discard the prophecies of those who thought by then that Nigeria might never be able to reunite. Two years before the war, the Student Christian Movement of Nigeria (SCM) had warned at its Uyo meeting in December 1965 that "God's judgment is inescapable where man violates the laws of the moral universe and of his own nature as ordained by God."[34] Among the features of the life-styles of the period, as enumerated by the SCM, which were portentous for the nation, included:

> Justice turned upside down, those in power acquiring wealth by questionable means; masses of our people oppressed; hooliganism and thuggery licenced and maintained at the expenses of tax payers; Federal and Regional elections conducted in the most questionable way; truth distorted or

evaded..., [therefore] we can no longer postpone the evil day. Judgment is now upon us in consequence of our moral irresponsibility and guilt.[35]

I have cited this incident to illustrate how religious perspectives can help to raise a seemingly mundane affair to the level of fundamental ethical principles, thereby jettisoning the idea that what is descriptively the case is necessarily normative. The SCM tried to accent the point that Nigerians needed to recognize that they do have a fundamental ability and responsibility to bond into self-disciplining political community. The distinction between "facts" and "value," between what is empirically observable and what is normative, has remained one of the cardinal issues in philosophical and theological ethics.[36]   In his own contribution to this debate, Reinhold Niebuhr argues that

> while egoism is 'natural' in the sense that it is universal, it is not natural in the sense that it does not conform to man's nature who transcends himself indeterminedly and can only have God rather than self for his end.[37]

To counterpoise the culture of narcissistic hedonism, Niebuhr argues that

> love [by which he meant solidarity for the pursuit of the common good] rather than self-love is the law of [human] existence in the sense that man can only be healthy and his communities at peace if man is drawn out of himself and saved from the self-defeating consequences of self-love.[38]

Unfortunately, this kind of prophetic fervor has been declining in the post-1970s history of religions in Nigeria. Religious life in the country, to the extent that one can speak of it, is now marked more by "sentimental self-flagellation" than by "substantive social consciousness." This is so because, like so much of the nation's life, "it suffers from social amnesia," a disease that "prevents systemic social analysis of power, wealth, and influence in society from taking hold" among the people.[39]

Contrary to popular expectations, the national ecumenical religious bodies mentioned above have failed to contribute to the shaping of national public life and to assist in the formation of a coherent moral framework within a pluralistic social order. They have not articulated a macro-morality that is intelligible beyond their immediate religious provenances. Instead, they have succumbed to the ethos of politicizing religion that is pervasive in the entire nation.[40] Thus the single most important task facing religious communities in Nigeria today is how to assist in developing and nurturing a new macro-morality sufficiently robust to accommodate larger interests of the nation and the specific fibers of religious tapestry.

The enduring impact of such contributions is however contigent upon the extent to which religious behavior is governed by the theological virtue of civility. It is not just sufficient to generate religious visions of political change, it is equally important that religious people see their involvement in the struggle for such a change "less as a voice of expertise and more...as one human voice among others," directed to the very public in which their own lives are involved.[41] They have to regard themselves as participants in a drama that involves numerous other actors, and realize that neither the Christian *ecclesia* nor the Muslim *umma* is the director of this drama, but God--"the God who created the worlds of politics, law, science, economics, and culture just as surely as God created the [religious communities] and gave [them] a mission."[42] In short, people of faith must learn how to combine religious fidelity with public civility.

While each religious discussant might enter public debate on his/her theological terms, there has to be a simultaneous recognition of the fact that the source of the social bond and fabric cannot be located in the tenets of any particular religious tradition, for God's presence and God's truth are not exclusively confined to any single religion and its institutions. There is what Laitin rightly describes as "the historical dimension of religious dissemination"[43] in consequence of which it would seem anomalous for any of pluralism's many goods to be absolutized or allowed to dominate others; rather, "the place of each must be recognized and respected in the framework of social existence."[44] Accordingly, efforts to shape public affairs that have not been tested by the rigors of intelligent public argument that presupposes the good will of one's neighbors risk degenerating into ideology and self-deception.

It is also mistaken to claim that cultures and religions are ultimately incommensurable. On the contrary, among the forced options in the current tempo that cannot be ignored without incurring even greater harm or dangers are interreligious conversations. According to Paul Knitter,

> To believe that we are all ultimately trapped within our own cultural-religious confines, with at the most the ability to shout across our borders but never to really engage in conversation, can lead to a type of cultural solipsism in which one is protected from criticisms and suspicions of others; or it can bring one to a new form of fidelism by which one has no grounds to criticize

one's own cultural-linguistic system, or to a potential-ethical toothlessness brought about by the lack of any basis on which to validly and coherently resist what appears to be intolerable in other cultural-linguistic systems.[45]

What this translates to in practical terms is that a particular religious community can often not attain its political goal. One dimension of the religious pluralist dilemma in Nigeria is how to justify the official recognition of certain aspects of religious requirements, e.g., the place of Islamic *Shari'a* in the country's judicial system. While the Muslims remain intransigent in their affirmation of the superiority of the *Shari'a* to the Common Law system, the Christians are also unyielding in their objection to establishing a religious law. One promising way of redefining this problem in a way that may please both sides is the approach proposed by the late Ustadh Mahmoud Mohamed Taha of Sudan. According to him, there are two overlapping messages in Islam, namely, an eternal and universal one of complete justice and equality for all human beings without distinction as to race, creed, or gender, and a transitional message of relative justice among believers in terms of the quality of their belief.[46] Mahmoud proceeded from this basic premise to declare the *Shari'a* as the transitional message, "which by now has served its purpose...[and] and must be superseded by the eternal and universal message, the practical implementation of which has, thus far, been precluded by the realities of human existence."[47] In a tone reminiscent of Ibn Khaldun, Mahmoud argued that "whereas the public law of *Shari'a* was appropriate for the previous stages of human society, it is no longer appropriate and must make way for another version of the public law of Islam."[48]

In his reflection upon the approach of Mahmoud (who was unfortunately executed by the Sudanese government of Nimeiri for holding an heretical view), Abdullahi A. An-Na'im, himself a Sudanese Muslim and Law Professor at the University of Khartoum, saw it as "a viable Islamic alternative."[49] On the one hand, it does not dismiss the public relevance of Islam as a religion, and at the same time "confront[s] the proponents of *Shari'a* with the inadequacy of their model because it will never permit national integration, which is the essential prerequisite for political stability, national security, and social economic development."[50]

While Nigeria and Sudan may be radically dissimilar in the way that power is distributed among the key ethnic and religious groups, they are similar in a number of other ways. They are both multi-ethnic and multi-religious, and in both countries, there is a strong advocacy for the establishment of religion as a state religion. I have argued elsewhere that the current official policy on the place of the *Shari'a* in the Nigerian constitution represents a compromise solution that avoids the two extreme positions represented by Christian and Muslim advocates.[51] In a religiously pluralistic context, it is categorically imperative for all segments of the population, religious and non-religious, to become agents of mature dialogue by subordinating their narrow interests to the civil well-being of all. Another relevant theological fact here is the emphasis that both Nigeria's world religions put upon the finitude of human knowledge through their different doctrines of sin. This theological epistemology provides a good moral basis for genuine civil interaction in a religiously pluralistic society. S. J. Samartha's extensive observations in relation to India are very pertinent here. According to him,

> Any notion that in a pluralistic society just one religion has the only answer to all the problems of human life at all times, for all peoples, and in all cultures is doubtful, despite the vehemence with which such a notion is propagated. Plurality of religions introduces an element of choice when faced with the profound perplexities of life to which people respond differently in different cultures. Alternative visions of life offer different possibilities of meaning and direction to human life. Moreover, in a pluralistic situation the possibilities of mutual criticism and mutual enrichment are greater than in a monoreligious situation.[52]

Whether or not any of these possibilities will occur will depend upon two contingencies. First, it will depend upon whether the state will be alert to its duty and responsibility by providing creative space for dialogue in order that a climate of profound tolerance might grow in the life of the nation. No matter how genuine the intentions of people of various persuasions may be, without an appropriate political context that encourages inter-communal cooperation, such efforts will surely be impeded and frustrated. Military dictatorship, civilian-bureaucratic autocrats, and some greedy religious leaders still constitute an ominous reality in Nigeria. Every effort must be made to debunk the myth underpinning the perpetuation of these dynastic demagogues.

Second, given the historical contributions of Islam and Christianity to Nigerian civilization, one hopes that their adherents will be courageous enough to correct the popular misconception that morality is merely a personal matter, and that the development of public policy is a purely secular or political endeavor, or merely economic or technological in scope. Thus, quite apart from their common monotheistic provenance, Muslims and Christians also have a common task to remind society that there are important moral and religious dimensions to each of the problems facing the country, and that these dimensions be taken into consideration in the development of public policy.

The contemporary Nigerian realities, as accurately described by Segun Gbadegesin, are manifested at three distinct levels of social existence-- economic, social, and political. At the economic level, there are "poverty and hunger, low productivity in the midst of wealth and natural abundance, and economic exploitation of individuals and nations."[53]   At the social plane is found "a cabal of hardened criminals."[54]   The political level does not fare better. Political violence, election rigging, and political intolerance are rules rather than exemptions in Nigeria. In Gbadegesin's words,

> 'Democratically' elected leaders detest opposition while dictators hate criticisms. Leaders seem now to be the only patriots as critics are declared saboteurs and are liable to indefinite incarceration.[55]

From the religious ethical standpoint, these realities reflect "a spiritual crisis [which is] located at the heart of the temporal order."[56]   They are symptoms of what Cornel West characterized as "an existential emptiness"[57] which religion cannot and should not ignore. In contrast to accommodationist forms of religion which usually aid and abet the socio-economic and structural- political conditions that produce this existential absurdity, a prophetic-critical religious spirituality "highlights systemic social analysis under which tragic persons struggle."[58]

By critically retrieving the prophetic potential of their respective religions, Nigerian Muslims and Christians can provide moral leadership in the common bid to uproot the underlying causes of the country's present problems. They can prove to be religiously productive and socially relevant if they attempt "to project a vision and inspire a praxis which fundamentally transforms the prevailing *status quo* in light of the best of [their traditions] and the flawed yet significant achievements of the present order."[59]

Concrete areas of society's life in which the moral resources of these religions can be registered include education and other social-welfare services. I shall now offfer a brief reflection on these inter-twined themes.

Religions and Social-Welfare Services in Nigeria

Several studies have shown the important role of religious institutions in the fields of health and education in Nigeria.[60] To be sure, schools and hospitals were initially used by their proprietors for proselytizing and missiological purposes.[61]   But they also provided at least a modicum of spiritual and symbolic cohesion for the social order. In pre-colonial northern Nigeria, for instance, the dominant Qur'anic education "underpinned and legitimated the Islamic state system established at the time of the Muslim reform movement at the beginning of the nineteenth century."[62] It was also "the main supplier of clerks, administrators, advisers, physicians, judges and scribes."[63]

It is common knowledge that Nigeria, as many other African countries, entered the boat of modernization through the agency of Christian Mission schools. There was, however, a curious pattern to this development in Nigeria. The colonial amalgamation of several nationalities into one country, the differential geographical distribution of religious patterns in the country, and the divergent philosophies of education held by Christians and Muslims introduced an element of competition, rivalry and mutual accusation into the social-welfarist activities of voluntary religious bodies in the country. This situation, plus the increasing assumption of the Nigerian state as "a distributor of resources,"[64] led to the government take-over of hospitals and schools established by religious institutions in 1977.[65]

The statist and controlled nature of the Nigerian economy restricted the capability of religious institutions to defy the government order, as many of them lacked the financial resources that would enable them to remain competitive in the provision of educational and health services.[66] Although the Catholic and Baptist Churches were each able to work out an agreement with the government whereby some forms of ecclesial influence is retained in their hospitals, other churches virtually acquiesced to the government directives, especially on health matters.[67] But the country's health delivery system has declined from bad to worse since the ill-fated decision was taken to make government the Alpha and Omega of people's life.[68]

While it may be difficult for most of the religious institutions in the country to run their hospitals if the government now decides to return them, given the current harsh economic realities facing the country, one may nevertheless suggest that the nation can still benefit immensely from a reconsidered policy that allows the participation of religious institutions in the supervision of these hospitals. At a practical level, religious representatives can serve on several committees, e.g., ethics committees, having responsibility to deliberate about ways in which the quality of health care systems can be improved. The quandaries of health, death, and survival are issues which ought not to be limited to either the state managers or the medical and nursing professionals. Because of the concern of religion for whole persons and their larger cultural circumstances, issues which seem trivial to the profit-oriented and career-conscious professionals may be cast in deeper existential light by religious ethics. Allocation of resources to the hospitals, the work ethic of the health-delivery professionals, the lexical priority of the economically disadvantaged persons as a factor in formulating policy about access to health, and the content of the medical and nursing schools' curricula are issues that can be greatly enriched by religious perspectives.

Likewise, the disarray that now marks Nigerian institutions of learning may not be unconnected with lack of clarity in official policy on education and the ostracization of religious-moral values in schools.[69] As I will argue below, the way in which religious authorities have reacted to the issue of education and religion has contributed to the perpetuation of a moral stalemate on the most important and vital organ of the nation's life. The frequency with which normal learning processes are interrupted in Nigeria is a clear illustration of the deterioration in the quality of the nation's education.[70]

The constitutional provision permitting "religious instructions" in schools hides more than it says.[71] The ambiguity of the provision revolves around the definition of "religious instruction." According to the Draft Constitution of 1979, religious instruction means "instruction relating to the advancement of the practice of any religion but does not include the teaching of religious studies or of religion as a discipline."[72]

From this definition, it can be inferred that religious instruction is limited to the seminary and Qur'anic education or Sunday school classes. One would expect this kind of religious instruction as a logical consequence of religious freedom generally, which is also provided for in the constitution. Despite this apparent constrictive allowance for religious instruction in the constitution, virtually every Nigerian University has a Department of Religious Studies, and Bible and/or Islamic Knowledge are taught in primary and secondary schools across the nation. The majority of those who teach these subjects have degrees either in Religious Studies or in the Theological Sciences of Islam or Christianity. Therefore, the fears of most religious institutions that the government take-over of schools would lead to the eradication of religious sciences in schools appear unfounded.

What has been lacking so far in the "religion and education" debate is a clear definition of what the goals of education should be, and how religion can best assist in achieving them. It is also important to examine the prospects and the integrative potential of public school system in a religiously pluralistic society. Contributions from the religious authorities have been marked by blatant rhetoric and morally arid concerns for retaining the symbolic vestiges of religious institutions--such as giving religious names to schools, swelling the number of confessional teachers in the schools, prayers at school, etc.[73] While these are by no means irrelevant issues, they are subordinate to the larger question of how religions in Nigeria might contribute to the achievement of *paideia* in the country's institutions of learning.

The conception of dialogic politics suggested above permits one to suggest that through "a close cooperation and a continuous dialogue among the various religious groups and sects"[74] in the country, they can contribute to "a kind of formation that involves not only schooling but also those patterns of social life that build character and inculcate virtue."[75] Questions about political reform are inexorably linked to the larger strategic and value concerns about how to mine both "national and religious histories and to search the practices of contemporary communities for elements of the paideia that is required to form new visions of the commonweal, those 'collective convictions about the shape of things to come' that can 'unleash incredible strength'."[76]

Moreover, it is important for the adherents and authorities of each religion in the country to articulate their role and objectives in a pluralistic setting. The quest for the kind of education that is oriented to public values, to those purposes that a community or society holds in common, may require an internal critique or renewal within every religious body. This intra-religious pedagogic metanoia may take the forms of theological reorientation, reform of religious education of the younger generation, drastic revision of syllabi for the study of religions in Qur'anic schools, theological colleges and seminaries, and developing links with other religious communities, so that all religions may make genuine contributions to the value basis of the nation and the growth of public morality.

When this creative and critical perspective is extended to the larger society, education, whether in religious or in liberal or scientific subjects, ceases to be merely a means to becoming a good Muslim/Christian, scientist or engineer, but one that also assists a person to cultivate "the civic self--the art of acting in concert with others for the common good."[77] As Nigerians and other Africans search for how to forge a consensus about how they should live together, they must also devise the means by which such a consensus, if and when found, can be continually tested and reformed. Religious institutions which occupy an important place at the baseline of society cannot and should not be left out or behind in this critical and innovative search. Writing about another society, Ariarajah suggested that perhaps

> the time has come to "institutionalize" the reconciling potential of religion as well. Inter-religious councils, multi-religious fellowships of religious leaders, peace education, studies in peaceful methods of conflict-resolution, education for justice and peace, exposure to each other's prayer and spiritual practices, etc., may have to be the new "institutions" that supplement the institutions that brought education, healing and service to communities. Peace does not come about by wishing

it; we have to be peace-makers. One has to work for and build peace, and strive to preserve it.[78]

Conclusion

All of this does not suggest that religious groups are always going to be able to agree on all issues perceived to be in the interest of everybody. Conflict of views is a fact that history will not let us deny. Even if Muslims, Christians, and other religionists are able to agree on the importance of making a genuinely public difference by refusing to permit a secularist domestication of their religions, they may still disagree on the mode and the extent to which religion should shape public policy. For instance, there is a substantial agreement between the Christians and the so-called secularists that juridical questions are distinguishable from those of religious morality. In contrast, Muslims see religion, law, and ethics as "extensively intertwined in a common Shari'a or Shar', 'the road leading to water' (or the source of life)."[79]

These perspectival differences between the adherents of the two leading religions in particular will affect the ways in which many domestic and foreign policy issues are resolved. To what extent, for example, should religious considerations be allowed to define the content of public education? How can the state achieve a coherent and effective foreign policy when there are some confessionalists who see their loyalty in trans-national terms? Should the government continue to be actively involved in the pilgrimage affairs at the expense of other non-religious tax-payers? These are sample questions that illustrate the enormity of the strains involved in handling inter-religious affairs in the country.

Besides these practical difficulties, there is the more poignant ethical problem associated with what Niebuhr called the sin of pride to which all human beings and groups are prone. All humans "are persistently inclined," he argues, "to regard themselves more highly and are more assiduously concerned with their own interests than any 'objective' view of their importance would warrant."[80] These prideful illusions are stronger in the religious realm than in other spheres of life. Religious intolerance persists in the country, not because there are too many religious virtuosos but precisely because religious contestants hide their more particular mundane interests behind religious absolutes. This moral-anthropological fact is pregnant with trouble, especially in the absence of a public consensus by which to "harness, equilibrate and deflect, as well as sublimate and suppress, self-interest."[81] Thus, despite the attractiveness of the ideals of dialogic politics and its conceptual affiliate -- mediating structures -- many forces are arrayed against the prospects of its fruition, not only in Nigeria, but in other culturally fragmented societies as well.

Finally, there is the stubborn persistence of the problem identified at the beginning of this paper, namely, the hegemonic pretensions of the state in post-colonial Africa, and by far the greatest enemy of the continent. When this reality is alligned with the factor of real or perceived inequity in the manner in which socio-economic benefits are distributed among various African national constituencies, the hope of transforming religious institutions from mere interest groups which perpetuate the practice of politicization to responsible mediating structures that shape people's moral sensibilities become extremely thin.   Yet, there is no substitute for this constructive religious approach to African politics, for if positive changes must occur in the material realm, the guiding compass must emerge from the ultimate source of value--RELIGION.

CHAPTER 4

ENDNOTES

1. Text of the speech in the *New York Times*, October 2, 1990, A6.

2. A. Bolaji Akinyemi, *In Search Of A New World Order*, NSIA Annual Lecture Series, no 1 (Ibadan: Vantage Pub., 1991), 17.

3. Ray Ekpu, "Opium of the People," *Newswatch Magazine* (Lagos), February 25, 1986, p. 10.

4. Don Ohadike, "Muslim-Christian Conflict and Political Instability in Nigeria," in *Religion and National Integration in Africa: Islam, Christianity, and Politics in the Sudan and Nigeria*, ed. John O. Hunwick (Evanston: Northwestern University Press, 1992), 109, 120.

5. Mark Juergensmeyer, *The New Cold War?: Religious Nationalism Confronts the Secular State* (Berkeley: University of California Press, 1993), 1-2.

6. Max Weber, *Sociology of Religion*, trans. Ephraim Fischoff (Boston: Beacon, 1963).

7. David Laitin, *Hegemony and Culture: Politics and Religious Change among the Yoruba* (Chicago & London: The University of Chicago Press, 1986), 24.

8. Sulayman S. Nyang, "Religion and social change in contemporary Africa," *Dialogue & Alliance* 2, 4 (1988-89), 31.

9. James O'Connell, "Nigeria," in *Religion in Politics: A World Guide*, ed. Stuart Mews (Essex: Longman, 1989), 196.

10. O. A. Olukunle, "The Impact of Religion on the Nigerian Society: The Future Perspective" (Paper delivered at the Twenty-Fifth Annual Religious Studies Conference, Ibadan, 17-20 September 1991), 2.

11. Adebanjo Edema, *Christians and Politics in Nigeria* (Ibadan: Codat Publications, 1988), vii.

12. Peter L. Berger and Richard John Neuhaus, *To Empower People: The Role of Mediating Structures in Public Policy* (Washington, D.C.: American Enterprise Institute for Public Policy Research, 1977), 2.

13. Ibid.

14. Ibid.

15. Franklin I. Gamwell, *Beyond Preference: Liberal Theories of Independent Associations* (Chicago and London: University of Chicago Press, 1990), 5.

16. James Luther Adams, "Mediating Structures and the Separation of Powers," in *Democracy and Mediating Structures: A Theological Inquiry*, ed., Michael Novak (Washington, D.C.: American Enterprise Institute for Public Policy Research, 1980), 2.

17. Ibid., 3.

18. Ibid., 4.

19. Berger and Neuhaus, *To Empower People* (1977), 2.

20. Cited in Max L. Stackhouse, "Religion, Society, and the Independent Sector: Key Elements of a General Theory," in *Religion, The Independent Sector, and American Culture*, ed., Conrad Cherry and Rowland A. Sherrill (Atlanta: Scholars Press, 1992), 12.

21. Michael Bratton, "Enabling the Voluntary Sector in Africa: The Policy Context," in *African Governance in the 1990s: Working Papers from the Second Annual Seminar of the African Governance Program* (Atlanta: The Carter Center of Emory University, 1990), 105.

22. See Harold Lasswell, *Politics: Who Gets What, When, How* (New York: Meridian Books, 1958); Billy Dudley, *Introduction to Nigerian Government and Politics* (Bloomington: Indiana University Press, 1982), 15.

23. Robin Lovin, "Social Contract or a Public Covenant?," in *Religion and American Public Life: Interpretations and Explorations*, ed. Robin Lovin (New York: Paulist Press, 1986), 141.

24. Antonio Gramsci's *Opera* were published in Turin in six volumes between 1947-54, although many of them were written in jail under the Fascists, in the 1930's and 40's. Translations of his *The Modern Prince* was published in London, and of his *The Open Marxism* in New York in 1957. It is pertinent to note that the term "sectors" does not appear in the dictionaries and encyclopedias of the social sciences as an analytical category before that time.

25. Dieter T. Hessel, "Making a Public Difference after the Eclipse," in *The Church's Public Role: Retrospect and Prospect*, ed. Dieter T. Hessel (Grand Rapids, MI: Eerdmans, 1993), 3.

26. *Perestroika without Glasnost in Africa*, Conference Report Series, vol. 2, 1 (Atlanta: The Carter Center, 1989), 7. The views were attributed to Michael Bratton.

27. Bratton, "Enabling the Voluntary Sector in Africa" (1990), 104.

28. Hessel, "Making a Public Difference after the Eclipse" (1993), 6.

29 J. Bryan Hehir, "The Catholic Bishops and the Nuclear Debate: A Case Study of the Independent Sector," in *Religion, The Independent Sector, and American Culture*, ed. Conrad Cherry and Rowland A. Sherrill (Atlanta: Scholars Press, 1992), 98-112.

30 C. O. Oshun, "Ecumenism: An Approach to Peaceful Co-existence," in *Religion, Peace, and Unity in Nigeria*, ed. Sam Babs Mala and Z. I. Oseni (Ibadan: Nigerian Association for the study of Religions, 1984), 121.

31 C.A.N. was formed for the purpose of (a) promoting a common understanding among all the Christians in the country; (b) standing together and projecting Christian ethics and also defending the rights of the Church; and (c) creating good fellowhsip of all Christians on the social level that will help all Christians to the better practice of their faith and the good of the country. For a comprehensive history and objectives of this association, see A. O. Makozi and O.J.A. Ojo, eds., *History of the Roman Catholic Church in Nigeria* (Ibadan: Macmillan, 1982), 93.

32. More than twenty aims and objectives of the NSCIA are listed in its charter, but those that are relevant to our purpose here include: Catering for and protecting the interests of Islam throughout Nigeria, serving as a channel of contact with the Government of Nigeria on Islamic affairs, fostering brotherhood and cooperation among Muslims in Nigeria and other parts of the world..., encouraging the establishment of institutions of learning wherein Islamic religion and culture as well as the Arabic language and other subjects of general education shall be taught, encouraging legitimate economic activities of all Muslims..., and engaging in any lawful activities in fulfillment and furtherance of the foregoing aims and objectives. For the complete list, see *Constitution of the Nigerian Supreme Council for Islamic Affairs* (Kano: Rasco Press, n.d.), 2-3. The constitution was adopted on 24 September 1985.

33. See, for instance, A. F. Walls, "Religion and the press in 'the Enclave' in the Nigerian Civil War," in *Christianity in Independent Africa,* ed., Edward Fashole-Luke et al. (Bloomington and London: Indiana University Press, 1978), 207-215; M. Y. Nabofa, "Christianity in Nigeria: Its Role in Nation-Building," in *Nigeria since Independence: The First Twenty-Five Years,* vol. IX, *Religion,* ed. J. A. Atanda, Garba Ashiwaju, and Yaya Abubakar (Ibadan: Heinemann, 1989), 104-106); M. M. Familusi, *Methodism in Nigeria, 1842-1992* (Ibadan: NPS Educational Publishers, 1992), 68-87; Laurie S. Wiseberg, "Christian Churches and the Nigerian Civil War," *Journal of African Studies 2,* 13 (1975): 297-331.

34. Christian Council of Nigeria, *Justice and Peace* (Ibadan: Daystar Press, 1971), 6.

35. Ibid.

36. This debate finds its *locus classicus* in G. E. Moore, *Principia Ethica* (Buffalo, NY: Prometheus Books, 1902 & 1988); C. L. Stevenson, *Facts and Values: Studies in Ethical Analysis* (New Haven: Yale University Press, 1963); Philippa Foot, *Virtues and Vices and Other Essays in Moral Philosophy* (Berkeley and Los Angeles: University of California Press, 1978).

37. Reinhold Niebuhr, *Christian Realism and Political Problems* (New York: Charles Scribner's Sons, 1953), 129-130.

38. Ibid.

39. Cornel West, *Prophetic Fragments* (Grand Rapids, MI: Eerdmans, 1988), x.

40. Peter B. Clarke, "Religion and Political Attitude since Independence," in *Religion and Society in Nigeria: Historical and Sociological Perspectives,* ed. Jacob K. Olupona and Toyin Falola (Ibadan: Spectrum Books, 1991), 224.

41. Conrad Cherry and Rowland A. Sherrill, "Introduction," in *Religion, The Independent Sector, and American Culture,* ed. Conrad Cherry and Rowland Sherrill (Atlanta: Scholars Press, 1992), 6.

42. Hollenbach, *Justice, Peace, and Human Rights: American Catholic Social Ethics in a Pluralistic Context* (New York: Crossroad, 1988), 13.

43. Laitin, 1986: 24.

44. Christopher F. Mooney, *Boundaries Dimly Perceived: Law, Religion, and the Common Good* (Notre Dame: University of Notre Dame Press, 1990), 26.

45. Paul F. Knitter, "Common Ground or Common Response? Seeking Foundations for Interreligious Discourse," *Studies in Interreligious Dialogue* 2, 2 (1992), 114.

46. Abdullahi A. An-Na'im, "Islam and National Integration in the Sudan," in *Religion and National Integration in Africa: Islam, Christianity, and Politics in the Sudan and Nigeria*, ed. John O. Hunwick (Evanston, IL: Northwestern University Press, 1992), 32.

47. Ibid.

48. Ibid., 33.

49. Ibid.

50. Ibid., 33-34.

51. Simeon O. Ilesanmi, "Challenge and Accommodation in Religious Politics: The Nigerian Experience," *Leidschrift: Dutch Journal of History* 10, 2 (1994).

52. S. J. Samartha, *One Christ, Many Religions: Towards a Revised Christology* (Maryknoll, N.Y.: Orbis Books, 1991), 47.

53. Gbadegesin, *African Philosophy: Traditional Yoruba Philosophy and Contemporary African Realities* (New York: Peter Lang, 1991), 138.

54. Ibid., 140.

55. Ibid. A clear proof of this situation is the promulgation of a new decree, signed into law on May 4, 1993, by the Babangida-led Government according to which "a person who levies a war against Nigeria in order to intimidate or overawe the president and commander-in-chief of the armed forces or the governor of a state is guilty of treason and liable on conviction to death sentence." *Newswatch* 24 May 1993, 14.

56. John Courtney Murray, *The Pattern for Peace and the Papal Peace Program* (Washington, D.C.: Paulist Press, 1944), 11.

57. West, *Prophetic Fragments* (1988), ix.

58. Ibid., x.

59. Ibid., xi.

60. For a comprehensive list of the relevant literature, see Gerrie ter Haar, "Religious Education in Africa: Traditional, Islamic, and Christian," *Exchange*, XVII, 50 (September 1988), 77-86.

61. Lamin Sanneh, *West African Christianity: The Religious Impact* (Maryknoll, NY: Orbis Books, 1983), 127-67.

62. Peter B. Clarke, "The Religious Factor in the Developmental process in Nigeria: A socio-historical analysis," *Geneve-Afrique* 17, 1 (1979), 51.

63. Ibid.

64. P. Brass, "Ethnic Groups and the State," in *Ethnic Groups and the State,* ed. P. Brass (London: n.p., 1985), 29.

65. In practical terms, the Government take-over of schools essentially meant that (a) the management of Schools was placed in the hands of district School boards of management, (b) the coordination, planning, financing and direction of the total education was placed in the hands of the State Ministry Department of Education, and (c) the integration of educational development and policy with national objectives and programs was made the responsibility of a Federal Ministry of Education. See *National Policy on Education* (Lagos: Government Printers, 1977), sec. II, nos. 86-87.

66. E. Ikenga-Metuh, "Religious Education in State-controlled schools in Nigeria," in *Religion, Peace, and Unity in Nigeria*, ed. Sam Babs Mala and Z. I. Oseni (Ibadan: N.A.S.R., 1984), 136-152).

67. For problems of logistics within the Methodist Church, see Familusi, *Methodism in Nigeria* (1992).

68. When Babangida seized power on 27 August 1987, he promised to improve the deplorable conditions of the nation's hospitals which, according to his own description, were worse than consulting clinics. To say the least, the conditions have hardly improved since then.

69. M. I. Mozia, "Religion and Morality in Nigeria: An Overview," in *Nigeria since Independence*, ed. J. A. Atanda, Garba Ashiwaju, and Yaya Abubakar (Ibadan: Heinemann, 1989), 172-73.

70. At the moment, more than half of the Nigerian Higher Institutions are still being forcibly closed on the order of the Federal Government due to a breached contract between the Government and the Academic Staff Union.

71. Section 37, subsections 2 and 3 of the Federal Constitution of 1989 says that:
(a) No person attending any place of education shall be required to receive religious instruction...if such instruction...relates to a religion other than his own, or a religion not approved by his parent or guardian; (b) No religious community or denomination shall be prevented from providing instruction for pupils of that community or denomination in any place of education maintained wholly by that community or denomination.

72. CDC, I: 22.

73. Peter B. Clarke and Ian Linden, *Islam in Modern Nigeria: A Study of a Muslim Community in a Post-Independence State 1960-1983* (Grunewald: Kaiser, 1984), 145-61.

74. Ikenga-Metuh, "Religious Education in State-controlled schools in Nigeria" (1984), 147.

75. Barbara G. Wheeler, "Introduction: A Forum on *Paideia*," in *Caring for the Commonweal: Education for Religious and Public Life*, ed., Parker J. Palmer, Barbara G. Wheeler, and James W. Fowler (Macon, GA: Mercer University Press, 1990), 2.

76. Ibid.

77. William F. May, "Public Happiness and Higher Education," in *Caring for the Commonweal: Education for Religious and Public Life*, ed., Parker J. Palmer, Barbara G. Wheeler, and James W. Fowler (Macon, GA: Mercer University Press, 1990), 244.

78. Cited in Samartha, *One Christ, Many Religions* (1991), 55.

79. Frederick S. Carney, "Some Aspects of Islamic Ethics," *Journal of Religion* 63, 2 (1983), 161.

80. Reinhold Niebuhr, *The Irony of American History* (New York: Charles Scribner's Sons, 1952), 7.

81. Reinhold Niebuhr, "A Dark Light on Human Nature," *Messenger* 13 (April 1948), 7.

PART II

HUMAN RIGHTS AND U.S. FOREIGN POLICY TOWARD AFRICA

"Ours is essentially a tragic age, so we refuse to take it tragically. The cataclysm has happened, we are among the ruins, we start to build up new little habitats, to have new little hopes. It is rather hard work: there is now no smooth road into the future: but we go round, or scramble over the obstacles. We've got to live, no matter how many skies have fallen."

D.H. Lawrence, Lady Chatterley's Lover

CHAPTER 5

DIVINING THE MYSTERIES OF AN ENIGMA: AN HISTORICAL DELINEATION OF AMERICAN FOREIGN POLICY TOWARD AFRICA

INTRODUCTION

The patter of tiny feet beat out a rhythmic cadence from bedroom to bathroom and back every fifteen minutes. Sadly, I had been staring deeply into the same chapter since we finished dinner. "Go to sleep, Peaches!," I shouted rather harshly. "O.K.," came the reply. The tiny voice seemed to giggle down the stairs and warm, at least temporarily, my frozen countenance.

"Somebody's in a foul mood," said Delia as she looked up from her work. "Actually, I'm in a pretty good mood," I responded without looking up from my mad scribbling. "Delia, do you have time to listen to something?" I asked. "Sure, I just finished my lecture notes and it would be good to rest my eyes." Then she leaned over to look at my notepad.

"Don't tell me this is more of that foreign policy garbage? Wasn't that stuff giving you a headache last week?" I shook my head in affirmation. "Yeah, but I think I've got it figured out now," I said flatly, still trying to finish the last of my notes. I put down my pen and could feel my eyes widen with anticipation. I must have looked like a man with a secret burning a hole in his pocket.

"American foreign policy toward Africa is best understood by observing the evolution of American involvement in Africa and the treatment of Africans in the United States!," I declared. "Whoa, whoa," Delia said as the bag of sunflower seeds fell from her lap onto the floor. "Don't you want to slow down for the rest of us?" "I'm sorry," I said as I leaned back on the couch, "but I'm so excited because this is finally making sense.

"I did as you suggested and looked back at the topic through my eyes. I examined the Black experience here and contrasted it with the ascendancy of European hegemony on the Continent. Upon reconsidering the entire issue, I realized why I was so frustrated at the start. Most diplomatic histories of American-African relations assume that American involvement on the

111

continent began during or immediately after World War II. What's worse is that few of these studies deal with the issue of race: those that do often examine race within the context of decolonization or the intransigence of the remaining white settler regimes in southern Africa. Only when I found a few recent dissertations did I find any historians who discussed American race problems against the backdrop of United States foreign policy."[1]

"By taking such a myopic approach to the issue, scholars have missed two key ingredients in American diplomacy: racism and the continuity of American contacts to Africa. Granted, European imperialism held sway in Africa until the debilitating effects of World War II - combined with the force of African nationalism - made empire too heavy a burden to carry. Nevertheless, America has always had some involvement with Africa. Moreover, the treatment of its captive African population was a critical element in the social atmosphere which gave birth to the power elites who formulated and executed American foreign policy."

Delia shook her head in mock disbelief. "Boy, you just said a mouthful. How did you conceptualize all of this?" I grinned, then started to explain. "It's like the waves of the ocean at high tide; at first,they start nibbling at the shore and before you know it, they've devoured the whole thing. American foreign policy toward Africa evolved in waves and if you can read the current, you won't get sucked down in the undertow."

A WORKING DEFINITION OF RACISM

Delia reclined as well and looked at the ceiling. "If racism is such a central component of American domestic and foreign policy, maybe you should define it." "Good point," I said as I rubbed my hands together and flipped through my notepad.

"Scholars like Dr. Francis Cress-Welsing and Neely Fuller have spent much of their careers tackling the issue of racism. Where Dr. Cress-Welsing - through her theory of color confrontation - has tried to determine why racism developed, Fuller has concentrated on unraveling just what racism is and exactly how it operates. Both agree that the element of power cannot be omitted when discussing racism.[2]

"Fuller postulates that racism/white supremacy is the most powerful force on the globe.

Of all the people [on the earth] . . . those white people who practice racism (white supremacy) have the greatest ability to use truth, and to use it in such manner as to produce justice and correctness, in all places, in all areas of activity, in the shortest period of time. The white people who practice racism know that they could, if they chose to do so, produce justice and correctness. . . . Knowing this, they have chose not to produce justice and correctness. They prefer to continue to practice white supremacy, though they fully understand that in order to practice white supremacy they must do so by promoting falsehood, non-justice and incorrectness. They apparently have judged that white supremacy is better than revealing truth.[3]

Fuller begins his treatise by stating that there are basically three types of people: white people (those who classify themselves as white), non-white people (those who are classified as not being white) and white supremacists (those people who classify themselves as white and practice racial subjugation against people classified as non-white). The racial subjugation practiced by white supremacists is against all non-white people, in a universal pattern (time and place), in any one or more of the nine areas of human activity: economics, education, entertainment, labor, law, politics, religion, sex and war.[4]

"For Fuller, the notion of race 'has little biological validity [and] is translated more correctly as 'organization', the sole purpose of which is to maintain white domination and world control,'" Delia interjected.[5] "That's right," I replied. "From here, Dr. Cress-Welsing is quite instructive as to the etiology of racism/white supremacy: a basic psychological fear of people of color, in general, and, most especially, 'Black' people."

I continued. "Cress-Welsing examines the domination of the modern world by Europeans from the perspective of a psychologist and recognizes a 'need' for such domination.

[I]t should be noted that, in the majority of instances, any neurotic drive for superiority usually is founded upon a deep and pervading sense of inadequacy and inferiority. Is it not true that white people represent in numerical terms a very small minority of the world's people? And more profoundly, is not "white" itself the very absence of any ability to produce color? I reason, then, that the quality of whiteness is indeed a genetic inadequacy or a relative genetic deficiency state, based upon the genetic inability to produce the skin pigments of melanin (which is responsible for all skin color). The vast majority of the world's people are not so afflicted, which suggests that color is normal for human beings and color absence is abnormal. Additionally, this state of color absence acts as a genetic recessive to the dominant genetic factor of color-production. Color always "annihilates" (phenotypically and genetically speaking) the non-color, white. Black people possess the greatest color potential, with brown, red and yellow peoples possessing lesser quantities, respectively.[6]

"Simply put, the Cress-Welsing Theory of Color Confrontation and Racism 'states that the white or color-deficient Europeans responded psychologically, with a profound sense of numerical inadequacy and color inferiority, in their confrontations with the majority of the world's people - all of whom possessed varying degrees of color-producing capacity.'[7]   By incorporating the ideas of these two intellectuals, we can formulate a working definition of racism:

> RACISM is a relationship system between two or more groups of people, based upon perceived racial differences, whereby the allegedly "superior" race exercises a requisite amount of power such that all the benefits of the relationship inure to the "superior" race and all the burdens fall upon the "inferior" race(s).

Based upon this explanation, 'racism' has four requisite elements: 1) the existence of a relationship between two or more groups of people; 2) observed 'racial' differences between these groups; 3) a value judgment, based upon these racial differences, which creates a Superior group and Inferior group; and most importantly, 4) the power of the Superior group to control the lives of the members of the Inferior group in one or more of the nine areas of people activity, so that all the benefits of the relationship flow in one direction and all the burdens flow in the opposite direction. Consequently, the behavior of a person or a group of people can be categorized as racist if, and only if, it meets all four elements.   As an aside, it is important to note that since the nine areas of people activity are interrelated, any domination in one area results in coercion in the other areas."[8]

AMERICAN RELATIONS WITH AFRICA AND AFRICANS

A. The First Wave - The Colonial/Antebellum Period

I rose to get some water for both of us and returned to my point before I returned to my seat. "American relations with Africa evolved within the context of the Atlantic Slave Trade. This nation was built on the land of indigenous people and by the labor of African people. Can we agree that Black people in this country have been, and remain, a subjugated group?" I asked rhetorically. Delia quietly concurred. "The enslavement of Africans was consistent throughout the original thirteen colonies. On the eve of the

American War of Independence, 4,000 slaves lived in Boston, New York and Philadelphia.[9] Clearly, slavery and the denigration of Africans was reconciled with Enlightenment precepts and prevailing religious dogma.[10] Yet, slavery alone does not explain this phenomenon.

Delia had been dying to say something and she finally broke in. "State domination of Africans in all phases of society mirrored the underdevelopment of African nations as the slave trade reached its zenith. The 'divide and conquer' strategies of the imperialists proved quite efficient as successive nations and ethnic groups succumbed to the onslaught of European encroachment." "That's true," I responded. "Furthermore," she continued, "those who collaborated in the endeavor found that they could not compete directly with the Europeans; the ethic of white supremacy prevented any potential alteration of the stream of benefits and burdens."[11]   I started anew as she sipped from the glass. "Even as slavery was abolished in the Northern states, so-called free Blacks remained pariah. Political, economic and educational subordination became the norm. Even travel restrictions and pass laws were used to frustrate Black aspirations for freedom.[12] The problem posed by the Africans, free or slave, went to the very fabric of the developing nations; simply put, the colonial leaders wrestled the issue of maintaining a population of color in a nation identified as exclusively white.[13] Within this vitriolic climate, the American Colonization Society ("ACS") emerged as a tantalizing elixir.

"Prior to the establishment of the ACS, Africans in this country had been leaving the United States and settling in numerous places around the globe. Free Blacks like Paul Cuffee actively aroused popular sentiment for a "back to Africa" movement in order to escape the humiliation offered by life in America."[14]   Delia placed her hand on mine. "George, some whites supported the colonization effort for purportedly humanitarian reasons. A second goal of colonization was to encourage 'Americanized' free Blacks to civilize their relatives."[15]   "Okay," I answered, barely muffling a chuckle. "Yet, the chief motivating factor - especially among the political elites of the time - was the salvation of the grand democratic experiment. In other words, the republican ideology of the day asserted that democracy could only flourish in a society with an all-white polity."[16]

Delia resumed her commentary. "The birth of Anglo-Saxonism - a pseudo-scientific rationalization for white supremacy - accompanied increased concerns about the African population in America. During the 1840's, the United States underwent its most extensive and rapid expansion, pushing further west from Mississippi to the shore of California. Part of the strategy of expansion simply was to overwhelm Native Americans in order to gain their lands." "However," I added, "American politicians actually discussed the possibility of using the area now known as Texas as a receptacle for the African population and eventually pushing the Blacks into what would be left of Mexico.[17] Although this never happened, the problem of what to do with the Africans persisted beyond America's approaching internecine conflict."

B. The Second Wave - 1865-1940

As I drained the glass, Delia pushed the conversation. "During the American Civil War, President Abraham Lincoln rendered his Emancipation Proclamation. Although it did not apply to African captives in the Border States and, without federal enforcement, meant little to slaves in the Confederacy, this document officially terminated slavery in the United States. Following the war, Africans tried to make a new place for themselves in American society, only to be denied.[18] Although their status as slaves officially ended, they remained socially dead beings.

"The promise of Southern Reconstruction quickly yielded to Southern Redemption as whites sought to rebuild their hegemony in that part of the country.[19] Blacks were relegated to the lower echelons of society. They were completely shut out of the political arena and those who sought to compete economically with whites were destroyed, literally and figuratively. Conditions had become so harsh that the Africans, again, began looking for a safe haven.[20] Many returned to the dream of African emigration, while others considered unsettled areas in Kansas and Oklahoma.[21]

"The period known as the 'Black Nadir' was fast approaching by 1884," I interjected. "In November of that year, the European powers met to settle their differences regarding their mad scramble for dominion in Africa. Although the United States had no political interests in the areas concerned, the President sent a delegation, led by an experienced statesman, to the Berlin Conference. Not only did the head of the American delegation sign the convention which marked the final agreement, he helped negotiate boundary disputes within the Congo Basin - of course, without any input from the Africans themselves."[22]

"European colonialism evolved into numerous forms, from the putatively benign to the overtly brutal. Regardless of its guise, colonization inevitably resulted in the appropriation of African labor, the corrosion or destruction of African cultural, political and economic institutions and the degradation of African life.[23] American missionary and economic efforts in colonial areas were not inconspicuous and exacerbated the negative flow of benefits and burdens."[24]

"Even as white Americans busied themselves by advancing the cause of civilization around the globe, they refused to address the suffering of America's African community," Delia said. "I recall a hauntingly familiar scenario in which African leaders appealed to the federal government for enforcement of the Civil Rights Acts of 1866. Of particular concern were educational funding and voting privileges.   An elections bill and a bill to provide federal aid for Southern schools (which were predominately Black) reached the floor of the Senate in 1890, only to die an ignominious death. The Republicans - at that time, considered the friends of the Blacks - sacrificed the legislation in order to ensure the passage of a hotly contested tariff bill."[25]

"   See how it's staring to fit," I exclaimed. "The United States slowly was becoming a major player on the world scene. Although the participation at the Berlin Conference was not welcomed by all members of the American political establishment, it was a step toward increased leverage within the scheme of global hegemony.[26] Growing interest in Africa among America's business, professional and military classes, though no threat to European hegemony, drew white American deeper into the development-underdevelopment cycle on the continent.[27]   As European colonial domination fully bloomed, Americans were slaughtering the last vestiges of Plains Indians and watching as the Germans crushed the Maji Maji rebellion."[28]

Delia's smile had sagged. She stared somewhat blankly as she finished my thought. "As World War I raged, race riots and lynchings in all parts of the United States stood as eerie testament to the fact that the African in America remained socially dead.[29] The Black intellectuals of the Harlem Renaissance grew disenchanted with the paternalism of the white Left.[30] The United Negro Improvement Association's quest, the next manifestation of the dream of reaching the Promised Land, perished as Marcus Garvey was marginalized and expelled from the country."[31]

C. The Third Wave - 1941-Present

We sat quietly for a moment. Then I tried to brighten the mood. "Black nationalism, again, bubbled to the global surface in the 1940's. A. Phillip Randolph was planning the first March on Washington and, even though it never took place, the civil rights leaders of the day were able to extract a few concessions from President Roosevelt.[32] Kwame Nkrumah organized the first General Conference of Africans in America alongside Nuamdi Arikiwe and Durosimi Johnson. By 1945, he had finished his education in the United States and was in England, preparing for the Fifth Pan-African Congress with George Padmore.[33] As the cries of self-determination emanated from the lips of the Allied leaders amid the din of World War II, African hearts began to swell. Nevertheless, the promise of the day would again yield to stark reality.

"Franklin Roosevelt was a staunch anti-colonialist. However, his zeal seemed based upon a desire to foster American economic stability rather than any yearning to free peoples of color from the yoke of imperialism.[34] The Truman administration was more than happy to step into the growing power vacuum left by the British and to accommodate the white settler regimes in southern Africa.[35] Eisenhower fretted a great deal about premature independence and his Secretary of State frowned on the neutrality of emerging Third World Nations.[36] Kennedy granted Nkrumah a significant aid package for the development of the Volta River Dam but only after forcing Nkrumah to 'accept at least verbally American principles in economics, politics and international relations."'[37] Kennedy's policies were so flexible that he saw fit to intervene in the Congo for fear that it would become another Cuba."[38]

Delia nodded, then spoke. "White paranoia of Black power led to U.S. government spying and clandestine operations at home and abroad. We can find an analog for the CIA disruption of African affairs when we consider the FBI's dirty tricks."[39]   "Again," I broke in, "the government sacrificed egalitarian principles to insure global and domestic stability. The Cold War was the perfect excuse for the United States to back away from any commitment to social justice."

At this point, Delia chimed in. "I think I know where you're going but you should mention that the Cold War did a great deal to reshape American domestic, as well as foreign, policy. As non-white countries chaffed under the weight of their bitter disappointment, they ridiculed the United States for its unwillingness to treat its African population as full citizens. Moscow used American racial intolerance as a propaganda tool. Sensing this challenge to Western hegemony, successive presidential administrations used the exigencies of the Cold War as a means of speeding the advancement of civil rights. The federal government's support of Black rights, visible in Justice Department arguments in Shelly v. Kramer and Brown v. Board of Education, came at a time when courts generally were restricting civil liberties in many areas."[40]

"Alright," I cheered. "As the Civil Rights movement drew to a close, the 'white backlash' of conservatism reappeared. All too similar to the period of Southern Redemption in the late 19th Century, Africans in the United States saw the government turn its back on their continued cries for power and equality. President Johnson had begun the escalation of combat in Vietnam and had steadfastly refused to support African freedom in southern Africa.[41] Johnson's reluctance to budge on southern Africa mirrored his ill-tempered refusal to seat the Mississippi Freedom Party delegates at the 1964 Democratic Convention.[42] During this same period, President Nixon implemented the 'Tar Baby' option in Rhodesia.[43] The Carter administration dabbled in 'idealism' for a moment, only to return to a stylized version of the anti-communism of its predecessors.[44] From there, the

Reagan doctrine led to escalations in Angola and African misery in the United States seemed to skyrocket.[45]

"It appears that throughout the Cold War, the United States intervened in African affairs in the name of anti-communism and without exactly knowing just 'who' was 'what.' Most scholars suggest that American fears were legitimate, while others suggest that, legitimate or not, mistakes were made. Does it matter that Lumumba was not a Marxist? At least one scholar says 'no'; the fact that any Third World leader was a radical nationalist was as frightening as if he were a Communist since American power elites were fearful of nationalists gaining economic leverage, encouraging other Third World nations to do the same and thereby altering the shape of the fiscal playing field.[46]

CONCLUSION

"So, what do we learn from all of this?" Delia inquired. "First, we learn that America's lofty egalitarian principles were never meant for us. Second, we understand that the compromise of those principles and the sacrifice of African life are central tenets of the American ethos. American foreign policy toward African states has followed the same pattern. This is not to say that change cannot occur. However, history shows us that change takes place within the context of racism/white supremacy and only to the extent that the concerns of white and non-white peoples combine." Delia frowned for a moment.

"That sounds like Derrick Bell's interest convergence theorem," she said. "Professor Bell noted that, with regard to human rights struggles, whites - and white institutions - who supported or participated in such activities have done so out of self-interest, as well as philanthropic motives. The putative success of these struggles often is a direct result of a convergence of interests on the part of Blacks and whites. Accordingly, white commitment to continued social change is often diminished by the degree to which their interests have been satisfied."[47]

"Exactly!" I shouted. "Thus, when we hear the national security establishment making noises about linking diplomacy to human rights, we should be suspicious. Consider the speech Anthony Lake gave in September 1994, when he said that the challenge to American diplomacy in a post Cold War world is to 'reshape and create new international security and economic structures . . . with the flexibility to withstand shifting threats to their stability . . . [a]nd . . . we must infuse these structures with the ideas and habits of democracy,' he sounds like any good liberal internationalist from Wilson to Roosevelt.[48] Given the history of white supremacy, this tells us that the United States may intervene in certain areas of the globe to replace totalitarian regimes with 'new, improved' regimes. The results of the intervention will do little or nothing about structural problems facing African nations and may leave them in worse condition by diminishing their revolutionary capacity.

"This is kind of scary stuff, huh?" Delia said, looking more than a little tired. "Naw, what's scary is not knowing," I replied. "I don't like swimming in rough surf."

CHAPTER 5

ENDNOTES

1. See e.g., Thomas Borstelman, "Apartheid, Colonialism and the Cold War: the United States and Southern Africa, 1945-1952," Duke University 1990 562pp., DAI 1991 vol. 52, no. 3, p. 1051-A and Daniel Henry Volman, "United States Foreign Policy and the Decolonization of British Central Africa [Zimbabwe, Zambia and Malawi], 1945-1965," UCLA 1991, 555pp., DAI 1991 vol. 52, no. 3, p. 1042-A.

2. Neely Fuller, Jr. The United Independent Compensatory Code/System/Concept: a textbook/workbook for thought, speech and/or action for victims of racism (white supremacy), (Washington, D.C.: Neely Fuller, Jr., 1969), pp. 25-29 (where the author discusses four types of power and explains that white supremacy/racism cannot be practiced without exercising power over people characterized as non-white). Francis Cress-Welsing, M.D., The Isis Papers: The Keys to the Colors, (Chicago: Third World Press, 1991), p. 1 (where the author states that "[i]n today's very small world at least three-quarters of the people are 'non-white' and the members of this 'non-white' majority population are subjected to domination throughout their lives. . . .").

3. Fuller, p. 6.

4. *Fuller, pp. 20-22*

5. Cress-Welsing, p. 3.

6. Ibid., p. 4.

7. Ibid., p. 4-5.

8. Fuller, p. 22.

9. Gary Nash, "Forging Freedom: The Emancipation Experience In the Northern Seaport Cities," in Ira Berlin and Ronald Hoffman, eds., Slavery and Freedom In the Age of the American Revolution, (Charlottesville, VA: The University of Virginia Press, 1983), p. 3.

10. See David Brion Davis, The Problem of Slavery In Western Culture, (New York:Oxford University Press, 1966), p. 186 and Slavery and Human Progress, (New York: Oxford University Press, 1984), pp. 130-131; Forrest

Woods, The Arrogance of Faith, (New York: Alfred A. Knopf, Inc. 1990), pp. 281-289; A. Leon Higginbotham, In the Matter of Color: Race & The Legal Process, the Colonial Period, (New York: Oxford University Press, 1978), p. 377.

11. St. Claire Drake, Black Folk Here and There, vol. 2, (Los Angeles: The University of California Press and St. Clair Drake, 1990), p. 251 (where the author relates the following story: "Yet when [King] Afonso [the 'Apostle of the Congo'] sought to trade with Portugal as an equal, even asking to purchase a ship, the Portuguese monarchy refused . . . [One of King Phillip III's advisors noted that Afonso] 'should not be sent workmen; it is not proper that he should have in his kingdom someone who knows how to work with stone and lime or with steel because this would be an occasion for disobedience.'"

12. Nash, p.3; Leon Litwack, North of Slavery: The Negro In the Free States, 1790 - 1860, (Chicago: University of Chicago Press, 1961), pp. 17-75.

13. Ronald Takaki, Iron Cages: Race and Culture In 19th Century America, (New York: Alfred A. Knopf, Inc., 1979), p. 14 (where the author reveals that "[Ben Franklin] noted that the number of 'purely white people' was proportionately very small. 'All Africa was black and tawny, Asia chiefly tawny and America (exclusive of the newcomers) wholly so.' The English were the 'principal Body of white People,' and Franklin wished there were more of them in America. 'And while we are . . . scouring our Planet, by clearing America of woods, and so making this Side of our globe reflect a brighter Light to the Eyes of Inhabitants in Mars or Venus,'
he declared, 'why should we in the sight of Superior Beings, darken its people? why increase the Sons of Africa, by Planting them in America, where we have so fair an opportunity, by excluding all Blacks and Tawnys, of increasing the lovely White?'").

14. Peter Duignan and L.H. Gann, The United States and Africa: A History (Cambridge: Cambridge University Press, 1984), pp. 81-83.

15. Ibid., pp. 85-96, 164-173 (where the authors discuss the role of Africans in the United States in the colonization movement and, in the latter pages, highlights the roles of individuals like Bishop Henry McNeal Turner); for opposing perspectives of diasporan Africans regarding colonization, see Edward Wilmot Blyden, Christianity, Islam and the Negro Race, (Edinburgh: Edinburgh University Press, 1967) and Martin Robison Delany, The Condition, Elevation, Emigration and Destiny of the Colored People In the United States (New York: Arno Press, 1969).

16. Takaki, pp. 39, 47 (where the author writes that, for men such as Thomas Jefferson, "[r]epublicanism required a homogenous population. Unless everyone could be converted into Lockeans or . . . 'republican machines', the republic would surely disintegrate into anarchy.").

17. See generally, Reginald Horsman, Race and Manifest Destiny: The Origins of American Racial Anglo-Saxonism, (Cambridge, MA.: Harvard University Press, 1981); see also Thomas Hietala, Manifest Design: Anxious Aggrandizement In Late Jacksonian America, (Ithaca, N.Y.: Cornell University Press, 1985), pp. 10-11, 27-31, 34-36 (where the author discusses the annexation of Texas and the various arguments made regarding the usefulness of the area).

18. See generally, Thomas Holt, Black Over White: Negro Political Leadership In South Carolina During Reconstruction, (Urbana, IL.: University of Illinois Press, 1979). See also, Eric Foner, Reconstruction: America's Unfinished Revolution, 1863- 1877, (New York: Harper & Row Publishers, 1988), pp. 425-444 (where the author discusses the activities of the Ku Klux Klan) and Edmund Drago, Black Politicians & Reconstruction In Georgia: A Splendid Failure, (Athens, GA.: University of Georgia Press, 1992), pp. 101-159 (where the author discusses the postbellum labor system and the emerging Conservative triumph in this former Confederate state).

19. William Cohen, At Freedom's Edge: Black Mobility and The Southern White Quest For Racial Control, 1861-1915, (Baton Rouge: Louisiana State University Press, 1991), pp. 22, 275-282; see also Nell Painter, Black Exodusters: Black Migration To Kansas After Reconstruction, (New York: W.W. Norton & Co., 1986).

20. Cohen, pp. 228-247 (where the author discusses the use of vagrancy laws, false pretenses rules and other labor-control measures); see also, Drago, pp. 114-122. See also Painter, pp. 39-67 (with regard to migratory patterns).

21. See generally Painter.

22. Duignan and Gann, pp. 133-134 (where the authors relate that the American delegate, John A. Kasson, "because of his neutrality and international impartiality . . . had a strong influence on the conference."). For more on the diplomacy surrounding the berlin Conference, see Edward Chester, Clash of Titans: Africa and U.S. Foreign Policy, (Maryknoll, N.Y.: Orbis Books, 1974), pp. 145-149.

23. With respect to the various colonial administrations and their styles of governance, see generally, E.D. Morel, The Black Man's Burden: The White Man in Africa from the Fifteenth Century to World War I, (New York: Monthly Review Press, 1969); Michael Crowder, West Africa Under Colonial Rule, (Evanston, Ill.: Northwestern University Press 1968) and Senegal: A Study In French Assimilation Policy, (London: Methuen, 1967); John Iliffe, Tanganyika Under German Rule, (London: Cambridge University Press, 1969); and Eveline Martin, The British West African Settlements, A Study In Local Administration, (London: Pub. for the Royal Colonial Institute, 1927); see also Barnett Singer, "A New Model Imperialist In French West Africa," Historian vol. 56, no. 1, Autumn 1993, pp. 69-86 (where the author talks, in part, about how Colonel Leon Faidherbe became governor of Senegal in 1854 because Bordelais merchants, seeking "to wrest the gum market from the Mauritanians," deemed him best able to defend their interests).

24. Duignan and Gann, 140-144 (where the authors discuss the American cotton trade in Zanzibar).

25. Gary Nash, The American People: Creating a Nation and a Society, vol. 2, (New York: HarperCollins Publishers, 1990), p. 662.

26. Duignan and Gann, pp. 135-139 (particularly where the authors state that "[t]he Americans who assisted in opening the Congo were filling roles in the tradition of the many other pioneers who subdued the wilds of North America.").

27. Ibid., pp. 144-163 (where the authors highlight the activities of American soldiers fighting in Egypt and in South Africa, American prospectors and engineers playing a pivotal role in the nascent South African mining industry and Edward McMurdo's building of a railroad from the Mozambique coast to the Transvaal frontier).

28. Dominic J. Capeci, Jr. and Jack C. Knight, "Reactions to Colonialism: The North American Ghost Dance and East African Maji-Maji Rebellions," in Historian 1990, vol. 52, no. 4, pp. 584-601.

29. Cohen, pp. 210-213, 293-294 (where the author discusses lynchings within the context of the "Black Codes" of the Southern Redemption period, the legal edifice supporting involuntary servitude and restrictions on mobility for Africans in the American South); see also Paula Giddings, When and Where I Enter: The Impact Of Black Women On Race And Sex In America (New York: Bantam Books, 1984), pp. 28-30, 83, 89-90 (where the author discusses

the groundbreaking work of newspaper woman and anti-lynching activist Ida B. Wells).

30. Harold Cruse, The Crisis of the Negro Intellectual: A Historical Analysis of the Failure of Black Leadership, (New York: Quill Books, 1967), pp. 23-63 (in particular, see the author's description of the ouster of W.E.B. DuBois from the NAACP in 1934 and Claude McKay's falling out with the American Communist Party).

31. Lerone Bennett, Jr., Before The Mayflower: A History of Black America, (New York: Penguin Books, 1982, 5th ed.), pp. 352-355, 522-526.

32. Ibid., pp. 365-367; see generally, Cruse, pp. 171-173.

33. John Henrik Clarke, African World Revolution: Africans At The Crossroads, (Trenton, N.J.: Africa World Press, 1991), pp. 102-110.

34. William Roger Louis, Imperialism At Bay, 1941-1945: The United States and the Decolonization of the British Empire (New York: Oxford University Press, 1978).

35. Thomas Noer, Cold War and Black Liberation: The United States and White Rule in Africa, 1948-1968, (Columbia, MO.: University of Missouri Press, 1985); for a marxist critique of American foreign policy in Africa, see William Minter, King Solomon's Mines Revisited: Western Interests and the Burdened History of Southern Africa, (New York: Basic Books, 1986); see also Borstelman

36. Noer, pp. 34-60; see also Thomas Noer, "New Frontiers and Old Priorities In Africa," in Thomas Paterson, ed. Kennedy's Quest For Victory: American Foreign Policy, 1961-1963 (New York: Oxford University Press, 1989) (where the author distinguishes between John Foster Dulles' adamant warning against Third World neutrality ["neutralism is a transitional stage to communism"] and John Kennedy's reform notion of neutrality).

37. Thomas Noer, "The New Frontier and African Neutralism: Kennedy, Nkrumah and the Volta River Project," in Diplomatic History 1984, vol. 8, no. 1, pp. 61-79 (the author also points out, on p. 62, that American advisors/envoys practically censored one of Nkrumah's December 1961 speeches; he adds that "[f]ew if any Kennedy advisors viewed the project solely in humanitarian or even economic terms. The major arguments for and against the project were couched almost exclusively in traditional Cold War rhetoric.")

38. William Blum, The CIA: A Forgotten History (London: Zed Books, Ltd., 1986), pp. 174-179 (particularly where the author discusses the findings of Africa scholar M. Crawford Young with regard to Lumumba and the coalition leadership "The destruction of the [Leopoldville] regime, a vigorous reassertion of Congolese control over its own destiny, and a vague socialist commitment were recurrent themes. But at bottom it appeared for more a frame of mind and a style of expression than an interrelated set of ideas."); see also Madeline Kalb, The Congo Cables: The Cold War in Africa -- From Eisenhower to Kennedy (New York: Macmillan Publishing Co., Inc., 1982).

39. With regard to the CIA activity in Africa, see Blum, chapters 24, 26, 32, 41, 42 and 46 (where the author documents in detail the agency's activities in Algeria, the Congo, Ghana, Angola and Zaire; for instance, with regard to an assassination plot against Patrice Lumumba, Blum writes on pp. 176-7 that "[i]n September [1960], the CIA sent one of its scientists, Joseph Scheider, to the Congo carrying 'lethal biological material'. . . specifically intended for use in Lumumba's assassination. The virus, which was supposed to produce a fatal disease indigenous to the Congo . . . was transported via diplomatic pouch."); for an insider's perspective on CIA activity, see John Stockwell, In Search of Enemies: A CIA Story (New York: W.W. Norton & Co., Inc., 1978); for an exclusive treatment of CIA activity in Africa, see Ellen Ray, et al., eds., Dirty Work 2: The CIA in Africa (Secaucus, N.J.: Lyle Stuart Inc., 1979) (where, among other things, the authors discuss CIA misinformation campaigns in Angola, CIA infiltration of trade unions and other revolutionary groups in order to promote internal suspicion and dissension and agency recruitment of Black professionals - at one of America's foremost Black colleges - for use in Africa). For an in-depth overview of the infiltration and disruption caused by COINTELPRO, see Brian Glick, War At Home: Covert Action Against U.S. Activists and What We Can Do About It (Boston: South End Press, 1989); for general information regarding spying on diasporan Africans, see Kenneth O'Reilly, Black Americans: The FBI Files (New York: Carroll & Graf, 1994) and Racial Matters: The FBI's Secret File On Black America, 1960-1972 (New York: Free Press, 1989).

40. Mary Dudziak, "Desegregation As A Cold War Imperative," 41 Stanford Law Review 61, 117 (1988) (where the author states that "[t]he Truman Administration recognized and responded to this threat by marshalling evidence in its amicus briefs on the foreign policy implications of the desegregation cases. The Eisenhower Administration took advantage of the denouement, prominently using Brown in its propaganda efforts.") The "friend-of-the-court" briefs filed by the Department of Justice (hereinafter

"DOJ") in the aforementioned cases are quite revealing. The DOJ brief in
Shelly stated, in part, that "[t]he Legal Adviser to the Secretary of State has
advised that 'the United States has been embarrassed in the conduct of
foreign relations by acts of discrimination taking place in this country." Page
19, Brief for the United States as Amicus Curiae, Shelly v. Kramer, 334 U.S.
1 (1948). The DOJ brief in Brown went even further, indicating that "[t]he
shamefulness and absurdity of Washington's treatment of Negro Americans
is highlighted by the presence of many dark-skinned foreign visitors. Capital
custom not only humiliates colored citizens, but is a source of considerable
embarrassment to these visitors. . . . Foreign officials are often mistaken for
American Negroes and refused food, lodging and entertainment. However,
once it is established that they are not Americans, they are accommodated.'"
Pages 5-6, Brief for the United States as Amicus Curiae, Brown v. Board of
Education, 347 U.S. 483 (1954). The DOJ continued its argument thusly: "It
is in the context of the present world struggle between freedom and tyranny
that the problem of racial discrimination must be viewed. The United States
is trying to prove to the people of the world, of every nationality, race, and
color, that a free democracy is the most civilized and most secure form of
government devised by man. We must set an example for others by showing
firm determination to remove existing flaws in our democracy." Page 6, Brief
for the United States as Amicus Curiae, Brown v. Board of Education, 347
U.S. 483 (1954). The cited material from the DOJ briefs may be found in
Michal Belknap, ed., Civil Rights, The White House and The Justice
Department, 1945-1968 (New York: Garland Publishing, Inc., 1991), vol. 18,
pt. 1, pp. 19-20, 197-198.

41. William Minter, "With All Deliberate Delay: National Security Action
Memorandum 295 and U.S. Policy Toward Southwest Africa," in *African
Studies Review* 1984, vol. 27, no. 3, pp. 93-110.

42. For a detailed treatment of Fannie Lou Hamer's tireless efforts to
surmount Johnson's political roadblocks, see Robert Weisbrot, Freedom
Bound: A History of America's Civil Rights Movement, (New York: Plume
Books, 1990), pp. 117-123.

43. Anthony Lake, The "Tar Baby" Option: American Policy Toward
Southern Rhodesia, (New York: Columbia University Press, 1976).

44. W. Scott Thompson, "U.S. Policy Toward Africa: At America's Service?"
in *Orbis* 1982, vol. 25, no. 4, pp. 1011-1024 (where the author details the
ambiguities in the Ford and Carter administrations' policies which resulted
from the conflict between "idealism" and "realism" and suggests that, as

"realism" triumphed, the later Cater policies actually paved the way for the Reagan doctrine).

45. Inge Tvetden, "U.S. Policy Towards Angola Since 1975" in *Journal of Modern African Studies* 1992, vol. 30., no. 1, pp. 31-52; see also Richard Weitz, "The Reagan Doctrine Defeated Moscow In Angola," in *Orbis* 1992, vol. 36, no. 1, pp. 57-68; for an assessment of Reaganomics, among other things on the African community in the United States, see Earl Ofari Hutchinson, The Mugging of Black America, (Chicago: African American Images, Inc., 1990).

46. Gabriel Kolko, Confronting the Third World; U.S. Foreign Policy, 1945-1980 (New York: Pantheon Books, 1988).

47. Derrick Bell, "Brown v. Board of Education and the Interest-Convergence Dilemma," 93 Harvard Law Review 518 (1980).

48. United States Department of State Dispatch, September 19, 1994, p. 2. For a treatment of Wilson's "liberal internationalism," see N. Gordon Levin, Jr., Woodrow Wilson and World Politics: America's Response to War and Revolution, (London: Oxford University Press, 1968).

CHAPTER 6

Creating a Human Rights Culture:
A Strategy for Socially Just Policy Toward Africa

At the Conference of Evian, (1938), called largely upon the initiative of the United States in response to the atrocities the German government was committing against its own citizens, the world stood horrified. As it turned out, the world's disgust, however, was not so much over the atrocities of Hitler and the Third Reich, but rather the goal of other countries to intervene in another state's internal affairs.

Government Reluctance to Promote Human Rights

This reluctance to promote, what has now come to be known as human rights, resulted in one of the most dreadful pogroms in history, more commonly known as the holocaust, resulting in the wanton massacre of at least ten million innocents.

In order not to allow such a ghastly continuance of events to happen again, members of the international community formed a United Nations, whose purpose in large measure was, and is, as stated in the United Nations Charter, Article 1, section 3 to promote and encourage "respect for human rights and for fundamental freedoms for all without distinction as to race, sex, language, or religion."

The authoritative definition of human rights, essentially left undefined by the Charter are the principles embodied in The Universal Declaration of Human Rights, signed by the General Assembly with no dissenting vote in 1948 with eight abstentions. To date, it appears that only South Africa, fearful that the international community does not appreciate the difficulties of the European community living in a foreign and primarily indigenous culture and Saudi Arabia, apprehensive that freedom of religion may be a pretense for evangelical religions to exploit their culture, has abstained. This Universal Declaration of Human Rights, I argue here, ought to serve as the basis for creating a human rights culture in the United States.[1] Such a culture in turn

129

would and should serve as a social change strategy to positively influence policy toward Africa.

Originally, member states wanted the Universal Declaration to be merely a hortatory document, urging governments to respect and promote human rights. After all, the Soviet Union had its hideous Gulag; the European countries, their colonial empires, which included, of course, most of Africa; and the United States, its rampant poverty and sprawling ghettos[2] which substantively comprised African-Americans. Certainly, a legally binding document would engender too close international scrutiny.

But as documents from the Dumbarton Oaks, Yalta, and finally the San Francisco conference, which founded the United Nations, strongly suggest, it was non-governmental organizations (NGOs) primarily representatives of religious groups and labor, that pressed, in spite of apparent government reluctance, for the promotion of basic human rights principles.[3]   Such government reluctance today is still apparent, as at the recent World Conference on Human Rights in Vienna (1993), NGOs were excluded from the drafting of the final document, the Vienna Declaration, and implementation measures and monitoring of government compliance with human rights principles were sorely lacking.[4]

The Universal Declaration as Customary International Law

Briefly, the Universal Declaration of Human Rights consists of thirty articles, comprising in essence, four crucial notions:[5] human dignity in Article 1, a major tenet of major world religions; negative rights, that is, the responsibility of government not to interfere with fundamental liberties, more particularly civil and political rights, like freedoms of speech, the press, and assembly, primarily the legacy of the Age of Enlightenment and the American Bill of Rights (also called first generation rights); positive rights, that is, the responsibility of government to intervene with basic rights to provide for health care, shelter, employment, education, special protections for children, and security in old age, primarily the legacy of the Age of Industrialization and the Soviet Constitution of 1917 (also called second generation rights); and finally solidarity rights, which address rights to development[6], a clean environment, peace, and international distributive justice, the legacy of the failure of domestic sovereignty in the latter part of the 20th century to solve global issues (also called third generation rights). Originally meant to be hortatory, however, the Universal Declaration of Human Rights is increasingly referred to as customary international law[7] thereby binding governments to abide by its principles.

This last set of rights it appears is the most pertinent to speaking about U.S. policy toward Africa and other primarily poorer nations of the world, more commonly referred to as the Third World (a phrase I don't like very much, we are really all one world), as it calls in essence for an equitable distribution of the earth's resources. It must also be noted that international distributive justice, is deeply embedded in African culture.[8] As the Universal Declaration of Human Rights states in Article 28: "Everyone is entitled to a social and international order in which rights...can be realized."

The Interrelationship Between Rights and Policy

Social policy scholars, such as Stone (1988) have argued that the United States is a rights based culture[9], due in large measure to its Bill of Rights, which has served as a model for much of the world. However, Americans' conceptions of rights is, quite frankly, sorely limited. As I indicated in my book, Human rights and social policy in the 21st century (1992), the U.S. constitution makes no mention of second and third generation rights, apart from protections for an author's interests. Given that research consistently demonstrates that notions of human rights can influence policy,[10] can these lacks account, for example; why there are at least three million homeless, thirty eight million lacking health insurance, approximately thirty percent of children in poverty, and according to a 1993 study by the Department of Education, evidence that approximately 47% of Americans may be functionally illiterate.[11]

The failure to also acknowledge solidarity rights may account for why the United States, which comprises only 4% of the world's population consumes approximately 40% of its resources. It is also the world's largest supplier of military arms. Is U.S. military intervention throughout the world, such as in El Salvador, Grenada, Panama, the Persian Gulf and, more recently, Somalia a means to protect the wealth of the United States and due, also, to a failure to formally recognize peace as a human right? According to the official document of the U.S. Department of Information in response to the Vienna Declaration, foreign invasion should not be considered a human rights violation.[12] This statement was after the Persian War, when pediatric hospital admissions tripled after the U.S. invasion. Why was the United States the only country to veto the U.N. Declaration on the Right to Development? Is this because the former U.S. Representative to the U.N. Human Rights Commission, Morris Abram (1990), had argued for the "priority" of civil and political rights and referred to the right to development as an "empty vessel?"[13]

Toward a Human Rights Culture

A human rights culture would acknowledge as Asbajorn Eide (1987), special rapporteur to the U.N. writing on the right to food that all rights are equal, interdependent and indivisible[14]. Or as Shridath Ramphal (1982), Commonwealth Secretary-General to the United Nations eloquently stated: It does the cause of human rights no good to inveigh against civil and political rights deviations while helping to perpetuate illiteracy, malnutrition, disease, infant mortality, and a low life expectancy among millions of human beings. All the dictators and all the aggressors throughout history, however ruthless, have not succeeded in creating as much misery and suffering as the disparities between the world's rich and poor sustain today[15]."

A human rights culture would acknowledge that war cannot serve as a pretext to enforce human rights, which in turn, may easily mask hidden agenda. Thus, President Clinton's discourse on the starving children of Somalia and more recently much public discourse on genital mutilation, widely practiced there, may be a pretext to invade that strategically located country.[16] Given also, for instance, that the longevity rate of African American males in the inner city is 42, lower than the average throughout the third world, in this country that has one of the highest per capital incomes in the world, can it not be said that hypocrisy, not humanitarian concern, is the driving force behind the enforceability of human rights? Violence according to Martin Luther King can only beget more violence.

The African Situation

At the recent U.N. Human Rights Commission meeting in Geneva the count against Africa in regard to human rights violations was at an all time high.[17] But can it not be argued that this is because the West is now discovering the vast mineral and other resources in that continent, which President Bromery amply discussed at the previous African Conference here, and human rights discussions may fuel public sentiment to intervene. While I certainly abhor the genocidal atrocities in Rwanda, it may also suggested that this count was a backlash in response to the African countries attempt to block U.N. initiatives to commemorate 1992 as the year of Columbus's discovery of the Americas.[18] As some of you may be aware, this attempt is consistent with the Banjul Charter on Human and Peoples' Rights, more or less a progeny to the Universal Declaration of Human Rights, adopted by the Organization of African Unity on June 27, 1981 whose purpose is "the total liberation of Africa, the peoples of which are still struggling for their dignity and genuine independence, and undertaking to eliminate colonialism, neocolonialism, apartheid...and to dismantle aggressive foreign military bases and all forms of discrimination (Blaustein, Clark, & Sigler, 1987)." In response then to the question is there a U.S. policy toward Africa, I say yes. This is a policy that is first the legacy of a narrow definition of human rights and one that may easily mask hidden agenda. (Quite frankly, Americans are prisoners to their past. The U.S. Constitution is an Age of Enlightenment document. The world has radically changed since then.) While it may be true, as Jimmy Carter (1994) remarked, "For every person killed in Bosnia, fifty are killed in Sudan, [but] because they are black, because they are African we do not hear about them, they are not on our list of priorities[19]," I cannot help but feel that we will hear about "them," but unfortunately, only if we have something to gain.

Surely, the exploitation of Africa has historical roots in the United States, the most obvious, of course, being slavery. But it must be remembered that, at least according to Howard Zinn (1980) in A People's History of the United States, this exploitation continued as, for instance, it was North Africa that foot the bill for the prosperity of millions of Americans during the so-called roaring twenties[20]. And, today, was the International Conference on Population and Development led, it appears, largely upon the initiative of the United States, meeting in Cairo, the epitome of insult to the African people, who notoriously consume less than their western counterparts? Should it not have been the International Conference on Overconsumption?

In Conclusion: A Call To Consciousness

But there is hope if a human rights culture evolves, a call to consciousness, that acknowledges and has what is a "lived awareness[21]" of the equality of all rights; first, second, and third generation. Let me conclude with the first words of the preamble to the proposed constitution for the State of New Columbia (U.S. Government Printing Office, 1983), presently the District of Columbia, which Jesse Jackson had expressed interest as possible governor. "We reach out to all the peoples of the world in a spirit of friendship and cooperation, certain that together we can build a future of peace and harmony."

CHAPTER 6

ENDNOTES

1. J. Wronka, "Human Rights and Social Policy in the United States: An Educational Agenda for the 21st Century," Journal of Moral Education, Vol. 23, No. 3 (1994), pp. 261-272.

2. T. Buergenthal, International Human Rights Law (St. Paul, MN: West, 1988).

3. T. Farer, "The United Nations and Human Rights: More Than a Whimper," in Human Rights and the World Community, ed. by R. Claude and B. Weston (Philadelphia: University of Pennsylvania Press, 1989), pp. 194-208.

4. D. Sullivan, "Women's Rights and the 1993 World Conference on Human Rights," American Journal of International Law, No. 88 (1994), pp. 152-167.

5. J. Wronka, Human Rights and Social Policy in the 21st Century: A History of the Idea of Human Rights and Comparison of the United Nations Universal Declaration of Human Rights with United States Federal and State Constitutions, (Lanham, MD: University Press of America, 1992).

6. See M. Agonafer, Contending Theories of Development in the Contemporary International Order/Disorder: Lessons from Kenya and Tanzania, (Lanham, MD: University Press of America, 1994).

7. Filartiga v. Pena, 630 F2nd 876 (1980) and E. Stamatapolou, "Indigenous Peoples and the United Nations: Human Rights as a Developing Dynamic," Human Rights Quarterly, No. 16 (1994), pp. 58-81.

8. A. Legesse, "Human Rights in African Political Culture," in The Moral Imperatives of Human Rights, ed. by K. Thompson (Washington, D.C.: University Press of America) and H. French, "Abidjan Journal: Does Sharing Wealth Only Promote Poverty?" in New York Times (1995, January 14), p. 14.

9. D. Stone, Policy Paradox and Political Reason (Boston, MA: Scott, Foresman, 1988).

10. D. Gil, Unraveling Social Policy, (Cambridge, MA: Schenkman, 1992), and A. Chapman, Exploring a Human Rights Approach to Health Care, (Washington, D.C.: Association for the Advancement of Science, 1993).

11. C. Wolkie, "Locked Out of a World of Words," in Boston Globe, (1993, October 24), I and U.S. Department of State, Civil and Political Rights in the United States: Initial Report of the United States of America to the U.N. Human Rights Committee Under the International Covenant on Civil and Political Rights, (Washington, DC: U.S. Government Printing Office, 1994).

12. United States Information Service, "U.S. Information Regarding the World conference on Human Rights," (Geneva, Switzerland: Author, 1993).

13. M. Abrams, "Realization of Economic, Social and Cultural Rights Contained in the Universal Declaration of Human Rights," and "The Right to Development," (Geneva, Switzerland: U.S. Representative to the U.N. Human Rights Commission, 1990).

14. A. Eide, "Report on the Right to Adequate Food as a Human Right," (New York: U.N. Human Rights Commission, 1987).

15. S. Ramphal, "Address to the United Nations," (Geneva, Switzerland: Commonweealth Secretary, 1982), p. 1.

16. J. Wronka, "Human Rights," Encyclopedia of Social Work (Washington, DC: National Association of Social Workers, in press).

17. Conference on Universal Human Rights: Accountability and Enforcement, December 10, 1994 (Cambridge, MA: Coalition for a Strong United Nations) and J. Crook, "The Fiftieth Session of the U.N. Commission on Human Rights," American Journal of International Law, No. 88, pp. 806-820.

18. Op. Cit, Stamatapolou.

19. J. Carter, "Address in Columbus, Ohio," (Atlanta, GA: Carter Center for Human Rights, 1994).

20. H. Zinn, A People's History of the United States, (New York: Harper and Row, 1980).

21. P. Colaizzi, "A Phenomenological Approach to Learning," in Existential-Phenomenological Alternatives to Psychology, ed. by R. Valle and S. Halling (New York, Plenum), pp. 78-92.

CHAPTER 7

United States And Africa:
Exporting Democracy in the New World Order.

Exporting Democracy has been an important goal of the United States foreign policy. But the prevalent International Climate makes it even a more appropriate goal for the only existing Superpower on the globe. Using Africa as an example because of the euphoria surrounding the increased democratic activities on the continent on one hand and the preeminence of the promotion of human rights and democracy on the foreign policy agenda of the United States on the other, we shall examine the implementation of such foreign policy goals in light of the uncertainties of the present international system.

This paper is premised on the fact that the historical contradictions in the United States foreign policy in Africa and the uncertainties of the New World Order impact on the attainment of U.S. foreign policy goal -- Exporting Democracy, therein.

"...As an African, you will understand it when I say that, in this New World Order, issues of conflicts, problem of Democracy and Human Rights in Africa is as much part of your National Interest because we are of the same Community, without regards to race or sex. Issues of tyranny, problem of Democracy should no longer be peripheral to your National Interest...."

Nelson Mandela
President of South Africa
[In his Address to the Joint Meeting of the US Congress.
October 6 1994.] (CNN Special Report).

President Nelson Mandela, in the above speech, reinforces the interdependent nature of the present world order, which is epitomized in the increasing rhetorics and desire of the United States to promote democracy and human rights.

Exporting democracy has been a very important aspect of American foreign policy goals for some time. But it has been plagued by inherent contradictions whereby tyrants   and dictators have been cuddled and supported in the name of making the world safe for democracy and containing Soviet expansionism.

Nelson Mandela, in his speech, also raised the fundamental question of the place of Africa in the American foreign policy scheme. It is the interactions between the pursuits of the American goal -- referred to by Mandela, as the promotion of democracy and human rights, on the Continent and the changing nature of the international environment that constitutes the focus of this piece.

The objective of this paper is to identify, therefore, the circumstances surrounding the export of democracy by the United States to Africa in this New World Order or Disorder. Hence we shall examine:

a) The United States Foreign Policy and the factors influencing its formulations and implementation, in an attempt to identify the linkage between the export of Democracy and the American sense of purpose in the International system.

b) The changing nature of the international system. By examining the chaotic nature of the New World Order in an attempt to identify its impact on the formulation and implementation of the American policy -- Exporting Democracy.

c) The United States Foreign Policy in Africa in relation to a) and b) above. By critically examining some policy issues in an attempt to characterize American Foreign Policy in Africa.

This paper is premised on the assumption that the United States policy objective of exporting democracy is a function of the nature of previous American policy options in Africa and the characteristic uncertainties of the present World Order. This paper, however, affirms:

a) That exporting democracy is rooted in American tradition.

b) That the uncertainties of the global order undermines American dominance and its attempts to influence other Nations, and that other important variables influencing U.S. foreign policies includes the increase in domestic priorities, the disintegration and incoherence within some international alliances and the preference for cooperations rather than confrontation in the new international environment.

c)   That   the   U.S.   Foreign   Policy   in   Africa   is   schizophrenic.
Schizophrenic to the extent that it is reflective of the characteristic of
American policy behavior in Africa.

I: UNITED STATES FOREIGN POLICY: PATTERNS & IMPULSES.

The end of the Cold War has not drastically changed the orientation
of United States foreign policy. In fact,the changing circumstances suits
American characteristic persistence and vacillation [as it suits its goals] in
its relations with other Nations.

This vacillation has undermined United States supremacy in global
politics. Its persuasive power, its influence has been eroded gradually. Its
position and command over International economic system has been strongly
challenged and deteriorating. And, as indicated earlier, the world has changed
but the basic tenets of U.S. foreign policy remains constant[1].

Like many others, the United States foreign policy encompasses: the
goals that its leaders seek to attain abroad; the values that gives rise to these
goals and the means through which these goals are to be pursued. And the
means to achieving these goals are in themselves a function of the varying
domestic and International developments.

The formulation of these goals, on the other hand, also embodies the
impulses of policy makers and political elites. Through its persistence, the
United States Foreign policy has demonstrated a capacity to respond to
changing conditions while in some cases reactive in pursuits of its established
goals[2].

An example of this is the containment of the Soviet Union, which was
the preoccupation of the United states under Truman and Eisenhower. This
turned into competitive coexistence under Kennedy and Johnson. It changed
from brinkmanship to deterrence under Nixon,Ford and Carter. During this
period detente became the watch word, with the containment strategy pursued
by reduction and rewards for compliant behavior rather than coercion and
force. But under Reagan, the focus was on strains in East-West relations
characterized by militant orientation towards containing Soviet adventurism,
whereas Bush exploited the weakening Soviet economy and political
disintegration to fashion support for its policy in the Gulf. And Clinton
inherits a much weaker but dangerously nuclear proliferated and disintegrating
Commonwealth of Independent States.

This foreign policy pattern is a product of causative agents, which J.N.
Rosenau considered as important influence on the foreign policy behavior of
the United States. These factors could be classified into five viz:

- The External Environment
- The Societal Environment

- The governmental setting
- The roles played by central decision-makers.
- The individual characteristics of foreign policy making elites[3].

These factors are also the input that give shape and direction to the behavior of a Nation abroad. The behavior of the U.S. is the output and therefore a dependent variable.

These inputs includes the conditions of the global environment, the nature of relationship between Nations and its impact on America and its response to such impact. The input also includes the ideological and geographical realities, the potential for aggression. It must be noted, however, that these factors (external) do not exclusively determine how the United States acts but do influence how decision maker may choose to act -- thereby stimulating policy decision.

The external environment is an important determinant of United States foreign policy.   American policy makers are reactive to the changing international system.   The New World Order is characterized by the absence of the Soviet Union and the usual anti-Communist posture of the United States.   Once the ideological dimensions fades, what is apparent is not peace and harmony as one would have expected but a global politics based on dominant powers competing for influence and pursuing their respective national interest[4].

In this new International environment we have seen conflicts between small states, the resurgence of domestic politics and inter-ethnic conflicts.   But it also displays the usual two features of the external environment :

a) Its decentralization: Nation-States continue to monopolize power in the absence of a central institution or authority. Nation-States have had to rely on bargaining and self-help (including the threat and actual use of force) in their quest for national security in a particularly insecure and competitive environment[5].   The premium is, therefore, on the quest for power as a means of defense and influence.   And, the utmost desire to promote and preserve its national interest.

b) Its Stratification: The International System is also stratified. Power is unevenly distributed and hierarchical in nature within the global environment. Nations are not equal, although in line with the legal myth, they are presume to be so. But only a few nations like the United States possess a vast proportion of power and influence to achieve their stated objectives and, on the other end of the scale, there are those with none and who are powerless and weak.

The United States came out of the Cold War as the only Superpower, which has made her (U.S.) less militant in an attempt to cooperate with other major powers, including Western Europe and Russia (this was effectively and successfully used against Iraq). The United Nations, therefore, became the means through which the United States can universally exercise her power of influence. This has led to critics inferring a "pentagonization of the United Nations".

This less confrontational approach and efforts at cooperative enterprise in the exercise of foreign policy by the United States, with precedence set in the Gulf War, tends to portray America as being less decisive.

The second important causative agent of foreign policy is the Societal Environment: The chaotic nature of domestic economy today, marked by high rate of unemployment, high interest rates and budget deficits has forced governments to be inward-looking in their policies, therefore reducing the usually dominant position of foreign policy in the priorities of United states Government. Elections are now won solely on domestic issues, and foreign policy prowess becomes secondary in electoral decisions. However, foreign policy competes with domestic politics in a post-election environment. President Clinton realized this after the euphoria of his election victory when he got saddled with problems in Haiti, Bosnia, Somalia, the Middle-East and Russia, among others, as well as domestic issues like health care, deficits and many more.

The nature and roles of governmental institutions is an important factor influencing foreign policy decisions as well. The Constitution which divides the making and implementation of foreign policy among the different branches of government. The extent to which these institutions cooperate and the inherent ideological divide do impact on foreign policy goals and how to achieve them.

The growth of the bureaucracy within the multitude of governmental agencies and organizations which regularly competes to enlarge their "slice" of policy-making pie , also impacts foreign policy implementation and formulation.

Also important is the rise of executive dominance in foreign policy and the corresponding reassertion of congressional authority. This and the sheer size of governmental institutions may, however, contribute to a fractionalized and inefficient decision-making structure[6].

These governmental variables constrains what the United states can do abroad and the speed with which it can do it. The size and bureaucratization can also militate against policy reversal. We saw the impact of such variable on the United States policy recently in Somalia. The role of the State

Department and its relations with its agencies and other governmental agencies and institutions like the Congress, the CIA and even the Presidency do have an impact on policy formulation and implementation.

The roles played by central decision-makers and the ideological predisposition of foreign policy-making elites also constitute an important influence on the foreign policy making process. The concept of "role" refers to the impact of such thing as the nature of office on the behavior of its occupant. This includes the individual character of decision makers responsible for policy formulation and execution, like the skills, personalities, beliefs and psychological predisposition which define the kind of people they are and the type of behavior they exhibit.

The ideological predispositions of the policy-makers coupled with the impulses and tendencies within the American central decision-makers are important influences on the goals of United States foreign policy. These tendencies are categorized as Isolationism and Internationalism. The U.S. foreign policy in Africa is no doubt influenced by one or more variations of these policy impulses, but some are likely to be more predominant than others from issue to issue.

For example during the Carter years, the debates on U.S. policy in Africa is predicated on the influences of the globalist and regionalist variations of the Internationalist tendency. I do not intend to engage in a lengthy discussion of these tendencies, but a brief identification of some are relevant to the understanding of the objective of American foreign policy pursuit-Exporting Democracy.

Isolationism

Since George Washington, Isolationism has remained a main current in the United States foreign policy debates. Even now that it is no longer as dominant, it usually resurfaces, as in the case of the Vietnam War, with the popular reaction against American involvement (which is then categorized as neo-isolationist). It resurfaced on the question of American involvement in Bosnia, Somalia and Haiti. There were such sayings as "*America cannot be the World's policeman*" and "*No more Vietnam*" (otherwise referred to as the Vietnam syndrome). It gained currency during the last presidential campaign. To candidate Bill Clinton, it was the "economy stupid" and to Ross Perot, it was the "the deficit reduction." A prominent sub-group tendency in the Isolationist currently is the "Pacifist Idealist". They are against the use of force and they have been active in the anti-war movement and in influencing American involvement in the creation of legal devices to prevent war (i.e, the U.N. Charter and other bilateral treaties).

Internationalism

The predominance of this tendency is extraordinary given the persistence of the pacifist and Isolationist impulse over the years. This group wants to pursue, promote and maintain peace by making more governments democratic which would, in turn, create and promote a conducive international climate for America.

II: THE NEW WORLD ORDER OR DISORDER.

The behavior of a State in the International system is determined also by its power and situation in relation to the rest of the states in the World. Such behavior is a product of internal processes as earlier indicated. But the end of the Cold War in 1989 brought dramatic changes to the American position in the World by forcing a rethinking of the concepts which has persistently guarded its foreign policy for decades.

The dramatic improvement in the American security position was also a product of the disorganization and the breakdown of the Soviet System. On the other hand, this situation enhanced cooperations between the two Superpowers, which made it possible for the United States to entertain some peculiar objective on the periphery -- as demonstrated in the Bush administration's confrontation with Iraq over Kuwait.

Another characteristic of the New World Order, as earlier indicated, is the increasing budget deficit which reflects a profound disorder within American body politics and a fundamental disequilibrium between the wants of the people and their willingness to sustain the sacrifice necessary to secure these[7].

With the absence of the ideological opposite [in the Soviet Union], it becomes a difficult task for America to induce change in the posture of other States in the International System because of the lack of existing danger. It can, however, induce the promotion of Democracy and Human Rights by using some of the instruments used during the Cold War, such as the threat or actual use of force, military intervention, economic and military assistance, arms sales, propaganda, diplomatic bargaining and clandestine operations. But the International system now demands a different set of values and means of achieving these values.

Exporting Democracy

In light of the current state of the World, advancing and promoting democracy is America's most effective foreign policy option, "in terms of not merely good deeds, but of self-interest as well"[8]. The premise, according to American policy makers, is that, the spread of democracy will provide and promote the pursuit of happiness, which will make for a friendlier world. This, in itself, will not and has not guaranteed a conflict-free world.

The United States has always prided itself as the bastion of Democracy. Its foreign policy is democracy-conscious which is rooted in its history[9]. The belief is that spreading democracy is in the interest of America, for it will rally support for its policies and actions from large numbers of peoples both at home and abroad.

The practical prospect for the spread of democratic ideals has manifested itself since the end of the Cold War. This is because democratic values exist also beyond Europe and the western hemisphere. In fact, in some cultures and especially in Africa, democratic values and traditions predates modern Europe. The question is whether U.S.-styled democracy can be exported. The roots of democracy are complex. Democracy is a way of life and a belief system that evolves and is maintained within its own cultural "milieu."

American export of democracy has been carried out through military occupation as was the case in Japan, Germany, Austria, Italy, Grenada, the Dominican Republic and most recently in Haiti. The U.S. has spread democracy as a by-product of War (as well as a by-product of the Cold War, even through the covert activities of its intelligence services [covert activities may have had the opposite effect in many instances). The United States has also fostered democracy through the National Endowment for Democracy (NED). It has also done so through foreign aid, which could be military and financial.

The use of telecommunication such as overseas broadcasting has been an effective tool in promoting Democracy. The United States Information Agencies (USIA), Radio Liberty and Radio free Europe have played important roles in these efforts. Other USIA agencies includes the Voice of America (VOA), Radio and Television Marti and the Fulbright Program for International Exchange of Students and Scholars. While these agencies have increased the American influence on the Elites through educational exchange (some of which have turned out to be dictators), the VOA in 1988 for example reaches an audience of over 127 million once a week.

Diplomacy has also served to promote Democracy, as demonstrated recently in South Africa, Haiti and Namibia. Apparently, if Democracy could take hold in Germany, Italy (non Anglo-Saxon countries], Japan (non-western), India (not a rich country) because of prevalent and preexisting democratic tradition, it is also possible for democracy to take hold in African States. It is, however, impossible to promote universally acceptable democratic values and institutions. Democracy has to take its root in the domestic socio-economic and political tradition of that particular society. For example, the democratic style in Japan is decidedly Japanese not American.

Democratic ideas have increased its appeal in the past decades.It is even growing stronger in "the democratic World like the United States," especially with victories of the civil rights movements of the 1960s. A global overview do indicate that the road to democracy is not a one-way street. Democracy is not a have and have not attribute of political systems[10]. However the survival of the political system and democracy is dependent on the extent to which civil and political rights are recognized and reformed. According to Arat, the desire for a western democratic model has also been overwhelming, that its global transformation over the past five hundred years and the subsequent differences of the historical junctions at which democratization processes were initiated by the old and new developers has been ignored[11]

Of importance is the existence of an egalitarian development strategy of the West adopted by the governing elite in young democracies, were expected to work in societies where mobility is higher, communication means are more advanced and accessible and the governments are held responsible and accountable. Moreover, the masses in developing countries today are not only enfranchised but also politically more alert and demanding than their European counterparts were a few centuries ago[12].

A pertinent question can be asked. Is democracy a product that can be sold or bartered?   Or, to what extent can the United States control the political functions of other Nations? Moreover, democracy (a l'Americaine) is as much a product of certain social circumstances like literacy, affluence, national unity and peace. It is also important to note that America will promote democracy in its own best interest and those interest are as defined by its policy makers. For example, The U.S. went to Haiti primarily because of the possible impact of the Haitian refugees on its economy and political fabric rather than a God-ordained mission of promoting Democracy.

III: UNITED STATES FOREIGN POLICY IN AFRICA

The United States foreign policy in Africa has been negligible despite the fact that it was a source of inspiration for anti-imperialist and nationalist movements after the second World War. At the onset, America did not want to interfere in the turf of colonial powers and respected their zones of influence throughout the Continent until independence and much later in some cases.

In 1958, the United States Senate established a Foreign relations sub-committee on Africa with John F. Kennedy as its first chairman. United States relations with Africa took off rather gradually until it was embroiled in the Congo crisis. In Congo it supported and helped stage-manage the removal and the murder of a democratically elected leader Patrice Lumumba because of his leftist leanings and install instead a military tyrant Mobutu Sese Seko who has remained in power ever since while looting his country, suppressing his people and violating human rights. And, it remained a close ally of the United States until 1993.

The United States foreign policy thus began its schizophrenic pattern of relationships with many African States. This is also manifested again by its incertitude, ambivalence and "neutrality" during the Nigerian Civil War. In Angola, the United States also demonstrated its double standard by supporting Jonas Savimbi against its legitimate leadership because of his anti-Soviet predisposition. On the independence of Namibia, the U.S. demanded the withdrawal of Cuban forces from Angola as a precondition for supporting the legitimate U.N. Supported proposal to end Apartheid South African illegal occupation of the country. A dominant inconsistency was manifested in the U.S.'s support for the Apartheid regime in South Africa despite the United Nations position on the racist regime and the universal abhorrence of the racist policies in Pretoria.

In 1990, American policy in Africa was also tested in Algeria, especially on the issue of Islam and democracy. The Islamic Salvation Front won the 1990 local election and was on its way to winning a landslide in the legislative election when the military took over and the democratic process was annulled. The Islamics were the target, but democracy was the ultimate victim[13]. The United States was very passive and "regretted" the annulment, but this ambivalence contrasted with the Bush administration's promotion of political pluralism and it shows the continued preference for a police state to an Islamic Democracy.

The danger in this type of contradictory and schizophrenic posture is that, American reluctance to pressure the military junta or even speak against it will be seen as an inherently anti-Islamic sentiment. This same scenario was similar to the U.S.'s accommodation of the flagrant violations of human rights for many years in Apartheid South Africa and the occupation of Namibia. America also cuddled Mobutu and Samuel Doe and ignores the fact that Egypt is not a democracy but a military dictatorship and supported its candidate to successfully attain the Secretary-Generalship of the United Nations. It becomes very difficult to view and assess American foreign policy without taking cognizance of its previous positions on the Continent. In fact, its future foreign policy success in Africa is very much dependent on :

- the extent to which it has redressed it previous policy miscalculations.

- its perceived commitment to African interest (which is still very doubtful despite humanitarian efforts in Somalia and elsewhere)

- its distancing itself from any attempt at imposing political solutions ,since colonialism and imperialism is still very fresh in the African mind and racism is still prevalent against its African-American population.

President Clinton's efforts will no doubt pave the way for a more pragmatic and effective policy success on the continent. Policy initiatives such as moving beyond humanitarian efforts by increasing American investments, debt relief initiatives, assisting black enterprises in South Africa, promoting democratic institutions through aid and necessary non-military assistance.

Conclusion

The preoccupation with domestic needs and its considered regions of priorities like Europe, Asia and Latin America, has pushed Africa even further out in the extreme periphery.

Inasmuch as democracy and human rights are desirable, America must not be seen as imposing its structure or ideals on the people of Africa. But America must develop the means of forcing African leaders to be responsible and accountable if African themselves are unable to do so as a result of political suppression in the hands of their own leaders. International pressures like sanctions -- political and economic, suspension from international organizations -- are possible means of inducing change in African leadership.

America must demonstrate its commitment and must be consistent about this in its relation to African States. But it must be understood that a foreign policy which seeks to promote democracy tends to impose its values on cultures that are different from their own. The United States must therefore assist individual African States in this effort through economic and technical aid and leave them to develop their own democratic models.

Democracy will come when most people believe that their government is not legitimate unless it has their consent. It will come when enough people feel strongly enough about democracy and the preservation of human rights to risk their lives or their positions to reject the authority of a government that has not been democratically elected. It will come when they feel strongly enough to insist on the freedom of opposition groups to organize and circulate information, the freedom of speech and the press and other basic human rights. For example, in Nigeria, the emergence of a democracy movement is a sign of an increasing people determination to resist and a possible beginning of a democratic process.

CHAPTER 7

REFERENCES

1. C. W. Kegley & E.R. Wittkopf (1987) American Foreign Policy: Pattern and Process[New York,NY: St Martin's Press] p.5.

2. Ibid.

3. J.N. Rosenau(1984), Scientific Study of Foreign Policy [New York,NY: Nichols] Chapter 1.

4. C.W. Kegley Jr., (1922),

5. C.W. Kegley & E.R. Wittkopf (1987), Op.cit., p.151.

6. op.cit., p.22.

7. S.L. Spiegel & D. J. Pervin (1994), At Issue: Politics in the World Arena [New York,NY: St. Martin Press].

8. J. Muravchik, (1991) Exporting Democracy: Fulfilling American Destiny [Washington,D.C.: The AEI Press] Chp.1-2

9. Ibid.

10. Zehra Arat, (1994), Democracy and Human Rights in Developing Countries [Boulder,CO: Lynne Rienner] Chp. 2.

11. Ibid., p.8

12. Ibid.

13. Robin Wright [1993/94], "Islam,Democracy and the West" in Helen Purkitt [ed] [1993/94], World Politics 1993/94 [Guilford,CT: Dushkin Publ.] p.

BIBLIOGRAPHY

1. Adelphi Papers, (1991/92), "America's Role in a Changing World", Adelphi Papers,#256,Part 1, Winter 1990/91.

2. Aluko J & Shaw T. (1986), _The Political Economy of African Foreign Policy: Comparative Analysis._(New York: St. Martin's Press).

3. Arat Z. F.,(1994), _Democracy and Human Rights in Developing Countries_,[Boulder,CO: Lynne Rienner Publ.].

4. Carnegie Council on Ethics & International Affairs (1992),"_Democracy and the New World Order_" Ethics & International Affairs, Vol.6, Winter 1992.

5. Ethics & International Affairs, Vol.8, 1994.

6. Dahl.R.A. (1984), "_The Democratic Mystic_"in _New Republic_, April 2, 1984.

7. Diamond, L.,(1992),"_Promoting Democracy_",Foreign Policy ,[1992] p.87

8. Eberstadt,N. (1988), _Foreign Aid and American Purpose_ [Washington D.C: AEIPPR].

9. Foreign Affairs, (1978),"_America and the World_",_Foreign Affairs,_ 1978.

10. Halperin,M.H., (1993)"_Guaranteeing Democracy_", _Foreign Policy_ 91.

11. Harvier,O. et al (1987), _The Reagan Doctrine and Beyond_, [Washington D.C: AEI].

12. Herokovitz,J. (1982),"_Nigeria: Power and Democracy in Africa_" Headline Series, #257, Jan/Feb. 1982.

13. Hill, K.L. (1985), _Concise Overview of Foreign Policy 1945-1985_ [Malaibaw,FL: R.E. Krueger Publ.]

14. Kegley, C.W. & Wittkopf,E.R. (1987), _American Foreign Policy: Patterns & Process_[New York: St. Martin's Press].

15. Kennan, G.F. (1959),_American Diplomacy: 1900-1950_, [Chicago: University of Chicago Press].

16. Lake, A. (1985), "*Third World Radical Regimes: U S Foreign Policy Under Carter and Reagan*", Headline Series, #272, FPA, Jan/Feb.1985.

17. Larson,J.F. (1987) "*Global Television and Foreign Policy*", Headline Series, #288, March/April 1987.

18. Mazrui,A. (1977), *Africa International Relations:The Diplomacy of Dependency and Change*, [London: Heinemann].

19. Muravchik,J. (1991), *Exporting Democracy: Fulfilling America's Destiny*, [Washington D.C: The AEI Press]

20. Nathan,J.A. & Kolwer,J. (1976), *United States Foreign Policy & World Order* [New York: Little Bow & Co].

21. Onwuka,R.I & Aluko,O. (1986), *The Future of Africa and the New International Economic Order* [New york: St. Martin's Press]

22. Rosenau,J.N, (1984), *Scientific Study of Foreign Policy*, [New York: Nichols].

23. *Comparing Foreign Policy:Theories and Methods.* (1978) [New york: Wiley].

24. Schatzberg,M.G., (1991), *Mobutu Or Chaos?: The U.S. and Zaire 1960-1990* [Lanham,MD: University Press of America].

25. Singer,M. & Wildavsky,A. (1993), *The Real World Order: Zones of Peace and Zones of Turmoil*, [Chatlham,NJ: Chatlham House Publ.]

26. Spanier,J. (1992), *American Foreign Policy Since World War II* [Washington DC: Congressional Quarterly].

27. Spiegel,S.L. & Pervin,D.J.(ed) (1994), *At Issue: Politics in the World Arena*, [New York: St. Martin's Press].

28. Tryin,M.D & Mwanba,Z.I. (ed) (1987), *Apartheid South Africa and American Foreign Policy*, [Dubusque,IOWA: Kendall/Hunt Publ.]

29. Robin,W. (1993), "*Islam ,Democracy and the West*", in Helen E. Purkitt (ed) (1993/94), *World Politics 1993/94* [Guilford,CT: Dushkin Publ.].

CHAPTER 8

How Heathens Treat Women:
Sati, Footbinding and the American Campaign
Against Genital Mutilation

We don't talk about heathens anymore. It's not just that the West has become more secular; it's that heathens belong to a rhetoric of empire long since discredited. The word is gone but the image of the heathen is still very much with us. This is nowhere more apparent than in the international debate regarding the African practice of female genital surgery (FGS)[1].

Many Western critics of FGS recognize this of course, and have gone to some lengths to be more sensitive regarding differing cultural and religious mores. Nonetheless, the debate surrounding FGS not only resurrects the image of the heathen, but also the old arguments and techniques of empire including the emphasis on emotion over data, the tendency to use the other to define oneself, the oversimplification that defines an entire culture in terms of a single practice, and the misuse of religious texts to denigrate customary laws. Indeed, the arguments regarding FGS today are startlingly similar to the British arguments denouncing sati[2] in late 18th and early 19th century India. The only thing missing is the word heathen.

This does not bode well for Africa or for African women. The British attacks on sati were part of Britain's most successful colonial conquest. By focussing on a single aspect of Indian life, the British not only managed to lend a high moral tone to colonial conquest, but also managed to ignore (or disguise) the magnificence and complexity of the culture they invaded. The anti-sati campaign was an effective propaganda tool on the homefront because it portrayed Indians and their culture as simplistic and childlike, in need of parental guidance and easy to control. It also justified direct intervention in Indian life despite British protestations of defending religious freedoms. It did not, however, end the practice of sati. (The last public case was in 1987.) It did nothing to improve the lives of the majority of Indian women and may actually have undercut what little customary power they had (The last publicized case of sati was in 1987.)

153

Such direct colonial conquests are no longer likely today, of course, and outraged statements by the U.S. on the subject of FGS probably do not indicate an intention to try to settle the matter through military force. However, the 1994 decision by the U.S. Agency for International Development to provide funding to eradicate FGS in Africa represents a new development. Those who provide the money so often set the agenda for how reforms are to be carried out. And it may not stop there. Already some feminist groups are urging the Clinton administration to go further, to use the threat of political and/or economic sanctions to force African states to ban the practice. The forcible intrusion of one nation, especially a nation as powerful as the U.S., into the internal affairs of another is something that needs to be approached with care. If the example of British India is anything to go by, direct U.S. involvement in FGS is unlikely to do Africa or African women any significant good.

That is not to say that outside pressure to eradicate undesirable practices in another culture must inevitably fail or wind up being used as a tool of imperialism. The American and European missionaries working in China in the late 19th and early 20th century played a small but significant role in ending the practice of footbinding[3] without adding much to the rhetoric of empire. Moreover, in retrospect it becomes apparent that they were not only successful in ending the practice of footbinding, but also set in motion a number of other changes that empowered Chinese women. Their experience suggests, however, that bringing about change in a culture other than one's own requires a non-national presence, considerable luck, the ability to compromise, a willingness to work with and for indigenous resistance groups, and a recognition that the role of the outside must and should be small and temporary. It also suggests that changing a long-standing tradition takes time. The anti-footbinding campaign was successful, but it took more than 70 years.

In this paper, I will take a fresh look at the international campaign against FGS by comparing it to two earlier campaigns against institutionalized violence against women: the British abolition of sati in India, and the missionary campaign against footbinding in China. My aim is not to pass judgment on any of these practices but to examine the actual results of each campaign in terms of what the reformers themselves hoped to achieve.

The image of the heathen was perhaps the most useful icon devised by 19th century Europeans. It was, of course, the ultimate justification for imperialism. The male heathen needed to be saved from himself, from his unenlightened (I.E. non-Christian) tendency to satisfy his primitive appetites at the cost of his future salvation. The female heathen was even more useful. She needed to be saved not only from herself but also from the male heathen to whom she represented one of those primitive appetites.   The pathetic figure of the female heathen pleading to be rescued from her own culture did much to diffuse what little homefront opposition there was to 19th century imperialism.   However, the image of the heathen, especially the female form, cannot be dismissed purely as a propaganda device for imperialism. It had and has greater power than that. By defining the other, the heathen, Westerners defined themselves. This worked equally well for supporters of the status quo and for reformers. For supporters of the status quo, the heathen proved their own culture superior. For reformers, the heathen provided a medium through which to express their own pain and frustration.   In the case of sati, Englishmen found in it proof that they were far more chivalrous and civilized. They would never treat a widow this way. By focussing on the physical horror of sati, they conveniently ignored the wretched lives English widows actually led due to the nature of English property laws. For early feminists, many of them working to change those property laws, the image of the sati was a compelling symbol for their own helpless rage. Either way, the discussions thus generated had little to do with the actual cultures or women involved. It is hardly surprising, therefore, that the solutions they developed did little to improve the situation.

Because the image of the helpless, female heathen was and is important to the Westerners personally, the debates surrounding her plight have a tendency to emphasize the emotional response and to ignore the need for factual data. This is apparent in both the British campaign against sati and in the current campaign against FGS. In both cases, the factual data is ignored, and sometimes distorted, to suit the needs of the campaign.

This is most evident in the British campaign to outlaw sati. The British were free with their figures but seldom consistent. They noted that the frequency of sati varied drastically in different regions of India, and then proceeded as if the startlingly high figures found in Bengal in the 1820s (more than one incident daily) were typical. In fact, later research has cast considerable doubt on the accuracy of the Bengali statistics. Kinder analyses have suggested that the incidence of sati may have risen sharply during this time as a nativist resistance to British rule. Other analyses suggest that British bureaucrats under the aegis of Governor-General William Bentinck, an avid opponent of sati, may have increased the statistics by listing any widow who committed suicide, in any way, at any time, for any reason as a sati. Most contemporary scholars agree that cases of sati were, in fact, rare. Some have even suggested that it had almost died out by the time the British arrived, and that the British created the myth of its continuing existence for their own purposes.[4]

The reportage on FGS is probably more accurate. Sufficient evidence exists that some form of FGS is practiced in many parts of Africa and the

Middle East. As in India, there are regional differences and because of the intimate nature of the issue, information is harder to come by. Nonetheless, the numbers usually range between 80 and 100 million women affected, more than enough to describe the situation as widespread. However that is where the accuracy stops. The problem lies in the definition of FGS. The term actually covers 4 different procedures: 1.) ritualistic circumcision in which the clitoris is lightly nicked and there is little or no long term damage, 2.) sunna, in which the clitoral prepuce is removed but the clitoris is usually left undamaged, 3.) clitorectomy in which the entire clitoris and often parts of the labia minora are removed, and 4.) infibulation in which all external genitalia are removed and the raw edges are sewn together leaving only a tiny opening to allow urine and menstrual fluid to escape.[5]

Obviously there is a great deal of difference in these four practices[6] that is not reflected in the statistics of 80-100 million women affected by FGS. Indeed, most writers structure their presentation for maximum dramatic or political effect by focussing on infibulation, the most extreme and damaging form of FGS. They usually begin by acknowledging that FGS covers 3 or 4 (the first two are often combined) different practices and then launch into a harrowing description of an infibulation under the most unhygienic conditions possible. The implication is that this is the norm. It may be, but no group has yet produced convincing evidence one way or the other.[7]

The emphasis on eliciting emotional over rational response is not only a substitute for exact figures, it seems to be a preference. In the Indian case, it led colonial bureaucrats to exaggerate statistics to correspond with their own, emotionally based expectations. The same may well be true in Africa, especially considering the greater ability of the modern media to elicit such response.

In the case of sati, the media was limited to sketches and verbal description. Indian depictions showed the sati sitting in divine detachment as the flames rise up around her, and even some British observers recorded that the sati seemed to feel no pain. In 1825 Dr. Richard Hartley Kennedy, Inspector General for the Bombay Hospitals, attended the sati of a woman he knew well. He went with the intention of dissuading her saying that

> if she felt any misgiving, my presence would prevent it from being too late, even at the supposed last moment ...but her look of reply was quite sufficient; she had not come without counting the cost...[She] exhibited not a sign of reluctance, but conducted herself as one who met her fate with as much inward feeling of alacrity and readiness, as she undoubtedly did with all outward show of superhuman fortitude...I think I should have heard any

unrestrainable shriek of extreme agony had it been uttered; and observed any convulsive movement, or desperate attempt to break forth, had it been made. I do not think that either took place.[8]

Kennedy was the exception, however. Most British accounts were harrowing and portrayed the sati as a victim both of her own superstition and the cruelty of her culture. The sati was most often portrayed as a child despite the fact that British records indicate most cases were above the age of 40. Some described the practice as a vicious form of mob murder. Walter Ewer, Superintendent of Police in the Lower Provinces of Bengal, provided a vivid picture of what happened should a widow refuse to mount her husband's funeral pyre:

> ...it will avail her little--the people will not be disappointed of their show; and the entire population of a village will turn out to assist in dragging her to the bank of the river and keeping her down on the pile. Under these circumstances nine out of ten widows are burnt to death.[9]

C. M. Lushington, the Magistrate at Trichinopoli, denied seeing such mob activities and focused instead on the innate weakness of women and the superstitious nature of Indians generally:

> The act I apprehend is always voluntary, provided a being in a state of stupefaction and delusion can be said to possess the power of volition.[10]

Some British women noticed that the question of voluntarism involved more customs than simply the act of sati. Katherine Mayo, in a more socially sophisticated effort to explain why women might choose sati, painted an equally appalling picture of what happened to the widow who failed to commit sati:

> The widow becomes the menial of every other son in the house of her late husband. All the hardest and ugliest tasks are hers, no comforts, no ease. She must take but one meal a day and that of the meanest. She must perform strict fasts. Her hair must be shaven off...she may be turned adrift. Then she must live by charity--or by prostitution into which she not seldom falls. And her dingy, ragged figure, her bristly, shaven head, even though its stubble be white over the haggard face of unhappy age, is often to be seen in temple crowds or in the

streets of pilgrimage cities, where sometimes niggard piety doles her a handful of rice.[11]

Recognizing that ending sati did little by itself to improve the lot of Indian women, she advocated widespread reforms involving women's education and increased job opportunities. However even she could not resist the temptation to use Britain's power to stop a practice she found so personally distasteful.[12]

Popular fiction soon picked up on the themes introduced by British abolitionists. Freed of any need to stick to facts, works of fiction used sati almost exclusively for shock effect. Jules Verne's novel, Around the World in Eighty Days, played up the cruelty of Indian society in describing the plight and rescue of the widow Aouda:

> "The poor wretch! exclaimed Passepartout, "to be burned alive!"
> "Yes," returned Sir Francis, "burned alive. And if she were not, you cannot conceive what treatment she would be obliged to submit to from her relatives. They would shave off her hair, feed her on a scanty allowance of rice, treat her with contempt; she would be looked upon as an unclean creature, and would die in some corner like a scurvy dog. The prospect of so frightful an existence drives these poor creatures to sacrifice much more than love or religious fanaticism..."
> The doors of the pagoda swung open, and a bright light escaped from its interior, in the midst of which Mr. Fogg and Sir Francis espied the victim. She seemed to have shaken off the stupor of intoxication, to be striving to escape from her executioner.[13]

Indeed, sati soon became such a staple of any story involving India that many Europeans believed that all Hindu widows were routinely burned on their husband's death although not even the most avid abolitionist had ever made such a claim.

A similar combination of emotionally laden narrative and the world of fiction also affects the discussion of FGS and is arguably more intense given the greater power of television over the written word to heighten drama and lessen factual input.

Television, however, cannot be blamed for everything. Even in written form the image of the heathen has made an unwelcome come-back in discussions of FGS. Perhaps the most notorious was the work of Fran Hosken whose sensationalized presentation caused a number of African feminists to walk out of an international women's conference in 1980. Hosken's casual dismissal of evidence that FGM had once been a Western practice, her insistence that all such cases must be linked to African immigration, and her "us helping them" approach led many non-Western feminists to criticize her for her colonialist attitude.[14]

Television, however, adds its own unique problems. In a documentary produced by the Inter-Africa Committee on Practices Affecting the Health of Women and Children

> The camera pans a bustling marketplace in Ibadan, Nigeria, the frame crowded with colors that shriek as loudly as the hawkers with their wares. The focus shifts to the granite hills in the distance, and then to a dusty street where a traditional African medic has set up shop out in the open. A sign in English advertises "Native Doctor." Mothers are lined up with their babies in arms to see this man who carves tribal marks and performs circumcisions. He sharpens his blade on a well-worn whetstone. A toddler is spread-eagle, naked before him. The girl's eyes are wide and fearful as she frantically searches the crowd of adults around her and realizes there is no rescue.
>
> The blade does its work. The baby's scream is unendurable. "Mamamamamamamamamama."
>
> Now we see the doctor's impassive face. He sits back on his haunches and motions for the next in line.[15]

In this case the problem lies not so much with the film itself which was produced by Africans, albeit Western educated Africans (the Inter-Africa Committee headquarters are in Geneva), but in the viewer. What the viewer, in this case Mary Ann French of The Washington Post, saw was not simply a protest against a specific practice, but an indictment of an entire culture from its shrieking (I.E. heathen) colors to its callous doctors and ignorant mothers who do not know enough even to protect their own children. She is not alone. A. M. Rosenthal of The New York Times has attacked FGS as "a violation of human decency," and an "atrocity."[16] William Raspberry of The Washington Post goes even further describing it as "a brutal (one is tempted to say savage) practice with no redeeming value," and wonders at "the willing complicity of women in this...awful practice."[17]

This was certainly not the response the Inter-Africa Committee hoped for. In a letter to the editor of The New York Times published on December, 24, 1993, Berhane Ras-Work, President of the Inter-Africa Committee protested the turn the discussion was taking:

Some writers consider the practice a crime and torture, and reproach Africans for not taking action to stop it. Another calls it a joyous occasion for the girls who undergo the operation...[but I] cannot help asking whether or not the writers have cared to inform themselves about the efforts Africans are making to deal with the problem.[18]

The variability of reader/viewer response is even greater when fiction is involved. Seble Dawit and Salem Mekuria, two African women active in the anti-FGS movement, criticized Alice Walker's novel, Possessing the Secret of Joy for dealing with FGM as an emblem of gender oppression rather than an issue in and of itself, for using it as

a powerfully emotive lens through which to view personal pain-- a gauge by which to measure the distance between the West and the rest of humanity.[19]

This is probably unfair to the novel which is by its very nature, personal. The fact that most of those characters who recognize the evil of FGS are either Western or Western educated is also justifiable in terms of fictional license. It is true, however, that Walker could have done more to note the presence of an indigenous opposition without greatly affecting the impact of her work.

More recently, Walker collaborated with Pratibha Parmar, a London based feminist film maker, to produce a documentary about FGS, Warrior Marks. Unlike Possessing the Secret of Joy this purports to be fact although the themes are identical: the health dangers, the loss of sexual pleasure[20] and the destruction of women's spirit. It does include interviews with African women who oppose FGS. Nonetheless, the film has been denounced by a number of African feminists for portraying a neo-colonialist vision of an Africa

where women and children are without personality, dancing and gazing blankly through some stranger's script of their lives. The respected elder women of the villages' secret societies turn into slit-eyed murderers wielding rusted weapons...[Walker and Parmar] portray the continent as a monolith...the background against which Alice Walker, heroine-savior, comes to articulate their pain and condemn those who inflict it.[21]

Whether or not that is an accurate description of the documentary, it is certainly true that the response of Western viewers reveals some alarming reversions to imperialist attitudes. One American viewer saw the film as a call

> to compel civilized countries to acknowledge that female genital mutilation is nothing less than ritual torture of girls--and to enlist international support to eradicate it.[22]

Another viewer added

> This is not just another quaint cultural practice that outsiders ought to leave alone. There is, as several panelists at the Howard screening noted, an important difference between culture and mutilation.
>
> Of course, calling it "mutilation" instead of the more benign "circumcision" hints of bias, maybe even cultural superiority.
>
> It's a risk I'm willing to take, and NOW is correct in raising it as a human rights issue...[23]

It may be correct to raise FGS as a human rights issue, but it is not necessarily wise. The viewer responses to Warrior Marks are disturbingly similar to the statement made by Governor-General Bentinck when he finally outlawed sati in Bengal in 1829. Although he confessed to some qualms about interfering in religious practices, he had made his decision "resting altogether upon the moral goodness of the act and our power to enforce it."[24]

The problem here is not only the Western assumption that they know what human rights or moral goodness are, but also the assumption that it is possible to eliminate a practice without considering other aspects of the culture, that the practice exists apart from the society and can be changed by external force. Such an argument has some major ramifications. First, it justifies forceful intervention in the affairs of another country. Second, it oversimplifies the culture, often to the point of defining that culture by a single practice. Third, it ignores the impact ending the practice may have on other aspects of life, an impact which can be detrimental to the very people (in this case, women) that the reform advocates are trying to help. And fourth, it ignores the fact that such efforts are seldom fully successful since they fail to address the real issues that lead to the practice in the first place.

In the case of the British in India, the force was direct and military. Sati was outlawed. Since a successful sati could clearly no longer be prosecuted, further laws were enacted stating that anyone who aided or abetted a sati "whether the sacrifice be voluntary or not, shall be deemed guilty of culpable homicide."[25] This is an interesting distinction. The British accused the Indians not of forcing women to commit sati but of failing to stop them.   In the same way, opponents of FGS accuse African governments not of mandating such surgeries, but of failing to ban them.   This is a far intrusive form.   It is one thing to demand that a government stop doing something, E.G. using torture.   It is another to demand that they take action to stop their own people from doing something that is not mandated by law.   That is not only intrusive but difficult, perhaps impossible, to enforce through political or military means.

A celebrated case of sati in 1913 indicates the problems involved.   An entire village had stood by or actively assisted while a Brahman widow mounted her husband's funeral pyre in the center of village, held his corpse in her arms and burned with him.   Although there were close to 2,000 witnesses, no one could be found to say who had fired the pile.   The police, although notified, arrived late.   They later explained that they had acted in fear, "the sati having threatened to curse them if they withheld assistance."[26]

Such open defiance was rare, however.   More often, sati became a private, secretive affair.   In 1876 a

> widow dug a pit inside her house, filled it with sandalwood, and dressed herself as a bride; she shut the doors, lit the pile, and leapt in.[27]

Even more common were cases where

> the newly widowed wife deliberately pours oil over her garments, sets them afire and burns to death, in a connived at secrecy.[28]

Poorer women used paraffin.

Banning sati did not end the practice, it merely forced it into hiding, and by doing so, robbed it of all dignity.   The Brahman widow who held the police at bay by threatening them with curses was a powerful figure.   The desperate woman who drenched herself in paraffin was a victim, albeit a defiant one.   Moreover, the necessary secrecy of the act made coercion much easier.   Some British observers in the 1920s charged that unwanted widows were often burned alive by their in-laws who knew that it was usually impossible to prove that she had not committed the act herself.[29]   Some contemporary critics have charged that the current wave of burning young brides in dowry fights owes much to the British attempt to end sati by force.

The possibility of such family homicides was increased by the property laws passed by the British.   Designed to develop a land-owning class on the

English model, the British barred widows from succeeding to their husband's property. This was perhaps inevitable since, despite their chivalrous self-image, the British system was as abusive to women as the Hindu. Ultimately, the British not only failed to recognize the way their own system abused women, their focus on sati blinded them to the economic and social advantages women enjoyed in many parts of India. As a result, they managed to produce a set of laws that emphasized the most abusive aspects of both systems.

Some British women recognized sati as a women's issue rather than a unique practice unrelated to the culture. Women like Katherine Mayo stressed the other factors that made sati preferable to widowhood. She advocated wide ranging reforms affecting education, child brides, attitudes toward remarriage and increased job opportunities for women. Such women undoubtedly had an impact, especially on the upper class Indian women they worked with, but their ability to persuade the colonial government to support their aims was limited both by their gender and by their refusal to admit the overwhelmingly patriarchal nature of their own institutions.

It may seem that this is a very different situation from that which faces Africa in the late 20th century. Direct colonialism by any Western power is unlikely. Military intervention by the U.S. or the U.N. is more likely, but so far economics and public opinion have ensured that such episodes will be brief. Certainly intervention over the issue of FGS is remote. Despite the efforts of some American and internationalist women's groups to get the U.S. or the U.N. directly involved in FGS during the Somalia intervention, both bodies declined.

More recently, however, the Clinton administration has moved to provide aid to African groups opposed to FGS. The U.N. too has supported the creation of African led groups like the Inter-Africa Committee on Traditional Practices Affecting the Health of Women and Children. There is nothing wrong with this provided that this support does not try to set priorities emphasizing the ending of FSG over the many other issues these groups address.

This is a very real possibility even without official intervention. When Representative Constance Morella visited a family planning center in Cairo in September, 1994, she was so impressed by the local doctors's denunciation of FSG and a CNN filming of a surgery on 10 year old Nagla Hamza, that she brought the matter up in an official meeting with Egyptian President Hosni Mubarak. Mubarak noted that FSG was already illegal and promised to look into the matter. CNN put their film on the air. By the time Morella deplaned in the U.S. Nagla Hamza's father and several other relatives had been arrested. A few days later, religious leaders agreed to back the ban provided doctors agreed.[30]

The event was hailed as a triumph for international feminism and the press. "That's probably the best argument for showing shocking and horrifying footage of any atrocity," said CNN spokesperson Paige Prill. Jaqui Hunt, president of Equality Now, a New York based organization opposed to FGS, agreed:

> We're happy the practice is being exposed...Obviously the Egyptian government and other mutilators are very sensitive to outside pressure and publicity.[31]

It is doubtful that this really achieved much. Aside from the question of what will happen once the publicity dies down, Egypt has already banned FGS in public hospitals as have several other African countries. Enforcement is lax but that is not the only problem. Many Egyptian doctors who oppose FGS still perform the operations. They note that banning FGS in hospitals without actually ending the practice, simply increases the chance that it will be carried out in unhygienic conditions. They add that they at least use sterilized instruments and anesthetic. In the age of AIDS, this is no trivial argument. Many of these doctors oppose a ban and instead advocate education at the grassroots level. Even those who support a ban on physicians performing FGS admit the need for ongoing education and predict that it will taken a long time, possibly several generations to eliminate the practice.[32]

Indeed, most indigenous African and Middle Eastern women's organizations do not focus on FGS as strongly as do outside forces. They recognize it as just one of the many forces that affect women's lives in Africa. Femnet, which represents 20 non-governmental women's groups operating in 24 African countries, sees empowering women, not banning FGS, as the major issue. Njoki Wainaina, the head of Femnet wants to use outside pressure to

> redefine development so that women are central to every effort, whether it is in health and family planning, agriculture, education or housing...foreign aid programs [should] hold governments responsible for making women full participants and beneficiaries of aid, with an emphasis on health, education and economic incentives.[33]

Although Femnet includes FGS among its concerns, its more broadly based approach could lead those who focus exclusively on that issue to exclude it from international support.

In the poorer nations, international support may well be able to set the agenda. That would be a pity. The wide variety of indigenous approaches to the issue of FGS testify to the complexity of the issue, to the diversity of the practices, regional variations, national interests and religious differences. International approaches, on the other hand, seek to find a single policy and reveal a tendency to view Africa as a monolith. It is not impossible that international support might be limited to those groups that share this view. Certainly this is what happened in India. British opponents of sati persisted in seeing the sub-continent as a nation state which it was not, and as a single cultural entity which it also was not. Even those who recognized that sati occurred more frequently in some areas than others and was affected by many other factors, still sought a single remedy that would work all over India. They applauded, publicized and supported Indian reformers who supported this view. Others were dismissed from consideration.

Probably the most applauded Indian opponent of sati was Rammohun Roy, a male, western influenced Brahman who wrote extensively on the subject in the early 19th century. Rammohan based his opposition on his extensive knowledge of the Hindu scriptures. He argued that sati was not commanded by the scriptures and that even where it was mentioned, it was an act of inferior virtue. He criticized those who favored sati of "taking refuge in usage."[34] As part of an indigenous discourse on sati, Rammohan's arguments were sound. It was the colonial construct that distorted them by making of them an officially sanctioned orthodoxy.

The British loved Rammohan's work and not only because it provided them with proof that Indians also opposed the custom. Its religious bent also fit most neatly into the way in which Westerners were prone to analyze social issues. Later, as the British became more knowledgeable about India, many of them would also use the Hindu scriptures to criticize not only sati but other customs as well, arguing that they violated India's own ethical and religious standards.

Unfortunately, this approach ignored two vital points. First, the Hindu scriptures were not analogous to the Bible or the Qor'an. There was no single body of writing from which all Indians derived their moral values. The Hindu scriptures were a loose compendium of stories and doctrines, often internally contradictory, none of which were even considered to apply to all people at all times. By treating these texts as a Hindu version of the Bible, Rammohan and his British followers, altered the nature of Hindu discourse in a way that may have much to do with the religious intolerance and violence that now exists between the Hindus and the Muslims.

Second, Rammohan's argument rested upon the premise that where written scripture contradicted usage, it was usage that was in error. Thus any woman who committed sati and the people who helped her were revealing their ignorance of their own religion. Other Indians disagreed, noting that Hinduism was as much a matter of practice and custom as of textual references. Their arguments, however, were dismissed from consideration by the British rulers.

In fact, Hindu scriptures contained little to empower women. Local customs, especially in areas that favored matrilineal descent and inheritance, often gave women more dignity than the written form would imply. Even sati gave women credit for a dignity and heroism quite absent from the 19th century Western view of women. By elevating the importance of the written form and devaluing the importance of custom, Rammohan and the British may have saved a few women from the flames, but they may also have worsened the situation for Indian women overall.   A similar misuse of religion and internal debates by outsiders plagues the international discourse on FGS. Indigenous reformers use religious argument as a tactic. This is especially true in Muslim countries where feminists regularly use quotations from the Qor'an, the Haditha and the long history of Islamic commentaries and law codes to justify women's rights. Moroccan sociologist Fatima Mernissi has recently published a dictionary of Qor'anic citations for feminists.[35] Biblical quotations, Jewish and Christian, serve the same purpose.

This is a valid enough tactic for indigenous reformers who structure their arguments to the appropriate groups. Moreover, it does not distort the aim of Jewish, Christian and Islamic scriptures as did the British use of the Hindu scriptures.   It becomes less valid, however, when it is picked up by outsiders and used to justify international intervention on the grounds that FGS violates the internal mores of the country concerned.

Islam is usually the religion to be so used.   In fact, FGS is not a uniquely Muslim custom.   Jewish, Christian and animistic Africans also practice it. Moreover, some Muslim countries, including Iran, Iraq and Saudi Arabia, do not practice it at all. FGS is a regional tradition, not a religious imperative. Yet those who argue for greater international efforts to ban FGS, regularly use Islamic texts to prove that such efforts are not in violation of the desires of the indigenous peoples.   For example, Stephen A. James of Princeton University   who notes that FGS is not an Islamic custom, nonetheless cites indigenous arguments based on Islam to conclude that

> We may take developments along these lines in Islamic countries as evidence that the condemnation of human rights violations within them need not necessarily be grounded in and imposed by 'alien', imperialist, Western cultures.[36]

James adds that a number of Islamic states have created their own religiously based definitions of international human rights and laments that

> these human rights schemes are typically unsatisfactory because they subordinate universal protections of individual human

rights to vague limits like 'the shari'a'(traditional Islamic law) or 'the limits of Islam. These limits are then conservatively and expansively applied by clerical rulers in Muslim countries...to augment and defend their own interest in a patriarchal, undemocratic and reactionary state rule.[37]

That may very well be, but in dismissing this approach to human rights as unsatisfactory because it can be flexibly applied, James also asserts the power of the written form over usage. In India, that argument disempowered women whose limited power was centered in usage. The same may well be true in many African countries where FSG, whatever its pains and dangers, sometimes does seem to provide a source of power both for the midwives who perform the procedure and for the girls who undergo it. Susan Rich of Population Action International was stunned to learn that Kenyan women were fully aware of the health risks involved, but unwilling to give it up because they saw it as an important rite of passage and because it was the only ritual for which women had full responsibility.[38] According to Leah Muuyu, a Kenyan activist who opposes FGS, 65% of Kenyan women want FGS to continue because it

> has such benefits among those who practice it. It gives women the power to feel cohesion in the community. The woman really belongs...[39]

Muuyu's group, like many in Africa, is working to establish a new ritual so that the ending of FGS will not mean a loss of what power Kenyan women have in their society. The new rituals are certainly more pleasant. The girls are secluded in a hut for a week or two during which they are taught the traditions of their people, regaled with special foods and given gifts. At the end, the girls emerge dressed in new clothes and wearing jewelry to signify that they are now adult members of the community. Elizabeth Alabi promotes a similar program in Nigeria. In addition to creating a new rite of passage, she also advocates working with midwives to make them teachers of the new tradition.[40]

Muuyu and Alabi's success is a hopeful sign. The real question is whether or not their positive, non-coercive approach will be recognized on the international front. They have received grants from the Ford Foundation, and so far that funding has helped but not changed their program. It remains to be seen whether the West can maintain that supportive, non-intrusive attitude.

This is not completely impossible. The experience of missionaries in China in the late 19th and early 20th centuries suggests that support for programs like Muuyu and Alabi's are the best hope for actually ending FGS. In China, the missionaries who wished to eradicate the practice of footbinding faced a situation very similar to that of feminist and other international organizations wishing to eradicate FGS.

At first glance their position appeared to be weak, certainly weaker than the British in India, a united, national entity that could back its reform efforts with military and political force. The missionaries were an international group, mostly Protestants from America and Northern Europe, with some Catholics thrown in to confuse the issue. They were not a cohesive group. Their religious and national differences were too great and their sense of isolation was as likely to cause dissention as to promote harmony. None of their governments had dominion over China which was still technically an autonomous state although the Western nations (and Japan) had divided it up among themselves into spheres of influence.

There was no consensus, either among the missionaries or on the homefronts, that footbinding was a major evil deserving everyone's best efforts. Chinese missionaries were generally interested in social reform as well as religious conversion, but male missionaries had the power to set policy and few of them showed much interest in a practice that affected only women; their priorities were economic and political reforms. An early attempt to inspire outrage in English missionary circles foundered when a misunderstanding developed that the practice involved the use of a special boot. By the time the technicalities had been straightened out, all emotional impact was lost.[41] Even among female missionaries, education, arranged marriages and infanticide drew a more positive response than the anti-footbinding campaign.

As a result, the natural foot advocates, as they came to call themselves, were few in number, inadequately funded and usually unable to use their national affiliations to promote their aims. They were, therefore, forced to work through and with other organizations, both missionary and Chinese. This involved a wide range of compromises. In order to get permission to open orphanages in Southern China, for example, missionaries had to agree to bind the feet of the little girls they took in to make them desirable as wives. They reasoned that this was the lesser of two evils since the children might die otherwise. Schools faced similar problems. Mission schools saw education as the main hope for Chinese women. They offered many incentives for female students, including a free education for their brothers. A few schools insisted their students unbind their feet, but most of them declined to make footbinding a further issue that might deter Chinese parents from educating their daughters at all.[42]

That seeming weakness was their greatest strength. In particular, the need to work through and with Chinese organizations was probably what ensured their success. This was not a carefully thought-out plan. Indeed, the early natural foot advocates initially made most of the same mistakes the British had made in trying to ban sati, beginning with the assumption that their role was to be central and controlling rather than marginal and catalytic. Their statistics were dubious at best. Because most missionaries lived in Chinese cities (where footbinding was far more pervasive than in rural areas), they assumed the practice was more widespread than it was. They also failed to take into account that the tightness of the binding varied from class to class. Lower class women bound their feet fairly loosely which made them less attractive on the marriage market but better able to walk and work. Nonetheless, the practice was widespread enough to make the missionaries' efforts worthwhile.[43]

In many cases, the missionary ladies failed to understand the delicacy of the issue. Bound feet had strong erotic connotations for Chinese men. Thus, when over-eager reformers like Alicia Little attempted to shock schoolboys into demanding wives with unbound feet by showing them slides of (to Western eyes) cruelly deformed feet, she was actually bringing "dirty pictures" into the classrooms. Chinese parents reacted predictably.[44] Fortunately such incidents were rare. Because there were so few of them, and because of the language problems involved, much of the public speaking was handled by the "Bible women."[45] Chinese themselves, Bible women understood the risque nature of the topic, spoke of it only in all female groups and then with the greatest tact and discretion.

Once the missionaries' aims were understood, they soon discovered that they had allies. Like the British in India, it had not occurred to them to wonder if an indigenous resistance existed. This mattered less than in the Indian case, since the Chinese movement was relatively ineffective until it combined with the missionary efforts. Chinese reformers encouraged by missionary zeal developed a natural foot platform based on existing cultural norms.

The early missionary tracts had based their arguments on the theme that since God had made man and woman the same, it was sacrilegious for parents to try to improve on the design. They added that by making women useless for work, the practice encouraged female infanticide. Some of the more feminist missionaries used arguments appropriated from the Western anti-corset movement to insist that women with bound feet were unhealthy and therefore made poor mothers.

Chinese reformers changed the format considerably. They dismissed the religious argument at once. Christianity was not China's religion. (The total number of Chinese Christians has never gone above 1%.)[46] They did introduce a religious theme from Taoism, however, arguing that Kuan-yin, the Goddess of Mercy, whose services were often called upon to relieve a young girl's foot-binding pains, was inevitably shown with large, healthy feet.[47]

They also ignored the argument linking footbinding to female infanticide. In fact, the Chinese preference for sons was far more complex than a simple need for another worker in the family. It was intimately connected to Confucian ancestral rituals, virilocal marriage and the desire to continue the family line; a daughter could not perform the rituals correctly, and when she married, she moved into her husband's home and her filial obligations were toward his parents. The Chinese reformers stressed the fact that a big footed woman was more useful around the house and therefore better able to serve her husband and in-laws.[48]   Later, as feminist and nationalist arguments gained support, they stressed the value of natural feet to allow a woman to pursue her own desires and to serve her country.

Natural foot reformers also often failed to grasp the full extent of the emotions involved in persuading young women to unbind their feet. It was not just that the process of unbinding feet was often as painful as the initial binding had been, or that the young woman might have some real fears and regrets about her future marriage prospects. Footbinding was generally something a mother did to and for her daughter. It was part of being a good mother. "If you care for a son, you don't go easy on his studies; if you care for a daughter, you don't go easy on her footbinding,"[49] said an old Chinese proverb. Nonetheless, the process was excruciating and often caused a rift between mother and daughter that might never heal. A song composed by Chinese natural foot advocates reveals the resentment many Chinese women felt about what their mothers had done to them:

A five-year-old girl
Bravely repressing bitter sobs,
Tearfully asks her mother:
You used to love me so tenderly.
Why do you now bind my feet,
As if you were binding a chicken?
The toes in my feet are broken,
And my heart breaks with them.[50]

When a Chinese girl unbound her feet, she symbolically rejected her mother's care, an act both mother and daughter frequently found difficult to accept. Hsieh Ping-ying, recalled the mixed messages of pain, coercion and care that accompanied the beginning of her footbinding.

Everything had been carefully prepared. A pair of small shoes embroidered with two plum flowers...were placed before me. Though this pair of shoes were made of vermillion silk, had very

thin soles and was very pretty indeed, I did not like it...I pleaded in tears and full of fear.
"I must bind your feet because I love you [said the mother]. If I do not bind your feet I shall not be doing the right thing by you. You must realize that a girl with huge feet will never be accepted by a husband.[51]

Later, when Hsieh went to a modernized boarding school she unbound her feet:

When my mother saw that my tiny bound feet had become large, flat, ugly things she was very angry and almost heartbroken...and all the more bitter for her because she had wasted all her trouble in past years in binding my feet...[52]

Hsieh looked back on her schooldays and the "sisters" who had helped her to unbind her feet as the single most important emotional point in her life. Unbinding bound feet was almost as painful as binding them had been, and the act became a rite of passage for many teenage girls in turn of the century China. For Hsieh, the support of the sisters who helped her to unbind her feet was vital. The alienation that developed between her and her mother was never really healed.

Chinese reformers worked to join parents and children in resisting footbinding. Ideally, joining a natural foot society was a family matter. Parents promised never to bind their daughters' feet nor to allow their sons to marry a girl with bound feet. Daughters asserted their right to unbound feet. Sons vowed never to marry a girl with bound feet. Even when parents refused to join their rebellious children in such vows, the society reminded them that they too would be parents one day by demanding that even the unmarried take the parents' vow. Such slogans as "If a child's parents do not pity her but bind her feet unmercifully, how can she be expected on some future day to pity her own children,"[53] reminded angry young women that their own mothers were simply the result of a corrupt system and not to be blamed personally.

The same mixture of love and rage is apparent in the relationship of traditional African women to their reformist daughters. Mary Ann French of The Washington Post described a Somali mother and daughter who had moved to America. The daughter, who had been infibulated at the age of 5, angrily described her experience while her mother, who spoke no English, sat beside her.

Even though she doesn't catch the words, the mother looks weary, as if she has heard this story many times before. She is unapologetic, although not unkind.

"There's a Somali proverb," the mother says softly, her daughter translating. "If you stop a tradition, it's similar to making God mad."

Her daughter fumes quietly at first, stealing accusatory glances at her mother, talking obliquely of "abuse." Then her voice rises.

"I think it's totally unfair," she says. "I find it totally useless...I can see before, when people lived in little tribes and villages and something happened to a woman, then it would make a big deal. But now with things changing...I don't see the reason why women have to suffer."

At this last, her eyes melt toward her mother. She moves closer and gently pats the elegant older woman here and there, gathering wool around her in preparation for the trip home.[54]

This is not a situation in which an outsider can offer much in the way of comfort or solution. The inclusive approaches suggested by women like Muuyu and Alabi who seek to involve entire villages in the creation of new rites of passage, offer the best chance for reconciling generations in a time of change. They are grassroots organizations, individually designed to reflect local customs and without noticeably strong ties to outside interests.

This last was probably the most important factor Chinese reformers added to the success of the natural foot movement at the turn of the century. Although most societies had some missionary connections and many depended upon mission societies for funding, this was not readily apparent. Some missionaries accepted this with better grace than others. Some continued to play a central role, but for the most part it was Chinese who led the meetings, drew up the platforms and petitioned the Empress to ban the practice which she finally did in 1902.[55] Some intellectuals, convinced that the Western affiliations of the anti-footbinding campaign were a stumbling block, produced historical evidence that the practice had been a foreign import during the Tang dynasty (617-907). Thereafter, they argued that

To eradicate the evil age of footbinding is to restore the intent of our ancient Sages, who elevated natural-footedness.

The natural footed is stronger, more patriotic, and can achieve heroic deeds.

The nation benefits from her vigorous spirit and devotion to study.[56]

With the introduction of this nationalistic note, the missionaries lost control of the anti-footbinding movement. Increasingly, Chinese girls unbound their feet not so that they could be better mothers or daughters-in-law, but so that they could fight to free their country from Western imperialism. Indeed, many of missionaries' finest achievements in education and social reform proved their worth by repudiating Western affiliations altogether in the name of national sovereignty.

Understandably, many missionaries resented this. There was, however, nothing they could do about it. They were in China on sufferance. The funding and support they gave to reform efforts like footbinding were significant, but not so essential that withdrawal of same could be used as a threat. None of their governments was really willing to go to war over their reforms. (Japan, which was, was not in favor of their reforms.) As a result, they did the right thing. They kept a low profile, and when indigenous efforts took over and changed the direction of their programs, they let it happen.

It is to be hoped that the U.S., the U.N. and the various other organizations interested in banning FGS will have the sense to do the same. Programs designed or carried out by outsiders are unlikely to have much effect at the local level especially in a matter so delicate.

This does not preclude outside involvement; it merely means that to be effective outside groups must be willing to provide support while accepting the leadership of indigenous groups. African-American and/or feminist groups fall into this category and so, probably, does the U.N. Like the Chinese missionaries, their goals are so diverse and their ability to cooperate among themselves so limited that indigenous leadership will probably prevail. Such groups may have the desire to force changes more rapidly than is wise, but they simply do not have the ability.

The U.S., however, is another matter. It is a sovereign state with its own interests and, perhaps even more significantly, it has a leadership answerable to an electorate. It also has the political and economic ability to exercise considerable control over internal African affairs. In a sense, this has already started with the Clinton administration's decision to allocate funds for groups opposed to FGS. In 1994, the U.S. Agency of International Development allocated $290,000 toward eradicating FGS, a small amount, but a sizable increase over the $50,000 allocated by World Bank, WHO and UNICEF in 1993.[57] There is nothing wrong with doing this, provided that the U.S. does not decide that the money gives them the right to say how these groups should or should not go about ending FGS. The U.S. might well try to control the direction such groups take by threatening to withdraw support from groups whose plans do not conform to American ideas of how things should be done. Past experiences do not give much room for optimism on this point. The U.S. has been known to create "indigenous" reform groups when the real thing failed to live up to its expectations.

Those expectations are apt to rise now that FGS has become a domestic issue for Americans. The case of Lydia Oluloro, a Nigerian who successfully resisted deportation on the grounds that her daughters would be infibulated if she returned with them, put FGS on the front pages. So did Rep. Pat Schroeder's (D-Colo.) introduction of legislature to ban the procedure in the U.S. There is no intrinsic problem with either of these actions; they represent legitimate domestic concerns in the U.S. However, Americans have a record of wanting to at least seem consistent. If these domestic decisions to control FGS at home become part of America's foreign policy, it could mean real trouble in Africa.

FGS is simply too specific an issue. Like the British campaign against sati, the anti-FGS campaign focusses on a single practice rather than the contributing causes. By doing so, it implicitly sets priorities for African reformers and also places itself in a position where compromise is difficult or impossible. If the U.S. really wishes to become involved, it might do better to allocate its funding toward improving African women's lives more generally, thus allowing indigenous groups to determine methods and priorities.

It is not difficult to foresee some of the problems that could develop if the U.S. insists on making FGS the criteria by which funding is justified. If, for example, an African women's group decides to use its money to open clinics where FGS can be performed safely and painlessly, tax-payer protests are almost inevitable even if the same organization is also engaged in education to try to stop the practice altogether.[58] Similar problems are apt to arise when spending does not seem closely related to FGS. If groups trying to create new rites of passage choose to use U.S. aid to buy new dresses or jewelry for young women, they may well find themselves the target of auditors or American politicians seeking a campaign issue at home.

The problem is not entirely the creation of the U.S. The indigenous groups themselves need to think carefully about asking for political or military assistance from the U.S. Some have already done so. Women Living Under Muslim Laws, an advocacy group operating in Provence, has urged the Clinton administration to implement economic sanctions against any African nation that has not banned FGS.[59] Their requests are understandable. They need not only funding, but sometimes diplomatic protection from their own governments which may be unsympathetic to the point of real oppression. Nonetheless, they need to bear in mind that all aid comes with strings attached.

The real key to the issue lies in America, however. If Americans really want to help end the practice of FGS, they need to do something they have historically found very hard to do. They need to remember that they are not the main event. They can provide some support in the way of funding and diplomacy. Even advice is not out of the question provided it remains at the level of suggestion. However, the main event will be in Africa and the main actors will be the African people. That is the way it should be and that is the way it must be in order to succeed.

CHAPTER 8

ENDNOTES

1. I have chosen to adopt Isabelle Gunning's term, female genital surgery, because of its carefully neutral tone. These practices are also sometimes called "female genital mutilation" which implies a negative moral assessment, or "female circumcision" which suggests, erroneously in at least 2 types, that the surgery is analogous to male circumcision.

2. Sati, sometimes rendered suttee, is a ritual in which a widow immolates herself on her husband's funeral pyre. It derives from the term sat meaning moral truth; the sati is one who remains faithful not only to her husband but also to her moral truth. The term can refer to the act, to the woman who performs the act or to a Hindu goddess of that name.

3. Chinese footbinding involved bending under the four small toes of a 5 or 6 year old girl and wrapping the foot tightly with bandages. As the child's foot grew, the bones broke and bent until she was literally walking on her own bent over toes. The triangular three inch foot thus produced was called the "golden lotus."

4. Radha Kumar, The History of Doing: An Illustrated Account of Movements for Women's Rights and Feminism in India, 1800-1990 (London: Verso Press, 1993), p. 9.

5. A. Slack, "Female Circumcision: A Critical Appraisal," Human Rights Quarterly, 10, 1988, 441-447. Cited in Stephen A. James, "Reconciling International Human Rights and Cultural Relativism: The Case of Female Circumcision," Bioethics, 8:1, 1994, 6-7.

6. Indeed there are vast differences in each category to say nothing of different rituals and methods.

7. Unverified statistics published by The Washington Post (Jan. 16, 1994) claimed that at the time of U.S. involvement in Somalia, 90% of Somalian women had been infibulated. One has to wonder how, why and if the U.S. military would undertake such a study at such a time.

8. R. Hartley Kennedy, "The Suttee: The Narrative of an Eye-Witness," Bentley's Miscellany, 13:75, 1843, 242-252. Cited in Paul B. Courtright, "The Iconographies of Sati," in Sati, the Blessing and the Curse: The Burning of

Wives in India, edited by John Stratton Hawley, New York: Oxford University Press, 1994, pp. 44-46.

9.   Peggs, India's Cries to British Humanity, Second Edition, 1830, pp. 14-15. Cited in Edward Thompson, Suttee: A Historical and Philosophical Enquiry into the Hindu Rite of Widow Burning, New York: Houghton-Mifflin Co., 1928, p. 54.

10.   Ibid., pp. 100-101.

11.   Katherine Mayo, Mother India, New York: Harcourt, Brace & Company, 1927, pp. 82-84.

12.   Ibid., p. 83.

13.   Jules Verne, Around the World in Eighty Days, New York: The Heritage Press, 1962, pp. 75-76, 83.

14.   Isabelle R. Gunning, "Arrogant Perception, World-Travelling and Multicultural Feminism: The Case of Female Genital Surgeries," Columbia Human Rights Law Review, 23:179, 1991-1992, 200-201.

15.   The Washington Post, Nov. 22, 1992, FO1.

16.   The New York Times, Nov. 12, 1993, A33.

17.   The Washington Post, Nov. 8, 1993, A21.

18.   The New York Times, Dec. 24, 1993, A26.

19.   The New York Times, Dec. 7, 1993, A27.

20.   Most feminists and virtually all Westerners assume that at least in cases of clitorectomy and infibulation, all sexual feeling is destroyed. This seems a logical conclusion but studies by Lightfoot-Klein and Ballal suggest that it may not be true, although both authors warn that women's responses may not be completely open and that some women may be referring to the pleasure they gain from pleasing their partner. See Ahmed Ibrahim Ballal, Psychological Effects of Female Circumcision, New York: Vantage Press, 1992; Hanny Lightfoot-Klein, Prisoners of Ritual: An Odyssey into Female Genital Circumcision in Africa, 1989.

21.   The New York Times, Dec. 7, 1993, A27.

22.   The Washington Post, Jan. 16, 1994, X04.

23.   The Washington Post, Nov. 8, 1993, A21.

24.   Kumar, p. 11.

25.   Kumar, p. 11.

26.   Thompson, p. 124. A woman about to commit sati was already partly divine and her curses had particular power.

27.   Ibid., p. 125.

28.   Mayo, p. 83.

29.   Thompson, p. 126.

30.   The Washington Post, Sept. 23, 1994, E3.

31.   Ibid.

32.   The Washington Post, Aug. 28, 1994.

33.   The Washington Post, Mar. 25, 1994, E3.

34.   Lata Mani, "Contentious Traditions: The Debate on Sati in Colonial India," pp. 102-15, in "Kumkum Sangari and Sudesh Vaid, Eds., Recasting Women: Essays in Indian Colonial History, New Brunswick: Rutgers University Press, 1990.

35.   The Washington Post, September 16, 1994, A27.

36.   Stephen A. James, "Reconciling International Human Rights and Cultural Relativism: The Case of Female Circumcision," Bioethics, 8:1, 1994, 23.

37.   Ibid., 25.

38.   The Washington Post, Apr. 13, 1993, Z9.

39.   The Washington Post, June 15, 1994, E15.

40   Ibid.

41.   Howard Levy, The Lotus Lovers: A Complete History of the Curious Erotic Custom of Footbinding in China, New York: Prometheus Books, 1991, p. 77.

42.   Jane Hunter, The Gospel of Gentility: American Women Missionaries in Turn-of-the-Century China, New Haven: Yale University Press, 1984, pp. 22-23; Levy, p. 86.

43.   Levy, pp. 90-93.

44.   Sterling Seagrave, Dragon Lady: The Life and Legend of the Last Empress of China, New York: Vintage Books, 1992, p. 9.

45.   Bible women were converts, trained and employed as assistants in the missions. Most were poor widows, barred from remarriage by tradition, for whom mission work represented a much needed job opportunity.

46.   Drucker, 183.

47.   Levy, p. 75.

48.   Ibid.

49.   Alison R. Drucker, "The Influence of Western Women on the Anti-Footbinding Movement, 1840-1911," Historical Reflections-Reflexions Historique, 8:3, 1981, 180.

50.   Levy, p. 86.

51.   Hsieh Ping-ying, Autobiography of a Chinese Girl, London: Pandora Press, 1986, p.43.

52.   Ibid., p. 61.

53.   Levy, p. 74.

54.   The Washington Post, Nov. 22, 1992, F1.

55.   This did not necessarily settle the matter. Sun Yat-sen also banned footbinding in 1912, Chiang Kai-shek in 1928 and the communists in 1950. It took over 70 years of consistent effort to end the custom; something opponents of FGS would do well to remember.

56. Levy, p. 76.

57. The Washington Post, June 15, 1994, E15.

58. This is not unique to U.S. foreign policy. Needle exchanges and condom distribution programs at home fall afoul of the same either/or, moralistic criticisms in the political arena.

59. Ann Louise Bardeck, "Tearing Off the Veil," Vanity Fair, 56:8, August, 1993, p. 127.

PART III

U.S. AND RUSSIAN POLICY TOWARD AFRICA

"The day of small nations has passed away; the day of empires has come."

Joseph Chamberlain, Birmingham, 1904

"Empires have fallen on evil days and nations have risen to take their place."

Rupert Emerson, Cambridge, Massachusetts, 1960

CHAPTER 9

Russia's Policy Toward Africa

Introduction

Russia became an independent state after the collapse of the Soviet Union in January 1992. Its policy turned out to be anticommunist and pro-Western. Russia is no longer interested in promoting international communism and great power expansionism. The Cold War is over and Russia became friendly with Western nations, particularly the United States. Russian foreign policy's priority became the development of ties with the nations which could contribute to the country's economic revival. African nations could help only in a limited fashion in this endeavor. As Russian Historian Vladislav Zubok indicated,

> Russia's present focus on the seven leading industrial powers and geoeconomic openings to Europe and the Pacific leaves little room for involvement with the Third World. It strategy... cannot after all, succeed with comparably weak countries. For the Soviet Union under Gorbachev and for Russia under Yeltsin, this global retreat from Africa and Latin America has resembled a hasty evacuation, as once dominant position has been reduced in many cases to a mere diplomatic presence. Former Soviet allies have been left in the lurch.[1]

Nevertheless, the Russians did not totally forget about Africa. In this paper current Russian assessments of the situation in Africa and Russo-African relations will be provided. Before examining the current stage of Russo-African relations, it is necessary to tackle the political, diplomatic and economic record of Soviet penetration in Africa.

Soviet Expansion In Africa

Soviet expansion began in mid-1950s, with Gamal Abdel Nasser's ascent to power in Egypt, Kwame Nkrumah's in Ghana, Sekou Toure's in Guinea. These regimes attracted Soviet attention due to a number of factors: they were anti-Western, left wing and radical with a big element of nationalism and some version of socialism. Their domestic agenda appeared in agreement with Soviet ideological requirements: the mentioned regimes pursued nationalization of major fields of economy, nationalization of foreign enterprises, reforms in agriculture, the establishment of a one party system. The Soviet theoreticians called these countries national democracies: although there was no substantial, numerous and strong working class (proletariat), the Soviets showed creativity in attaching "progressive" labels to such regimes. The Soviet Communist Party's officials used to argue that proletariat would be strong and dominant in such nations later. For the time being, the countries, like Nasser's Egypt, were marching in the "right" direction because there were other leading and progressive internal elements, including "progressive" bourgeoisie, the army, peasantry and certain intellectuals as a substitution for proletariat in such countries.[2]

According to Arkady Shevchenko, the highest ranking Soviet defector, a former Under Secretary General Secretary of the United Nations,

> For more than two decades Africa was viewed by Moscow as the most turbulent outpost in the capitalist world, and therefore the weakest. Exploiting local turmoil created opportunities to expand Moscow's zone of control without incurring high costs. Some money and advisors and a supply of relatively cheap weapons could buy disproportionate influence with new and shaky governments or anti-colonialist guerrilla forces.[3]

Shevchenko also made other interesting observations concerning Soviet policy in Africa. He maintained that Foreign Ministry officials "dealing with that area were among the most conformist, least imaginative diplomats he knew".[4] In addition,

> ...our diplomats in Angola were so poorly supplied from Moscow that their families at home were shipping powdered milk, one of the essential commodities they could obtain no other way. Colleagues in the ministry knew that such neglect was common in African posts. As a result, few wanted to take jobs there. The personnel department had great difficulties

finding qualified staffers to expand the Soviet presence in Angola, and the ministry cafeteria was full of grumbling diplomats fearful of being ordered into such hardship.[5]

Soviet officials described Moscow's policy in most favorable terms, while all Africa's woes were blamed on the West. This is a typical Soviet estimate of Soviet and Western policy towards Africa:

> Fatally weakened by the slave trade, the continent's economic development was further held back by colonialism. Many people lost faith in their skills, agricultural methods stagnated, and by the end of the nineteenth century, the colonialists were in possession of almost all Africa's territory, plus an endless supply of cheap labor.[6]

Former Soviet Minister Andrei Gromyko also indicated that when WWII came to an end very few African nations were independent: Ethiopia, Egypt, Liberia and the Union of South Africa. Since then about fifty African nations joined the UN and, according to Gromyko, the USSR always had been working towards developing friendship and cooperation with these nations.

> By contrast, the former colonial powers adopted a policy... of 'leaving in order to remain'. The tragic events that took place in 1960 in Zaire... are memorable in this respect... the colonialists quickly discovered... that the new government of Patrice Lumumba intended to have genuine independence... An army revolt was organized so that the colonialists... could send in heavy units of Belgian troops whose task was to secure the establishment of a puppet government in Katanga.[7]

Gromyko concluded his argumentation saying:

> The Lumumba government was not to the taste of the United States either, but Washington resolved to act on a grander scale, and to bring the whole country, rather than simply Katanga, under its domination. It chose to as its instruments direct terrorism and subversive activity, together with manipulation of UN forces... The plot which the USA hatched against an outstanding son of Africa... is a glaring example of how much Washington's claims to the 'moral leadership of the world' really mean.[8]

Assessing prospects for Soviet penetration, Jonathan Adelman and Deborah Palmiere pointed out,

The Soviet Union enjoyed advantages in competing with Western influence in the region. First, the Soviet Union lacked a colonial past. Second, it did not have a history of involvement or trade with supremacist regimes in South Africa or Rhodesia. Third, the chronic weakness of unstable African regimes plagued by tribal, religious and ethnic divisions and weak economies, seemed promising for the Soviets.[9]

According to a former high ranking KGB agent and a defector, Oleg Gordievsky,

the principle new opportunities for the spread of Soviet influence in the Third World during the 1970s were in Africa. The break-up of the Portuguese Empire and the overthrow of the Emperor Haile Selassie brought to power self-proclaimed Marxist-Leninist regimes in three major African states: Angola, Mozambique, and Ethiopia.[10]

Indeed, the Soviets appeared to achieve some salient successes in Africa, including the establishment of Marxist regimes in Angola and Ethiopia. On April 25, 1974 a revolution took place in Portugal which brought an end to this last colonial empire. While in most Portuguese colonies Portuguese rule was replaced by a local government peacefully, Angola encountered a different fate. There were three major factions fighting for power and the pro-Soviet MPLA (the Popular Movement for Liberation of Angola) prevailed to a major extent because the Soviet Union and Cuba actively supported it. The rivalling factions were UNITA (National Union for the Total Liberation of Angola) and FNLA (National Front for the Liberation of Angola). In 1975-1980s Cuba maintained tens of thousands troops in Angola and this proved to be a decisive factor in the MPLA's victory. The Soviets were also enthusiastic about Mengistu Haile Mariam's regime in Ethiopia. The Marxist-Leninist orientation of this regime enabled the Soviet Union and Ethiopia to sign in November 1978 a long-term friendship treaty. In 1984 Mengistu established the first communist party in Sub-Saharan Africa: its official name is the Workers' Party of Ethiopia.

In the 1970s, several African countries thus embraced Marxism as their doctrine and proclaimed themselves to be engaged in the task of building socialism. Six-Angola, Mozambique, Madagascar, the Congo, Benin, and Ethiopia-even went as far as to adopt Marxism-Leninism as their guiding framework and stressed their fidelity to the broad outlines of the Soviet experience in building socialism. Nine others-Algeria, Libya, Cape Verde, Guinea-Bissau, Guinea, Sao Tome and Principe, Zambia, and the Seychelles-became self-avowed socialist regimes, though stressing the centrality of their own national conditions in the actual implementation of socialist goals and avoiding explicit identification with Leninism. All of them did, however, elevate the state into the central organ of socioeconomic change and organized political power around a single and militarized party.[11]

However, despite some visible accomplishments, the Soviets were experiencing numerous problems and difficulties. Even countries sympathetic to the Marxist-Leninist cause realized that the Soviet Union is much weaker economically than the West and tried to gain Western aid. Angola and Mozambique are cases in point. According to Adelman and Palmiere,

> Over the years, ... Angola tried to balance its trade ties and pro-Soviet foreign policy by increased ties with the West. Although Cuban troops remained to protect the regime, they merely highlighted Moscow's weakness and minimum base for expanding its influence.[12]

Later, already during Yeltsin's rule even Pravda conceded that Soviet policy toward Africa was unsuccessful. The previous regime, according to the newspaper, "...instead of careful and thoughtful work in development of mutually advantageous cooperation, introduced gigantic projects, built mausoleums, party schools and delivered arms..."[13] Its policy turned out to be a fiasco.[14]

Gorbachev's Period

During Gorbachev's years the Soviet Union partially changed and adjusted its foreign policy. It no longer pursued a victory of pro-communist forces in regional conflicts. Instead, Gorbachev called for a settlement on the basis of national consensus and free elections. In Ethiopia Gorbachev called on Mengistu to negotiate the continuing ethnic conflicts with Eritreans and Tigreans and apparently either drastically reduced or curtailed Soviet military advisers' participation in this ethnic conflict.

In the Angolan conflict the Soviet Union agreed to a compromise. In December 1988 the Soviet Union signed the Brazzaville accords, which linked the Cuban withdrawal from Angola to Namibia's independence and South Africa abandoning its control there. A Soviet newspaper Moskovskyie Novosti (MN) gave a critical analysis of the results of the Soviet policy in Angola.[15]

Fifty nine Soviet military advisors and billions of dollars were wasted. The Soviet Union heavily invested in Angola and received back very little. MN points out that American sources maintain that the Soviet Union spent a sum equal to $20 billion on maintaining the largest 200,000 men army in Africa. In contrast to the previously quoted assessments, MN claims that Angola blindly had followed the Soviet model and that brought about its economic demise. After the conclusion of a peace agreement between the warring factions with the participation of Portugal and the Soviet Union, Angola could become attractive to foreign investors: its natural resources include gold and diamonds, copper and iron, oil and manganese. Angola also enjoys a favorable geographical location and cheap labor force. MN also mentions Angola's coffee, valuable types of arboreal and exotic fruit. MN complains that despite excellent relations with the ruling regime, the Soviets managed to get almost nothing out of that. The only exception was the joint Soviet-Angolan fishing company. The newspaper points out that inflexibility and limits of Soviet foreign trade organizations quickly shattered the Angolans' optimistic illusions and most profitable contracts were given to the Western companies. The Soviet role was to provide free or low-rate loans, building and restoration of bridges, assistance in establishing the health and education system and, of course, the training of the military personnel and arms supplies.

Under Gorbachev, the Soviets were more willing than before to expand ties with pro-Western regimes like that in Kenya, Ivory Cost, Liberia and Senegal. As Brzezinski pointed out,

> In Africa, the remaining islands of socialist commitment were either stagnating or seeking to disengage from socialist commitment. The drive toward privatization was gaining momentum in almost every one of the African countries that had once embarked on the Soviet-oriented road toward state socialism. After a quarter century of independence, many "socialist" countries in the developing world were poorer in terms of per capita gross national product than they had been at the outset.[16]

This is why Gorbachev decided to improve ties with "capitalist" African countries. Actually, during the final years of Gorbachev's rule there was no ideological load attached to Soviet foreign policy toward Africa. The Soviets were ready to deal even with South Africa.

> In late March 1989, Soviet Deputy Foreign Minister Anatoly Adamishin became the most senior Soviet official to visit South

Africa since the two countries broke off diplomatic relations in 1956. A growing dialogue between Moscow and Pretoria has been carried out ever since the Soviet emphasized the need for a peaceful solution to South Africa's racial problems. Although long a supporter of the African National Congress..., Moscow has urged its leadership... to rely on political means... [17]

In July 1990 Moscow made a deal with South African De Beers to sell uncut diamonds to this largest diamond cartel in the world. The Soviets accepted $1 billion advance against future deliveries and showed that economic and profit considerations were central in Gorbachev's foreign policy.[18] Moskovskiye Novosti analyzed Soviet policy toward South Africa.[19] Yuri Yurkalov, the head of the African section in the Soviet Foreign Ministry, described the Soviet position towards Republic of South Africa at that time. He emphasized the fact that the USSR was supporting struggle against apartheid, but preferred that political means be used in the fight for the democratization of South Africa. Yurkalov pointed out that his country was not going to abandon its support for the ANC. At the same time the diplomat stressed the fact that the Soviet position on South Africa was determined by a new general approach - renunciation of confrontation in relations with the West. One could register that the Soviet position was still cautious: it was in no hurry to reestablish ties with South Africa. In the same newspaper Historian Irina Filatova virtually endorses the official position: she thinks that a quick restoration of relations with South Africa could mean that the Soviet Union was distancing itself from the traditional strong anti-apartheid stand.[20] It is fair to say that in South Africa Gorbachev's Soviet Union made some steps toward normalizing ties with Pretoria. But on this issue Moscow was slower in introducing innovations than in other foreign policy issues: arms control, Eastern Europe, regional conflicts. MN gave some interesting data concerning Soviet ties with Africa and Southern Africa. There were 26 thousand African students in the former Soviet Union, including 2850 - from the South of the continent. 1600 - students from Angola, 700 - from Mozambique, 350 - from Zambia, 200 - from Zimbabwe, 50 - from South Africa. (they came on the ANC request, altogether 200 South Africans received education in the former Soviet Union on the ANC request.) The share of the Soviet Union in the imports of Angola and Mozambique is about 10%, Zambia and Zimbabwe - about 1%, South Africa - 0%.[21] Examining Russo-African economic relations, a supplement to Moscow News, MN Business gave this assessment: the trade volume with Africa went down from 3.4 billion rubles in 1984 to 2 billion rubles in 1990.[22] Africa made up 22% of our machinery, equipment and transportation exports to developing and industrialized nations. "Even now the production of our mechanical engineering constitutes 50% of the whole value of our exports to

Africa."[23] However, Africa's share in the Soviet Union's trade was less than 3% even in the best times. By December 1991 the Soviet Union maintained more or less significant economic ties with six out of fifty one African nations: Egypt, Libya, Algeria, Guinea, Ethiopia and Morocco. The trade volume with each of these countries was more than 90 billion rubles and formed almost 85% of "our trade with Africa."[24] However, trade with Moscow was not that important for these African nations, because it formed just 2-3% of their entire foreign trade. 40% of the Soviet import from Africa was a form of compensating Moscow for the loans it had earlier awarded to African countries. The newspaper gives some recommendations how to keep and expand Soviet(Russo)-African economic and trade ties. It points out that both parties experience shortage of hard currency. Therefore, barter deals could be a solution. MN Business also calls for involving Western businesses in Soviet(Russo)-African cooperation, taking advantage of Western experience and contacts in Africa.[25] MN Business also indicates that 67% of the African debts belong to the countries of the so called socialist orientation which are least likely to pay, including Angola, Ethiopia, Mozambique and others.[26] However, the situation is not hopeless. The newspaper suggests that in exchange for delay of debt payments, the African countries could provide special concessions allowing Russian companies an access to African markets. MN Business indicates that "the budget efficiency of some African goods is very high." The following kinds of tropical agriculture are of particular interest to the Russians: coffee, cacao, citric plants, bananas and oil-bearing crops. Produce processing industry is also important. It includes canned meat and canned vegetables, wine, cotton and leather products as well knitted garments. The same could be said about the rubber import and the import of African mining enterprises. MN Business recommends these products in local African currency as part of debt cancellation.[27]

Yeltsin's Period

Yeltsin's Russia did not make Africa its foreign policy priority. There were major disappointments in the past concerning Africa. Algeria was a case in point. Moskovskiye Novosti pointed out that Algeria was a typical example of a country of "socialist orientation" where things turned out to be particularly sour.[28]   The features that defined the socialist orientation were "the dominant state sector in economy, anti-imperialism and nonalignment in foreign policy, a well armed and trained army with Soviet participation, the revolutionary bureaucratic model of state system or to say more exactly an authoritarian regime with socialist trappings."[29]   There was a single political party in the country, MN laments, the FNO, Front of National Liberation. The

Soviet Communist party continued and developed its friendship with FNO, which methodically strengthened its power, destroying either left (the communists) or right (Islamists) opposition. The result of the FNO rule was not impressive. Economic and political situation was getting worse and worse. Moscow's influence was decreased dramatically. The same situation developed in Angola, Mozambique, and Ethiopia. Moscow under Yeltsin's anticommunist regime was developing a new foreign policy, which had repercussions for Africa. Yeltsin did not want to continue the communist party's policy, which was characterized by "the blatant discrepancy between our real goals and the bombastic verbal camouflage..."[30]   Russia's relations with the West, first and foremost the United States became a national priority. This tendency was reflected in the Russian authorities' neglect concerning African and Asian studies in Russia. 115 scholars from the Institute of Oriental Studies, for whom Africa is one of the major fields of specialization, wrote a letter, which stated that the majority of scholars specializing in Asia and Africa found themselves beyond the poverty level and that a Russian scholar is in a humiliating situation when he has either to live on the level of misery or change his occupation.[31]   The rational for such situation can be explained this way: the country is in bad shape economically. The authorities face a dilemma whom to pay: the bus drivers or scholars. The country will not starve without scholars. But it will starve without drivers. The choice is self evident.[32]   A prominent scholar Svetlana Prozhogina stated that the occupation of an Asia or Africa scholar not only lost prestige. It became even dangerous to have this profession: you can easily get unemployed and your knowledge can be completely useless.[33]

Despite these difficulties, Moscow did not fully abandon this continent. One of the problems inherited from the former Soviet Union was the debts the Africans owed Moscow. MN indicates that within 16 years the Soviet Union invested heavily in Angola and received nothing for its efforts. Moscow had assumed the role of a "reliable milch cow" and this resulted in a natural outcome: the Angolans pay on time to Western partners and delay their payments to the Russians.[34]   For instance, while the Brazilians got oil for participation in the construction of a major electrostation; "we got a pledge that we would get compensation for our expenses in the future."[35]   MN indicates that since Russia is unlikely to receive in the foreseeable future either money or goods as payment, there are two options available: first, to sell the Angolan debts 15-20 cents for a dollar and use the money for our urgent needs; to drastically reduce our presence in Luanda and forget about Angola. The more so, as Russia is unlikely to buy oil or diamonds in this country. Second, to write off some debts and to get some of them in receiving from Angola real estate and land on Angolan territory as well as favorable fishing conditions.

According to MN, during the Russian Foreign Minister Andrei Kozyrev's visit to Angola in March 1992 a decision was made about the closure of the Russian military mission in Luanda. Since 1989 there are no Russian military advisors in Angola. There are, however, military experts, about 70-75 people, 45 among them are doctors. They receive hard currency for their work. In addition, MN claims, Moscow still has some influence in the form of traditional ties with the MPLA and personal contacts with the Angolans who studied in Russia and feel attachment to "us".[36] MN points out that Moscow should use this influence to establish a profitable economic penetration to Angola.

Some Russian enterprises became so motivated by economic considerations that they were ready to risk human losses to save contracts with Angola. Pravda reported an episode when the Russian company Technopromexport allowed the Russian technical specialists to stay at a hydro-electro station in a dangerous area Kopanda, which was captured by the UNITA troops and the Russian experts became hostages.[37] In the same issues Pravda indicated that among the UNITA members the Russian image was tarnished by former Soviet aid to the MPLA. A young UNITA soldier, almost a teenager, was about to shoot Russian specialists, shouting at them: "You are all Cuban helpers. You repaired Cuban tanks. My brother was killed. Return al the diamonds they paid you with right away. Return all the pistols. Otherwise, I will kill all of you."[38]   Only an officer's interference saved the Russians.

As far as Republic of South Africa is concerned, there were noticeable changes in the Russian perceptions of South Africa and its policy. For instance, as Vitalii Portnikov pointed out, the South African policy of creating homelands was not as absurd and racist as it seemed before.[39] Portnikov refers to Bophuthatswana as a case in point. He mentions that the established elites in this homeland do not want to change their current status. They claim that Bophuthatswana is a non-racial society, where mixed schools, including colleges and universities operate. Whites and Blacks serve in the army together. The Whites form 10% of the homeland's population. The leaders of this homeland, according to Nezavisimaia Gazetta, explain nonrecognition of their homeland by the international community by pressure of the ANC and the South African Communist Party. Lukas Mangope, the homeland's President, made this statement during the meeting with UN Secretary General Butros Ghali. Portnikov indicates that the very fact that such meeting took place testifies to a real political weight of the homelands and to its ability to fight for survival[40]   In another issue of this pro-government newspaper Historian Yakov Plais examines a possible political scenario after the elections scheduled for April 27, 1994.[41]   He is concerned that the situation is not favorable for a smooth and constructive transition of power from Blacks to Whites. The competence of the new authorities will not be as high as that of the previous government. Possible wholesale or partial nationalization might cause economic problems. In addition, the Black majority is divided between Nelson Mandela's followers and the followers of Chief Mangosothu Buthelezi and this might cause grave problems. Such analysis of the situation in South Africa became possible in Russian pro-government mass media only in Yeltsin's times, when all old communist slogans and standard vocabulary had been finally dropped. Earlier, mass media and scholarship in this country claimed that RSA will be on its way to prosperity once the ANC takes over. Now Russian pro-government mass media tries to show even-handedness in describing different political forces in Republic of South Africa.

In May 1993 the Organization of African Unity celebrated its 30th birthday. In Moscow the following organizations held a meeting devoted to this anniversary: the Movement for Cooperation and Solidarity of the Peoples of Asia and Africa, the Russian Society of Solidarity and Cooperation of Peoples of Asia and Africa, the International Association of the Funds of Peace and the Russian Fund of Peace.[42] Pravda points out that this time the celebration of the OAU anniversary was different from the ones held in recent years, including, for instance, the last year celebration. First, the character of conversations concerning Russo-African cooperation changed. Earlier, they complained that this cooperation reached an impasse and that it is maintained on a low level. At present they assert that the impasse has been overcome. The representatives of the legislative and executive branches share an opinion: it is necessary to strengthen ties with Africa. In addition, an unexpected slogan was put forward: we need to emulate the experience of African countries. However, Pravda's commentator Sergei Filatov wonders what kind of experience the Russians should emulate. Second, according to Pravda, one of the Russian Foreign Ministry's leading officials said that as a permanent member of the Security Council Russia must have firsthand information about Africa and that is why Moscow does not close embassies in the African continent any longer. The same official said that Moscow's interests are different from Western ones. According to Sergei Filatov, "we did not hear things like this from Foreign Ministry for a long time."[43] Earlier, Pravda criticized Russia's Foreign Ministry for joining sanctions against Libya and following the United States in its foreign policy in general and in its African policy in particular. Pravda indicated that as a result of Russia's participation in sanctions against Iraq, Yugoslavia and Libya Russia was to lose $18 billion.[44] Russia will not receive hard currency for arms delivery to Libya and for training her military personnel.[45] MN adds that Russia has in fact sacrificed its old and comprehensive ties with Libya by supporting sanctions. According to the newspaper, almost all modern weaponry at the Libyans' disposal was made in the former Soviet Union. The departure of the military specialists from the Commonwealth of the Independent States makes it impossible to receive the payment of $3,5 Billion for the arms earlier delivered to Libya.[46] MN points out that this outcome is the punishment for Moscow's support for the Qaddafy regime, which had been maintained for many years. Overall, evaluating Russia's policy toward Africa, Pravda asserts that the general line is to cut its missions, from embassies to intelligence personnel. The newspaper indicates that Russia has neither strategy nor even a tactical guideline towards Africa, which makes Russia a supernumerary in the region where earlier she had enjoyed a superpower status. "It is not an accident that, as one of our diplomats acknowledged, Russia has one reaction when the word "Africa" is mentioned - it gives one the sheevers."[47]

Pravda also covered the African view of Russia in present times. An interview with Dixon I. Katambana, Kenya's Ambassador to Moscow is a case in point. Katambana indicated that he was appointed Ambassador shortly before the August 1991 coup attempt in the Soviet Union. Since then he follows the developments in Russia with enormous interest. He states similarities between Russia and Kenya: "Shortage of food, the problem of exerting political pressure on the government with the goal of forcing it to do more for the people, the government's lack of political strength."[48] Concerning Kenyan-Russian ties, the Ambassador mentioned that the volume of economic ties is not as big as it should have been. However, he believes Russia has a number of goods which Kenyans would be happy to purchase: agricultural equipment, some electrical products and "certain other things." At the same time, the Ambassador complained that African diplomats feel insecure and unsafe in Russia. In March 1992 one of the embassy's employees was badly wounded in his apartment. However, Russian militia does not take serious steps against such criminal activities. Such behavior of local authorities makes an impression that they do not care about the safety of foreign diplomats.[49]

It should be mentioned that unfortunately racism became visible in Russia even before revolutionary changes took hold during Gorbachev's and Yeltsin's rule. American journalist David Shipler writes:

> ...racist attitudes are held about blacks, who are rarely seen by Russians outside Moscow, where there are African students and diplomats. A friend once spotted a peasant family on the Moscow subway, all standing around a black man and staring at him. They had obviously never seen a black man before... "If you see a black student with a Russian girl," said an eighth grader, "We say, 'Vot Nakhal' (This is an impudent fellow)." And the language is full of antiblack idioms and epithets. If

someone does not want to do the menial chores, he may say, "I don't want to be a Negro in this institute," or " I do not want to be a Negro for you." Someone working hard is likely to hear youngsters chant, " Work, nigger, work, the sun is still high." A teenager who came from a liberal-minded dissident family told me seriously, "Although I have never met a nigger, I have very bad images of them." I asked for some adjectives, and he gave the following: lazy, stupid, unattractive. "Of course," he said, " Negroes are big."[50]

In recent years crimes committed against African students have been reported. Moskovskiye Novosti reports that in August 1992 a militiaman shot an African student from Zimbabwe, who studies at the University of Peoples' Friendship named after Patrice Lumumba. According to MN, the city's prosecutor lied in his presentation on a TV program when he said that the militiaman was defending himself against drunk Africans. The facts testify to the opposite. MN points out that a newspaper Moskovskii Komsomolets published blatantly racist materials which "contributed to the dirty character of this crime."[51] The newspaper underlines the fact that "...our state has not yet paid a penny to the family of the deceased. The Zimbabwe government paid several thousand American dollars for the transportation and funeral of the deceased."[52] MN also describes the murder of a student from Ruanda Jean Claude Nsengiyuma (27 year old), who came to Moscow several years ago and studied at the Department of Journalism at Moscow University.

Conclusion

Russia under Yeltsin is developing a new approach towards international relations. Old communist stereotypes and concepts have been thrown in the trash heap of history. Cooperation with the West, the United States in particular, became a priority in Russian foreign policy. Under these circumstances Africa apparently is not high on the agenda for Yeltsin's administration which desperately tries to get out of the economic crisis and hopes that assistance from the West, Japan, South Korea, oil rich countries would make a difference. How can Africa fit into the current picture of Moscow's foreign policy priorities? The submitted materials show that although Moscow does not compete with West for influence in Africa and there is no longer any ideological rivalry between Moscow and Washington, Russia still has vested interest in Africa: it wants to collect debts inherited from the previous regime and to pursue mutually advantageous economic cooperation. Russia has some forces in Africa to rely on: many years of the Soviet Union's involvement in Africa gained friends for Russia in certain areas in the continent. Russia has an objective to take full advantage of what remained from its predecessor's influence in Africa. However, Russian prospects for establishing a strong position in Africa appear to be bleak and uncertain, the difficult internal economic situation being the main reason for such pessimistic forecast.

CHAPTER 9

ENDNOTES

1. Vladislav Zubok, "TYRANNY OF THE WEAK," Russia's New Foreign Policy, World Policy Journal, vol. IX, no. 2, Spring 1992, p. 206.

2. For an excellent account of Soviet earlier efforts to penetrate the African continent, please see, D. C. Beller and M. Rejai, Communism in Subsaharan Africa, pp. 210-242, in Dan N. Jacobs, Editor, The New Communisms, Harper & Row, New York, 1969.

3. Arkady N. Shevchenko, Breaking with Moscow, Ballantine Books, N. Y., 1985, p. 362.

4. Ibid., pp. 364-365.

5. Ibid., p. 165.

6. Andrei Gromyko, Memoirs, Doubleday, N.Y, 1989, p. 265.

7. Ibid., pp. 265-266.

8. Ibid., p. 266.

9. Jonathan R. Adelman, Deborah Anne Palmiere, The Dynamics of Soviet Foreign Policy, Harper & Row, N. Y.,1989, p. 208.

10. Christopher Andrew And Oleg Gordievsky, KGB Inside Story, Harper Perennial, N.Y, 1990, p. 554.

11. Zbigniew Brzezinski, The Grand Failure, Scribner's, N. Y., 1989, p. 212.

12. p. 211.

13. Pravda, 31 December, 1992, p. 5.

14. Ibid.

15. MN, 30 June 1991, p. 12.

16. Brzezinski, p. 214.

17. Alvin Rubinstein, <u>Soviet Foreign Policy since WWII</u>, Harper & Collins, 1992, p. 192.

18. Ibid., p. 193.

19. <u>MN</u>, 16 April 1989, p. 7.

20. Ibid.

21. Ibid.

22. <u>MN Business</u>, no. 0/2, December 1991, p. 15.

23. Ibid.

24. Ibid.

25. Ibid.

26. <u>MN Business</u>, no. 0/1, December 1991, p. 15.

27. Ibid.

28. <u>MN</u>, 2 February 1992, p. 12

29. Ibid.

30. Shevchenko, p. 362.

31. <u>Nezavisimaia Gazetta</u>, 27 July, p. 6.

32. Ibid.

33. Ibid.

34. <u>MN</u>, March 15, 1992, p. 13.

35. Ibid.

36. Ibid.

37. <u>Pravda</u>, 9 December 1992, p. 3; <u>Pravda</u> 10 December 1992, p. 6.

38. <u>Pravda</u>, 10 December 1992, 1992, p. 6.

39. Nezavisimaia Gazetta, 28 July 1993, p. 4.

40. Ibid.

41. Nezavisimaia Gazetta, 23 July 1993, p. 4.

42. Pravda, 27 May 1993, p. 3.

43. Ibid.

44. Pravda, 24 February 1993, p. 1.

45. Ibid., p. 3.

46. MN, 3 May 1992, p. 13.

47. Pravda, 24 February 1993, p. 3.

48. Pravda, 12 December 1993, p. 3.

49. Ibid.

50. David K. Shipler, Russia, Broken Idols Solemn Dreams, Times Books, N. Y. 1989, p. 338.

51. MN, 13 December 1992, p. 16.

52. Ibid.

Chapter 10

A Regional Action Plan for Africa:
A Report of Activity During Global War Game-1993
July 1993

Summary

Africa presents no direct threat to U.S. national security, but if apparent insoluble political-military problems are allowed to deteriorate further, Africa will become a burden to the United States. However, if means can be found to transform the region into a self sufficient, more prosperous economy, Africa can become an important market for U.S. goods and a larger part of the global economy.

During Global War Game-1993 at the U.S. Naval War College, the challenges presented by contemporary Africa to the security and economic well-being of the United States and its allies were explored. A working group composed of civilian and military personnel met to formulate a possible interagency approach to prevent and resolve potential crises within Africa and to define a coherent role for U.S. policy. This paper reports on the process and product of Global War Game-93's Regional Action Plan for Africa. The views expressed in this paper are those of the game participants and not necessarily those of the Naval War College and the Department of the Navy.

Global War Game

The Global War Game (GWG) series was designed at the height of the Cold War to explore the United States global defense capability. The main thrust of the series is to identify the issues that are pivotal to national interests. These issues were then applied in the context of global conflict -- now regional conflict. Following each game, an effort is made to analyze these issues with a view toward identifying alternative strategies or ways to improve upon existing operational concepts.

The domain of research for the GWG project ranges from policy through strategy to operations (military campaigns). It is an opportunity for senior military and civilian personnel within the federal government to investigate ideas and concepts that may vary from current strategy or policy wisdom. With the understanding that these games are only an approximation of the behavior of governments facing potential conflict, the scenarios developed for these games are considered only as a context for issues to be explored.

The GWG series was conceived in 1978 as a structure to explore defense issues and to provide a larger perspective than the tactical view that was prevalent in the Navy at that time. The first game was designed specifically with a Navy focus, but, by obvious necessity, the series quickly evolved into a much broader military and political forum. During the first five year series, GWG was used as a test bed for an emerging maritime strategy. The second GWG series, 1984-1988, was a continuum of the first series. Its purpose was to explore issues involved in waging protracted warfare in the decade of the 1990s. The third series, beginning in 1989 and ending this past summer, focused on the world's changing political, military and economic relationships.

Global-93, the fifth and last game in the third GWG series, was held at the U.S. Naval War College, Newport, RI, from July 12-30, 1993. Focused on "the globalization of change," this game continued the twofold effort of the series: (1) to identify the issues that may be critical to U.S. national interests throughout the next decade, and (2) to examine U.S. policy and strategy in light of those issues to determine changes required to achieve national objectives. Nearly twelve hundred participants were involved in this three week game.

Global-93 was played as three inter-related games, constituting a set of "building blocks," that would synthesize national and regional perspectives and reconcile differences between existing and proposed policy initiatives.
In Week 1, inter-agency working groups, operating as elements of the National Security Council (NSC) and the National Economic Council (NEC), made recommendations to the player-President regarding U.S. economic and national security interests in the new global arena. Players were provided with a draft statement developed by senior students at the Naval War College that estimated the geostrategic environment over the next decade and proposed both a National Military Strategy and National Economic Strategy for the United States. At the end of the week, these proposed strategy documents were revised to reflect the issues and concerns identified by the various working groups.

In Week 2, a second set of working groups developed Regional and Selective Action Plans to deal with potential crises for the Americas, Europe, the Newly Independent States/Former Soviet Union, Asia/Pacific, Africa, and the Middle Fast. Each Regional Working Group, using the strategy documents and national issues generated in Week 1, assessed the Regional Action Plans against a range of crises and intra-regional concerns and then modified and refined those plans based on game observations and findings. In Week 3, senior players met at two policy levels. First, as nominal Deputies' Committees of the NSC and NEC, they considered the national issues and regional action plans generated in Weeks 1 and 2. Then, the most consequential issues were submitted to senior executive players in the context of a full NSC/NEC meeting. At this meeting, policy recommendations appropriate at the national decision-making level were then developed and proposed.

This paper contains a summary of work accomplished by the African Regional Working Group during Week 2 of Global-93. It also contains an appendix that provides a brief summary of the cross-cutting security issues of the six regions examined during the game.

Global War Game 1993: Report on Africa

Africa is important to the United States for economic and sentimental reasons, even though it poses no direct threat to national security and appears to offer little but insoluble political-military problems. If allowed to deteriorate further, Africa may become a burden to the United States, but if means can be found to transform Africa into a self sufficient, relatively prosperous economy, Africa can become a market for U.S. goods and part of the global economy. That is the proper goal of U.S. policy toward Africa.

Organization

During Week 2 of Global-93, a working group of 20 players created a Regional Action Plan for Africa. The Africa Working Group was headed by a career diplomat with extensive ambassadorial experience, and included African specialists, many of them mid-grade military officers in the Africa foreign area specialty program. Most members of the working group had served in Africa, and had first-hand current knowledge of the region. Several international military officers who had served in Africa also participated in the work.

For the purposes of the game, Africa was defined to encompass the entire land mass -- from the Mediterranean Sea in the north to the Cape of Good Hope in the south, and from Dakar in the west to Eritrea in the east. This is different from the customary arrangement by the Department of Defense. DOD groups North Africa (Mauritania, Morocco, Algeria, Tunisia, Libya, Egypt, and Sudan) with the Middle East region for analysis; the nations south of the Sahara Desert are treated as "Sub-Saharan Africa." In this instance, combining North Africa and Sub-Saharan Africa allowed the working group to address common issues for the entire continent, while still recognizing the differences between North Africa and Sub-Saharan Africa. The organization of this report conforms generally to the work of Week 2 participants. The first section is a discussion of U.S. interests in Africa, followed by sections on North Africa, Central Africa, Southern Africa, and an Economic Policy for Sub-Saharan Africa. A section for Somalia is also included. The final section summarizes the major elements of a coherent U.S. policy toward Africa.

United States Interests in Africa
The United States has no vital interests in Africa. No African nation nor group of nations could attack the United States directly, although Libya may possess the means by the end of the decade. Terrorism sponsored by Libya and Sudan does pose a threat, but one that can be contained provided proper counter-terrorist measures are adopted.

While no strategic military threat exists, the United States does have interests in Africa, and they are primarily economic and humanitarian in nature.

Africa is of interest to the United States essentially because it is so poor. Africa -- particularly the area south of the Sahara Desert -- is in dire condition and getting worse. It is beset with internal strife, ineffective leaders, corruption, environmental degradation, and a multitude of health problems, including AIDS, malaria and tuberculosis. In addition, because of unchecked population growth, Africa's population of 800 million people will double by the year 2025.

One major U.S. interest in Africa, simply put, is to avoid the certain future cost of providing massive humanitarian relief if present downward trends continue. The United States cannot ignore the existence of 800 million mostly poor, despondent, and suffering human beings in Africa. Ultimately, such a human cataclysm will have to be addressed by the United States and the other wealthy nations of the world. Furthermore, more than 12 percent of the American population have ethnic ties with Africa. No American President can ignore the need to relieve the suffering of Africans before what is seen as merely bad, deteriorates in to a worse condition. This is particularly true of administrations elected on a platform of human rights, promotion of democracy, and concern for the less fortunate. Therefore, it is in the interest of the United States, to do something; the sooner something is done, the smaller the problem to be solved.

Another major interest in Africa is the transformation of this liability into an asset -- a relatively successful regional economy capable of participating in the global economy and buying American goods.   If Africa becomes self-sufficient, we will not be required to provide monetary aid; if Africans achieve even a modest level of prosperity, they can buy our goods and services and thus help our economy.   In this respect we must act out of economic self interest to boost Africa's economy to avoid reacting out of sentiment to provide massive humanitarian relief later.

One current problem is that no visible coherent overall U.S. policy for Africa is obvious; this leads to a situation where individual nations and problems are addressed separately, rather than through a coordinated regional strategic plan.   Another unfortunate tendency -- a likely holdover from the Cold War -- is the primacy of political-military issues in developing African policy.   Consideration of the latest rebellions and scandals consumes the foreign and military policy specialists, while economic issues for Africa are relegated to limited development projects.   Economists engrossed in the fine points of dealing with Japan, the European Community, and Russia seldom find time to consider the broader economic implications of Africa.

An unfortunate tendency exists when the United States and other Western nations deal with Africa.   These states assign responsibility to former colonial overlords; the United States has responsibility for Liberia, the British are "assigned" Nigeria, and Italy plays a special role in Somalia. The French have retained this practice, relish it, and maintain successful relations with most of their former colonies.   However, a policy of implied spheres of influence, based on previous colonial responsibilities, is unsuited for the future.

Regional Working Group participants recognized that Africa is, and will remain, the lowest priority among global regions for U.S. interests and funding.   The predicament for the players, therefore, was to develop an acceptable policy for Africa within the scope of limited resources.

North Africa: Islamic Radicalism

The nations of North Africa are predominately Arab and Moslem, mostly moderate states, that cope fairly well with difficult economic conditions. The obvious exception is Libya, a rogue state with a secular dictator. All of these governments are threatened by the thrust of Islamic radicalism.   The players preferred the term "Islamic radicalism," instead of the more familiar term "Islamic fundamentalism."   Islamic radicalism connotes violent anti-Western and anti-capitalist ideas, while Islamic fundamentalism, is intended to mean a return to the basic values of Islam that are not necessarily violent or aggressive. Islamic fundamentalism per se is not a threat, but Islamic radicalism -- like all radicalism -- is.

If Islamic radicals were to gain power in the Maghreb, the entire sub-region could become like Iran, festering a hatred of the West, and the United States in particular, to shore up repressive and antiquated regimes. It is possible also that the ideology of Islamic radicalism could unite Arabs against Israel, which would certainly dim any hope for enduring peace in the Middle East. This could provoke another Arab-Israeli war where the United States might be forced to intervene to protect Israel. Increased anti-U.S. terrorism may also be an outgrowth of Islamic radicalism. Two Islamic radical nations -- Iran and Sudan -- are believed to be sponsors of terrorism.

Egypt is a key nation because it links Africa and the Middle East, and controls the Suez Canal. Egypt is a moderate secular nation that supports U.S. goals on Middle East peace, access to Persian Gulf oil, and thwarting terrorism. Egypt is under assault by Islamic radicals seeking to undermine the government. Attacks on tourists and government officials are two terrorist tactics used by Egyptian radicals in their attempt to seize power. If Egypt succumbed to the radicals, the moderate governments of other Middle East and North African nations could also become destabilized, and the Middle East peace process halted. The availability of Persian Gulf oil would be uncertain. Terrorists would find it easier to operate. The maintenance of a stable, moderate, democratic Government in Egypt is important to our interests. Egypt is already a major recipient of American foreign aid and should continue to be supported in its efforts to maintain moderate rule and improve its economy.

Sudan has a radical Islamic government that opposes the United States and is believed to sponsor terrorism. For may years Sudan's Arab Moslem north has engaged in a war with its southern provinces, populated by black Africans that are Christians or animists. This conflict has generated massive suffering among the peoples of southern Sudan. The United States should attempt to facilitate this war's resolution through the Organization of African Unity (OAU), the Arab League, and the United Nations. Separately, we should act as necessary to contain the terrorist threat emanating from Sudan.

Libya is a unique threat. Ruled by an idiosyncratic dictator, Libya harbors illusions of power and indulges these dreams with a large arms program paid with oil revenues. Libya likely has developed chemical weapons and is a source of weapons technology for kindred nations, such as Iraq and Sudan. The United Stated should contain Libya, minimize its ability to make its mischief internationally, and insist that the perpetrators of the PanAm Flight 103 bombing be brought to justice.

Algeria, Tunisia, Morocco, and Mauritania are generally moderate nations that are preoccupied with domestic problems and pose no threat to the United States. These nations are susceptible to takeover by Islamic radicals, who may achieve power by legal means but thereafter refuse to cede power in the face of popular discontent. Should these nations become radicalized, the United States and Europe would face major difficulties in stopping terrorist activity, resulting in   economic losses -- including the disruption of oil from North Africa. Radical regimes in these nations could stimulate the flight of refugees to Europe, exasperating an already serious problem. In time of crisis, the flow of shipping through the Mediterranean Sea could be threatened. The United States should support efforts by these governments to improve their economies and resist takeover by Islamic radicals.

With stable moderate governments, North Africa is a region with great potential for economic growth from agriculture, oil, and, increased manufacturing. The advent of radical Islamic regimes intent on anti-Western agitation and domestic regression would have a negative impact on the region's ability to achieve this potential. The United States should support local governments in their efforts to meet the economic aspirations of their peoples while resisting Islamic radicalism.

Central Africa: Chronic Ungovernability
The fundamental problem of Central Africa is chronic ungovernability. Artificial states, created for the most part by colonial powers, have moved into a new and difficult stage of development. Most of the immediate post-colonial leaders have passed on, and a new group of leaders have taken power. The socialist propensity of many of the earlier leaders has been discarded by the new leaders; unfortunately, this has been replaced with a new ideology of greed, corruption, and power. Africa is rife with conflict, self-perpetuating military takeovers, and power elites that have scant regard for their people. Tribal antagonisms repressed during the colonial era have reappeared, instigated earlier by Cold War conflicts but now perpetuated by selfish leaders determined to retain power at all costs. Some of the more important problems are as follows:

Liberia. Rebels who overthrew the corrupt regime of Samuel Doe -- who came into power after overthrowing an earlier corrupt regime -- threw the country into chaos and suffering through indiscriminate killing and looting. Only the combined efforts of several West African nations, led by Nigeria, have been able to provide the conditions for resolution of this problem. The outlook is slightly favorable, providing Nigeria continues to lead the Western African coalition. If Nigeria drops out, the United States should be prepared to step in and support the establishment of stable government in Liberia.

Nigeria. The apparent decision of General Bagangida not to relinquish power, despite losing an election, has cast doubt on the continued stability and prosperity of this African nation -- potentially, a strong economic power. Pervasive corruption and cynicism contribute to the present instability. The ultimate outcome is in doubt, and the consequences of civil war and economic disaster in Nigeria could affect the stability of the rest of West Africa. Besides offering diplomacy, the United States can not play a major role in the outcome.

Angola. The decision of rebel leader Jonas Savimbi not to accept his defeat in an apparently fair election has spoiled hopes that this nation would coalesce and set a good example for others. Fighting continues between the government and the Savimbi rebels. Neither side can win militarily, so the outlook for continued indecisive fighting is strong. This could lead to a spread of the conflict outside of Angola, as Savimbi looks to increase his chances of success. The United States supported Savimbi during the Cold War and has some responsibility to persuade this former client that continued warfare is futile. Direct intervention, however, would be neither useful nor decisive, except for protecting the Cabinda oil fields, if necessary. The United States should instead work through the international community and support the UN Observer Force once peace is restored.

Zaire. The country is in chaos because of Mobutu's insistence on remaining in power. Rather than yield to the opposition, Mobutu and his adherents choose to exploit tribal animosities and force mass migration. It is possible that the nation may separate into three or four pieces. The United States can play no substantive role in this situation aside from encouraging Mobutu to step aside in favor of a legally elected government. If a representative government does come to power in Zaire, we should be prepared to move quickly to demonstrate support and provide assistance.

Mozambique. The process of making peace between the government and rebels is underway but could come unraveled by events in South Africa. The country is saddled with huge problems of refugees, damaged infrastructure, and an economy in chaos. The United States should avoid unilateral military involvement but should work through the international community and support the UN peacekeeping mission in Mozambique. As the situation improves, increasing the number of American civilians in the Peace Corps and other low-cost programs would be useful.

Rwanda and Uganda. There is internal tribal strife in Rwanda and neighboring Uganda. The United States should support UN efforts to resolve the conflict and restore stable governance. Continued warfare will damage the interests of all parties.

The ability of the United States to solve these important problems is limited. The United States is unlikely to use direct military intervention in these crises as it does not meet the criteria stated by Global 1993 Week 1 participants. These players determined that the United States must be assured that the benefits of a proposed action are clearly identified, there is reasonable assurance of success (within resource limitations), and there is consensus at home and abroad for direct U.S. intervention. Thus, we can do little to resolve these problems, aside from applying diplomatic pressure and supporting humanitarian assistance programs. Regardless, diplomacy and economic assistance have proven ineffective even at mitigating the worst aspects of the domestic terror inflicted by some of these governments. This might be offset by low level military assistance program, centered on training and military-to-military contacts, designed to demonstrate an acceptable civil-military relationship. Persistent cautious pressure to improve domestic conditions, and provide effective governance, might have some positive effect over the long term. In the meantime, the United States can only respond to specific events with short-term solutions.

The goal of promoting democracy -- particularly U.S. style democracies -- in Central Africa tends to be unrealistic. What most African nations need are government leaders that place the interests of the people, and the nation, ahead of their personal   interests for increased wealth, position, or class. Corruption is endemic. Cultural ties of family, clan, and tribe take precedence over allegiance to nation-states. Tribal justice, group equity, and survival have been superseded by a form of Western values without the benefits that these values are supposed to bring. The result is a melange of ruling styles that too often result in governments that restrain their economies and oppress human rights. While maintaining a hope for a liberal Western-style democracy, for many of these states an interim goal to achieve basic effective governance would be more feasible.

South Africa: Transition to Multi-Racial Democracy

The most serious potential problem facing the United States in Sub-Saharan Africa is South Africa's transition from white rule to a multi-racial democracy. Although the National Party, led by Prime Minister DeKlerk, agreed to a transition timetable, there are serious potential problems, particularly widespread fighting between the African National Congress (ANC) and the Inthaka Freedom Party (IFP). Radicals in the ANC are impatient at the slow pace of the process and eager to remove -- or kill -- the whites once the ANC assumes power. Extremist white Afrikaaners also have formed armed groups such as the Afrikaaner Volksunie (AVU) to resist black rule. The situation in South Africa is fraught with peril and the climax will occur in April 1994 when a national Election is scheduled that will lead to a black-major government.

There are three possible reactions to the April 1994 elections -- each equally probable:

- Peaceful Transition. The ANC assumes power peacefully, and reaches an accord with the IFP and the moderate whites. White extremists elect not to fight.
- Dissolution. Two dissident groups break away to form their own separate nations after the ANC wins a majority at the polls. The IFP forms an independent Zululand, and the AVU forms a new Boer State

in eastern and central Transvaal. The ANC and the moderate whites in South Africa elect not to contest the separation of the two new nations, and a fragile peace ensues while the new arrangements take hold, although some incident could plunge the country into conflict.

● Civil War. Following the ANC victory at the polls, the IFP and the AVU refuse to accept ANC rule and try to form separate states, but this is resisted by the South African Government. The South African Defense Force (SADF), the AVU, and the IFP engage in warfare that degenerates into a nationwide civil war. The rough parity among the armed forces of the contending factions prevents a decisive military victory by any party and the fighting continues open ended.

Either of the latter two scenarios would likely require U.S. military forces to conduct a Noncombatant Evacuation Operation (NEO) to remove about 250,000 U.S. passport holders and other expatriates. A NEO of this magnitude is a formidable operation that may require resources beyond those readily available to the Department of Defense. Under these conditions, moreover, the cooperation and assistance of the South African Government could not be taken for granted.

Under these circumstances, a NEO is consider the minimum U.S. military response. Additional missions that might be directed could be more difficult to accomplish and may require additional assets. Included in these possibilities is participation in a UN peacekeeping force, deployment of naval, air, and ground support forces for other peace operations (under UN auspices or unilaterally), or the introduction of military forces of sufficient quantity and capability to prevent additional bloodshed. While the possibility of a large scale military operation is remote, it may warrant some attention in planning. What is more important, the probability of civil disorder in South Africa is sufficient to warrant a serious program of preventive statecraft to increase the likelihood of a peaceful and successful transition to a new government.

Somalia

The current United Nations peacekeeping operation in Somalia poses a difficult problem for the United States -- the UN operation has no clear definition of what constitutes a successful outcome. Conditions that allow U.S. for disengagement are not clear. Withdrawal without meeting "success" criteria would diminish U.S. credibility in Africa and elsewhere, but remaining in Somalia without a clear objective and a program to meet that objective will face increasing domestic opposition -- particularly if the number of U.S. casualties increase. By an overwhelming margin, the American people supported the limited mission of humanitarian relief, but are now puzzled and anxious about the broader peace operations aspects of that mission. The United Nations must develop and define a clearer set of objectives. These objectives must determine what is "successful" restoration of order to Somalia, "successful" reconciliation of the warring factions, and "successful" political and economic reconstruction. After agreeing to participate in a UN operation, the United States is committed to the success of that operation. UN objectives, therefore, must be thoroughly examined and clearly understood by the U.S. political and military leadership before accepting the operation and deploying forces. The United States focused too much on short-term objectives in Somalia at the expense of the long-term conditions for success.

In retrospect, it was unduly optimistic to expect that even limited humanitarian operations could be carried out successfully in the conditions of anarchy prevailing in Somalia. At the onset, a more realistic estimate of the situation should have focused on the need to disarm the various factions and establish a stable political order as preconditions for a long-term humanitarian relief effort. It would have been easier to do this when the United States had 25,000 troops in Somalia than it is now, but it still can be done.

The UN has limited capability for peacemaking operations involving combat. It is good at carrying out peacekeeping operations once combat is over, but it must make improvements in its ability to plan and to provide command and control for these operations.

For its part, the United States needs to define its own criteria for success in Somalia, including the following:

● Establishment of civil institutions and domestic governance.

● Elimination of manmade famine.

● Freedom of access by non-governmental organizations.

● Effective internal security and police forces.

● A framework for peace between the warring clans.

After achieving these conditions, the UN will be left with a peace to keep when American combat forces are withdrawn from Somalia.

Once peace is achieved, additional effort is needed to provide for long-term success. An inter-agency task force should address the underlying problems in Somalia and establish policies and programs to promote economic stability and growth. The United States should work closely in this endeavor with key regional players and promote Somali solutions to Somali problems. Somalia should be provided with assistance to solve migration, refugee, and public health problems.   Support would also be required to assist the Somali's reintroduce their goods and services in the African and world markets.   The ultimate success of the combined U.S.-UN operation will be a peaceful and self-sufficient Somalia.

Economic Development Strategy.

It is in our interest that Africa develops economically to a point of self-sufficiency, and if possible become prosperous enough to buy American goods and service as part of a global market.   The major goal of the United States in Africa is to promote economic growth.   The way to accomplish this is to focus available resources towards a few nations that have the best prospects for success.   Preconditions for economic growth are political stability, effective governance, cessation of armed conflict, and acceptance of free market mechanisms.   Only a few African nations meet these criteria, and it is with these nations that the hopes of the continent must rest.   As prosperity grows in these states, the benefits of economic growth may become apparent and encourage neighboring states to become less dependent on Western aid.

The targets of U.S. interests in Africa are selected nations that are regionally important and have demonstrated enough economic success to serve as driving forces for other nations to follow.   These states, and the sub-regions they are intended to influence, are:

Southern Africa: **South Africa.**   If the transition to a new government is accomplished peacefully, South Africa is in a good position to resume and accelerate its already impressive economic growth.   Because of its mineral wealth, well-developed infrastructure, and business and financial institutions, South Africa is the most modern industrialized African state.   Economic growth under a stable multi-racial government would drive development in neighboring countries, particularly in areas of investment and trade.   The beneficial effects of South African growth would be felt in Mozambique, Zambia, and possibly Angola.

Middle-Africa: **Gabon, Cameroon, and Angola.**   These coastal states all have considerable oil resources and viable economic infrastructures that could support their growth if political stability is achieved in Angola.   Increased growth in this region would enhance stability in neighboring states and become a linchpin between oil producing countries in west.and southern Africa.

West Africa: **Nigeria.**   Already a developed nation with a free market economy, Nigeria needs to move toward better governance and reduced corruption for its economy to expand.   An economically healthy Nigeria is key to stimulating growth in other West African nations that have already made

some progress, such as Senegal, Ghana, and the Ivory Coast, and to set an example for lesser developed nations.
North Africa: **Egypt.** Egypt is a vital link between Africa and the Middle east. An Egypt that is stable and prosperous is important for continued economic growth in other North African nations. This is necessary to protect against Islamic radicals exploiting the poor of the region. The outlook is not good, for Egypt has serious economic problems only partially mitigated by massive U.S. assistance.

For each of the nations targeted, the economic development strategy emphasizes the following eight elements:

Debt. Reduce the foreign debt burden by joining with other creditor nations to facilitate economic adjustment programs and debt rescheduling. Once these states' debts have been addressed, a restructuring program could be applied to other nations.

Capital. Encourage loans of investment capital to African entrepreneurs, emphasizing the need for private investment. Educate American business people about available investment opportunities.

Trade. Expand trade with targeted nations, particularly with agricultural products and low-technology goods. Increase share of U.S. trade with Sub-Saharan Africa from 8% to an initial goal of about 20%. Encourage consumption of more African commodities and products in the United States and other trading nations.

Domestic Markets. Encourage market based domestic economies in targeted nations by assisting them to improve financial, distribution, and credit systems.

Infrastructure Development. Provide investment and loan guarantees for the development of national and regional infrastructure -- roads, airports, airfields, and communications networks -- by national governments and regional organizations.

Population. Encourage these nations to stabilize population growth consistent with economic expansion and internal development.

Public Health. Support programs to combat disease. Assist in community-based health, including sanitation, immunization, public education, and AIDS prevention programs in these states.

Environmental Protection. Encourage sound environmental practices and standards that contribute to economic development.

United States Policy Toward Africa.
In conclusion, Unites States policy for Africa should stress the following basic elements:

●Develop a long-range comprehensive national policy for Africa and organize an interagency coordinating committee with wide membership to monitor progress and make necessary adjustments.

●Support economic development and growth; prosperity is a precondition for political stability.

●Focus U.S. programs and support on a few selected target countries that meet preconditions for success. Address major cross-cutting issues, such as public health and environmental degradation, in an economic context as part of the economic growth strategy.

●Oppose terrorism sponsored by nation-states or insurgent groups.

●Oppose the development of weapons of mass destruction and discourage the proliferation of conventional arms on the continent.

●Contain Islamic radicalism.

●Encourage the development of effective governance in problem nations leading ultimately to democratic rule.

●Work with the United Nations, the Organization of African Unity, and local African regional groups to help them devise African solutions to African problems.

●Assign responsibility for Africa to a single unified (or sub-unified) command charged with being prepared to undertake limited military missions, such as non-combatant operations, nation assistance, humanitarian relief, and military training and assistance.

●Plan for U.S. responses to undesirable consequences of the April 1994 elections in South Africa, including the possibility of evacuating U.S. citizens and friendly nationals under difficult circumstances.

Implementation

African nations should be encouraged to work together to resolve their problems with limited international assistance. The key to helping Africa move from dependency to a self-supporting condition will be to provide economic development assistance to specific target nations where the preconditions for economic growth exist. U.S. interests in the region will be best served by fostering renewed confidence, restoring peace, and raising economic well-being for all.

The specific threat of terrorism incited by Islamic radicalism should be met by a combination of deterrence, intelligence, military readiness, and psychological strategies. Preemptive military strikes may be an option, particularly when faced with evidence that weapons of mass destruction are targeted at U.S. interests or citizens.

The transition to black majority rule in South Africa will be another source of tension and potential crisis. If the transition is accompanied by violence, the U.S. and its allies will be critically concerned with the safety of their citizens, and might have to consider a massive non-combatant evacuation operation (NEO).

U.S. policy should declare its support for UN sponsored and other peace support operations, emphasizing logistics and other forms of non-combat assistance.

APPROACHING REGIONAL CONTINGENCIES WITHIN A GLOBAL FRAMEWORK

Although they were considered independently, an underlying distinction emerged between those regions in which security issues were salient -- Europe, Russia/Eurasia, Asia, and the Middle East -- and those in which such issues were subsidiary to broader political and economic concerns -- the Americas, Asia/Pacific and Africa.

Cross-Regional Issues: Many issues appeared across several regions as efforts were made to deal with projected regional contingencies, though they carried different weights depending on the situation being addressed.

REGIONAL/SELECTIVE ACTIVE PLANS
CROSS CUTTING ISSUES

Issue	Africa	Americas	Europe	Asia	Mideast	Russia/ Eurasia
WMD issues take precedence over all others				●	●	●
Consider response option for WMD use			●	●	●	●
Balancing unilateral requirements against multilateral constraints	●	●	●	●	●	●
Political stability prerequisite to trade and market access						
Promote democratization through economic means	●	●	●	●	●	●
Refugee problems and risk of mass migration	●	●	●	●	●	●
Expand interagency & internat'l organization coordination	●	●	●	●	●	●

Weapons of mass destruction (WMD) appeared as the paramount security issue. In cases where WMD posed a real or potential threat -- in the former Soviet Republics, in North Korea and in the Middle East -- these weapons tended to overshadow longer-term strategic planning. Even in those instances, however, operational issues were enmeshed in the larger political and economic consequences for the region, especially when considering appropriate response options to WMD use.

In virtually every region, contingency plans for potential unilateral actions had to balance against the efficacy of cooperative security. In some instances, such as a crisis in Russia/Eurasia, no matter how desirable direct action may appear to be in a given contingency, there is likely to be little latitude for unilateral U.S. engagement. In other areas, such as the Middle East, unilateral action was considered essential because of the immediacy and severity of the threat. In most instances, however, contingency plans anticipated some balance of American leadership within multilateral and/or regional security arrangements.

In regions where security issues were less salient, there was greater opportunity to consider long-term objectives using all elements of national power. In all regions, economic growth was considered to be essential to the process of democratic development and to national and regional stability. In particular, it was felt that such stability was the key to alleviating the growing security threat posed by refugees and economically induced mass migration. Major initiatives for these regions (e.g., military professionalization, humanitarian assistance, fostering market and resource access through international and regional mechanisms) seek to build the foundations for democracy. Associated with these broad initiatives were concerns that greater interagency and international coordination is needed.

Chapter 11

PROMOTING THE DEMOCRATIZATION PROCESS IN AFRICA: A NEW
ROLE FOR THE U.S. IN THE NEW WORLD ORDER?"

Over the course of the past four decades, foreign policy discussions in
the United States were overwhelmingly preoccupied with the global military
equilibrium or bipolar balance of power that existed between the U.S. and
U.S.S.R. The very language of policy makers, academics, and the news media
even suggested that this global alliance system was somewhat stable and
non-threatening-- so much so that it could be called a "Cold War."
     On the other hand, for the peoples of that residual category loosely
defined as the "Third World," especially those in Africa, the status quo was
anything but stable and predictable. For decades, dozens of nations in Latin
America, Africa, the Middle East and Asia experienced a seemingly endless
series of crises, tragedies, and humanitarian disasters that the U.S. could
conveniently subsume under larger priorities related to the crusade against
communism.
     With all of this in mind, it is ironic that the onset of the 1990s has
brought an about face in the popular discourse of American policy makers
and the erstwhile news media. After a 40 year absence, it only now seems
appropriate to be acknowledging the complexities of deep political and
economic problems in the Third World. Suddenly, we are confronted with
lively debates in Congress over the root causes of tragic civil wars in Liberia,
Cambodia and Yemen, where once we heard nothing but detailed discourses
on the Soviet arms build-up and broad platitudes about the spread of global
communism. Hard-nosed critiques of missile capabilities and Star Wars are
increasingly drowned out by compassionate statements and concern for
hunger, indebtedness, decertification, and vanishing rain forests in the diverse
landscape of Third World states.
     Nowhere is this more in evidence than in Africa. Practically overnight,
we see a newfound concern for a whole litany of distressing micro-level
problems that have been around for decades, but are only now finding the
light of day:

221

(a) civil wars as states split apart at the seams currently exist in 14 states (out of 33 worldwide) as a result of ethnic fragmentation in states long held together by the force of outside power players.

(b) sputtering transitions to democracy in over two dozen societies long under authoritarian rule.

(c) population explosion unchecked and placing increasing pressures on impoverished governments-- Africa has the highest fertility rates (over 3%) of entire world.

(d) natural resource depletion increasing at an alarming rate and threatening long-term health of entire globe, with rainforests disappearing, widescale soil erosion, decertification in areas bordering the great Sahara.

Freed from Cold War shackles, the Clinton administration is facing the decades-old problems in Africa as if they were an entirely new agenda. This is most graphically illustrated by the recent deployment of 16,000 troops in Somalia, but also may be seen in dozens of other commitments in aid and assistance worth over $800 million per year that are currently in place or being negotiated throughout the continent. Secretary of State Warren Christopher stated in an address in May of 1993 that the Clinton administration is searching for a "productive new relationship with Africa." At present, the lack of any clear, unifying theme directing U.S. foreign policy is best explained as a natural reflection of the sheer magnitude and gravity of the issues and the lack of real experience in dealing with them.

Given the multi-dimensional nature of social, economic and political problems in Africa, what would be an appropriate organizing framework for American foreign policy? Among the numerous suggestions currently being aired, by far the most reasonable direction would be to shift foreign policy toward an all-encompassing focus on fostering democratic governance throughout the continent. Only by taking an aggressive stance on promoting human rights and participatory governance will the foundations be properly laid for progressive policy reforms in other areas of national development.

Root Cause of Instability

The international market economy has never been kind to Africa, nor have the Western powers that have frequently intervened and bullied these countries in pursuit of their own interests. But this has been the state of affairs for most countries in the Third World throughout the past 40 years. There are many states in Latin America, Asia, and even the Middle East that have moved beyond these deficiencies and are now carving out for themselves a place in the world community. In contrast, we have the 50-odd states of Sub-Saharan Africa. Among them are 32 out of the 40 most impoverished nations on the earth. Between 1960 and 1990, the African share of global gross national product actually dropped from 1.9% to 1.2%. Even the overall gross national product of Africa totalling some $150 billion is overshadowed by an external debt load has risen to a staggering $174 billion. In one country after another, the public infrastructure is crumbling, essential services are in stagnation, bureaucrats are unresponsive and uncaring, and chronic political instability seems ever-present. At present, one half of all refugees in the world are Africans, most fleeing the side-effects of devastating civil wars.

The future also looks grim. Although population growth is projected to rise from 548 million today to 2.9 billion by the year 2050, Africa has been experiencing a net loss in income over the past 10 years due to massive, pre-calculated disinvestment on the part of foreign business interests and investors. Plagued by poor services and political instability, along with capital and operating costs 50-100% higher in Africa than in other parts of the Third World, there is little incentive for businesses to remain here to make use of Africa's vast source of cheap labor.

Why is it that Africa has fallen so far behind? It is certainly not for want of natural resources, a favorable climate or an adequate labor force. What is different about Africa is that few of these countries have any kind of coherent state structure. Indeed, it is difficult to locate more than a handful of governments that enjoy the enthusiastic acceptance and legitimacy of the people. African societies are faced with social breakdown and economic chaos because there is little loyalty or emotional attachment to state authority, and by implication, little respect for the ideology, institutions, and law that comprise its existence.

All of this is a result of the confluence of a number of complex historical factors rather unique to the African landscape. A legacy of colonialism and abusive dictators meant that there was simply no cultural integrity between the rulers and the ruled at any level beyond the local community. National-level politics has been the sole preserve of the elite-- in most cases, a small minority of educated intellectuals, professional politicians, and military strongmen who have held the offices of state almost exclusively for personal and communal gain. For decades, government corruption, incompetence and inefficiency have been the rule rather than the exception in these states. Disgusted and disillusioned by frequent crises at the national level, abrupt changes in government and official policies that have little or no connection with their lives, most people have chosen to desert their governments en masse-- retreating to the sanctity and security of regional, ethnic, religious or kin-based communities in order to give meaning to everyday life. People simply allocate their time and energy toward parochial ends while seeking to evade the arbitrary and unjust authority of the state. The consequence of these circumstances is the much-noted "collapse of the state" in Africa, where governments find themselves ruling over highly fragmented societies in which the realm of social control is severely limited, and often only attainable through the use of heavy-handed coercion.

For more than three decades, the superpowers and the United Nations alike have given credence to the absolute and inviolable sovereignty of each of these states. This went on even if the authority of these states was largely a legal fiction, both for those states that persisted under the enduring leadership of a single strongman dictator (Zambia, Kenya, Tanzania, Gabon, Senegal and Zaire), and for those where one government after another collapsed of its own weight (Benin, Chad, Nigeria, Ghana, and Congo). Ever patient, the world community gave its nodding acceptance -- no questions were asked, and little real concern was shown for the plight of the unfortunate people in each country. The only real concern was whether the current set of rulers in a given state bowed to the abstract ideology of capitalism or communism. For those states that fell to Marxist dictators (Ethiopia, Angola, and Mozambique), there were years of bloody civil wars were fostered in the interests of the global chess game. For those in the camp of France, Britain, Belgium and other American alliance partners, there was plentiful financial, economic and military aid to prop up the "friends" of Western capitalism.

Democracy as the Critical Missing Element

With the thankful passage of the Cold War, the signal deficiency of these states today remains in the absence of a healthy, legitimate state structure. In tandem with this is the equally egregious missing element of an amenable civil society. By this, reference is made to that melange of interest associations, labor movements, political parties, and other organizations that allow people to transcend ties of creed and kinship and work together at the national level in relatively productive relationships. For decades, these societies have been instilled with authoritarian traditions, where rulers have sought only to dominate, extinguish, or at the very least, emasculate autonomous political forces outside of their control. Yet it appears that in the late 20th century, even African governments that claim to speak for the people increasingly must compete with an assertive citizenry perfectly prepared to speak for itself. Undoubtedly, this has been encouraged by revolutionary advances in international communications technology and information processing as much as anything else. There is a rapid and virtually unobstructed flow of information both to and from Africa due to the nearly ubiquitous reach of CNN, the BBC, fax machines, internet, video cameras and cellular phones. Indeed, like Coca-Cola, the word "democracy" is understood virtually everywhere, without need for translation. Africans, however little formal education they may have had, have been well-schooled in the practices of repressive dictatorship and arbitrary rule-- they fully realize that truly accountable and fair government must incorporate the will of the people.

How can these societies hope to implement true economic restructuring programs, health care and educational development, population control, and any number of other critically important policy initiatives in the absence of a strong, coherent state structure that carries on a successful interlocution with the society at large? Indeed, these reforms are unattainable without the active participation of the populace, and the articulation of its genuine needs and hopes through a responsive participatory political system. It is only when these barriers are overcome that the societies of Africa may truly begin to deal with the enormous social and economic problems they are facing.

There is no quick and easy magic formula of constitutional reform that is uniformly applicable to all of Africa. Many of these societies have had plenty of time to experiment with failed constitutional models imported from the West. There is clearly a need for Africans themselves to innovate in the design of new constitutions that do the job of incorporating the participation of the people in a way that ensures just, accountable governance from their leadership.

It would be wrong to assume that Africans themselves do not see the need for this kind of government. The swift and spontaneous collapse of the Soviet Union and repressive dictatorships in Eastern Europe in 1989-1990 left an indelible impression on the disparate peoples of Africa. Many took to the streets in an unprecedented fashion, seeking peaceful change and structural reforms with a boldness never before witnessed. National conferences were held in some francophone countries entirely outside of government supervision. In other countries, protests and mass civil disobedience campaigns were waged with great skill and precision. All over Africa, dictators and military strongmen have been compelled to acknowledge the will of the people, stepping down in some cases in humiliation, or at the very least, submitting to the call for multi-party elections and press freedoms.

New Focus in American Foreign Policy

If agreement can be found that democracy is the critical missing element in Africa, what kind of foreign policy guidelines might be helpful for the United States? The past record of American involvement in the Third World is certainly of little help. Few efforts have been made at promoting participatory democracy and human rights, save in those cases where it has been politically expedient to do so. Rather, most experience has been in training local military and security forces in the ways of dictatorship, promoting the interests of American multinational corporations, and dumping poor nations with loads of unwanted American grain.

A complete turn-around from previous experience is clearly needed to address this new agenda. We are therefore living at a time when creative new ideas are at a premium in our foreign policy establishment. I would like to propose the following initiatives as being essential elements of any such policy:

Conflict Resolution. In those cases where countries are undergoing the tragedy of civil war, we must join hands with the United Nations in adopting a more assertive role as mediator. There is a wealth of past experience to draw upon in this regard, given the long record that the United Nations has had with peacekeeping operations over two dozen trouble spots around the world.

Historically, this has been a delicate issue, given that it has always been the exclusive right of governments to do as they please within their own borders. In the 1990s, though, this notion seems to be outdated, especially in light of events over the past four years. In Somalia, efforts were coordinated under UN auspices to take on a new, more assertive kind of intervention between warring parties. The international mediation of the civil wars in Mozambique, Angola and Namibia are other cases in point.

While the US has a critical role to play in future cases where intervention is mandated, it should not go it alone. Only a body as representative as the UN has the legitimacy to handle this responsibility. Even better, there is far more room here for regional organizations to shoulder a significant segment of responsibility. The recent intervention of the Economic Community of West African States (ECOMOWAS) in the Liberian civil war sets an important precedent for Africa as a whole. On the other hand, the U.S. must realize that little concrete action of this type will take place without bold leadership from the President. No other country at present has the same degree of prestige and international authority to initiate such efforts and coordinate support.

Constitutional Development. Where there is a genuine commitment for adopting democratic reforms, the international community must offer any and all support possible for the establishment of an institutional framework for democracy. This will not be an easy task, since the U.S. really has little past foreign policy experience in this area, nor does the United Nations.

What kinds of assistance can be given to foster democracy? Clearly, the jury is out as to what works best in preparing a lasting framework of democracy. At present, the U.S. has in place its National Endowment for Democracy, but its record has not been completely consistent due to partisan political biases over the years. Perhaps more suited to this task would be the reinvigoration of existing UN agencies that might provide aid and assistance in the design of democratic constitutions, including training seminars and educational assistance. Additional field support could be provided in the form of modern electronic balloting technology, and sending out teams for the purpose of election monitoring. There have been several notable cases of success already through comprehensive efforts sponsored by international agencies that include both non-governmental aid and multilateral assistance from Western states in Ghana, Cote d'Ivoire and Zambia.

Ultimately, an extended period of experience with the institutional trappings of democracy is critical so that eventually, new traditions can spread among the people embodying such ideals as tolerance, moderation, and equality. In this regard, fertile ground for democracy may be tilled by supporting substantial investments in "human capital" that are so often missing in these societies. This means funding for universal education, health care provision, sanitation, urban planning, and other projects that will provide a satisfactory level of survival for the people at large.

On the other hand, any effort to provide assistance must be managed carefully. The world community should resist the idea of offering tangible incentives to induce compliance. There is already a long and dishonorable record of unscrupulous bureaucrats accepting hand-outs in return for feigned compliance with the demands of external donors. The case of Rwanda is a tragic reminder of the way such transitions may break down after a superficial transition has taken place.

Economic aid and assistance. It is unrealistic to expect these countries to adopt attitudes of tolerance and moderation if they are facing severe economic hardship. Extreme demands are made on politicians because there are extreme needs in the daily lives of the people.

There is a pressing need for adopting entirely new economic policies that can provide the foundation for genuine development in Africa. To this end, traditional notions of aid, which amounted to nothing more than dumping inappropriate technology and food assistance as a sop to domestic political interests in the United States, should be dropped. Instead, efforts should be made to encourage and support sustainable development-- projects that are appropriate to the technological level and existing capacity of these societies. Just as importantly, we should offer to open up our markets to African participation through export/import incentives. This means stripping back the protectionist walls that exist on our domestic consumer economy so that impoverished Third World nations might gain from global trade for their commodities and merchandise that have for so long been kept out by force of law. Western nations must also be willing to make concessions on debt repayment and provide room for these nations to rebound from the destructive cycle of debts run up by unscrupulous dictators and irresponsible politicians of the past.

Conclusion

The current status of Africa is quite alarming. In addition to longstanding economic, social and environmental problems, it is also a time of state collapse and disintegration. This should not come as a surprise. The world is bearing witness to a pent-up supply of discontent that has arisen out of the internal contradictions that have existed in these countries since their inception. After four decades of artificial preservation created by the superstructure of the Cold War alliance structure, these atrophying states are now falling apart of their own weight.

The seeming disorder and lack of clarity of the post-Cold War era should not be seen as a hindrance to sound foreign policy by the Clinton administration. Rather, in this time of great change, it has been given an unparalleled opportunity to refocus traditional policy priorities in new directions for Africa and the rest of the Third World. At perhaps no other time than the African independence era has the U.S. been given a better opportunity to foster genuine economic and political development in these states. It would be inadvisable to perpetuate the distressing realities of the present by withdrawing from the great responsibilities that fate has placed on American shoulders as the leading voice of freedom in the world community of nations.

CHAPTER 11

REFERENCES

Christopher, Warren. 1993. "A New Relationship with Africa: Address to the,23rd African-American Conference. Reston, Virginia." Reprinted in Africa Report (July-August), pp. 36-39.

Rotberg, Robert I. 1993. "The Clinton Administration and Africa." Current History 92 (May), pp. 193-197.

Morrow, Lance. 1992. "Africa: The Scramble for Existence." Time September 7, pp. 39-46.

This condition has been widely documented and studied. See for example, Wunsch, James S. and Dele Olowu, eds. 1990. The Failure of the Centralized State:Institutions and Self-Governance in Africa. Boulder: Westview; and Rothchild, Donald and Naomi Chazan, eds. 1988. The Precarious Balance: State and Society in Africa. Boulder: Westview.

Hammerskjold Foundation. 1987. "The State and the Crisis in Africa: In Search of a Second Liberation." Development Dialogue (2), pp. 5-29.

See the essays in Ergaz, Zaki, ed. The African State in Transition. New York: St. Martins.

Sklar, Richard L. 1987. "Developmental Democracy." Comparative Studies in Society and History, (29), pp. 686-714.

For a general analysis of this topic, see Huntington, Samuel P. 1991. "How Countries Democratize." Political Science Quarterly 106 (Winter), pp. 579-661. For the case of Africa, see Ayoade, John. 1986 "The African Search for Democracy." In Dov Ronen, ed., Democracy and Pluralism in Africa. Boulder: Lynne Rienner; and Ake, Claude. 1991. "Rethinking African Democracy." Journal of Democracy 2, pp. 32-44.

PART IV

SOUTH AFRICAN RELATIONS: "A DIAMOND IS FOREVER"

"The struggle itself toward the heights is enough to fill a man's heart. One must imagine Sisyphus happy."

Albert Camus, The Myth of Sisyphus

Chapter 12

The Past as Epilogue: A New Signpost for United States'
Africa Policy in the Post-Cold War Era

I. Introduction

United States foreign policy is adrift because a new rudder to replace
the Cold War grand strategy of containment has not been crafted. In
particular, U.S. policy for Sub-Sahara Africa has no direction[1]. Sub-Sahara
Africa lacks both strategic importance and a powerful domestic constituency
in the U.S.[2] Ironically, the end of *de jure* apartheid in South Africa removed
the one issue which gave purpose to that domestic constituency that did
exist.[3] Christopher Coker argued in 1991:

> Once apartheid fades into memory, once it becomes a subject
> of historical enquiry rather than contemporary criticism, once it
> is blurred or erased, South Africa will lose its meaning [to the
> U.S.], with Southern Africa following in tow.[4]

This paper suggests an alternative framework for U.S. Africa policy
that completes the break with Cold War policy, but challenges the current
policy. I argue that U.S. foreign policy for Africa should focus on regional
stability, and to this end, should advocate, and when possible promote,
regional cooperation and integration in Africa. I use southern Africa as an
example to make this argument.

First, regional cooperation and integration will promote economic
development in southern Africa in a way that complements the International
Financial Institution's (IFIs) structural adjustment programs (SAPs) in Africa.
Eight southern African countries have undertaken extensive structural
adjustment programs,[5] and each belongs to one or another regional
organization promoting cooperation and/or integration. Second, economic
development is the necessary, if not sufficient, condition for the success of
stated U.S. policy objectives, such as democratization and a conflict prevention

and resolution. Third, the policy outlined here is more cost-effective because the many points of light (and sources of funding), and diffused objectives, of U.S. policy are passed through a conceptual prism that facilitates a more focused and a more comprehensive policy. Finally, this policy is also relatively consistent with African demands and thus diplomatically more efficient.

The argument is made is five parts. First, I briefly outline the sources of instability in southern Africa. Second, I review U.S. Cold War foreign policy for Africa. Third, I examine the promotion of economic liberalization in Africa, and its relationship to the prospects for democratization. Fourth, I discuss ethnicity in Africa as it is influenced by, and as it influences, economic development, regional integration and political stability. The fifth section argues that promoting regional cooperation and integration in southern Africa pulls together the different strains of current U.S. Africa policy into a comprehensive and efficient policy.

Unlike the reactive policy of containment, the promotion of regional stability will entail the formative process of identifying the underlying, and multiple, causes of instability in Africa, and then designing a unified policy framework that addresses those causes. A formative policy will challenge two American foreign policy traditions: the reactive policy of containment, as well as the institutional myopia of our elective officials who usually think in terms of six, four or two years.

II. Instability in Southern Africa

There are multiple and reinforcing causes of instability in Africa. The long-term sources of instability in southern Africa are: economic underdevelopment, ethnic rivalry, political underdevelopment, and regional disparities in economic development. Because these sources flow together to create a strong undertow of instability, they must be addressed under a single policy framework.

Economic stagnation is a primary cause of instability. A New York Times article, the first of a three part series on Sub-Sahara Africa entitled, "Survival Test: Can Africa Rebound?" stated: "The economic failure is undercutting a drive for political liberalization, raising ethnic rivalries to a dangerous level and forcing countries to impose inflammatory austerity programs, often under the dictates of Western financial institutions."[6]

Economic development is an apposite policy objective by itself, but is also necessary for the success of stated U.S. foreign policy objectives in Africa: conflict prevention and resolution, controlling problems of ethnicity, and democratization.

Thomas Calleghy's metaphor of "weak neighborhoods" captures the character of African's economic decline:

In declining neighborhoods, even strong houses are eventually affected negatively--certainly their property value goes down; while in improving neighborhoods, even the weakest house may eventually be affected positively--its value might even go up without any major renovation.[7]

A regional approach to economic development is necessary, and regional cooperation and integration will attenuate the underlying causes of instability.

III.   The Cold War and U.S. Policy Towards Africa

Michael Clough argues that U.S. policy most importantly "must be grounded in an understanding of the past failures of U.S. policy in Africa."[8] U.S. Africa policy must also be guided by the lateral successes of U.S. Cold War foreign policy, such as the reconstruction of Europe, and remain alert to antecedent polices that are relevant to current African realities.

U.S. Africa policy has historically swung between the extremes of benign neglect and malign manipulation. There also have been short bursts of positive policy innovation, such as the Kennedy Administration's regional approach. In fact, Herman J. Cohen, Assistant Secretary of State for Africa in the Bush administration, argued that encouraging regional economic integration was a constant in U.S. policy during both the twenty year period preceding Ronald Reagan, as well as under Reagan. However, Cohen also lists this as the last of the five main elements of traditional U.S. policy for Africa.[9]

Geopolitical considerations generally shaped U.S. policy for Africa during the Cold War. The level of foreign aid to Africa, and to which countries it went, was determined by the exigencies of the Cold War. As Richard Sincere states:

The Foreign Assistance Act of 1961, which set up AID meant, that no longer was U.S. economic aid to be limited to disaster relief or famine relief: it was meant to be a tool of foreign policy, to promote economic growth, encourage free enterprise and democracy, and to serve as a weapon in the growing arsenal fighting the encroachment of Communism around the globe.[10]

The Kennedy Administration nonetheless adopted a policy for Africa that went beyond the confines of the Cold War. U.S. interest in Africa during the Kennedy Administration is reflected in the increase of aid from practically nothing in 1960 to $1.3 billion in 1962.[11] More importantly, this assistance was to support regional economic integration.[12]

However, this approach was brief and U.S. policy for Africa is best characterized as benign neglect until the sudden arrival of the Cold War in Africa in the 1970s. As Michael Clough states "... the United States was more active in Africa from the mid-1970s through the mid-1980s than at any time in its history."[13] The level of U.S. interest during this period is reflected in the rise in foreign assistance. Between 1975 and 1984, U.S. bilateral assistance to Africa increased 250% and by 1985 the U.S. was the largest aid donor to Sub-Sahara Africa.[14] However as Jeffrey Herbst states: "Since geopolitical concerns, rather than African realities, were what interested top policy makers, actual aid programs were seldom the result of a coherent, long-term vision."[15]

U.S. foreign assistance to Africa during the Cold War was usually bilateral. In 1988 Carol Lancastor argued that the United States was the only donor in Sub-Sahara Africa whose aid was both widely dispersed and concentrated in a handful of geopolitically important countries;[16] in that year 60% of U.S. aid to Africa was bilateral.[17] The long-run effect of bi-lateral assistance was the entrenchment of rulers such as, Daniel arap Moi of Kenya and Mobutu Sese Seko of Zaire, who now most stubbornly resist democratization. U.S. policy inadvertently contributed to the strength of patrimonial rule in Africa because rent-seeking by political elites was abetted by the flow of foreign aid that went directly to the individual country's governments.[18] The persistence of patrimonial rule in Africa inhibits the prospects for both democracy, and for economic reform.

Africa was only one part of the geopolitical chess board and the grand strategy of containment had different applications across different parts the world.

The "conditions" laid down by the Americans...included demands that the participating countries undertake internal financial and monetary reforms, stabilization of currencies, the establishment of proper rates of exchange, as well as "steps to facilitate the greatest practicable [sic] interchange of goods and services among themselves, adopting definite measures directed toward the progressive reduction and eventual elimination of barriers to trade within the area...[19]

The first part of this statement could be describing an IMF structural adjustment program (SAP) for Africa; it is, in fact, describing conditionality that accompanied the Marshall Plan.

Unlike post-Cold War SAPs in Africa, regional integration and cooperation were an integral part of post-World War II structural adjustment in Western Europe. The general consensus among U.S. policy makers was that economic recovery in Europe depended on economic cooperation and integration in Western Europe.[20]

IV. U.S. Policy and Economic Development in Southern Africa

A. Political Liberalization and Economic Development

Which comes first, democracy or economic development? For U.S. foreign policy, democracy is at least rhetorically *a priori*. In Michael Clough words:

> Promoting democracy has been a recurring theme of American diplomacy at least since the days of Woodrow Wilson. What makes the current era different is that a growing segment of the foreign policy Establishment (sic) believes both that the global triumph of liberal democracy ideals is now inevitable and that the United States has the power and the freedom to make promotion of democracy its first priority.[21]

However, African countries are expected not to merely reform their polities, but simultaneously reform their economies through economic liberalization. How compatible are these two goals?

Thomas Ohlson and Stephen J. Stedman state: "Economic adjustment and political democracy may be contradictory and incompatible programmes."[22] Jeffrey Herbst states,

> In fact, the relationship between overall economic growth and political freedom is quite complicated. Many of the best economic performances in the Third World over the last twenty years, especially the East Asian Tigers, could not be considered politically liberal.[23]

Thomas Callaghy, has most convincingly argued that in Africa an inherent tension exists between economic reform and democratization.

> But is political conditionality a good idea, especially regarding the prospects for major economic change? A major contradiction between economic and political conditionality may indeed exist, one that Western governments either do not see or ignore.[24]

If, in the African context, democratization and economic liberalization are incompatible, but both are integral to U.S. policy, the next question is: which takes precedence? The answer lies in which of the two is logically *a priori*. Stephen Stedman poses the question in this way:

> In situations where a narrow transition has taken place in unamenable circumstances, *can democracy survive if it does not lead to economic growth, lessen inequalities, and create national unity and norms of tolerance?* Second, *in the absence of these good things, how likely are democratic processes to be stable?*[25]

The answer is, not likely. Economic development may not necessarily lead to political liberalization, but it is probably necessary to sustain it. Economic decline in Africa must be arrested and that means economic reform must be made to work.

B. Structural Adjustment and Economic Development in Africa
Africa is entering what John Ravenhill calls the second decade of adjustment.[26] For Africa in the 1980s, "national economic policy and strategy have been formed in the context of highly conditional basically (if unevenly) neoliberal Stabilization Programs (Stabs) and Structural Adjustment Programs (SAPs)."[27] The U.S. has played a major role in this process.

SAPs and Stabs, generically known as economic reform, have had mixed results in Africa. The World Bank's recent study, *Adjustment in Africa: Reforms, Results, and the Road Ahead*, argues that in African countries which have undertaken and sustained major policy reforms, structural adjustment has worked.[28] The report states: "Of the twenty-nine countries studies in this report, the six with the most improvement in macroeconomic policies between 1981-86 and 1987-91 enjoyed the strongest resurgence in economic performance."[29] The implication is, of course, that if the other twenty-three countries followed suit they too would witness improved economic performance.

Independent of structural adjustment's success, or lack of success, as Zimbabwean economist Tony Hawkins states, "... no viable alternative strategy is on offer."[30] Declining U.S. interest in most of Africa means that the IMF and World Bank will become increasingly important instruments of U.S. foreign policy and U.S. policy must then complement economic reform in Africa.

The debate over economic reform in Africa has been framed by contrasting the Lagos Plan of Action (LPA), an indigenous Africa policy prescription, with Accelerated Development (AD), an external policy prescription. According to the Secretaries of Africa's three principal organizations, the Organization of African Unity (OAU), the African Development Bank (ADB), and the U.N.'s Economic Commission for Africa (ECA), the export-oriented strategy of *AD* was in direct conflict with the internally oriented *LPA*.[31] In Thomas Callaghy's words:

> This disagreement erupted with surprising vigor in what could be called "the bloody spring of 1989." A major battle ensued between the World Bank and the UN's Economic Commission for Africa (ECA) as the former tried to defend structural adjustment and the latter attacked it and presented its own alternative strategy [LPA].[32]

Third World countries favor regional economic integration (i.e. *LPA*) because in most cases they are too small to build viable separate national economies. The larger countries, although theoretically more capable of separate national development, are constrained by their position in the world economy. Regional economic integration is Africa's response to chronic underdevelopment and thus, as might be expected, regional integration as a panacea has had enduring strength.[33]

The World Bank's response to the, at times, acrimonious debate over *AD* was the 1989 study, *Sub-Saharan Africa: From Crisis to Sustainable Growth, A Long Term Study*. As John Ravenhill states, this report endorses at length the OAU/ECA's demand for regional economic integration.[34] However, although the gap between African leaders and external actors on the best development strategy has narrowed, there is still a fundamental difference. The World Bank sees regional integration as a step towards full participation in the international economy and greater international competitiveness.[35] African policy-makers, on the other hand, have consistently argued that it is participation in the world economy that has led to the continent's economic stagnation. African regional integration offers a solution to the trap of unequal exchange relations because, by eschewing trade relations with the industrialized countries, the developing countries, by definition, escape the dependency syndrome.

While most of the countries of Sub-Sahara Africa participate in regional economic integration of one form or another, the vast majority of African governments in the 1980s have entered into structural adjustment agreements with the (IMF) and/or World Bank.[36] In fact, African debt to commercial banks is relatively small, 35% of total, unlike that of Latin America debt, and therefore Africa is even more susceptible to IMF influence.[37]

Because the influence of the International Financial Institutes (IFIs) in Africa will continue, three questions must be addressed. First, can structural adjustment on an individual country basis work? Second, if not, can the inherent weaknesses of SAPs be ameliorated by a regional approach? Third, how does structural adjustment in a more regional context affect the underlying political logics that many analysts blame for Africa's economic stagnation.

The three principal guidelines to SAPs in Africa are: getting macroeconomic policies right, encouraging competition, and using scarce institutional capacity wisely. Furthermore, the key macroeconomic policy is putting exporters first, for instance, by reducing import barriers. Protectionist trade policies, it is argued, reduce the internal level of competition that is a prerequisite for increasing productivity. Most African countries have failed to diversify their export base and remain, therefore, reliant on a few primary export commodities. Statistics for Africa, indeed, paint a bleak picture.

> Export volumes grew by only 1.5% each year from 1980-1986 but this increase was more than offset by declining terms of trade for Africa's commodities; as a consequence the purchasing power of the exports fell each year in the 1980s so that at the end of the decade they stood at only 76.7% of the level of 1982. In other words, movements in the terms of trade have cost African countries close to 25% of the purchasing power of their exports in the last decade.[38]

In the World Banks's stark summation: "Africa is simply not competitive in an increasingly competitive world."[39]

To create a wider export base through greater diversification, more investment is necessary. In fact an *implicit bargain* has existed between the IFIs and the major Western countries on one hand, and Africa on the other, that promises that new foreign direct investment and commercial lending will follow in the wake of sustained structural adjustment.[40] But, individual markets are relatively small, and Africa's return on investment fell from 30.7% in the 1960s to 2.5% in the 1980s,[41] Consequently Africa does not attract significant domestic or foreign investment. To put Africa in comparative perspective, the amount of external financing done in 1991 through bonds for South Asia was $1.9 billion, for Africa zero.[42]

There is a significant, and relatively unexplored, paradox in the *implicit bargain* that rests in the link between foreign investment and competitiveness. The notion of competitiveness, central to the long term success of economic reform, is implicitly framed in terms of an individual country's competitiveness. However, what makes a country competitive is competitive industries. As Professor Tony Hawkins of the University of Zimbabwe states: "After all, it is firms, not nations, that make investment decisions, employ people, market products and compete in international markets."[43]

Regional economic integration can provide the economies of scale, and therefore the factor efficiency necessary for production; it does not necessarily make that industry competitive. This is because two aspects of the market must be distinguished, the technological aspect and the economic aspect. The technological optimum size of a market is linked to economies of scale and, at times, on economies of intra-industry specialization. It will, therefore, differ across industries. However, even if the market is brought up to an optimal level for a given industry in terms of production techniques this does not ensure that the market is also at optimum size economically. This is because much of the benefits of larger markets come from the effects of competition. Therefore, to reap these benefits, the market may have to be a multiple of the technological optimum.

Thus, the size of the market must be large enough to house competitive industries. This creates the paradox of the *implicit bargain.* Competition is necessary for successful long term economic reform (SAPs), and therefore larger markets are necessary, and in the case of Africa with its small fragmented markets some form of economic integration. But in regions characterized by relatively high risk, and a poor return on investment, multinationals look for captured regional markets. The underlying logic of successful markets, and by implication SAPs, competition, is diametrically opposed to the logic that drives foreign investment - the pursuit of market shares (i.e. monopolies) and profit.

Stacked on top of the economic illogics of SAPs are the prevailing political logics. It is generally acknowledged that SAPs in Africa have vast political ramifications that transcend the potential economic benefits. This is because, as Jeffrey Herbst states:

> Most African leaders operate in political systems where votes do not matter. Instead, rulers try to institutionalize their regimes by establishing webs of patron-client relations to garner the support necessary to remain in power.[44]

If both democratization and economic reform are necessary for stability in Africa, then effecting change in the political logics of the African state is necessary. Regional economic integration can help redefine domestic politics.

In the post-colonial era, African states have used a system of differentiated tariffs and quotas to apply different levels of protection to different industries in order to reward clients.[45] Free trade, therefore, goes against the patrimonial grain of the African state. Christopher Clapham states:

With a convertible currency and an open market for agricultural produce, for example, conflict over the control of foreign exchange allocations and parastatal marketing boards becomes redundant. Reduced state patronage also reduces competition within the states for control of central government.[46]

But economic liberalization, including freer trade, must be gradual. SAPs have sent shock waves through the political economies of Africa. Most countries in Africa attempting SAPs are emerging from long periods of import substitution. The shift to export oriented industrialization (EOI) can cause an immediate, and significant, drop in employment in the formal sector.

There are economic and political reasons to cushion those shocks. African economies are far from being able to compete internationally. Competition could first be promoted at the regional level where the macroeconomic policies of the individual countries can be more reasonably be expected to converge. Instead, of rapid economic liberalization over time, liberalization should occur over time and over space. Sanjaya Lall states: There is evidently a need to combine the benefits of international competition with the need to foster infant activities."[47]

Finally, because regional economic integration presented as an African alternative, the conscious promotion of regional liberalization by the U.S. makes it more difficult for African leaders to fall back on the "foreign devil" excuse (ie. IFIs and SAPs) for rejecting economic reforms, and democratization.[48]

B. Regional Economic Integration in Southern Africa

The *AD - LPA* dichotomy is false because, as with post-World War II Europe, economic reform and economic integration are complementary. A discussion document written by the South Africa "Macroeconomic Research Group," which was a think tank for the ANC during the transition to democracy, recognized that the *AD - LPA* debate had to be transcended. It stated:

> The primary aim of integration cannot be to rescue failed import substitution strategies. Growth and development will require the elaboration of strategies to increase the value added of export products and become more effective and competitive in world markets.[49]

However, the document also cautioned that regional integration had to be judged on criteria beyond the degree to which the region is open to external penetration.[50]

Repeated failures demonstrate that economic integration is not a panacea for Africa's chronic economic underdevelopment. Most importantly, the myth of South Africa as the engine for regional economic growth in southern Africa must be debunked.

There are two glaring weaknesses to the assumption that South Africa will be a benevolent hegemon promoting regional economic development in southern Africa. First, although there are strong indications that South Africa will cooperate with its neighbors there are limited reasons to believe that South Africa is either willing or able to shoulder the responsibility for regional development. Second, and closely tied to the first, is the notion that regional economic integration will, *ipso facto*, benefit the region. There are real concerns by South Africa's neighbors, that South Africa will dominate the region. Each of these considerations will be briefly examined.

During the transition to democracy, the ANC often stated its intention to promote regional development in southern Africa in an equitable manner.

A central proposal of this chapter is that we cannot build the South African economy in isolation from its Southern African neighbors. Such a path would benefit nobody in the long run.[51]

Nonetheless, within South Africa debate continues over how to structure its post-apartheid regional relations.

The current debate in South Africa focuses on the rationalization of existing regional institutions: the Common Monetary Area (CMA), Common Market for Eastern and Southern Africa, Comesa, (formerly the Preferential Trade Area, PTA), the Southern African Development Community (SADC, formally SADCC), and the South African Customs Union (SACU).[52] The most extensive proposal on the rationalization of the four regional institutions is A Vision for Economic Integration and Cooperation in Southern Africa, prepared for the Department of Trade and Industry by Professor Gavin Maasdorph in March 1994. The focus of this report is on SACU as the center of a renegotiated and differentiated regional cooperation scheme. Maasdorph's report is a product of economic realism and in fact seems to be accepted by the relevant government ministries, ie. Finance, Trade and Industry, and Foreign Affairs.

However, political logics will interact with economic logics to determine South Africa's role in the post-apartheid regional dispensation. In the first half of 1994 a working committee of the Transitional Executive Council (TEC) for regional integration was formed.[53] The TEC working committee consisted of two members of the ANC, two representatives of the Development Bank of South Africa, (DBSA), the ex-Director General of Trade and Industry, and an economics professor from the University of

Stellenbosch. The Maasdorph report was not uncritically accepted by the working group,[54] and relative political pressure are just beginning to be felt. As expected, South Africa joined SADC soon after the May 1994 elections. This is not surprising given SADCC's origin in the Frontline States and the ANC's long participation in SADCC (SADC) meetings. However, at this time South Africa's membership in SADC is *pro forma*, as SADC itself is in the process of restructuring.

Other powerful actors in South Africa are against any formal approach to regional cooperation. For instance, the South African Chamber of Business commissioned a study on post-apartheid South Africa's regional role, which concluded that SACU should be used as the nucleus for regional cooperation and for bilateral trade agreements with South Africa's neighbors. The institutional model that this report argues best fits South Africa's regional needs is the Organization of Economic Cooperation and Development (OECD), which has a very limited institutional structure.[55]

There is widespread support for less formal cooperation in the Government bureaucracy, that is still a powerful force. Dr. Desmond Kroch, advisor to the South African Reserve Bank and a member of South Africa's National Economic Forum, argued that it is not in South Africa's interest at this stage to engage Africa, "to bite more than it can digest." He viewed the rest of Africa as a liability.[56]   Dr. S.J. Naude, ex-Director-General of the Department of Trade and Industry, argued that domestic constraints would limit South Africa's ability to act as an engine for regional growth. He states that the rash promises of some politicians for regional integration would be faced with real economic restrictions.[57]

At the other end of the political spectrum in South Africa, Labour is likely to resist the formation of a common market which would mean free factor movement across borders, including labour. South Africa would have to absorb 0.5 to 0.75 million low income people,[58] and as it already faces a severe unemployment problem the recent trend has been for tighter immigration control. The Congress of South African Trade Unions (Cosatu), a powerful faction of the ANC alliance, will likely want job protection and creation for its members.

Thus, while South Africa is actively exploring ways to enhance cooperation with its southern African neighbors, the extent and kind of cooperation is still being debated within South Africa.

The second problem with the assumption that South Africa will lead the sub-continent to economic prosperity is that its neighbors are at once anxious for South Africa to be the "engine of growth," and disconcerted by South Africa's regional dominance. The reconstitution of the Southern African Development Coordination Conference (SADCC) into the Southern

Africa Development Community was an explicit response to this concern. The regional dominance of South Africa is unquestioned; it accounts for 75% of the total GNP of the SADC region and its GNP per capita is six times that of the average of the SADC countries.[59] South Africa also dominates intra-regional trade.

The unequal distribution of costs and gains is a principal explanation for the failure of Third World integration movements. The most advanced of the developing countries will arguably receive a disproportionate share of the integrated region's aggregate gains.[60] That the more developed country will attract more foreign capital compounds the inequity of most regional integration schemes. The more developed country has options not available to the less developed. Richard Higgott argues, "the existing vertical linkages with Europe are likely to prove, in the short run at least, more significant for the pursuit of export oriented industrialization (EOI) in Africa's semi-industrialized states than its horizontal linkages with regional neighbors."[61] Sub-Sahara's market is worth approximately $250 billion; South Africa's market is worth approximately $100 billion, or over 40% of Africa's total.[62]

Regional integration has positive potential for southern Africa but, South Africa domestic constraints and the problem of its regional dominance, must be considered. The international system will likely have to help navigate these troubling currents. The "MERG Report" concluded:

> ...it is extremely likely that an equitable regional programme will only be possible if it is supported by external resources, particularly to finance programmes aimed at the most impoverished countries.[63]

South Africa's immediate concerns with redistribution at home, and its neighbors concern over South African dominance abroad, means that for regional economic cooperation to benefit the entire region, outside assistance will be necessary.

V. Regional Integration and the Attenuation of Regional Instability

Ethnicity is the greatest threat to the internal stability. of African states. There are generally two categories of explanations for ethnopolitics: primordial, and instrumental. The former explains ethnic conflict by referring to long simmering animosity between groups; the latter focuses on elite manipulation of ethnic identities for political and material ends. Ethnicity in most African states is instrumental rather than primordial.[64]

The intervening variable between elite manipulation and ethnicity is the state. The centrality of the state in African politics means that, in Jeffrey Herbst's word's, "one of the factors promoting ethnic strife is the need different groups feel to mobilize in order to press the state on important allocation issues."[65]

The Inkatha movement in South Africa is a good example of the predominantly instrumental nature of ethnicity in Africa. Herbert Adam and Kogila Moodley state:

> Leader-follower relationships among the majority of Zulu supporters of *Inkatha* are mainly based on reciprocal instrumental advantages and ethnic symbolic gratifications. The movement's poor and illiterate constituency depends on patronage, handed out by strong leaders and local power brokers in return for loyalty, regardless of ideological outlook or ethical behavior.[66]

The machinations of Mangosuthu G. Buthelezi during the May 1994 elections, and immediately afterwards, reflect this fact. Buthelezi, as leader of the nominally independent homeland of KwaZulu, built his patronage network on the back of administrative funds from apartheid South Africa. One of the major reasons for his eleventh hour participation in the May, 1994 national elections was his realization that the post-apartheid South African state would end subsidies to an independent Kwa-Zulu Natel.[67]

The political logics of the African state fan the flames of ethnicity, and the arbitrary boundaries of the African state encourage the spread ethnic conflict across state borders. Because the ethnic conflicts are not likely to be confined by state boundaries, particularly in Africa, an overt regional approach to dealing with Africa has innate advantages. Finally, in the worse case scenario David Welsh posits that:

> Wider economic associations, becoming perhaps, also political associations (initially confederations, possibly later, federations) offer a potential safety net to the political entities that could result from dismembered states.[68]

Regional cooperation can both diminish the premium placed on capturing the patrimonial state that encourages ethnic mobilization, and directly address the innate regional dimension of ethnicity in Africa.

V. The Past as Epilogue: A New Signpost for United States' Africa Policy
    Supporting regional cooperation and integration in southern Africa can unify disparate strains of U.S. policy, while promoting greater stability in the region.

A. U.S. bilateral relations with southern Africa
    The unifying theme of U.S. post-Cold War policy for Africa appears to be *democratization*. Under the Clinton Administration, *democracy* is the prefix to most policy shibboleths. National Security Advisor Anthony Lake explaining the current Administration's policy of enlargement, states:

> A strategy of enlargement is based on a belief that our most fundamental security interest lies in the expansion and consolidation of **democratic** and market reforms (my emphasis).[69]

George Moose, Assistant Secretary of State for African Affairs in the Clinton Administration, stated: "fostering democracy" was the central plank of the administration's policy.[70] The second and third key areas of U.S. Africa policy he listed were conflict resolution, followed by, trade and investment. At the same Hearings, John Hicks, Assistant Administrator, USAID, stated: "...Building democracy has a prominent place in the agency's post-Cold-War foreign aid strategy."[71]
    However, under Clinton the real focus of U.S foreign policy in the Third World, and in general, is international economic relations. It is also where the administration has been most successful. An editorial in the New York Times stated that:

> To put it bluntly, Mr. Clinton's foreign economic policy tends to be everything that the rest of his foreign policy is not; his goals have been generally well-articulated, the payoff for the American public clear cut, and the passions of the President obviously engaged.[72]

The Clinton Administration foreign economic policy has two dimensions, aid and trade. In Antony Lake's words, the Clinton administration believes, "... that trade - and not just aid - must be the basis for much of our effort toward the developing world."[73] In the long term, the focus will likely shift further to trade, and therefore foreign aid must work to stimulate trade.[74]
    Because a central plank in the Administration's free trade agenda is its designation of ten countries as "Big Emerging Markets," and one of them is South Africa, southern Africa is included in the Administration's foreign

economic trade policy. In fact, the South African <u>Cape Times</u>, reporting on the appointment of Millard Arnold as U.S. "commerce czar" for southern Africa, stated: "The appointment is in line with U.S. President Bill Clinton's programme of linking foreign policy with trade potential for American business and industry."[75]

Singling out one country is consistent with reducing the aggregate level of foreign assistance by identifying potential winners. However, South Africa will not flourish in a decaying neighborhood. Since the end of the five-year-old ban on new U.S. investment in South Africa in 1991, 47 American companies have reentered South Africa, for a total of 154 U.S. companies with an equity presence there.[76]   However, and more revealing, of the 209 U.S. companies that left South Africa between 1985 and 1990, only a fourth have come back.[77] Those that have returned, "are essentially storefronts for goods made elsewhere."[78] The level of investment is a reflection on the cautious approach engendered by South Africa's transition.

The well developed civil society that pushed for an end to apartheid has also pushed hard for a post-apartheid dividend. For instance, in the first six months of 1994 South Africa lost 1.2 million worker days to strikes, up from 700,000 a year earlier.[79] Ironically, South Africa's relatively well developed civil society, which some argue, is representative of a healthy democracy, may impede the flow of investment into South Africa. While the quantity of investment is influenced by the perception of an as yet unsettled political economy, the type of investment is linked to South Africa's potential regional role.   This potential, however, has two faces, and both have implication for regional economic integration.

> Robert Davies describes the first face:
> The insistence on the need for unrestricted free movement of capital throughout the region appears, for example, to have much less to do with plans by South African companies to make investments in the region than a desire to reinforce South Africa's image as the "natural gateway" and partner for foreign investment in Southern Africa.[80]

Prior to the May 1994 elections in South Africa, The Investor Responsibility Research Center (IRRC) in Washington. D.C. cautioned against the thinking that U.S. investment would flood into post-apartheid South Africa.   The Center argued that the companies most likely to soon start business in South Africa would be one that could distribute their products there without a local manufacturing base.[81]

The second face of South Africa's regional role is its potential as the regional engine of growth. As one U.S. official stated:

> South Africa has the potential not only to provide a better life for all its people but also to serve as an engine of growth for the southern Africa region.[82]

In a similar vein Antony Lake stated:

> ...we should be on the lookout for states whose entry into the camp of market democracies may influence the future direction of an entire region; South Africa and Nigeria now hold that potential with regard to Sub-Saharan Africa.[83]

The underlying assumption of this view is that South Africa will invest in southern Africa. However, the growth rate of South Africa's gross fixed investment between 1980 and 1990 was -4.3%[84]; in the near future, South Africa can not be expected to be a net capital exporter to the region.

For South Africa to play the "engine of growth role," foreign capital is necessary. This in turn, engenders challenges for the second dimension of U.S. foreign economic policy, aid. South Africa does have the technical expertise and infrastructure to promote regional development. But these attributes must be nurtured in a way that does not further augment the disparity between South Africa and its neighbors.[85]

U.S. aid policy, however, is inconsistent on this issue. First, there is a strong focus on South Africa. Aid marked for South Africa is estimated to be close to $700 million over the next three years.[86] The Administration's foreign assistance request for Sub-Sahara Africa for FYI 1995 under the heading "International Sustainable Development and Humanitarian Programs" was $784 million,[87] some of which could go to South Africa. The FYI 1995 budget includes $16.9 million for the African Development Foundation for grants, loans and loan guarantees directly to people and/or organizations that promote development through self help, for which South Africa could also apply.[88] South Africa would not be eligible for funds from the approximately $21 million slated for the African Development Fund, a concessional lending affiliate of the African Development Bank (ADB), 80% of which funds are earmarked for countries with per capita GDP of less than $510.00.[89]   nI an interview with President Clinton on CNN's "Global Forum with the President", CNN reporter Bernard Shaw asked whether other nations will feel slighted if aid to South Africa is increased. Clinton responded:

> ...South Africa can be a beacon of economic development and prosperity for all southern Africa, can help to build interest in American and other business people in investing in all of

southern Africa and can help to build a constituency for expanded assistance throughout Africa.[90]

There is an implicit commitment to regional growth, in the enhanced commitment to South Africa. This is reflected in various statements on foreign assistance.

In contrast to the focus on individual countries, the second tendency of U.S. aid policy for southern Africa is a regional approach.[91]

Thus, for instance, the *International Relations Act of 1993* argued that additional emphasis should be placed on the strengthening of Mozambique's transportation sector through assistance to SADC.[92] The *Development Fund For Africa* stated: "...that funds appropriated under this heading which are made available for activities supported by the SADC should be made available..."[93] The Overseas Private Investment Corporation (OPIC) is supporting a $75 million equity investment fund, called the Africa Growth Fund, for southern Africa with a focus on South Africa.[94]

USAID, also, has supported a regional approach. In a major address to the SADC Conference of Ministers meeting in Gaborone in 1994, USAID officer Brian Atwood suggested a new U.S. regional initiative. He stated:

> ...the U.S. Government will undertake a special initiative for the Southern African region. Our goal is to develop new programs and strategies to enhance your efforts to broaden and strengthen economic cooperation and achieve sustainable growth.[95]

Generally, USAID has had to cut back on the number of its individual missions in Africa. It makes economic sense to take a regional approach given the current public opinion in America about foreign assistance.

B. The U.S. and Multilateral Assistance to Southern Africa
The U.S. must not only rationalize its own economic foreign policy for southern Africa but, as well, must work in tandem with multilateral organizations. Shortly before the May elections the Overseas Development Institute predicted that there would not likely be additional aid flows from the OECD countries to South Africa on the scale necessary to make a significance.[96] The IMF and World Bank are therefore particularly important.

The U.S. strongly influences the policies of the IMF and World Bank, and much of U.S. influence in Africa is filtered through those institutions. For instance, the 1993 Budget allocated twice as much for the IMF as it did for

international development and humanitarian assistance.[97]   Assistant
Secretary for African Affairs, George Moose, stated: "Clearly the IMF and
the World Bank have a substantial role to play in South Africa's economic
recovery."[98]   Not only does some form of regional cooperation logically
follow from the IFI's SAPs for Africa (as already argued above), but,
increasingly, the World Bank itself, is promoting regional cooperation and
integration in southern Africa. The U.N. has also argued that regionalism is
one way for developing countries to cope with the effects of the world
economy.[99]

C. Regional Security and U.S. Policy in Southern Africa

The Clinton Administration appears to be relatively successful in
articulating an economic foreign policy.   However, such policy cannot be
divorced from more direct national security concerns such as conflict
prevention and resolution.   In the 1980s, war related damage to the economies
of southern Africa was at least $90 billion.[100]   Aid, and growing trade,
cannot work its magic in such circumstances, but neither can the U.S. be the
world's policeman.[101]   There is a growing recognition in Washington of the
potential for conflicts within African to spread across borders.

U.S. Assistant Secretary for African Affairs, Herman J. Cohen, stated
in March 1993:

> Of critical importance is the reinforcement of Africans' own
> ability to resolve their internal and regional conflicts.
> Consequently, much of our assistance concentrates on building
> the conflict-resolution capacity of existing organizations such as
> the OAU and ECOWAS.[102]

Cohen reviews eight countries where the U.S. has been extensively engaged
in peace-making - four of those are in southern Africa.[103]

Deputy Secretary of State, Strobe Talbott's, fall 1994 trip to five
African countries, was partly to emphasize the importance of regional peace
keeping.[104]

Finally, closely related to the prevention of conflict is the suppression
of ethnic conflict.   Secretary of State Warren Christopher has called for
preventive diplomacy to keep ethnicity from spreading.[105]   Regional
problems demand a regional approach.

Conclusion

United States foreign policy is in search of a grand strategy to replace
the Cold War relic of containment.   In the case of Africa, that search is made

more difficult by relative disinterest, poorly defined policy objectives, and too many points of light.

The world economy is increasingly being defined by regional trading blocs and the completed Uruguay round of GATT may be the last of its kind. Trade liberalization will continue largely on a regional basis.[106]   The U.S. must not only expand its own market by broadening NAFTA, but also think in terms of inter-regional competition for markets. The EU has already begun to take steps to create free trade links with Latin America.[107]   The U.S. should not concede the southern African market to Europe and by fostering the growth of a regional market in southern Africa, the U.S. will concomitantly forge a closer trading relationship with Africa.

The current Administration needs a conceptual lens that will foster a well-focused Africa policy. Promoting regional cooperation/integration, and thus regional stability is a cost-effective policy. As USAID director Brian Atwood recently argued, worldwide economic expansion is in the U.S. interest.[108]   In the post-Cold War era the United States should as assiduously build bridges to new markets, as during the Cold War it built walls to contain communism.

CHAPTER 12

ENDNOTES

1. The negative reaction to the Clinton Administration's June, 1994 conference on Africa is indicative of the lack of a well formulated U.S. Africa policy. Representative Donald Payne (D- NJ), the chief foreign policy spokesmen for the Congressional Black Caucus stated: "I have no idea what the focus of the conference is or what its intended goals are." The New York Times, June 27, 1994, p. A9. A headline in the London Financial Times stated: "White House Irritates Advocates for Africa," June 28, 1994.

2. The Congressional Black Caucus has taken a leadership position on U.S. policy for Africa. For instance, Jeffrey Herbst states that aid to Africa increased in the early 1990s due to the effort by the Congressional Black Caucus. Jeffrey Herbst, *U.S. Economic Policy Toward Africa* (New York: Council on Foreign Relations Press, 1992), p. 14. However, the Congressional Black Caucus is one of 28 caucuses for which the Republicans have promised to cut funding; The NAACP has recently voted to establish a mission in South Africa. *The New York Times*, July 13, 1994, p. A8. However, it to is facing severe financial constraints. There is an umbrella organization that seeks to build a U.S. constituency to promote African interest, "The Constituency for Africa," (CFA), which was founded in 1990 and became independent in 1994.

3. This is point is most poignantly reflected Randall Robison's, the head of Trans Africa, protest fast over Presidents Clinton's Haiti policy. Trans Africa leapt to the public consciousness in November 1984 when Robinson organized a protest outside the South African Embassy in Washington,. D.C.

4. Christopher Coker, "'Experiencing Southern Africa in the twenty-first century," *International Affairs* 67, 2 (April 1991), p. 283.

5. Thomas Ohlson and Stephen John Stedman, *The New Is Not Yet Born: Conflict Resolution in Southern Africa* (Washington, D.C.: The Brookings Institution, 1994), p. 3.

6. John Darnton, "'Lost Decade' Drains Africa's Vitality," *New York Times*, June 19, 1994, p. 1.

7. Thomas M. Callaghy, "Reform in a Weak Neighborhood: Economic Change and Democratization in Africa," Paper presented at the ISOP Conference on "Regime Change and Democratization Revisited in Comparative Perspective," U.C.L.A. May 19-21, 1994, p. 4.

8. Michael Clough, *Free at Last? U.S. Policy Toward Africa and the End of the Cold War* (New York: Council on Foreign Relations Press, 1992), p. 4.

9. Herman J. Cohen, "A View from the Inside," in Harvey Glickman, ed., *Toward Peace and Security in Southern Africa* (Philadelphia: Gordon and Breach Science Publishers), pp. 215-216.

10. Richard Sincere, *Sowing the Seeds of U.S. Economic Aid in Africa* (D.C. International Freedom Foundation, 1990), p. 1.

11. Jeffrey Herbst, *U.S. Economic Policy Toward Africa*, (New York: Council on Foreign Relations Press, 1992) p. 3.

12. Ibid., p. 4.

13. Michael Clough, *Free at Last*, p. 11.

14. Carol Lancaster, *U.S. Aid to Sub-Saharan Africa: Challenges, Constraints, and Choices* (Washington, D.C.: The Centre for Strategic and International Studies), p. 1.

15. Herbst, *U.S. Economic Policy*, p. 2.

16. Lancastor, *U.S. Aid*, p. 24.

17. Ibid., p. 28.

18. World Bank, *From Sustainable Growth*, p. 60. "In neopatrimonial regimes, the chief executive maintains authority through personal parentage, rather than through ideology or law., Michael Bratton and Nicholas van de Walle, "Neopatrimonial Regimes and Political Transition in Africa *World Politics* 46 (July 1994), p. 458.

19. John Gamble, *The Origins of the Marshall Plan* (Stanford: Stanford University Press, 1976), p. 269.

20. For an excellent historical account of U.S. promotion of regional cooperation and integration in post-World War II Europe see Michale J. Hogan, *The Marshall Plan: America, Britain, and the reconstruction of Western Europe, 1947-1952* (New York: Cambridge University Press, 1987), pp. 41-44.

21. Clough, *Free at Last*, p. 58.

22. Thomas Ohlson and Stephen J. Stedman, "Towards Enhanced Regional Security in Southern Africa," in Bertil Oden, ed., *Southern Africa After Apartheid: Regional Integration and External Resources* (Uppsala: The Scandinavian Institute of African Studies, 1993) p. 89.

23. Herbst, *U.S. Economic Policy*, p. 64.

24. Callaghy, "Reform in a Weak Neighborhood," pp. 13-14. For a more extensive treatment of this question, including detailed empirical analysis, see Thomas M. Callaghy, "Political Passions and Economic Interests: Economic Reform and Political Structure" in Callaghy and Ravenhill, eds., *Hemmed In: Responses to Africa's Economic Decline* (New York: Columbia University Press, 1993), pp. 463-519.

25. Stephen John Stedman, "South Africa: Transition and Transformation," in Stephen John Stedman, ed., *South Africa: The Political Economy of Transformation* (Boulder: Lynne Rienner Publishers, 1994), p. 10.

26. John Ravenhill, "A Second Decade of Adjustment: Greater Complexity, Greater Uncertainty," in Thomas M. Callaghy and John Ravenhill, eds., *Hemmed In: Responses to Africa's Economic Decline* (New York: Columbia University Pres, 1993), p. 18.

27. Reginald Herbold Green, "The IMF and the World Bank in Africa: How Much Learning?," in Callaghy and Ravenhill, eds., *Hemmed In*, p. 54.

28. *Adjustment in Africa: Reforms, Results and the Road Ahead* (New York: Oxford University Press, 1994), p. 1.

29. Ibid.

30. Tony Hawkins, "All Cards on the Table," <u>Southern African Economist</u> 8 (February 1993), p 46.

31. Ibid., p. 85.

32. Thomas Callaghy, "Africa: Falling off the Map," <u>Current History</u> (January 1994), p. 33.

33. In 1976 the Kinshasa Declaration was signed calling for an African common market as a prelude to an Economic Community. In 1980 the Economic Commission for Africa promulgated the Lagos Plan of Action (LPA). The LPA was an alternative development plan for the countries of Africa that envisioned cooperation through integration and self reliance. The

goal was an African Economic Community by the year 2000. In June 1991 the Abuja Treaty was signed reaffirming the LPA, but pushing back the creation of an Common Market until 2020, and a Pan-African monetary and economic union five years later.

34. John Ravenhill, "A Second Decade," p. 25. In fact the World Bank held a workshop on regional integration and cooperation as part of the study. See *The Long-Term Perspective Study of Sub-Saharan Africa: Volume 4. Proceedings of a Workshop on Regional Integration and Cooperation* (Washington, D.C.: The World Bank, 1990).

35. Ibid., p. 25.

36. Thomas Callaghy and John Ravenhill, "Introduction, Vision, Politics, and Structure: Afro-Optimism, Afro-Pessimism or Realism?" in *Hemmed In*, p.2.

37. David Gordon, "Debt, Conditionality, and Reform," in eds., Callaghy and Ravenhill, *Hemmed In*, p. 98.

38. John Ravenhill, "A Second Decade of Adjustment: Greater Complexity, Greater Uncertainty" in Callaghy and Ravenhill, eds., *Hemmed In*, p. 31.

39. *Sub-Sahara Africa: From Crisis to Sustainable Growth*, (Washington, D.C.: The World Bank, 1989), p. 3.

40. The term, "implicit bargain" is Thomas Callaghy's. See for instance, "Political Passions and Economic Interests," in eds., Callaghy and Ravenhill, *Hemmed In*, p. 476.

41. Callaghy, "Reform in a Weak Neighborhood,P. 8.

42. Ibid., p. 9.

43. Tony Hawkins, "Industrialization in Africa," in ed., Douglas Rimmer <u>Africa 30 Years On</u> (London, James Curry, 1991), p. 148.

44. Herbst, "The Structural Adjustment of Politics in Africa,". p. 949. See also, Richard Sandbrook, <u>The Politics of Africa's Economic Stagnation</u> (New York: Cambridge University Press, 1985), p. 67.

45. Herbst, "The Structural Adjustment," p. 949. See also Christopher Clapham, "The African State," in Douglas Rimmer, ed., <u>Africa 30 Years On</u> (Heinemann: Portsmouth, NH, 1991), p. 97.

46. Clapham, The African State, p. 103.

47. Sanjaya Lall, "What will Make South Africa Internationally Competitive," in Pauline Baker, Alex Boraine, Warren Krafchik, eds., South Africa and the World Economy in the 1990s (Washington: D.C. The Brookings Institution,), p. 55.

48. For IFIs as foreign devil see G.K. Helleiner, *The IMF and Africa in the 1980's* (Princeton: Princeton University, International Finance Section), p. 2.

49. Robert Davies, Dot Keet, Mfundo Nkuhulu, *Reconstructing Economic Relations with the Southern African Region: Issues and Options for a Democratic South Africa* (Cape Town: A MERG Publication, September, 1993), p. 40.

50. Ibid.

51. *Reconstruction and Development Programme* (Draft: For Discussion Purposes Only, For ANC Regions and Departments Only), 17th February, 1994, p. 6. See also Nelson Mandela, "South Africa's Future Foreign Policy," Foreign Affairs 72 (November-December), 1993.

52. The Southern African Development Coordination Conference (SADCC) was formed in 1980, and changed its name to the Southern African Development Community (SADC) in 1992. At the initiative of the ECA, the Preferential Trade Area for Eastern and Southern Africa States (PTA), now Comesa, was formally established in 1984. The Southern African Customs Union (SACU), originally formed in 1919 and renegotiated in 1969. The CMA was established in 1986 to work in tandem with SACU. It links Lesotho, Namibia and Swaziland in a "parallel currency union." Botswana was a member of CMA's precursor, the Rand Monetary Area, but withdrew in 1975.

53. The TEC was a parallel or shadow government created during the negotiations at Kempton Park that was to oversee the transition from the National Party government to the government of national unity that would follow the April 1994 election.

54. Personal communication with a member of the working committee.

55. The Africa Institute's report for the South African Chamber of Business (Sacob) is very similar to what Maasdorph argues is the general consensus among economist" for South Africa's integration into the region. Maasdorp, Project, pp. 45-46.

56. *Interview*, (Pretoria) 20 April 1994.

57. *Interview*, (Pretoria) 20 April 1994.

58. Gavin Maasdorph and Alan Whiteside, "Project on Rethinking Economic Cooperation in Southern Africa, *Regional Integration Conference* (Harare, 1992), p. 52.

59. Andre du Pisani, "Post-Settlement South Africa and the Future of Southern Africa," Issue: Journal of Opinion 21, 1-2, 1993, p. 61.

60. Albert Hirschman, The State of Economic Development (New Haven: Yale University Press, 1958). See also Gunnar Myrdal, Economic Theory and Underdeveloped Regions (London: 1957) on the notion of "spread" and "backwash;" and Bala Balassa, Economic Development and Integration (Mexico: Grafica Panamericana, 1965), p. 123. Amitai Etzioni explains that in more successful cases regional integration is able to postpone redistribution issues, Amitai Etzioni, Political Unification (Huntington, N.Y.: Krieger, 1974), pp. 324-327.

61. Richard Higgott, "Africa and the New International Division of Labor," in, eds., Callaghy and Ravenhill, *Africa in Economic Crisis*, p. 297.

62. Business Day November 22, 1993, p. 10.

63. *Reconstructing Economic Relations*, p. 48.

64. Harvey Glickman, "Issues in the Analysis of Ethnic Conflict and Democratization Process in Africa Today," Draft Introductory Chapter to the volume, Ethnic Conflict and Democratization in Africa (revised version as of November 1994).

65. Jeffrey Herbst, "The Structural Adjustment of Politics," World Development Vol. 18, 1990. p. 955. For an edited volume that deals directly with the security implications of ethnicity see Michael E. Brown, Ethnic Conflict and International Security (Princeton: Princeton University Press, 1993).

66. Herbert Adam and Kogila Moodley, "Political Violence, 'Tribalism', and Inkatha," *Journal of Modern African Studies* 30:3 (1992), p. 508.

67. Since the May elections Butheliezi's hold on Kwa Zulu Natel as slipped. *New York Times*, October 21, 1994.

68. David Welsh, Domestic Politics and Ethnic Conflict," in Michael Brown, ed., *Ethnic Conflict*, p. 58.

69. Anthony Lake, "A Strategy of Enlargement and the Developing World," *U.S. Department of State Dispatch* October 25, 1993., p. 749.

70. *Hearings of the African Affairs Subcommittee of the Senate Foreign Relations Committee: Subject, The Situation in Sub-Sahara Africa*, Federal Information Systems Corporation Federal News Service, March 24, 1994.

71. Ibid.

72. Thomas L. Friedman, "What Big Stick? Just Sell?" *The New York Times*, October 2, 1994, p. A3.

73. Anthony Lake, "A Strategy of Enlargement and the Developing World," Address to the Overseas Development Council, Washington, D.C., October 13, 1993. *U.S. Department of State Dispatch*, October 25, 1993.

74. The Republican controlled Congress reportedly will seek to cut the 1994 $13.7 billion foreign aid budget by 15 to 20 percent. And, the $1 billion in annual aid to Africa seems to be targeted for the most severe cut. *The New York Times*, December 12, 1994 "Foreign Aid and G.O.P.: Deep Cits Selectively," p. A6.

75. Cape Times (Cape Town) April 8, 1994, p. 9.

76. Bruce Stokes, "South African Gold," *National Journal* June 11, 1994, p. 1336.

77. Ibid., p. 1341.

78. *The New York Times*, August 3, 1994, p. D2.

79. Ibid., p. D2.

80. Robert Davies, "Emerging South African Perspectives," in Oden, ed., *Southern Africa*, p. 79.

81. The Star (Johannesburg) October 23, 1993, p. 8.

82. Joan Spero, U.S. Secretary for Economic, Business and Agricultural Affairs, "The U.S. and the Global Economy," *1994 U.S. Department of State Dispatch* September 26, 1994.

83. Ibid., p. 661.

84. McCarthy, "South Africa as Cooperative Partner," *Regional Integration Conference* (Harare, 1992), p. 8.

85. The concern of regional players over a South Africa centric American policy is reflected in a statement by a member of the SADC secretariat: "You seem to have also accepted the Western concept that South Africa is the linchpin and everything revolves around South Africa,"   Personal communication (SADC Secretariat), September 13, 1994.

86. *The New York Times*, October 6, 1994.

87. *Budget of the United States Government: Appendix Fiscal Year 1995*, (Washington, D.C.: Government Printing Office), p. 76.

88. Ibid., p. 88.

89. Ibid., p. 70.

90. *Public Papers of the President*, May 3, 1994.

91. Although the U.S. apparent coincidence of interest with South Africa in the region, particularly during 'constructive engagement of President Reagan and his Under Secretary pf State for Africa, Chester Croker naturally had an anti-SADCC bias, the U.S. became the second country to open a regional office to manage a SADCC aid budget. Ibbo Mandaza and Arne Tostensen, Southern Africa: In Search of a Common Future (Gaborone: Southern African Development Community), p. 89-92.

92. *International Relations Act of 1993*, 103rd Congress, House Rept. 103-126 (Part 1 of 2).

93. *Budget of the United States Government: Appendix Fiscal Year 1995*, (Washington, D.C.: Government Printing Office), p. 76.

94. Hearing Testimony, May 24, 1994, Ruth R. Harkin, President Chief Executive OPIC, Senate Appropriations/Foreign Operations FY 1995, Foreign Operations Appropriations.

95. Brian Atwood, "U.S. Offers 'Special Initiative' for Southern Africa," *USIA Wireless File*, January 28, 1994, pp. 2-3.

96. Business Day (Johannesburg) April 20, 1994, p. 3.

97. Budget of the United States Government: Analytical Perspectives, Fiscal Year 1995, "Table 7-1: Budget Authority by Function & Program, pp. 151, 155.

98. George Moose, "U.S. Support for New Business Opportunities in South Africa," U.S. Department of State Dispatch November 1, 1993. p. 770.

99. Ohlson and Stedman, The New Is Not Yet Born, p. 8.

100. Ibid., p. 4.

101. Various estimates of the cost of South Africa's destabilization of southern Africa during the 1980s state that the amount of foreign aid to the region equals the cost of destabilization. See Peter Meyns, "The New World Order and Southern Africa in the 1990s," in Anthoni Van Nieukerk and Gary van Staden, eds., Southern Africa at the Crossroads: Prospects for the Political Economy of the Region (Johannesburg: South African Institute for International Affairs, 1991), p. 76.

102. Herman J. Cohen, "Peace-Keeping and Conflict Resolution in Africa," U.S. Department of State Dispatch April 19, 1993.

103. Ibid., p. 271.

104. Howard W. French, "In Africa, the U.S. Takes a Back Seat" The New York Times, October 28, 1994., p. A6.

105. The New York Times, February 7, 1994, p. 1.

106. The New York Times December 12, 1994, p. A1.

107. The New York Times December 7, 1994, p. D2.

108. Brian Atwood, Speech at the U.S. Summit on Africa Aid," February 3, 1995.

Chapter 13

A Diamond Is Forever: The Triumph of Mandela, The Survival of Chief Mangosuthu Buthelezi and F.W. de Klerk, and How the African National Congress Ended Up on the United States Payroll

Mandela is the president of South Africa, an event of monumental significance in world history. It is a great personal triumph for him and a vindication of his struggle. But now that the South African elections are finally over, it is high time the record was set straight about what really happened and why.

With the press concealing as much as it reported, with ideologues of all stripes rushing around to rationalize their hypocrisies, and with American politicians spreading around largesse as if the money was their own, it is rather remarkable that the results were so perfect, so historically so symmetrical. But because those with power, or who are connected to it, do not want the facts about the funding of the election to be known because it would reveal a pattern of deception and control, both to influence the outcome and to moderate the African National Congress, and because those on the radical left don't want it known that the ANC has compromised itself by joining the list of organizations taking money from the United States, because they think it will hurt the cause of revolution, everyone involved, across the ideological spectrum, has joined in a kind of game to cloud the minds of the observers.

Most hypocritical was perhaps the attempt to make a devil out of Chief Mangosuthu Buthelezi by characterizing him as the tool of the oppressors and an obstructionist in the transition to democracy. His anomalous situation in post-apartheid South Africa led to suggestions that he was an enemy of democracy and the cause of dissension that has led to violence in an attempt to disrupt the electoral process that black South Africans have struggled for decades to achieve. Chairman of the Inkatha Freedom Party and chief minister of KwaZulu, this prince and leader of the nation founded by Shaka Zulu was then cast in the role of villain and reactionary. But it was not always so.

The triumph of Nelson Mandela and the African National Congress in South Africa was, for many years, viewed in certain circles as an extremely undesirable result. During the Cold War, the power of the South African Communist Party in the ANC made the ANC unacceptable as a holder of power in a post-apartheid South Africa. Yet, because apartheid and the white supremacist Nationalist Party were anathema to the rest of Africa and because white racism fueled the sentiments for communism among the black majority in South Africa, a reliable black alternative to the ANC became essential. As Harry Rositzke, CIA station chief in New Delhi from 1957 to 1962 and coordinator of operations against Communist parties abroad from 1962 until his retirement from the CIA in 1970 wrote in 1977: "In Africa, an area of primitive, unstable states, Soviet influence is substantial in Somalia, Guinea, Nigeria and Angola. The support of black independence movements against the Rhodesian and South Africa governments may extend that influence. The training of five thousand African students each year in the Soviet and East European universities is a direct investment in the future leadership of a largely illiterate continent."[1] Noting the "Chinese competition the Soviets face in... the South Africa liberation movements ," Rositzke argued candidly for covert action: in the Third World: "Do we try to make a deal with the leftists-covertly at least to start? Do we take any covert political action to ensure the continued supply of chrome from a black Rhodesia that threatens to boycott its sale to the United States if we do not withdraw our investments in South Africa? However unlikely these scenarios, we cannot forecast what will   happen in the economic world to threaten our prosperity."[2]   These insights led to a policy that did not distinguish between anti-communism and opposition to apartheid. Indeed, they became synonymous in South Africa as that policy came to a head in the Reagan administration.

As Gregory Treverton has observed: "For the Reagan administration, the intended signal was anti-communism. For it, there was nothing incompatible about supporting anti communism in Angola and anti-apartheid in South Africa."[3] This was because United States anti-apartheid policy was always   primarily   a   tool   of   its   anti-communism   policy.   And   that anti-communism policy was directly related to the preservation of American "prosperity" and economic self-interest, as Rositzke explained. To this end, the CIA   funneled money into Africa Bureau, a London-based anti-apartheid group headed by the Rev. Michael Scott, an Anglican priest dedicated to ameliorating the harsh apartheid policies of South Africa in South West Africa. Dan Schecter, Michael Ansara and David Kolodney wrote in 1970, "The United States remains involved in channeling money to various factions within southern-African liberation movements, hoping, of course, to mold them in pro-Western directions."[4]

Long before the Reagan administration, white liberals in the United States and South Africa understood the threat of communism in South Africa and took action, in concert with the CIA, to undermine that threat, even if this delayed, by necessity, the end of apartheid. And ultimately, Buthelezi became a key figure in that effort. The leading American liberal politician to first become actively involved in the anti-apartheid movement was then United States Senator Hubert Humphrey.

In 1960, a press agency, International Features Service, was established, largely to disseminate the thoughts of Hubert Humphrey to the people of the Third World, including Africa. International Features was quickly reorganized as a not-for-profit organization, Peace for Freedom, liberally supported with CIA funds through the International Development Foundation and the Price Fund.[5] Another organization that was launched with CIA assistance was the United States South Africa Leadership Exchange Program (USSALEP) when the African-American Institute, a CIA conduit,[6] agreed to add USSALEP to its existing projects. A key functional area of USSALEP was, and is, "flexible independent exchanges, providing opportunities for leaders in any variety of fields to confer with colleagues."[7] In 1983, Harris Wofford, currently U.S. Senator from Pennsylvania and then, as now, a member of the management committee of USSAELP, stated to me that Buthelezi deserved support because he had stayed in South Africa, unlike leaders of the ANC, and had not engaged in violence.[8] Wofford handed me the USSALEP bulletin and made it very clear that he was speaking not only for himself, but for his organization.

Wofford served as President Kennedy's special representative to Africa from 1962 to 1964 before he became associate director of the Peace Corps. The implication was clear: Buthelezi was with us but Mandela, who often espoused pro-South African Communist Party sentiments, was not. And a major non-governmental backer of USSALEP was AMAX, the American mining giant, on whose board has served both Presidents Ford and Carter.

It was in 1959 that Allard Lowenstein, then a foreign policy aide to Senator Humphrey, traveled to South Africa and South West Africa to gather data on the effects of apartheid in both territories. During the course of this trip, Lowenstein was approached by the CIA in South Africa and requested to smuggle a "Cape colored" student, a member of the anti-SWAPO Herero tribe from Rehoboth, South West Africa, out of South Africa.[9] Beukes would later be accused of subverting SWAPO when it expelled him in 1976.[10] Lowenstein would later write a book on his South African experience entitled Brutal Mandate. A leading American liberal who had served as president of the National Students Association and a civil rights activist, Lowenstein was recruited to the CIA in 1962 as an expert on southern Africa.[11] From 1962 to 1967, Lowenstein traveled to southern Africa and had contacts with various southern African personalities both in Africa and the United States, providing the Agency with his assessment of their political leanings and their reliability. The ANC, which had taken up armed struggle on December 16, 1961 with the founding by Nelson Mandela of Umkhonot We Sizwe, "Spear of the Nation," and with its Communist support, was becoming a threat. Mandela was a cult figure of the left who had enormous appeal. Until his capture, his ability to elude the police had made him a folk hero.

In the spring of 1962, Lowenstein was contacted by both the American Committee on Africa and the CIA-supported American Society for African Culture, which were joining forces for a demonstration and protest march on behalf of Nelson Mandela, Walter Sisulu, and the seven others who had been arrested by the South African police when the ANC underground headquarters was discovered. While the United States did not want Mandela martyred, neither did it want him in power. The arrested leaders were on trial and faced the possibility of the death penalty, which in South Africa was administered by hanging but because of the organized pressure, Mandela and Susulu were not executed but sentenced to life in prison, with Mandela remaining on Robben Island as the preeminent figure in the African National Congress.

With the day to day operations of the ANC passed to Mandela's far less charismatic law partner, Oliver Tambo, who had fled to Zambia, the ANC was seemingly neutralized without the United States to blame. The CIA was looking for alternatives to the ANC. To the ANC's left, the CIA directed money to the ultra-black nationalist Pan Africanist Congress, which had organized the demonstration, from which the ANC abstained, that led to the Sharpeville massacre in the spring of 1960.[12] As early as 1961 Mandela discounted the Pan Africanist Congress because, he asserted, "there is no doubt in my mind that they preached an extreme form of racialism."[13] Mandela believed the abandonment of non-violence and the introduction of the use of force to be justified because, "[N]o leader is going out to say we want peaceful discussions because the government is making that kind of talk senseless. Instead of getting a favorable response, the government is more arrogant. The African reaction can only be a show of force." Notes of the secret interview given by Mandela to Patrick O'Donovan were provided to Lowenstein in London by Mary Benson, an anti-apartheid activist.[14]

To rival Spear of the Nation, which had begun a campaign of sabotage against "the symbols of apartheid" staging rocket attacks against police stations, the PAC launched Poqo, a mass movement modeled on the Mau Mau in Kenya. Claiming a membership of 150,000, it engaged in acts of terrorism and although it never could achieve the strength of the ANC, it would come back to haunt South African politics by initially refusing to take part in the first one person one vote non-racial elections in the country's history. Having become a Frankenstein's monster of the CIA, the Pan Africanist Congress ceased to be an acceptable alternative to Mandela and the ANC, but it continued to pose a sufficient threat to possibly disrupt the electoral process.

Throughout the Sixties, Lowenstein made considerable use of his expertise on revolutionary movements in southern Africa in ways that would have an important impact on United States policy. From his vantage point in the intelligence community, he argued for an anti-Communist alternative on the left, becoming a key figure, in the parlance of the Agency, of the "good wing" of the CIA. As one CIA operative described this element in the Agency to Harris Wofford, "If you only knew what we're really doing, the liberals and the leftists, the democratic leftists, what we're supporting around the world, you'd see that we represented the 'good wing' in the CIA."[15] And, in his pursuit of an anti-Communist left alternative in South Africa, while he acknowledged that the blacks had ample reason to resort to violence,[16] he faulted the ANC, as did the Agency, on the grounds that it was engaging in armed struggle with support from the Soviet Union and The People's Republic of China, not to mention its alliance with the South African Communist Party.

In his 1966 swing through southern Africa, Lowenstein conferred with representatives of the ANC in Dar es Salaam, whose quarters in which they met featured a large portrait of Mao Zedong. When Lowenstein asked them how he could be of help, the black South Africans told him that what they needed was money for arms. They were engaged in armed struggle and wanted weapons, not the limited support Lowenstein had provided in the past, and which China had eclipsed. It was at this point that Lowenstein concluded that the ANC was unreliable and uncontrollable and therefore totally unacceptable.[17] But as the entire Cold War liberal structure began to come apart during the Vietnam war, Lowenstein turned his efforts to getting rid of Lyndon Johnson and to replacing him with Bobby Kennedy and to his own political career, winning election to Congress in 1968. He would not return to the South African scene until the late seventies when, following a stint as one of President Jimmy Carter's ambassadors to the United Nations, he traveled extensively in southern Africa at the behest of the CIA and Harry Oppenheimer, scion of the South African De Beers and Anglo-American gold mining and diamond empire.

In the interim, the fruitless search for an alternative to the ANC continued as violence escalated in South Africa and it became increasingly threatened by the possibility of a revolution led by the South African Communist Party and the ANC. It was during this period that the fortunes of Buthelezi began to rise. Although in the pay of the government of South Africa as chief minister of the KwaZulu government, Buthelezi steadfastly refused to permit KwaZulu to be turned into a "homeland," which would have been an acceptance of the government's apartheid policies. It was this posture of at least nominal independence, as well as his identification with the mythic Zulu people, that led him to be able to play both sides with consummate skill. Never a sycophant to the National Party, which had formalized a system of total racial segregation and which had controlled South Africa since 1948, when the old United Party of Jan Smuts had been defeated, he appealed to those who never had any use for white liberals like Helen Suzman, whose Liberal party had been outlawed and who maintained a life of luxury in the midst of a system she purported to detest.

As the cast of "Wait A Minim," the South African musical comedy mocked, "the only thing the liberals hate more than apartheid is the blacks." Buthelezi, highly intelligent and articulate, played the role of the radical conservative to the increasing attention of the United States. Capable of appearing fiercely traditional one minute in tribal dress and handsome and immaculate in a Saville Row suit the next, Buthelezi began to capture the imagination of the power brokers. He not only spoke all the languages of South Africa, he seemed to speak to the economic and political needs of the country, with its astonishing diversity, as well. There was a vacuum and he appeared to be the only player capable of filling it. With Buthelezi and his ideas for a federal republic of South Africa, investment would be safe, whites and blacks could be placated. Even his appeal to royalty, his professed loyalty to the King of the Zulus, Goodwill Zwelethini (also his nephew), impressed whites who sought modest change in the context of stability and blacks, for whom royalty had always held a certain attraction as a dimension of African pride. If a black African leader for South Africa could have been created by the Reagan administration, it would have been Buthelezi.

With Reagan in the White House and William Casey at CIA, the "good wing" would be out and the hard line in. There was no such thing as a left alternative to communism in this ideology, only a right alternative that was indeed "right." Under Reagan, Buthelezi would fit the mold, as Zavimbi did in Angola, where South Africa and the CIA together aided his efforts against the leftist government, with its pro-Soviet sympathies.   Indeed, conservatives world-wide began to support Buthelezi, with particular support coming, according to a former U.S. "Africa hand," from Germany through such conservative semi-political foundations as the Adenauer Schiftung and the Ebert Schiftung17a, much in the manner that Casey was able to get other countries such as Saudi Arabia to aid the Contras in Nicaragua. Buthelezi had been, according to this source, promised a "Greater Natal" by hard-line apartheid Prime Minister Botha, who offered him the possibility of having white areas such as Durban in his power base. With such an increase in his domain, in an election, were it to happen, he would be able to command at least the five percent that was ultimately established as a basis for a seat in the cabinet and be a sufficient force, along with white representation in the cabinet, to moderate the policies of a leftist government under Mandela and block either nationalizations or confiscatory tax policies.[18] But before this scenario began to take hold, the liberals gave it one more shot to find an alternative to Mandela and the ANC that was not so conservative as to alienate the majority of blacks, who might still turn to the far left. At this point, in Seventies, Lowenstein once again entered the scene, with Buthelezi playing to both liberal and conservative factions. According to South Africa expert Professor William Foltz of Yale University, during the 1970s, Buthelezi was being "courted by South African big business and some American corporations."[19] He mentions AMAX, the mining giant with extensive South African holdings that was also a USSALEP backer through its AMAX Foundation,, as one of these. The leadership effort in approaching Buthelezi, Foltz explains, was not American business interests but the liberal part of South African industry, particularly Harry Oppenheimer, whose Ernest Oppenheimer Memorial Trust, the charitable arm of Anglo-American, was also backing USSALEP, Helen Suzman, and Clive Menell, chair of Anglovaal Holdings, Ltd. a mining giant, who lives across the street from Harry Oppenheimer in South Africa and who entertained Buthelezi in the presence of Professor Foltz in his home. Foltz explains that it was Buthelezi's refusal to let KwaZulu be a homeland that made him attractive to the Oppenheimer crowd, as he could not be seen as a tool of apartheid. Although highly ambitious and thin-skinned to slights, real or apparent, Buthelezi was regarded by them as a "reasonable and interesting alternative, at least a serious player."

Wofford was right: USSALEP, which had been launched with the CIA's help, and which had been passed along to the powerful South African and American corporate interests so it proclaim by 1980 that "USSALEP receives no funding, direct or indirect, from the United States, South African, or any other government," was now behind Buthelezi, seeing nowhere else to go. By the mid-seventies, the exploitation of uranium in South West Africa had made South Africa's role there a major international issue, as the large block of nonwhite Third World countries pressed for its independence.

In April of 1975, Lowenstein attended a key symposium on "The Outlook for Southern Africa, which was backed by the Johnson Foundation that was funded by USSALEP and the Johnson and Johnson pharmaceutical company and held at the Johnson Wingspread conference facility in Wisconsin. The symposium explored ways to prevent the worst from happening from the point of view of the American, South African and British companies that invested heavily there. South Africa was described as "the Saudi Arabia of minerals,"[20] and South West Africa had once again become vitally important to the West because of Britain's dependence upon it for uranium. Rio Tinto Zinc, a multinational mining company based in Britain, was exploiting that uranium at the Rossing mine, the world's largest single source of uranium.

Lowenstein's analysis at the Wingspread symposium was classic "good wing." Will we identify with the oppressed people, including those of South Africa?" Because Africans were finding that the only way to produce change was through violence, this was playing "into the hand of the Soviet Union and China," who were providing money and training which were, in fact, producing results. Lowenstein asked the rhetorical question,"Can we influence Africans to accommodate their demands in less violent ways? Only if we pressure for the necessary reforms at an acceptable pace. This means finding ways for South Africa to get out of Namibia and Rhodesia, to permit Black regimes to develop in both states. Instead of 'buffer states' there might emerge on the border of South Africa the appearance of privileged sanctuaries so that the pressure for change within South Africa would be stepped up. As the international dimensions proceed, they are the priority; the domestic ones should follow. Eventually, changes within South Africa will have to occur. If they do not come non-violently and in a rapid, evolutionary way, they will be forced with sabotage, violence and warfare."[21]

After his stint at the United Nations, where he clashed with Andrew Young over United States policy in Zimbabwe/Rhodesia (Lowenstein was strongly opposed to Robert Mugabe and wanted a role for white liberals), and visited South Africa where he held lengthy meetings with young Afrikaner Nationalists, Lowenstein came back in from the cold. It was not only through his involvement with the powerful white liberals of South Africa, but his relationship with Frank Carlucci, appointed deputy director of the CIA by Jimmy Carter and who had been stationed in South Africa when Lowenstein traveled there in 1959, that enabled him to continue his work in southern Africa in the summer of 1979. This vitally important trip was financed by Anglo American, which paid Lowenstein $7,000 for his services,$1,000 to his aide, Mark Childress and $1,000 to Lowenstein's secretary. Included, for the summer's expedition, was a comfortable house in Johannesburg with recreational facilities and domestic servants, and full transportation, including return air fares on the Concorde for Lowenstein, Lowenstein's three children and Childress. All of this was arranged by Hank Slack, the American Director of Anglo American and the former son-in-law of Harry Oppenheimer.[22] Lowenstein was working closely with Deputy C.I.A. Director Frank Carlucci, who stated categorically that "Lowenstein would report to me."[23] And there was much to report. Lowenstein first consulted with Theo-Ben Gurirab of SWAPO, at SWAPO headquarters in New York and departed for South Africa. There he held meetings with Buthelezi, Harry Oppenheimer, Helen

Suzman, Pik Botha, the South African Foreign Minister and P.W. Botha, the South African Prime Minister. He also met with Mandela, still incarcerated on Robben Island.[24] Richard Moose, Jimmy Carter's Assistant Secretary of State for Africa, told Sam Adams, formerly of CIA, that Lowenstein was talking to "a lot of opposition groups."[25] What Lowenstein was doing was laying the ground work for a flexible American policy in South Africa, forged with the wealthy South African white liberals and the "verlicht" Afrikaner Nationalists to dismantle with structure of apartheid without Marxist revolution. Lowenstein's role in this venture was cut short when he was shot to death in 1980 by Dennis Sweeney, a former recruit in the civil rights movement in Mississippi, but the legacy of his involvement remained a potent one.

Frank Carlucci, who admired Lowenstein and was greatly influenced by him, shared Lowenstein's assessment that the problems of South Africa could be "worked out."[26] And Buthelezi had good reason to believe that he was, at the very least, part of the solution and not the problem.

With the election of Reagan in 1980, United States and South African intelligence (BOSS, the South African C.I.A.) increased cooperation on behalf of Jonas Zavimbi, with the CIA authorized $15 million for UNITA.[27] With his German money coming in, Buthelezi was becoming the darling of American conservatives, including Jeane Kirkpatrick, Reagan's Ambassador to the United Nations, a "sound anti-Communist alternative."[27] The Washington Times and the Wall Street Journal would take up his cause. But according to William Foltz, there was a significant split in the Reagan administration, with Reagan's Assistant Secretary of State for Africa, with Chester Crocker, "opposed to Buthelezi," "playing a much more complicated game."[28] Foltz explains that Crocker thought it wise "not to see any single person as the answer."[29] And although he credits British Ambassador to South Africa at that time, Sir Robin Renwick, as being "highly skillful" in his efforts to prevent violence and bring about a peaceful solution in South Africa (Renwick is generally acknowledged with having obtained Mandela's release from prison, a task made easier by the fact that his government had not imposed sanctions on South Africa, thereby giving it some leverage with the white regime in Pretoria), Foltz argues that the "whole situation was sliding rapidly" and that the "logic" of the Reagan administration's policy was "coming apart."[30]

The support of American industrial interests for Buthelezi began to diminish as it appeared that he might not be able to deliver in the face of enormous public support for Mandela. The final push, Foltz, explains, was the 1986 sanctions legislation, which altered the situation irrevocably. With Mandela now a legend among American blacks as a symbol of the triumph through struggle over apartheid, he could no longer be shunted aside. His ANC was the ultimate force in South Africa, and Buthelezi, with his base limited to the Zulus, was without a national organization capable of overcoming it. But with his financial support still coming from Germany, Buthelezi was, according to Foltz, able to retain the services of the powerful Washington p.r. firm, Black, Manaforte, with him and his people still using the rhetoric of the Cold War, "not about the ANC but the ANC and the Communists."[31] But the mining companies were, according to Foltz, no longer interested and Buthelezi's support was limited to "the fast buck people in Natal."[32] And while Buthelezi may, at one point have been able to get the 5% needed for a cabinet position, the "old Africa hand" believed, he argued (incorrectly, it turned out) that Buthelezi would be "hard pressed" to carry the Zulu vote. Because the young Zulus are now more urban than rural and identify increasingly with the ANC, he maintained that Buthelezi's power base was substantially eroded, notwithstanding continued German support and support from private American conservative groups.[33]   Foltz puts it more forcefully: "He (Buthelezi) is playing a destructive and scandalous role now."[34] But who was actually paying for that role and, in effect, funding the blood bath that lasted until Inkatha reentered the elections?

Reenter USSALEP, now no longer stating that it does not to receive funds from any government directly or indirectly, but indicating overtly that it is funded, in part, by the United States Agency for International Development and the National Endowment for Democracy. In its 1992 Program Update, (Vol.1, No.1, 1993), in a short note entitled "Transition to Democracy Project," USSALEP proclaims: "The $8,000,000 cooperative agreement, under which subgrants of $4.8 million for the African National Congress (ANC) and $2.6 million for the Inkatha Freedom Party were to be disbursed by September 30, 1992, was extended for an additional 15 months in order to utilize the full amount obligated by USAID. The purpose of the project is to build administrative capacity within the ANC and the IFP organizations to enable them to participate more effectively in the negotiations leading to a new constitution and democratic government. Due to the very stringent disbursement conditions (which, for example, eliminated the category of salaries as a permissible expenditure category under the original budgets), coupled with administrative/absorptive capacity limitations of the sub-grantees, only approximately 45% of the $7.4 million could be expended during the originally scheduled, 13-month project life. "The monies disbursed to date have been used to:(i)acquire or rent office space to house central and regional staff, (ii)purchase and install computer hardware and software and train personnel needed to establish effective management information systems, and (iii)pay for sundry travel, consulting and workshop expenses relating to the above and to the formulation of policy options and negotiation positions.. "USAID and USSALEP are presently in discussion with the subgrantees to identify new areas of expenditure not previously included in their budget proposals. Among those being considered is the critical one encompassing peace initiatives."[35]

Hired as Project Manager of the Transition to Democracy Project was Stanley Kahn, a South African sociology professor of the faculties of both the University of Witwatersrand and Cape Town, who had served as executive director of the Funda Centre in Diepkloof, Soweto and who was the recipient of a USSALEP Alan Pifer Fellowship to visit the United States to "survey the contribution of community colleges to adult education."[36] Kahn has been promoted to Director of USSALEP South Africa. Kahn may be a fine fellow, but it still sounds a lot like "walking around money." And if salaries were being paid to ANC and Inkatha, who was getting the money? Buthelezi? Mandela? And if these groups were getting the money, who decided that more than twice as much should go to the ANC as to Inkatha? It is also worthy of note that Harris Wofford still serves on the Board and Council of USSALEP, which dispenses the funds from the AID budget that Wofford votes for as a Senator. His past legal practice has involved major clients in Africa. Apart from this seeming conflict of interest, it should be of concern to American tax payers that their money is going to influence the outcome of an election in a foreign country, however overt this funding might now be. All the old players are still there, Harry Oppenheimer, who funds USSALEP through The Anglo American & DeBeers Chairman's Fund, Clive Menell, Chairman of Anglovaal Holdings Ltd.(contributor and Board and Council member), and an old Buthelezi backer, and Hack Slack, now president and CEO of MINORCO in London (contributor and Board and Council member), as well as all the major industrial concerns, American, International and South African, that control the vast mining interests of South Africa and the rest of its economy. The result of all of this funding of the competing parties? R.W. Johnson, a native of South Africa and a fellow in politics at Magdalen College, Oxford, who is on leave from Oxford to write about current South Africa and also to serve as national co-director of the Launching Democracy project, a public information service for all South African political parties, sponsored by the Institute for Multi-Party Democracy (one wonders about the source of its funding), observed: "Some of the killing is political: currently the largest set of victims are Inkatha officials killed by the ANC, though the most publicized recent killing was that of Chris Hani, the SACP (Communist) leader, by the white Right. The Azanian People's Liberation Army, the armed wing of the Pan Africanist Congress, carries out anti-white atrocities from time to time, and, of course, Inkatha takes its vengeance on the ANC with fair regularity."[37]

While this was going on, with whites panicking, and a state of emergency declared in KwaZulu because of an inability of Mandela, Buthelezi, King Goodwill Zwelethini and de Klerk to come to an agreement on how to resolve the impasse and get Inkatha back into the election process,[38] Buthelezi denounced what he described as "a lengthy Machiavellian manipulation commenced, right at the start of our negotiations, with attempts to marginalize our Inkatha Freedom Party."[39]   If he was referring to the inequitable distribution of the AID money between the ANC and Inkatha, he certainly made up the difference from the Germans. And how effective giving money to the ANC will be in wooing it from the South African Communist Party ally remains to be seen. Mandela insists the ANC is not Communist, but that it remains loyal to its oldest ally and friend.[40]   Moreover, the relisting as a USSALEP sponsor of the African American Institute, a CIA conduit in the past that helped launch USSALEP, also means that CIA money still, in all probability, flows covertly to certain organizations in South Africa. The most likely candidate is the CIA's old client, the Pan Africanist Congress, whose overt support the ANC would never accept, to keep it in the electoral process and then accept the results. But the amount of money given to the Pan Africanist Congress, has surely been minuscule, given its lack of a function at this point of history. The purpose was not to get it votes, but keep it quiet.

After the supposed failure of former Secretary of State Henry Kissinger (now an international business consultant) and former British Foreign Minister Lord Carrington (who has served on the board of Rio Tinto Zinc, which controls the Rossing uranium mine in Namibia) to bring Buthelezi into the elections, all seemed to be lost,[39(a)] but an amazing last minute reprieve was finally achieved, and the elections went forward in the midst of bombings by white extremists. Helping the Independent Election Commission to supervise them to make sure they were "fair" was S.A.F.E., or South African Fair Elections Fund, funded largely by American interests and headed up by liberal Kennedy loyalist, Ted Sorenson, who had $7 million at his disposal for "voter education." According to Ian Williams of the New York Observer, "many if those involved in SAFE haven't concealed their hopes for an A.N.C. landslide."[40(a)] And while Williams reports the A.I.D. funding of both the ANC and Inkatha, he neglects to even mention USSALEP, the eminence grise of the whole sordid business. But even with A.I.D. funding much of the election and SAFE providing additional assistance to assure the right kind of acceptable "left" victory, and while Ron Brown, Clinton's man at Commerce, announced $140 million in aid to South Africa (a good portion of this will find its way into the pockets of North Carolina academics and their institutions, Duke, Chapel Hill and North Carolina State, who are participating in the $350 million South African research and manufacturing center to be built in Muizenberg, a suburb of Cape Town, which has the backing of the ANC,[40(b)] (no wonder arch-conservative, anti-Communist Senator Jesse Helms of North Carolina has failed to denounce the U.S. AID funding of the Communist-backed ANC- he makes an unlikely pair with Harris Wofford), the ANC and Buthelezi both shouted "fraud" as the election came to a close.

(Actually, the only institution that should cry fraud is North Carolina's predominantly black university, Jesse Jackson's alma mater, North Carolina A& T, which has mysteriously been excluded from the A.I.D. boondoggle.) Meanwhile, one party that began to pick up surprising support in the final hours was the old bastion of white supremacy, the National Party, as it appealed to the "colored" vote, those of mixed race who tend to be better educated and to own property, and to conservative blacks. F.W. de Klerk, ("F.W." as he is referred to affectionately) holding black babies, managed to remind South Africans of every color that "majority rule" in Africa can be less than paradise. Rwanda, Somalia, Angola, Zaire and the Sudan are shattering reminders of the chaos so often associated with post-colonial "liberation." He has managed to do the impossible; prevent the ANC from getting the two thirds seats in parliament it needed to ram through its economic agenda that is supported by the South African Communist Party. In five years, de Klerk's party will be in a position to form a coalition with Inkatha not unlike the Democratic Turnhalle Alliance in Namibia (formed with Lowenstein's support and assistance), which also managed to prevent the prevailing revolutionary group, SWAPO, from getting the two thirds it needed to nationalize the mineral wealth. Once again, white American liberals have failed to appreciate the innate conservatism of some black Africans and their willingness to work with whites, even their former oppressors, out of fear that they might lose their property to a "revolutionary" regime, even one financed by the United States government and supported by Jesse Helms and Harris Wofford, the "Odd Couple" of American politics.

If a post-Mandela ANC splits apart, as some South Africans have predicted, and with the South African Communist Party marginalized, a National/Inkatha Party could well become a real force in South Africa. There is a certain logic to this; the Boers and the Zulus have always had a common enemy; the British and their English speaking South African allies in the mining industries. But as the Boers and Zulus are pro-business, they pose no threat to the great companies and families that have controlled the South African economy since the Boer war. Meanwhile, Mandela has begun to make all the right noises, from the point of view of his American supporters. He has pledged not to confiscate the property of whites and not to tax in a way that will discourage foreign investment and profit. He has also made it clear that he will not tolerate disorder; he expects everyone to go back to work and back to school. Mandela did not spend all those years in prison to preside over a country in chaos and anarchy. Like Buthelezi, who is actually a close friend of his, Mandela is a descendent of African royalty, and if the ANC and Inkatha have accepted U.S. dollars, as they have, from the Americans who caused the perpetuation of apartheid for Cold War reasons, there is more than enough irony in this to justify their actions. Mandela has started to resemble his predecessor in African liberation, Jomo Kenyatta, who was jailed for a very long time on charges of being a Mau Mau terrorist and then released in time to stop a violent revolution. It was Kenyatta who suppressed his opposition and allowed the whites to keep control over the Kenyan economy. But if Alec Erwin, a white Communist ANC candidate can declare that there "was nothing sacrosanct" about limiting the budget deficit to 6% of the GNP, as the IMF had required the ANC to pledge prior to granting a loan, and if the ANC can stop mentioning this IMF requirement as part of the ANC's program,[40(c)] clearly more was necessary to make sure the worst did not happen. The election results, which all the parties have now accepted as "free and fair," produced some surprises, with the ANC polling 62.5%,less than the 67% required for control over the constitution, but more than enough to control patronage and 12 cabinet seats. de Klerk and the NP, which won control of the Western Cape, got enough votes over 20% for de Klerk to be one of the two executive vice presidents and 4 cabinet seats, and probably a higher percentage of the black vote than the Pan Africanist Congress, a relic of Cold War history, which received scant support in the election. Also disappearing into oblivion was the Democratic Party, which is nothing more than the reconstituted old Liberal Party that Allard Lowenstein had backed. Once banned by the primitive white racist South African government and later reinvented as the Progressive Party with the help of Harry Oppenheimer, it is basically the personal vehicle of Helen Suzman, who has spent as much effort fighting the ANC as apartheid. But Mandela has indicated that he would consider offering cabinet posts to representatives of parties which polled less than the required 5%, a carrot to the Pan Africanist Congress if they agree to behave themselves. Inkatha received over 10% enough to put Buthelezi in the cabinet and give Inkatha a total of four cabinet seats, a result his critics said was impossible. His total was augmented, and de Klerk's reduced, by the fact that some white Afrikaners voted for Buthelezi on the national level and the NP on the provincial level to bolster black opposition to the ANC. The white separatist Freedom Front ended up with about 3%, indicating that the white racist call for a boycott of the elections was only marginally successful. Together, these three provide an opposition of over a third of the voters, not counting those who boycotted the election.[41] Buthelezi, whose Inkatha also carried KwaZulu/Natal, which his critics claimed he would never be able to do, summed up: "I'm grateful that up to now, in spite of all the skullduggery and the cheating, so far it has not flared up into any conflict or violence."[42] And it is not likely to.

Buthelezi is now the Home Minister, which puts him in charge of internal affairs and makes him the boss of Sidney Mufamadi, the black chief of the police who is also a member of the central committee of the South African Communist Party. And if South African Communist Party chairman

Joe Slovo is now head of Housing and Welfare and Joe Modise, the black commander of Spear of the Nation is Minister of Defense (albeit assisted by the existing chief of staff, General Georg Meyring, a white Afrikaner, who remains in his post), Derek Keyes, de Klerk's white Afrikaner Minister of Finance will continue to run the economy in the same position. Mandela's selection of the ANC's Thabo Mbeki as the other executive vice president left the able Cyril Ramaphosa out of the cabinet and the government entirely, although he remains as the chairman of the ANC, in which capacity he is in charge of drafting the new constitution. An incredible balancing act, overall, there is something for almost everyone, at which the CIA must be heaving a considerable sigh of relief.[42(a)] With the Cold War over, who cares if a couple of Communists clank around in the South African government as long as things are basically under control?

The Goldsmith Commission, which had investigated the role of the police in the violence prior to the elections, meanwhile, is looking ahead to 1999, when the "real" elections will take place. There will be a need for new leaders who comprehend the serious economic problems of the country, as perceived by the International Monetary Fund. USSALEP no doubt stands ready to provide these leaders. The only question is whether the United States government will continue to finance their campaigns. But while the pundits debate the meaning of the election, De Beers continues to control 80 per cent of the world's diamond trade, "with 50 percent of these diamonds by value coming from the company's own mines in South Africa, Botswana and Namibia,"[42(b)] and Jonathan M.E. Oppenheimer, Harry Oppenheimer's grandson and the son of Nicholas F. Oppenheimer of Johannesburg, deputy chairman of the great mining giants, the Anglo American Group and De Beers Consolidated Mines, Ltd., the latter founded by Cecil Rhodes with the backing of the Rothschilds, who represents the next generation of Oppenheimers, continues his work as a management trainee at N.M. Rothschild & Sons in London.[43]

Politicians may come and go, but as the De Beers ad says on television, "a diamond is forever."

CHAPTER 13

ENDNOTES

1. Harry Rositzke, The CIA's Secret Operations-Espionage, counterespionage and covert action (New York, Readers Digest Press, 1977) p. 254.

2. Rositzke, supra, at 256, 266.

3. Gregory F. Treverton, Covert Action-The Limits of Intervention in the Postwar World (New York, Basic Books, 1987) p. 220.

4. Dan Schecter, Michael Ansara and David Kolodney (African Research Group) "The CIA as an Equal Opportunity Employer," in Dirty Work 2, The CIA in Africa Ellen Ray, William Schaap, Karl Van Meter, Louis Wolf, eds. (Secaucus, N.J. Lyle Stuart, second printing, 1980) p. 51, first published in Ramparts in 1970 and referring to The Politics of Unity by I. Wallerstein).

5. Schecter, Ansara and Kolodney, supra.

7. "The USSALEP Story 1958-1980."

8. Interview with Harris Wofford, May 18, 1983.

9. My sources for this were: Tom Gervasi, who served as a counterintelligence officer assigned to the Army Security Agency and the author of Arsenal of Democracy I (New York, Grove 1978) and Arsenal of Democracy II (New York, Grove, 1981), and who was writing a history of the CIA at the time of his death, allegedly from lead poisoning from handling toy soldiers he collected; Sam Adams, who served with the CIA in the Southern Africa Branch, DDI, at the time Lowenstein worked for it, and then switched to the Southeast Asia Branch, and who was writing a history of the role of the CIA in Vietnam at the time of his untimely death from an alleged heart attack. Gervasi's book was never published, while Adams' unfinished manuscript was finally published in 1994, years after his death, denying him the opportunity to both complete it and defend it against his critics. The book has so far attracted little attention. Adams was at my house in Bridgehampton for dinner not long before his death. He was in excellent health. See Sam Adams, War Of Numbers (Steerforth Press, South Royalton, VT, 1994). See also William Chafe, Never Stop Running-Allard Lowenstein and the Struggle to Save

American Liberalism (New York, Basic Books, 1993, note 13, p. 494: "It is noteworthy that the NSA's international vice president, who was working for the CIA, once again asked Lowenstein to do some student government chores while in South Africa." Chafe does not elaborate further, but as Lowenstein attended the Congress of the National Union of South African Students while in South Africa during the trip and had kept up his ties to the CIA-backed U.S. National Student Association, the smuggling out of Beukes would constitute such a "chore."

10. Interview with then SWAPO Representative to the United Nations, Theo-Ben Gurirab, May 5, 1983. Curiously, Gurirab, whom I interviewed at SWAPO's headquarters in New York and a close advisor to Sam Nujoma, the SWAPO leader and currently Namibia's head of government, referred to William Buckley as one of his closest friends in New York. Buckley has acknowledged serving in the CIA.

11. Gervasi and Adams, note 9, supra, were my sources for this. This is confirmed by a document in Lowenstein's CIA file which I obtained via the Freedom of Information Act. Document No. 10, dated 19 February 1962, a memorandum addressed to the Chief of Personnel, Security Division, OS, from the Chief of the Contact Division, OO, states: "It is requested that priority security checks be procured on Subject as described in the attachment. Our deadline is 23 February 1962 for approval to contact Subject on an ad hoc basis. Subject, reportedly has stated that he has done some work for CIA. If he were used in a (whited out) capacity, then this is an indiscretion regarding which our field representative would like to know something about the background before contact is made." Other portions of the document are whited out. This document has been confirmed to me by two former CIA station chiefs (Moscow and Saigon) as a "recruitment document." The "work" for the CIA to which Lowenstein was referring is clearly the smuggling of Hans Beukes out of South Africa. AS the former Moscow station chief explained to me, Lowenstein was not a CIA "agent," which is a term of art referring usually to foreigners under contract with the Agency for specific periods of time and for specific purposes, but rather a "consultant" to be used on an "ad hoc" basis. Such people, I was told by the former Moscow station chief, are generally older than the normal recruits to the Agency. Lowenstein's situation at the time of his recruitment was that he was in his thirties, an academic who taught courses on the politics of southern Africa. Academics in such situations have been routinely recruited to the CIA. While such persons can be used as analysts, the former Moscow station chief explained, they can also perform "operations," as Lowenstein did, including the providing of funds to political organizations. Ironically, while the CIA was recruiting Lowenstein, the FBI, on March 29, 1962, concluded that Lowenstein had never been

connected to the CIA, noting that as late as January 9, 1961, the CIA had advised the FBI that Lowenstein never had a relationship with the intelligence agency. Evidently, the FBI checked no further after that date, as Chafe indicates when he concludes, "None of this evidence is definitive." Chafe, supra. Further, in a letter dated January 23, 1985 to Bancroft Littlefield, a former Lowenstein aide who had married Lowenstein's ex-wife after she had divorced Lowenstein, lee Hamilton, chairman of the House Intelligence Committee said: "Based on representations made to me, I can say that Mr. Lowenstein was never an agent (italics added) of the CIA" Chafe, supra, note 20, page 509. To Chafe, this is also not conclusive. As explained, Lowenstein was not a CIA agent and was not recruited as one. He was recruited as an expert consultant. When I requested a copy of the letter from the CIA to Hamilton, Thomas K. Latimer, Staff Director of the U.S. House of Representatives Permanent Select Committee on Intelligence, wrote on August 5, 1985: "Mr. Hamilton has asked that I respond to your letter of July 30, 1985 regarding certain correspondence to this committee from Mr. Briggs of the Central Intelligence Agency. The correspondence you referred to is classified and therefore cannot be released. I regret that we cannot be of assistance to you in this matter." They are clearly hiding something. Further, the exchange between the CIA and the FBI is an example of the ongoing war between those two agencies over turf and budget.

12. The International Confederation of Free Trade Unions (ICFTU), whose executive board was taken over by the AFL-CIO, gave the money for the establishment of The Federation of Free African Trade Unions (FOFA-TUSA) in 1959, which was intimately connected with the PAC. Barry Cohen, "the CIA and the African Trade Unions," AFRICA magazine, September 1976, Dirty Work 2, supra p. 77. Jay Lovestone, who served as the Director of the Department of International Affairs for the AFL-CIO "was one of the Central Intelligence Agency's most important men." Joan Davies African Trade Unions (Harmondsworth, Penguin, 1966) p. 201. A former member of the Communist Party, U.S.A., Lovestone, who was actually expelled from the Party, waged the Cold War from his vantage point in the American labor movement. In "Fight US. Subversion of Trade Union Movement in Africa!" B.S. Nyameko directly accused the CIA of creating the Pan Africanist Congress to undermine the Communist-backed African National Congress. He wrote; "Throughout Africa labour organizations are infiltrated by CIA agents posing as private individuals or under non-official cover, as employees in private companies or as U.S. Embassy staff in the Information Department and Labour Attache men succeeded in establishing the PAC in 1959 to disrupt our ANC." The African Communist, No 87, Fourth Quarter, 1981, pp. 56-57.

13. Patrick O'Donovan secret interview with Nelson Mandela, May 30, 1961.
It is widely believed that the CIA fingered Mandela to the South African
police, which would have been an inside job, almost certainly one of the white
liberals pretending to be supporter. Lowenstein was privy to the secret
interview and may well have participated in the fingering of Mandela.

14. Richard Cummings, the Pied Piper-Allard K. Lowenstein and the Liberal
Dream (New York, Grove, 1985) at 136.

15. Interview with Harris Wofford, supra. Other CIA "good wingers" of that
generation included the Rev. William Sloane Coffin, Jr. (See Coffin, Once To
Every Man, New York, Atheneum, 1977), author and naturalist Peter
Matthiessen, for whom the Paris Review was his cover and who, according to
James Linville, the Managing Editor of the Paris Review, is "haunted by the
CIA." Conversation with James Linville, Oxford, Miss. April 1993, at 40th
anniversary celebration o The Paris Review' (The New York Times first
reported Matthiessen's CIA employment), Gloria Steinem, who worked for
three years for the Independent Research Service, an organization totally
supported by the CIA and whose purpose was to disrupt Communist youth
festivals. This was first disclosed by Ramparts and later reported in The New
York Times in 1967. See Press Release, May 9, 1975, Redstockings of the
Women's Liberation Movement: Letter from Jane Barry of Redstockings, 19
February 1987, and ultra liberal author/activist Robert Sam Anson (Interview
with Robert Sam Anson, May 1985). The theoretical intellect behind "good
wing" ideology in the CIA was Harry Rositzke, who argued that democracy
and capitalism were not necessarily synonymous and that the United States
should support progressive social democratic or democratic socialist
approaches in critical countries. See Rositzke, supra. at 268.

16. See Allard Lowenstein and John Marcum, "Force: Its Thrust and
Prognosis," in South Africa In Transition, (New York, Praeger, 1966): "In the
absence of internal collapse in Portugal and of external intervention in South
Africa and Southern Rhodesia, the period of violent upheaval may be
prolonged. Neither collapse nor intervention now appears likely, and the
legacy of European settlement in southern Africa may consequently be hatred
and destruction of catastrophic proportions. This prospect will not dissuade
Africans from force. It will be recalled that Americans fought an extended
War for Independence that was prompted by grievances that look paltry
compared to those now present in southern Africa." Praeger, the publisher of
the paper, which was given at a conference at Howard University in 1963
sponsored by the American Society of African Culture, a CIA front, was later
revealed by Ramparts to have had a CIA affiliation.

17. Interview with Hal Minus, Lowenstein aide on 1966 trip, March 1981.

17a. Telephone interview, 5 April 1994.

18. Paul Taylor of The Washington Post has provided an excellent overview of the South African scene prior to the elections in "Outlook," Washington Post, Sunday, April 3, 1994.

19. Telephone interview with Professor William Foltz, April 4, 1994.

20. South Africa: Policy Alternatives for the United States." Report of a Wingspread Conference convened by the Johnson Foundation, April 1975, Racine, Wisconsin. Others in attendance were George Hauser of the American Committee on Africa, Africanist Gwendolen Carter and Donald F. McHenry of the Carnegie Endowment for Peace and later Andrew Young's deputy and then replacement at the United Nations in the Carter administration. See also Alun Robert, The Rossing File (London, Namibia Support committee, CANUC, 1980).

21. Wingspread Report, supra.

22. Letter to Hank Slack from Ernest Wentzel, June 12, 1979; telephone interview with Ernest Wentzel, Johannesburg, Aug. 9, 1983.

23. Interview with Frank Carlucci, July 19, 1983.

24. Memo by Mark Childress, undated.

25. Moose quoted by Adams, telephone conversation with Adams, 1982.

26. Interview with Carlucci.

27. See Treverton, Covert Action, supra, at pp. 220-221.

27. Interview with Professor William Foltz, supra.

28. Foltz, supra.

29. Foltz, supra. See, generally, Chester Crocker's memoir, High Noon in Southern Africa (1991).

30. Foltz, supra.

31. Foltz, supra.

32. Foltz, supra.

33. Foltz, supra.

35. USSALEP 1992 Program Update, Vol. 1, No. 1, January 1993, p. 1.

36. USSALEP 1992 Program Update, supra, p. 7.

37. R.W. Johnson, "Beloved Country-R.W. Johnson in South Africa," London Review of Books, Vol. 15, No. 13, 8 July 1993, p. 3.

38. See Bill Keller, "Zulu King, Rejecting Budget for Patronage, Refuses to Halt Election Boycott," The New York Times International, Saturday, April 9, 1994, p. 6; Paul Taylor, "zulu Leaders Still Opposed to Vote," The Washington Post, Saturday, April 9, 1994, p. A18.

39. Managosuthu Buthelezi, "We Reject Unfair South African Election," Viewpoints, Newsday, Friday, april 1, 1994, p. A41.

39(a). See Steven Greenhouse, "Kissinger Will Help Mediate Dispute Over Zulu Homeland," New York Times, Tuesday, April 12, 1994, p. 8.

40. Allister Sparks, "south Africa: The Secret Revolution," The new Yorker, April 4, 1994, p. 67.

40 (a). Ian Williams, "CEOs and Barbra Fund South African Dream," New York Observer, May 2, 1994, p. 18.

40(b). The Chronicle of Higher Education, April 27, 1994, A36.

40(c). See R.W. Johnson, "Here for the crunch-R.W. Johnson in South Africa," London Review of Books, 28 April 1994, pp. 3, 5-6. Johnson points out that Ben Turok, "another white Communist, best known for his denunciation of the (World) Bank and the (International Monetary) Fund for 'attempting to install bourgeois democracy and so-called free markets in the Third World,' was installed as the top ANC official for economics. Johnson argues that the ANC will either have to borrow or print more money to finance its grandiose development plans, a policy that runs counter to the position of both the

World Bank and the IMF and which could damage the economy in a country that is presently "prudent and under-borrowed."

41. See New York Times, Monday, May 2, 1994, pp. A1, 10.

42. Francis X. Clines, "Mandela and de Klerk Meet on Picking a New Cabinet," New York Times, Wednesday, May 4, 1994, A8.

42(a) See Bill Keller, "Mandela Picks Old Comrades To Fill His New Government," The New York Times, Saturday, May 7, 1994, pp. 1, 8 (Which old comrades?); Bill Keller, "Mandela Completes Cabinet, Giving Buthelezi Post," The New York Times, Thursday, May 12, 1994, A8.

42(b) Suzanne Possehl, "Diamond Deal Stirs Regret in Russia," The New York Times, Business Day, Saturday, May 14, p. 37.

43. The New York Times, Sunday, December 26, 1993, Style, p. 10 ("Miss Ward, Mr. Oppenheimer"). For a history of Cecil Rhodes and the Oppenheimers, see Geoffrey Wheatcroft, The Randlords (New York, Atheneum, 1986) and Anthony Hocking Oppenheimer and Son, New York, McGraw Hill, 1973).

Note to the Notes

Finance Minister Derek Keys has announced his intention to resign in the fall of 1994, citing "personal reasons." New York Times, Wednesday 6 July 1994, A4. He will be replaced by Chris Liebenberg, who is also white and a prominent former bank chairman. As Keys is a member of the National Party and Liebenberg is technically an independent, de Klerk will have the right to name another Nationalist to the cabinet to keep his total of six. In actuality, he will have seven, as Liebenberg is very much part of the old establishment, a quick gain by de Klerk to increase his growing influence. Liebenberg is expected to follow Keys' pro-business policies.

The Democratic Party, the personal vehicle for Helen Suzman of the old Liberal Party, while not part of the national government, since it failed to win enough votes to gain representation in the cabinet, did win control of the city council of Johannesburg, where it is actively involved in crushing the squatter rebellion of poor blacks who seek to have the national government provide them with land, as the ANC had promised during the campaign.

Allard Lowenstein's connection with the CIA did not begin with his trip to South Africa and Namibia in 1959. It began in 1951, as a recently released CIA document reveals. An inter-office CIA memo from Milton W. Buffington to CSP (Lewis S. Thompson) dated 17 February 1951 (CIA Cold War Records, The CIA under Harry Truman, Michael Warner, ed., History Staff, Center for the Study of Intelligence, Central Intelligence Agency, Washington, DC 1994) discloses that at a CIA conference on the National Student Association held by Allen Dulles, the Director of the CIA and Dr. William Y. Elliot, it was decided that the CIA should obtain a draft deferment for the staunchly anti-Communist Lowenstein, who was threatened with conscription at the time of the Korean war, in order to allow him to serve s president of the National Student Association, thereby enabling him to thwart the efforts by left-wing students, led by the International Vice President, Herbert Eisenberg, to gain control over the organization. The memo makes clear that the CIA had accomplished the "penetration" of the National Students Association, and intended to "subsidize" specific NSA international projects. The CIA control of the NSA's international programs stems from this date, during which time Lowenstein was serving as the NSA's president. The NSA, through its international division, would develop close links with the south African National Union of Students and would afford Lowenstein the opportunity of developing close contacts that would be of considerable importance to him and the CIA. For example, Ernest Wentzel, who was pivotal in planning Lowenstein's trip to South Africa in 1979, when Lowenstein was reporting to CIA Deputy Director Frank Carlucci, was an old National Union of Students contact.

In Britain, an enigmatic Kenyan with the unlikely name of Washington Okumu is now being credited with mediating the deal between Mandela and Buthelezi to bring Inkatha back into the elections (See CAM, The University of Cambridge Alumni Magazine, Easter Term 1994, p. 36). A graduate of Harvard with a Ph.D. from Cambridge, where he was at King's College, Okumu has homes in London and Nairobi and is executive director of the Jubilee Centre, a Cambridge, England based "Christian research group." A what? But there was another reported possible enticement for the Zulus' return to the election process; the deeding to King Goodwill Swelethini by de Klerk of a large and valuable estate in KwaZulu/Natal.

* * *

Richard Cummings has worked for the Office of General Counsel, US AID, Near East South Asia region and has taught at St. Catherine's College, Cambridge, Addis Ababa University, Ethiopia, The University of the West Indies, Barbados and Pace University School of Law, where he has taught

International and Foreign Relations and National Security Law. A graduate of Princeton and Columbia Law School, he holds a Ph.D. in Social and Political Sciences from Cambridge University and writes on intelligence matters, international affairs and world politics.

Chapter 14

Can Political Democracy Co-exist with Economic Concentration?
The Case of South Africa

Using examples in the banking industry, the paper discusses the issue of concentration of ownership and control of large corporations in South Africa. Contending that the newly found political democracy is jeopardized by this concentration, the paper suggests that the private sector must be proactive in addressing this problem before the government takes the initiative. It proposes several practical ways by which this can be accomplished.

Introduction

In the aftermath of the historical elections that were recently held in South Africa (SA), the world watches as the new Government of National Unity (GNU) charts the course toward the establishment of a non-racial, non-sexist, democratic social order in the country's post-apartheid era. Now that political democracy has been attained, the next challenge for the country's GNU will be the restoration of economic *equity* without significantly compromising economic *efficiency*. Without a doubt, the goal of economic equity cannot be fully realized without addressing the distribution of economic power in and around large corporations in SA. It is with that goal in mind that this paper proposes to address this issue, specifically focussing on questions such as: who controls large corporations in SA, and for the pursuit of what goals? How can the interests of workers, investors, and society at large be best served by large corporations? Implied in this dialectic is the issue of corporate self-interest on one end, and national priorities on the other. To resolve this conflict, some have suggested the adoption of the stakeholder approach to corporate governance. Briefly, the stakeholder approach posits that corporations are social institutions whose responsibilities cannot be limited only to one group of stakeholders, i.e., the share- and bondholders. In their decision-making, managers are responsible for weighing and balancing the

287

interests of all stakeholders broadly defined as individuals or groups that can affect or can be affected by the goals, policies, practices, actions, or decisions taken by the corporation[1]. Given the far reaching influence that large--especially the multinational--corporations have in national economies, other writers have recommended that the stakeholder model be augmented with the "social contract" approach which is applicable to both domestic and multinational corporations[2]. The social contract approach helps to distinguish between fundamental, social contract related duties of an organization and supplemental, derived duties to investors. Because they constitute the moral basis for the legitimacy of the corporate existence, social contract-based duties will often override derived duties[3].

The paper begins by discussing the dynamics of power and corporate control. It then lays the basic tenets of Mintzberg's Conceptual Horseshoe model[4] which is used as a scaffolding upon which we discuss ways and means by which power can be distributed in and around large corporations. Next, the paper will turn to the concentration of economic power in SA, with specific reference to the Banking industry. This section indicates how ownership and control of corporations has become increasingly concentrated. Arguments for and against corporate concentration are presented, and implications of corporate concentration for a future South Africa are discussed. The paper contends that the private sector must be proactive in addressing the issue of the concentration of corporate power, suggesting some practical ways by which this can be accomplished.

Power

The extant literature on power in corporations is wide and varied. This section gives a brief definitional overview of what is understood by power in the context of the paper and the implications of its concentration in large corporations.

Defining Power

The concept of power, which is of fundamental importance in the running of organizations, has been treated in different ways in the social sciences. Scholarly writings about power are prolific and yet diverse, with the result that our understanding of the construct and its implications has remained limited. Hopefully the recent growth in interest especially in the concept of empowerment will help direct the focus of scholars who are interested in the enabling aspects of power[5]. In general, definitions of power refer to the existence of an asymmetrical influence relation between the behavior of two people; the ability of person X to make person Y do those things that person Y would otherwise not do; or the net dependence of person

A on person B[6]. These definitions imply that power is the ability to produce an intended effect, or the ability to employ force[7]. What power seems to boil down to is a "potential" force which, when put to use in organizations is known as organizational politics[8]. The running theme through many of the definitions is that power enables one (individual or group) to better achieve the outcomes one desires. The research further categorizes the sources of power elaborating on the merits of each[9]. One such categorization is French & Raven's five power bases which can be further divided into personal power bases (expert power and referent power), and position power bases (reward power, coercive power, and legitimate power). Social exchange theorists interpret power as a function of dependence: when A's performance outcomes are contingent not only on their behavior but on others' (say B's and/or C's) performance or responses, then B and/or C have power over A[10].

Power in Use

To understand how power is used in different corporate settings, two power paradigms can be delineated. These are the power accumulation paradigm and the power sharing paradigm[11].

The power accumulation paradigm. Some scholars have noted how, over the years, the broadening of the definition of power has made it synonymous with control[12]. Under the power accumulation paradigm, the tendency is to accumulate as much power as possible in order to use it to effect the desired outcomes. In other words, it is used as a control mechanism. However, the type of compliance obtained when power is used this way is usually contractual, involvement in the task, calculative, and those who comply are usually alienated[13]. At the extreme, power accumulation leads to corruption especially where there is no concomitant responsibility and accountability. This immediately brings to mind Lord Acton's famous cliché: power tends to corrupt, absolute power corrupts absolutely. Scholars have warned that if corporate power is not used responsibly, society might withdraw the legitimacy they give to corporations. This belief has been enshrined in the well known "iron law" of responsibility: "In the long run, those who do not use power in a manner which society considers responsible, will tend to lose it"[14].

The power-sharing paradigm. An alternative paradigm to power-accumulation as a means to get things done is the power-sharing paradigm. The underlying tenet of this paradigm is that in order to bring about the desired behaviors of others, a process of distributing and sharing of power, rather than accumulating it, may be more effective[15]. Unlike the power-accumulation paradigm, the driving force of the power-sharing paradigm is that power is not a zero-sum game but it actually increases the total amount of power in the organization[16]. Accordingly, sharing power actually creates a bigger "power pie" and results in an empowered workforce which can unleash its creativity in the operation of the total organization. This is, in fact, one of the fundamental attractions of the Total Quality Management concept[17]. In a country such as SA, which is grappling with how power can be distributed more equitably, the empowerment paradigm would be more germane. It seems logical that by empowering others, an environment can be created in which a sense of self-efficacy will result and mutual trust and respect will be the by-product.

When applied to corporations, however, power assumes more significant proportions because of the pervasiveness of the modern corporation. Writers like Galbraith noted how the world order is changing into one in which people increasingly serve the convenience of the same large corporations which were meant to serve them[18]. In this regard Deetz, in his book *Democracy in an Age of Corporate Colonization* notes:

> The modern corporation has emerged as the central form of working relations and as the dominant institution in society. In achieving this dominance, the commercial corporation has eclipsed the state, family, residential community, and moral community....Corporate practices pervade modern life by providing personal identity, structuring time and experience, influence education and knowledge production, and directing entertainment and news production[19].

The norms and values that emanate from corporations have the potential to restructure the customs and practices of society as a whole in ways that parallel the church in medieval times. Moreover, corporate power can impact society at different levels. For example, Epstein identified four such levels which he labelled macro (the totality of business corporations), intermediate (groups of corporations as in a cartel), micro (the firm), and individual (the chief executive)[20]. Each of these levels has a certain amount of intensity that drives the level of complicity desired by the power player involved. This leads to questions regarding concentration of power in and around large corporations.

Concentration

Concentration has typically been measured by economists in terms of the proportion of an industry's output, value added, sales, assets, market share, or employment accounted for by the largest four or eight organizations[21]. For example, in some instances economists use the Herfindall index to measure the extent of industrial market concentration[22].

Accordingly, the more concentrated a market, the more economic power is in the hands of a few dominant organizations. Other researchers have studied concentration of power by measuring the ratio of managers, proprietors, and officials to the total work force in a city[23]. In this case it was found that concentration of power was positively related to the probability of the city undertaking and completing urban renewal projects which are in the interests of the managers/proprietors. Another measure related to the distribution of resources in a given country is the Gini Coefficient which measures the extent to which income distribution departs from a uniformity. For example, if distribution were to be perfectly uniform, the Gini Coefficient would be zero. On the other hand, if resources were inequitably distributed, the Gini would approach unity.

By any of the above measures, there is no question that the distribution of resources and control in SA are grossly inequitable, with power concentrated in the hands of few. When one considers market concentration, one finds that SA's eight largest corporations control more than eighty percent of the nation's major business activity through either direct ownership or pyramid-like cross ownership structures[24]. McGregor noted that about 80 percent of the JSE is controlled by Sanlam, Old Mutual, Liberty Rembrandt, and Anglo-De Beers[25]. Anglo American Corporation (AAC, $14.6 billion capitalization) is not only the biggest company on the Johannesburg Stock Exchange (JSE) but it is also the controlling share holder of the diamond cartel leader DeBeers Consolidated Mines Ltd., the second-largest company on the JSE. DeBeers, in turn, owns shares in the food concern Premier Group Holdings Ltd., another company that is controlled by Anglo American[26]. This criss-crossing of ownership happens not as an exception but with remarkable regularity[27]. Because of the historical imbalances in education and restrictions in property holding rights and employment opportunities under apartheid, the second indicator of concentration of power--the ratio of proprietors and managers to the rest of the population--also indicates high concentration. Similarly, the Gini Coefficient has been reported to be around 0.6 for SA, indicating that income is highly inequitably distributed in South Africa, with whites being the biggest beneficiaries. It is noteworthy that ownership concentration is not a new phenomenon in SA but has existed for a long time. The most recent restructurings in the banking sector of the economy are interesting and worth singling out.

Restructuring of the Banking Sector

Up until the mid-1980s, the SA legislation prevented mutual building societies from entering the commercial banking sector. Their business operations were limited to the issuance of insurance policies and housing loans. The key legislature that precipitated the entrance of building societies into commercial banking was based upon the recommendations of the De

Kock Commission whose fundamental position was that deregulation would spur the stagnant economy. The Building Societies Act was passed in 1986 with provisions for conversion from mutual-based to equity-based ownership structures. Concomitant with the wave of restructuring was a trend toward mergers and acquisitions. Smaller banks were being taken over by the larger building societies-turned-banks. For example, United Building Society merged with Volkskas Bank to form United Bank. Then United Bank began a bid to acquire Allied Bank. The biggest beneficiary of this acquisition was Anton Rupert's Rembrandt Group since it owned significant interests in both banks. The move drew significant outcries in the financial sector that the Rembrandt Group wanted to monopolize the financial services sector of the economy. It also resulted in a counter-bid from another player, the First National Bank (FNB) controlled by Anglo American Corporation. United Bank finally outbid FNB resulting in the birth of a new giant, Amalgamated Banks of South Africa (ABSA) which took the overall leading position of the financial sector along with four other banks, i.e. SBIC, FNB, Nedcor, and Bankorp. Since then the ABSA has acquired Bankorp reducing the total number of banks controlling more than 80 percent of the financial sector to "the big four." The composition of the financial sector of SA in terms of market share is presented in Figure 1[28].

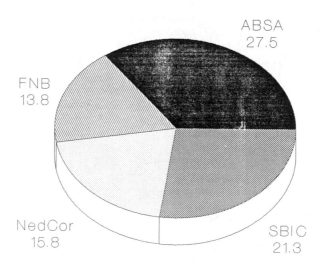

The discussion above demonstrates just how much corporate ownership still remains concentrated in the banking sector in SA. With redistribution being one of the goals of the GNU in post-apartheid SA, strategies will have to be devised about ways and means of reconciling the reality of the existence of these highly concentrated economic sectors with the ideal of equity restoration. Unbundling of the conglomerates need not come at the expense of economic performance as the following example demonstrates.

The Unbundling of Gencor

The propensity of the unbundling of conglomerates to unlock shareholder wealth is demonstrated by the case of Gencor Ltd., the world's second-largest mining house after AAC. In the fall of 1993, Gencor divested itself of all its non-mining assets totalling $0.6 billion. These included a paper pulp company (SAPPI Ltd.), an oil company (Engen--formerly Mobil before the latter divested from SA), a food and engineering company (Malbak), and an investment company (Genbel). After the divestiture, Gencor's stock rose from approximately 5.20 to 8.60 rand a share[29]. It follows that the unbundling of conglomerates would have a positive impact on the expansion of the economic pie which is a necessary precondition for the distribution of wealth in the country. The next section is a review of the elements of Mintzberg's horseshoe model.

The Conceptual Horseshoe Model

This section borrows heavily on Mintzberg's Conceptual Horseshoe Model (CHM) in which he proposed a range of ways whereby corporations can engage in the distribution of power within the communities in which they exist[30]. These include options such as to "nationalize" the corporation, to "democratize" it, to "regulate" it, to "pressure" it, to "trust" it, to "ignore" it, to "induce" it, or to "restore" it. Mintzberg visualized the options as being in the shape of a horseshoe, with "nationalize it" on the left end, "restore it" on the right, and "trust it" being in the center symbolical of the natural balance between social and economic goals. The options are listed on Table 1 and will now be discussed in turn.

Nationalize it. Why is it that state-run companies are now regarded as taboo? Perhaps the biggest reason is the recent collapse of the former Soviet Union which seems to confirm that command economies are much less efficient than market economies. In SA, state controlled enterprises have existed and some still continue to exist. There are several reasons why it was necessary to have such organizations in the past. Three of them are: in areas where certain critical industries would never have been started or kept responsive to national needs without government involvement (e.g. Sasol); when processes of production and distribution could be most efficiently carried out through supply by a single entity (Escom); and when activities of an organization must be intricately intertwined with government policy, that organization is best managed as a direct arm of the state (Armscor)[31]. The African National Congress (ANC), the biggest winner (62.5 percent of the popular vote) in the recent elections, was once in favor of nationalization as means of fundamentally restructuring the SA economy. An uproar from potential investor abroad combined with a heightened need for foreign investments to stimulate the economy prompted the ANC to change that position and pronounce a preference for a free-enterprise economy with possible "state participation in certain specific areas of the economy, like mining, the financial institutions, and monopoly industries"[32]. Given the realities on the ground, we think that "nationalize it" is the least preferred option for SA, one should be held out as a last resort to be followed when there is absolutely no hope for distribution of economic power.

Democratize it. This is a less extreme position the aim of which is to broaden the corporate power base by expanding it to other stakeholders both internal and external to the corporation. Examples are customers, workers, or even neighbors down the road. Of course, there has always been a natural, built in tension between the free market economic system and democracy. Free markets, on one hand, are driven by economic efficiency, self interest, and impersonal mechanisms. Democracy, on the other, is driven by goals of equal say, rule by majority choice, and a desire for fairness. Left unfettered, the former would lead to greater inequality in wealth and opportunity, whilst the latter would result in a relatively uncompetitive economy[33]. The "democratize it" option should thus be seen as placed within that dialectic.

The reader is parenthetically reminded not to lose sight of the different connotations that the term democracy impute in African and Asian contexts as a result of the historical legacy of colonization. In Africa, for example, the colonial powers withheld democratic rights from blacks because of the "rampant illiteracy", and their inability to "think concretely, coherently, and logically."[34] Within that context, SA corporations have had a history of companies preferring to use liaison committees whose role on boards has been mainly to "liaise" on behalf of the workers. Since such liaison committee members were usually not democratic representatives of the workers, agreements reached with them usually lacked the credibility necessary to gain acceptance by the workers on the shop-floor. A good example is demonstrated in the strong criticism levelled at Ford Motor Company's withdrawal by its SA work-force and some black trade unions who accused Ford of being paternalistic. In this instance, Ford had taken the precaution to consult their worker representatives about their pending divestiture from SA but, unfortunately, it turned out that these "representatives" did not have the mandate of the broader workforce[35]. The recent experience of corporate executives who have had to deal with black trade unions in SA has shown that collective bargaining is something that comes naturally to many balcks. As one executive noted after trade unions were legalized in the late 1980s, "blacks have taken to negotiations the way ducks take to water." To be meaningful and effective, however, democratization should be coupled with labor force education as well as ongoing training of the labor leadership.

Regulate it. Different types of regulation have different objectives, affect different segments of the population, and involve different costs, and have different methods by which they are accomplished. In the economic sphere, regulation can be used to curtail anti-competitive behavior in highly concentrated industries (e.g. price-fixing); to allocate limited space (airlines, broadcasting); to prevent predatory pricing (transportation); to provide services to areas that would be ignored by the market place (railroads to rural areas). In the social sphere, regulation is used to set limits on externalities effects on third parties (e.g., air and pollution); to set minimum safety standards for products and processes; to establish and protect the rights of employees to collective bargaining with management; and to monitor, investigate, and settle cases of discrimination in the workplace[36]. On the negative, regulating the corporation has several disadvantages. It is known that regulation tends to lead to a non-competitive environment, higher consumer prices, reduced innovation and investment, and rising unemployment[37]. Applied appropriately, however, regulation can help reduce private sector excesses and the need for periodic house-cleanings sometimes made necessary by these excesses. SA has witnessed misappropriations in the form of such deplorable scandals as the Muldergate Scandal in which the SA taxpayer's money was used to further the political agenda of the Nationalist Party.

Pressure it. Unlike regulate it, pressure it is designed to provoke the corporation to act beyond some base level behavior, usually in an area that regulation misses completely, especially in areas of social needs. In the vanguard of this activity is an array of public interest groups which purport to speak on behalf of consumers, tax payers, and other underrepresented citizens. These groups have been characterized as anything from "politically organized liberals," to groups which seek the collective good that will "not selectively and materially benefit the membership"[38]. "Pressure it" as a means to change corporate behavior is informal, flexible, and focussed; yet because of its ad hoc nature and the variety of groups involved, it may lead to contradictory demands being placed on management. "Pressure it" is considered to be to the left of center because it tends to lead to confrontation rather than cooperation. Several consumer groups and advocacy groups exist both in the U.S., SA, and elsewhere in the world as examples of this option. The PUSH (People United to Save Humanity) group founded by the Rev. Jesse Jackson is one example in the U.S. Internationally, perhaps the best known examples of the advocacy groups are the INFACT Group which pressured corporations such as Nestlé for marketing infant formula as a substitute for breastfeeding in less-developed countries, and Anti-Apartheid Movement of the last two decades. The latter movement had representation in many countries around the world and claimed the credit for having successfully pressured several companies to withdraw from SA. With all their short comings, pressure groups are a necessity in the interest of the maintenance of societal checks and balances.

Trust it. Based upon the principle of social responsibility, this position posits that the corporation has no need to be irresponsible. There is thus no need to "nationalize it", "democratize it", or "regulate it." "Trust it", along with the other positions to the right of the CHM ("induce it", "ignore it", and "restore it"), is more in line with the Milton Friedman dictum whose fundamental assertion was that the social responsibility of business is to increase its profits since the promotion of economic autonomy and freedom of economic choice facilitates political freedom[39]. In that spirit, "trust it" assumes that corporate executives have the innate predisposition to strike a balance between social and economic goals, i.e., they are ethical and can thus be trusted to make the socially responsible decisions vis-à-vis the societies within which their operations exist. This view has been attacked from the left (corporate managers have the tendency to impose their own interpretation of public good on society[40]), and from the right (corporations have no social responsibility beyond maximizing the corporate profit[41]). The excesses of the 1980s have caused a lot of public skepticism toward executives as revealed by many surveys which indicate that the public believes that corporate executives have become more unethical. Couple this with the fact that corporations in SA have coexisted with *apartheid* for close to half a century, it seems naive to expect that simply giving them *carte blanche* trust them is likely to bring about the desired redistribution of power. Already in the lead up to the first democratic elections, many of the large corporations have been accused of blackening their boards, i.e., appointing blacks into directorships who do not have enough knowledge about the functioning of these corporations. But the strongest reason for advancing the "trust it" option is that there is no alternative but to expect that executives would obey the letter and spirit of the law in helping to advance the country's superordinate goals of equity distribution.

Ignore it. Assuming that social needs are met in the course of pursuing economic goals, this option calls for no change in corporate behavior. This assumption is based on the belief in trickle down economics. The distinction between this option and the "trust it" option is that the former upholds that to do good is the right thing, and the latter upholds that it pays to be good. This options encourages enlightened self interest, by encouraging average behavior or the *status quo*. Given the history of corporate negligence for the human and civil rights of disadvantaged South Africans, this option is one that SA can least afford.

Induce it. Contrasted with the "regulate it" option, this approach brings to mind the carrot and stick approach as a means of gaining compliance--with "regulate it" being the stick, and "induce it" being the carrot. Whereas "regulate it" penalizes the corporation for what it does, "induce it" rewards the corporation for doing what it might not otherwise do. Of all the options, this is the least ideological since it merely conceives the corporation as an economic instrument whose power can be unleashed at society's request. In SA, if this induces the corporation into the kind of action that results in the distribution of power and restoration of equity, then it should be pursued wherever relevant.

Restore it. The assumption underlying this option is that managerial control is illegitimate and must thus be replaced by more valid forms of external control, and that the corporation's rightful owners are its shareholders. This assumption finds supports from scholars such as Friedman who also believe that this option is the only case where free enterprise and freedom can co-exist. Where vibrant competition exists, unlimited entry is possible, information is open, consumer sovereignty flourishes, and labor mobility is unhindered. The problem with these assumptions lies in what was pointed out by Schumpeter years ago[42]. It is that when they become successful (and thus grow in size) corporations might actually end up being antithetical to the model of market enterprise typified by several small businesses in competition with each other, and coordinated by the invisible hand mechanism. What was true in the 18th century when Adam Smith wrote *The Wealth of Nations*, no longer holds in contemporary times characterized by the existence of large institutional investors, and large conglomerate corporations, often in a collusive, co-respecting relationship, and with a market mechanism coordinated by the "visible hand"[43]. At any rate, in a truly democratic society why must it only be the shareholders who are entitled to having a say in the running of the corporations? What about the customers, the workers, people whose neighborhoods will be affected by the negative externalities of the corporations?

Summary. It seems that the issue to be addressed here is not which option should be chosen in order to make large corporations be responsive to their host nations. Rather, the question should be what mix of options must be adopted to accomplish the goal of redistribution of power in a country such as South Africa. From a managerial and organizational perspective, Mintzberg has suggested that these positions should be thought of as forming a portfolio from which society can draw to deal with the issue of who should control the corporation and how. A practical way to do this might be the application of a contingency approach whereby options will be chosen contingent to the shifting national priorities. As Mintzberg noted, it may be appropriate to add a new twist to the old adage: if the [horse]shoe fits, wear it.

Discussion and Suggestions

Since end of Nelson Mandela's long term of imprisonment in 1990, we have seen SA entering a new era in which one by one the pillars of apartheid were demolished culminating in the ascendancy of the "Prisoner to President." As the euphoria over the historical elections settles down, questions will begin to emerge about how realizable the pre-election promises were compared to the heightened expectations of many previously disenfranchised. Can it be guaranteed, for example, that in post-apartheid SA the composition of corporate management will approximate the demographic mix of the country in the short term? Left on their own, can private sector corporations play their role in the restoration of socio-economic equity in response to the needs of the country?

The record shows that in spite of several years of private sector initiatives to rectify the inequities, very few black managers have made it to top levels[44]. This can also be discerned in recent publications which paint a rather dismal picture concerning the demographic composition of the managerial and board of director ranks in some of the large corporations in SA where representation of the black majority is almost negligible. For instance the board of Anglo-American Corporation not too long ago only had one black director out of fifty[45], and only 6 percent of FNB managers were black[46]. How will the aspirations of the disaffected black population be accommodated[47]? The paradox of the situation is that a majority of the customers and workers served and employed by these corporations, is black. But the commercial sector is traditionally not run on democratic principles-- managers are promoted based on merit, CEOs are appointed.

Concerns about power and control of large corporations are not new, but can be seen in the works of several earlier writers who noted the problems of the separation of ownership and control, as well as the paradoxes implicit between the theory and practice of democracy in capitalist economies[48]. Similar concerns can be comprehended in the works of more recent writers about the impact of global corporations around the world[49]. The writers posit that large corporations dominate modern life by providing personal identity, structuring time and experience, influencing education and knowledge production, and directing entertainment and news production[50]. The social outcome is the holding up of corporate experience as the norm, and the artificial suppression of conflict that might have arisen had the various stakeholders had an opportunity to articulate their experiences from their own world views. It is the unequitable distribution of economic--and therefore socio-political--power that has led several scholars to question whether large corporations are predisposed to contribute to the general well-being of their host countries[51]. In the case of SA, it would be lamentable for the majority to lose their democracy to external corporate structures just as soon as they have gained it from internal political ones. Fortunately, hope has begun to emerge in the management scholarship in the form of writings about the need to rethink the meaning of organizational science[52], the humanization of strategic management[53], and the need for more eclectic approaches in theorizing about topics such as entrepreneurship and innovation[54].

The final question left to be answered is the issue of what can be done to ensure the distribution of power around large corporations in SA? Among the various courses of action available to catalyze the distribution of power are encouraging Employee Stock Ownership Plans, and aggressive affirmative action programs in corporate South Africa. Outside the corporations some of the methods can be the coupling of privatization of formerly state-owned corporations with the issuance of vouchers as was done in Russia, and the creation of business incubators to encourage and nurture small business start-ups.

●● Employee Stock Ownership Plans (ESOPs).

An ESOP is a benefit plan through which employees receive company stock, either in return for various wage and benefit concessions, or as additions to existing compensation[55]. The stock plan can typically become part of a pension plan or be drawn upon after termination[56]. When ESOPs were first introduced in the U.S. through an act of Congress, the Employee Retirement Income Security Act (ERISA) of 1974, they had two main objectives. First, they were to be used as a vehicle for the distribution of stock ownership of a company beyond the traditional stockholders (managers and professionals) to workers who were unlikely to invest in stocks on their own initiative. Distribution was intended to expand ownership of capital not just by redistributing existing wealth but by creating more of it. The second intention was the transformation of worker-management relationship from an adversarial one to a cooperative one through increased worker participation in decision making. Of course, ESOPs do have disadvantages, but not only would they contribute to the distribution of power in SA, but they promise to deliver other by-products such as the likely improvement in productivity rates and labor-management relations[57]. Fortunately, ESOPs have been introduced in a number of SA companies with remarkable success. Approximately one third of all companies traded in the JSE have some form of ESOP, and the number is increasing as the resultant productivity gains become more publicized..

● **Affirmative Action.**
The original intention of affirmative action was to ensure equal opportunity for members of groups that had been subject to discrimination. But affirmative action takes equal opportunity one step further in that, everything else being equal, preference is encourage for members of the formerly excluded population. Many objections to affirmative action have emerged over time mostly around its inefficiency and unfairness. But the situation of blacks in South Africa is quite unique in that they have been subjected to the most blatant exclusionary measures over the last forty six years. The results are the very glaring disparities that can be seen between the black and white citizens of the country. The 1991 Labor Relations Act was passed to prevent any discrimination in the work place on the basis of race and gender. But legislation by itself is not enough. Even the newly found political democracy will not alter the historical economic imbalances. Economic empowerment can, and aggressive affirmative action is an essential ingredient in that process. As the GNU facilitates access to education at all levels to blacks, access to upper-level jobs in the private sector will be a crucial step in breaking the legacy of job reservation under apartheid. Companies such as African Life, South African Breweries, and others have begun the way towards such affirmative action programs. The step has not been an easy one as the example of Cape Town based Pick 'n Pay demonstrated. While a strong advocate of the upward mobility of blacks, Pick 'n Pay had to contend with work stoppages by lower-level employees who were demanding pay raises. Private sector companies will play an important part in implementing in the destribution of power around corporations through affirmative action. It must, however, be remembered that affirmative action is not an end in itself, but a means of dealing with an intolerable situation[58].

● **Vouchers.**
Privatization has been heralded as one of the ways in which to reinvigorate the economy. But where economic power, i.e. income, has been concentrated in a few hands, privatization might work counter to the distribution of power. John Mayhard Keynes long showed that capital markets could operate efficiently both under conditions of high employment or low employment, meaning that left on their own, markets can establish efficient equilibria even with high unemployment. One way by which to invigorate the economy and, at the same time, stimulate the distribution of power is by

targeted privatization of certain previously government controlled enterprises. But this should be accompanied with simultaneous distribution of vouchers redeemable in exchange of shares of stock in the privatizing company as was recently done in Russia. The 1992 Russian Privatization Plan which called for rapid conversion of 14,000 state-owned enterprises employing 15 million people. How was the Russian privatization program carried out? It was basically carried out in three stages[59]. Stage 1 ordered all state-owned firms of more than 1,000 employees, or whose January 1, 1992 book value was $300,000 or more, to reorganize. Step 2 required companies to choose from two methods of corporatization. Corporatization has been defined as the process whereby employees and/or management decide if they wanted to remain a minority shareholder in their company, or buy the controlling block of shares in their company[60]. They could give their employees non-voting shares worth 25 percent of their companies' capital for free, plus an option to buy a further 10 percent of voting shares at a 30 percent discount; or the workers and managers together could buy 51 percent of their firms' assets. Step 3 took care of the demand side by issuing vouchers worth up to 3 months' average pay (10,000 rubles) to each of Russia's 150 million citizens[61]. The vouchers were to be used to bid for ownership, sold for cash, or pooled into investment funds. In spite of the criticisms levelled at the Russian privatization plan, it has been characterized by researchers from Rutgers University as a "success story."[62] These researchers reached that conclusion after an 18 month study of 200 large state-owned enterprises that had privatized. They found that, contrary to popular belief that the Russians would sell their vouchers for food, many of the vouchers were used to buy stakes in the privatizing companies. Only in very few cases were they used for shadowy purposes. The Russian experience is instructive to other economies willing to go the privatization route.

● **Small Business Incubators (SBIs).**

Small businesses comprised a significant part of the SA economy but after the discovery of diamonds and gold the spirit of entrepreneurship was crushed under heavy legislature. One way to rekindle the entrepreneurial spirit is through the creation of small business nurturing centers, or small business incubators. SBIs are a flexible method of encouraging the development of new businesses and fostering economic development in the community. Situated in community halls, college campuses, or other governmental agencies, SBIs provide affordable space and shared support, professional advice, and developmental services to entrepreneurs. Several advantages are offered by SBIs such as shared facilities, networking, and providing an umbrella of sustenance especially in the early stages of the venture[63]. In SA, the idea can be linked to efforts already in existence through organizations such as the National Stokvel Association of South Africa (NASASA)[64].

Conclusion

The foregoing discussion was intended to demonstrate that economic power in SA is highly concentrated in the hands of few. This situation has resulted in the creation of a large class of economically powerless citizens which unfortunately correlates highly with race. Such a situation is runs in contradiction to the sustained existence of political democracy which, as Plato once noted, can only continue to exist where there is a large middle class. It is this lack of a middle-class that perhaps helps explain why multiparty political democracy has been such an elusive goal in many developing nations.

Through our application of Mintzberg's conceptual horseshoe model, the message was that corporations would do well to initiate the process--albeit with help from the GNU--of ensuring the distribution of power to a broader section of the SA population. Special attention needs to be given to grooming talented individuals from the historically disenfranchised majority. This way, as more people become involved economically, political democracy will have a better chance of survival and the economy will reap the fruits of stability. If this is ignored, several scenarios are possible. One possible scenario is the widening of the gap between expectations of the masses and outcomes they receive, thereby creating tension which predisposes the situation to political upheaval. Another possibility is government intervention in areas of the private sector where it is least qualified to make strategic decision. Both these scenarios must be avoided since they would inevitably plunge the country into severe social turmoil or a deeper economic recession. A window of opportunity now exists to ensure long-lasting stability in SA through the distribution of power around large corporations. But that window may close sooner than expected.

Table 1
Applicability of the Conceptual Horseshoe in South Africa

ELEMENT	REASON FOR USE	DOWNSIDE	IN S. AFRICA
Nationalize it	To direct critical industries. Also where services, products can be produced efficiently by one firm and can't be produced privately	Inefficiencies possible	Only in a few cases and/or as the last resort.
Democratize it	To broaden the power base	Different meanings. Passive representatives	Yes
Regulate it	To curb corporate abuse. Minimal need for periodic housecleanings	Anti-competitive Price fixing	Yes
Pressure it	Induces ethics and social responsiveness	Too many groups working cross purposes	Yes
Trust it	Corporate executives can strike a balance between ethics and efficiency	Executives less ethical. May be indifferent to Social responsi-bility.	Yes
Ignore it	Sole Pursuit of Profits is Right	Enlightened self-interest. "Life would be nasty."	SA can't afford it
Induce it	Reward corporations for doing right. Corporations are instruments to be unleashed by induction	Corporations may do the minimum necessary	Yes
Restore it	Managerial control is illegi-timate. Shareholders are rightful owners. Their choices must dictate direction.	Free markets, unlimited entry, open information not always possible	Unfettered, may lead to maintenance of in-equalities

303

CHAPTER 14

ENDNOTES

1. See Freeman, R.E. (1984). *Strategic Management: A Stakeholder Approach.* Boston: Pitman; Alkhafaji, A.F. (1989). *A Stakeholder Approach to Corporate Governance: Managing in a Dynamic Environment.* Westport, CT: Quorum Books; and Carroll, A.B. (1993). *Business & Society: Ethics and Stakeholder Management.* Cincinnati, OH: South-Western Publishing Company. For a transactional cost view see Cornell, B, and Shapiro, A.C. (1987). Corporate Stakeholders and Corporate Finance. *Financial Management.* Spring: 5-14.

2. Donaldson, T. (1989). *The Ethics of International Business.* New York: Oxford University Press, chapter 4.

3. For a fuller discussion see Donaldson, T. (1989). *The Ethics of International Business.* New York: Oxford University Press, pp. 47-53.

4. Mintzberg, H. (1984). Who Should Control the Corporation? *California Management Review.* 27(1), pp. 90-114.

5. See, for example: Bennis, W. & Nanus, B. (1985). *Leaders.* New York: Harper & Row; Block, P. (1987). *The Empowered Manager.* San Francisco, CA: Jossey-Bass; Burke, W. (1986). Leadership as Empowering Others. In Srivastra, S. (ed.). *Executive Power.* San Francisco, Jossey-Bass; Conger, J.A. & Kanungo, R.N. (1988). The Empowerment Process: Integrating Theory and Practice. *Academy of Management Review*, 13, pp. 471-482; Nielsen, E. (1986). Empowerment Strategies: Balancing Authority and Responsibility. In Srivastra, S. (ed.). *Executive Power.* San Francisco: Jossey-Bass.

6. Dahl, R. (1957). The Concept of Power. *Behavioral Science.* 2(3), pp. 201-215. Stogdill, R. (1974). *The Handbook of Leadership.* New York, NY: Free Press. Bass, B. (1990). *Bass and Stogdill's Handbook of Leadership.* New York, NY: Free Press.

7. Stogdill, (1974). See also Epstein, E. M. (1973). Dimensions of Corporate Power: Part I. *California Management Review.* Winter.

8. Pfeffer, J. (1992). Understanding Power in Organizations. *California Management Review.* 34 (2): 29-50.

9. See French, J. and Raven, B. (1959). The Bases of Social Power. In D. Cartwright (ed.), *Studies in Social Power.* Ann Arbor, MI: Institute of Social Research, University of Michigan, pp. 150-167. See also Cartwright, D.

(1965). Influence, Leadership, Control. In J. G. March (ed.). *Handbook of Organization*. Chicago, IL: Rand McNally. See also Epstein (1973).

10. On the Social Exchange Theory see the following works: Blau, P.M. (1964). *Exchange and Power in Social Life*. New York: Wiley; Emerson, R.M. (1962). Power-Dependence Relations. *American Sociological Review*. **27**, pp. 31-41; Homans, A. (1974). *Social Behavior: Its Elementary Forms*. New York: Harcourt, Brace, & Jovanovich. Molm, L.D. (1991). Affect and Social Exchange: Satisfaction in Power-Dependence Relations. *American Sociological Review*. **56**, pp. 475-493. On power and Dependence also see Pfeffer, J. (1981). *Power in Organizations*. Marshfield, MA: Pitman; and Thompson, J.D. (1967). *Organizations in Action*. New York: McGraw-Hill.

11. Rudolph, H. R., and Peluchette, J. V. (1993). The Power Gap: Is Sharing or Accumulating Power the Answer? *Journal of Applied Business Research*. 9(3), pp. 12-20.

12. Tannenbaum, A. (1968). *Control in Organizations*. New York: MacGraw-Hill.

13. Etzioni, A. (1961). *Comparative Analysis of Complex Organizations*. New York: Free Press.

14. Davis, K., and Blomstrom, R. L. (1966). *Business and its Environment*. New York, NY: McGraw-Hill, pp. 174-175.

15. Conger, J. A., and Kanungo, R. N. (1988). The Empowerment Process: Integrating Theory and Practice. *Academy of Management Review*. 13, pp. 471-482; Rudolph, H. R., and Peluchette, J. V. (1993). *Op. Cit.*

16. Hollander, E.P., and Offermann, L.R. (1990). Power and Leadership in Organizations. *American Psychologist* 45 (February): 179-189.

17. For a fuller discussion of TQM see Creech, B. (1994). *The Five Pillars of TQM*. New York: Truman Talley/Dutton; also see Crosby, P.B. (1994). *Completeness: Quality for the 21st Century*. New York: Plume.

18. Galbraith, J. K. (1974). *The New Industrial State*. London: Pelican Books.

19. Deetz, S.A. (1992). *Democracy in an Age of Corporate Colonization*. Albany, NY: SUNY Press, p. 2.

20. Epstein, E.M. (1973). *Op. Cit.*

21. See for example, Adelman, M.A. (1951). The Measurement of Industrial Concentration. *Review of Economics and Statistics.* 33, pp. 269-296.

22. See Demsetz, H. (1983). *Ownership Control and the Firm.* Cambridge, MA: Basil Blanchard, pp. 202-222. To compute the H-index, the individual market share of each firm, expressed in fractional terms, is squared and added. The industry is concentrated when the H-Index approaches 1.

23. Hawley, A.H. (1963). Community Power and Urban Renewal Success. *American Journal of Sociology.* 68, pp. 422-431.

24. See Innes, D. (1984). *Anglo American and the Rise of Corporate South Africa.* New York: Monthly Review Press.

25. McGreggor, R. (1991). *Takeover Talks.*

26. Ford, Constance M. (1994). Pressure on South African Companies to 'Unbundle' Holdings Has Waned. *Wall Street Journal.* January 20: C1, C21.

27. See Innes, D. (1984). *Anglo American and the Rise of Corporate South Africa.*

28. Segal, S. (1993). *Finance Week* (SA). July 8-14, p. 38.

29. Ford, C.M. (1994). *Op. Cit.*

30. Mintzberg, H. (1984). *Ibid.*

31. The Sasol Plant which was created as a "window" for research in the coal to oil conversion. Escom is the Electrical Supply Commission. Armscor was created as a response to the international arms embargo against SA.

32. See Wycliff, D. (1990). Mandela Says Movement is Open to Future with Mixed Economy. *The New York Times.* Friday, June 22, pp. A1, A20-21.

33. See Steiner, G.A. & Steiner, J.F. (1994). *Business, Government, and Society: A Managerial Perspective*: 80. New York: McGraw-Hill.

34. For a more elaborate treatment of this topic see Abraham, W.E. (1962). *The Mind of Africa.* Chicago, IL: University of Chicago Press.

35. See Mangaliso, M.P. (1988). The Relationship of Environmental Turbulence, Strategy Preference, and Performance. Unpublished Ph.D. Dissertation. University of Massachusetts, Amherst, p. 147.

36. Examples of regulatory agencies in the U.S. are: the Consumer Product Safety Commission; the Environmental Protection Agency; the Occupational Safety and Health Administration; the National Labor Relations Board; and the Equal Employment Opportunity Commission established under the Civil Rights Act of 1964.

37. See Swartz, T., and Bonello, F. (1988). *Taking Sides.* Guilford, CT: The Dushkin Publishing Company.

38. Steiner, G.A., and Steiner, J.F. (1994). *Op. Cit.* For one view see Brimelow, P. (1987). A Man Alone. *Forbes* (August 24): 44. For another, see Berry, J.F. (1977). *Lobbying for the People.* Princeton, NJ: Princeton University Press.

39. Friedman, M. (1970). The Social Responsibility of Business is to Increase its Profits. *The New York Times Magazine.* September 13, pp. 32 ff.

40. Braybrooke, D. (1967). Skepticism of Wants, and Certain Subversive Effects of Corporations on American Values. In S. Hook (ed), *Human Values and Economic Policy.* New York, NY: New York University Press, pp. 224.

41. Friedman, M. (1970). The Social Responsibility of Business is to Increase Its Profits. *The New York Times Magazine,* September 13, 1970.

42. Schumpeter, J. A. (1934). *The Theory of Economic Development.* Cambridge, MA: Harvard University Press.

43. Chandler, A.D. (1977). *The Visible Hand: The Managerial Revolution in American Business.* Cambridge, MA: Harvard University Press; also see Baran, P.A., and Sweezy, P.M. (1966). *Monopoly Capital.* New York: Monthly Review Press.

44. Mangaliso, M.P. (1992). The Corporate Social Challenge for the Multinational Corporation. *Journal of Business Ethics.* 11(7), pp. 491-500.

45. *The Economist* (1990). A Survey of South Africa, p. 18. It is interesting to compare the situation in SA with that in the U.S. An recent report [Huey, J. (1993). How McKinsey Does it. *Fortune*] showed that out of 465 partners

of the U.S. consulting group McKinsey & Co., only 2 were black and only 12 were women.

46. Segal, S. (1993). First's Thirst. *Finance Week.* July 8-14, pp. 38-39.

47. In extreme cases these are represented in slogans such as "we will take over the factories!"

48. See the works of Berle and Means (1932), and Schumpeter, J.A. (1942). *Capitalism, Socialism, and Democracy.* New York: Harper & Row. (Revised edition, 1976.)

49. See the work of Reich, R.B. (1992). *The Works of Nations.* New York: Vintage Books; Deetz, S. (1992). *Democracy in an Age of Corporate Colonization.* Albany, NY: State University of New York Press; Barnet, R.J., and Cavanagh, J. (1994). *Global Dreams.* New York: Simon & Schuster. For an earlier criticism of global corporations, see the works of Barnet, R.J., and Müller, R.E. (1974). *Global Reach: The Power of the Multinational Corporations.* New York: Simon & Schuster; and Mattelart, A. (1979).

50. Deetz (1992). *Op. Cit.*; Barnet & Cavanagh (1994). *Op. Cit.*

51. For example, see Barnet & Müller (1974). *Op. Cit.*

52. Daft, R.L. & Lewin, A.Y. (Forthcoming). Where are the Theories for the "New" Organizational Forms? An Editorial Essay. *Organizational Science.*

53. Gilbert, Daniel R. Jr. (1992). *The Twilight of Corporate Strategy.* New York: Oxford University Press.

54. See Mangaliso, M.P. (1992). Entrepreneurship and Innovation in a Global Environment. *Entrepreneurship, Innovation, and Change.* 1(4), pp. 437-450, and several articles in volume 1 of this journal.

55. See Blasi, J.R. (1988). *Employee Ownership: Revolution or Ripoff.* Cambridge, MA: Ballinger. For a review of the book, see Hammer, T.H. (1989). *Academy of Management Review* 14 (4): 588-600.

56. See Sayles, L.R. & Strauss, G. (1981). *Managing Human Resources*: 414-417. Englewood Cliffs, NJ: Prentice Hall.

57. See Buchholz (1988). *Op. Cit.*

58. Nagel, T. (1981). A Defense of Affirmative Action. Testimony before the Subcommittee on the Constitution of the Senate Judiciary Committee. June 18.

59. *Economist* (1992). Russia under the Hammer. November 28, pp. 69-70.

60. See Strauss, Cheryl B. (1992). Russia Releases Details of Privatization Program. *Investment Dealers Digest.* 58 (48), p. 18.

61. Walker, Martin (1992). Taking Russia Private. *Europe.* 321, pp. 10-13. The value of the voucher in terms of equivalence in weeks of pay varies from 6 weeks to 3 months.

62. Blasi, J. (1994). Privatizing Russia - A Success Story. *The New York Times.* June 30, p. A23.

63. For further discussion see Allen, D.N., and McCluskey, R. (1990). Structure, Policy, Services, and Performance in the Business Incubator Industry. *Entrepreneurship.* Winter, p. 61 ff; Brandt, E. (1991). Incubators: A Safe Haven for New Businesses. *Journal of Property Management.* January-February, p. 52; Freundlich, N. (1990). Business Incubators Bring up Baby. *Business Week.* May 28, p. 65.

64. See Mangaliso, M.P. (1993). Cultural Exigencies in Management and Organizational Discourse. Entrepreneurship, Innovation, and Change. 2 (4), pp. 321-334. For a history of the formation of NASASA see Lukhele, A. K. (1990). *Skokvels in South Africa.* Johannesburg, South Africa: Amagi Books.

PART V

"The complaint of the poor nations against the present system is not only that we are poor both in absolute terms and in comparison with the rich nations. It is also that within the existing structure of economic interaction we must remain poor, and get relatively poorer, whatever we do....The demands for a New International Economic Order is a way of saying that the poor nations must be enabled to develop themselves according to their own interests, and to benefit from the efforts which they make."

Julius K. Nyerere

Chapter 15

Deconstructing Development:
From Underdevelopment to Maldevelopment

Despite the ambiguity surrounding the meaning and attributes of development, there is a common ground among all less industrialized countries (LICs): their uppermost objective is to "develop." Commonality ends, however, when theoretical choices for strategies of development must be made to that end. Since the second World War, three major development paradigms have emerged. They offer different options to development planners and political leaders in the LICs.

The first, and more widely applied, strategy can be referred to as the neoclassical (also labeled classical, structuralist or modernizationists) approach to development. This strategy has been premised, since Adam Smith, on human preferences, on the given endowments of productive resources that human beings privately own, and on the productive capabilities (the available technology) that enable humans to produce what they desire in an environment of political stability.[1] Human nature is, therefore, the theoretical entry point around which the argument of this school revolves.

The second strategy has been termed the dependency (or neo-Marxist) approach. This school views power as its theoretical point of entry and essence, and constructs its theoretical argument on that basis. It is diametrically opposed to the prescriptions, tactics, and strategies of neoclassical theorists.[2]

The third strategy, termed the orthodox Marxist approach, uses either class, power, or consciousness as its point of entry and essence. Orthodox Marxists base their production of knowledge about a particular society on one or more of these three aspects. Paradoxically, this school bears striking resemblances to the neoclassical approach in that it affirms the determining influence of the human being's power (God given power) on economic events.[3]

Thus, each is different in its focus, or organizing idea, and each is similar in its reductionist logic. Consequently, the implementation of economic and political development policies in the LICs based on and guided

313

by any one of these paradigms will lead, even if economic growth and political stability is registered by this means, to maldevelopment rather than to "sustainable development."[4]

In what follows, I will proceed in the following format. First, I will present a capsule summary of the three dominant paradigms mentioned above. Second, I will critically analyze these paradigms from the deconstructionists perspective. Third, on the basis of these premises, I will conclude by calling for a deconstruction of the development paradigms mentioned above.

1. The Neoclassical Paradigm

Neoclassical (also classical, structuralist or modernization) development utilizes entry concepts of choice and scarcity with a particular essentialist theoretical procedure (deductive logic) so that development is theorized as a phenomenon of the entry concepts. Thus neoclassical theory's entry concepts function as essences. Human beings are assumed to be rational and to maximize their resources. According to the theory, they exercise their free choices in the context of a given scarcity, which propels all economic activity forward.[5] Human beings choose what they want to consume and produce what is rational to produce, of course, by rationally responding to market forces. Rational institutions, or in other words, political and economic systems, can be created that correspond to the rational human nature, whose primary goal is to accumulate capital and wealth. In the process, it is assumed that such institutions will also advance and secure the democratic rights of both capitalists and workers alike. In such organized institutions, the market is assumed to take care of the economic growth of the country for reasons spelled out by Adam Smith and David Ricardo.[6] That the market rewards the "productive"--as it is measured by efficiency and innovation in order to stretch the margin of profit--sectors of the society and punishes the "unproductive" sectors of the society (this includes thinkers with no immediate profit to show) is accepted and considered unproblematic.

Internationally, it is argued that the development processes of the LICs can get the necessary "push" if investment capital is allowed to move freely and if nationalist barriers are not allowed to inhibit the flow of investment capital in the international market.[7] In a context where there exists industrial countries (ICs) and LICs, the former could then transfer capital to the latter and generate wealth there, via economic growth, for the benefit of both parties.[8] The market will force individuals, or society, in both ICs and LICs to initiate such international trade relations if the utility gain from such trade is greater than without it. According to this school, barring any interferences, such as market imperfections created by external economies, monopolies, irrational institutions, or nationalist politics and culture, the pattern of trade is fully determined by conditions of scarcity and choice.

In neoclassical paradigm formulation, the success of a country's development was conceived solely in economic terms and measured by the rate of growth of its Gross National Product (GNP). Gross National Product, a measure of the total output claimed by the nationals of a country,[9] is assumed to show the well being of a nation-state. Thus, the strategy used by LICs to achieve their goal of development focused largely on economic growth in the belief that an increase in GNP will percolate down to the poorest of the poor and eventually eliminate poverty, inequality and unemployment. In such neoclassical conceptions, production is encouraged to expand untrammelled; further production is considered profitable, and, assuming man's natural innovativeness, new ways of stretching the profit margin are constantly created.

Associated with such neoclassical conception of development was the concept of modernization.[10] For proponents of modernization (structural development theory) the emphasis is mainly on either some kind of given economic structure, say, dualism, or an aggregate lack of investment capital, or the size of the market.

Political developmentalists, educators and economists within this school thought that particularly appropriate work ethics, proper social and family attitudes, as well as, an appropriate political system were more conducive to development than other elements of social development.[11] LICs, therefore, differed from the ICs because their society did not exhibit these modern attitudes. In order to be on the right path of development, LICs had to make sure that their people acquired modern attitudes,[12] i.e., adopted the culture, values and paths of development of the already existing ICs. Such a view is well expressed by Daniel Lerner: "the process of social change [takes place when] less developed societies acquire characteristics common to more developed societies."[13] Similarly, Wilbert Moore observed that "what is involved in modernization is a total transformation of a traditional or pre-modern society into the types of technology and associated social organization that characterize the advanced, economically prosperous, and relatively politically stable nations of the western world."[14] Edward Shils' definition of modernization best captures the kernel of the neoclassical's position. To him, "'modern' means being western without the onus of dependence on the west. The model of modernity is a picture of the west detached in some way from its geographical origins and locus."[15] Hence, development equals modernization equals a shift from agricultural economy to industrial economy.

The central theme of the above discussion is a unidirectional, linear conception of the processes of development through which human society evolves from traditional (preindustrial) to modern (industrial) society. Since development is thought to proceed in a linear fashion, it follows that every country that wants to develop must necessarily pass through a series of stages that were once passed by the now ICs, i.e., capital accumulation, ever-increasing industrialization, a drive to maturity, and a constant move toward a modern wealthy economy with mass (high) consumption. This view was propounded in works like Rostow's Stages of Economic Growth, and it has had a powerful influence on the political elites and development planners in the LICs.[16]

The idea of "take off" captured the LICs' imagination and presented them with an operational tool to map out their development strategies. In this school all countries were presumed to follow the same pattern of economic development, and the different countries of the world were grouped in a hierarchical classification. The poorer LICs were presumed to have a long way to go to reach the "take-off," as defined by Rostow, the point at which they would have developed the dynamism to sustain economic growth.[17]

Still another neoclassical position, which has a strong hold on the thinking of the political elites and the development planners, is to view the processes of development as monocausal. Such a view is evident in the idea of the "vicious circle of poverty," where the scarcity of capital is seen as an obstacle to development that condemns LICs to remain permanently at levels of economic subsistence.[18]

The corollary to this is that the solution lies in the virtuous cycle of capitalism, which makes productive behavior rational, and hence leads to economic growth and political stability. The task is, therefore, to find the necessary capital and to invest it in those countries. Not only that, to break the vicious cycle, these countries are encouraged to install "strong" (a euphemism for "repressive") and stable governments that can provide the long-range planning necessary for rational growth patterns.[19]

Political stability is presumed to encourage an influx of foreign investment as well as foreign technical and economic assistance. To this end, the Harold-Domar model became the development plans of a large number of LICs.[20] Governments and development planners in the LICs have found the Harold-Domar model[21] and the Rostowian model of stages of growth convenient for development planning. Although they recognize the interconnection between economics and noneconomic factors, they remained committed to the former because it is easily measurable and prone to manipulation. These models assumed capital by and large as the prime prerequisite to economic growth.

The basic contradiction in the international economy, therefore, is between two self-reinforcing cycles: the virtuous cycle of capitalism, which makes productive behavior rational and hence leads to economic growth and political stability, versus the vicious cycle of noncapitalist economic nationalism, which interferes with the rational logic of market-responsive individual behavior and hence leads to economic stagnation (or "backwardness").[22] The social task of rational economics is to tirelessly reveal the nature of two cycles. Its task is to expose the irrational reasoning that promises economic benefit from restrictions on economic freedom or that misunderstands capitalism as the source of the problem of economic stagnation rather than as the source of the solution.[23] The underlying assumption of this position was that it would not only explain the situation causing the development problem, but also that it would suggest policies to change that situation. However, after decades of research and policy formulations, change did not take place in the LICs as expected. In fact, the economic and political situation in these countries went from bad to worse, precipitating a veritable crisis for the neoclassical and modernization paradigms. Many development scholars concluded that the neoclassical and modernization paradigms are unable to fully explicate the problems of the existing LICs' development; thus they sought a new explanation.[24] The result was the emergence of a dependency/world system paradigm.

2. The Dependency Paradigm

The dependency (or neo-Marxist) paradigm arose in reaction to the failures of the optimistic growth models proposed by classicals, neoclassicals and structuralists (or modernizationists) discussed above. It is an eclectic body of thought incorporating several hues of opinion; even the individual authors within this tradition are not often consistent in their arguments.[25] There are differences in their approaches, degrees of emphasis, and policy recommendations.

In this paradigm the inequality in wealth and power between the ICs and the LICs is seen as a key reason for transferring a huge amount of LDC (surplus) wealth to the ICs, regardless of ICs' consent. The result is not only the development of the ICs (this paradigm's center) but also the underdevelopment, or dependent and distorted development, of the LICs (the periphery).[26] In short, the neoclassical (and modernizationist) strategy of development leads inexorably to neocolonialism.

Moreover, the dependency theorists claim that the modernizationist's assumption that development takes place only by following the western model is both an ahistorical understanding--because it ignores the colonial experiences of the LICs--and a false understanding of the ICs development processes.[27] Indeed, they claim that the ICs, the capitalist ones in particular, prevent the LICs from choosing their own development path.[28] If non-western countries like Japan have escaped the present condition of LICs, they argue, it is because they have managed to escape colonialism.

Andre Gunder Frank, in his essay, "Sociology of Development and Underdevelopment of Sociology," attacked not only the sociologically oriented modernization theories of Parsons, Levy, and Moore but also attacked neoclassicals and modernizationists such as Hoselitz, Hagen, McClelland, Rostow, Nash, et al.[29] Frank contends that, despite differences in their explanations of modernization theory, these writers were united in their acceptance of an ideal-type methodology, a trickle-down notion of social change, and a specific type of orientation to end underdevelopment. Frank's essay not only runs counter to modernization theories but also attacks some Marxist interpretations (to be discussed in the next section) which share this dual vision of LICs with some neoclassicals and modernizationists.

Frank's views are also shared by many other dependency theorists. Amin, an African scholar, for instance, argued that the impact of ICs on the economy of LICs creates "peripheral capitalism," a social system in which the total articulation of the capitalist mode of production is hindered, thus resulting in distorted economic development.[30] From the same school, Rodney, a Guyanese scholar, provides the most incisive analysis of how Europe underdeveloped Africa by siphoning off its surplus.[31] Sunkel and Paz affirms Frank's original thesis by arguing that development is a global, structural process of change and underdeveloped countries are those countries which lack an autonomous capacity for change and growth, and which depend upon the center for these.[32]

Emmanuel argued that underdevelopment is caused by the absence of high wages in LICs. Low wages neither stimulate sufficient market and large outputs, nor cause the development of a capitalist goods sector in LICs. Thus for Emmanuel, if private capitalists agree to pay high wages, then these countries can achieve economic development.[33] His theoretical approach involves identifying an independent variable and relating other phenomena to that variable as its effect. In the last pages of his book, Unequal Exchange, Emmanuel states:

> Any system of analysis must ultimately be based on one or more data taken from outside the system. These data are independent variables. Without them analysis comes to a dead end and the argument becomes circular.[34]

Emmanuel specifies differential wage rates as his essence from which all other model determinations are explicitly derived as its (the model's) simple effects. Thus, he writes, "wages are the independent variable, and prices (and so the terms of trade) are the dependent variables of the system."[35] This simple causal chain is, according to Emmanuel, "Marx's position, which forms the basis of my thesis."[36] Classes, in Emmanuel's theory are determined by their relationship to this wage rate. Those who receive the wage rate comprise the working class. Those who receive the remainder--after the wage is paid-- comprise the capitalist class.[37] Thus, class is defined in reference to type of income, and the possession of "essential" conditions of existence. Exploitation is considered by him as the outcome of monetary flow (in the form of higher wage payments) from the periphery to the center.

Then there is Wallerstein's world-system and world economy approach in which he divides the world capitalist system into three vertically structured states, the core, the semi-periphery, and the periphery.[38] According to Wallerstein's thesis, closely related to that of Frank, the essential difference between the three world segments lies in the power of their respective state machineries. The periphery has the weakest power; the core, the strongest; and the semi-periphery, the medium power. Wallerstein assumes these inequalities eventually lead to the transfer of surplus from the periphery to the center, thereby further enhancing the power of the core state.[39] The semi-periphery, between these two antagonistic points, serves as a buffer zone to prevent a possible collision between them. Any attempt by the periphery to be the center of a socialist economy is blocked by the "world-capitalist-system."[40]

It should also be pointed out that, for Wallerstein, a class analysis of peripheral societies is of secondary interest, since the class-structures of those societies have already been specified according to first principles once their peripheral status has been established.[41] A peripheral location in the world economy necessarily entails a reliance on coerced labor, which implies class structures and relations adapted to coercive labor control.

Despite the existence of various competing views on the dependency theory, there are certain specific points on which all the writers are agreed. First, they cite power as their point of entry and essence, around which they focus their organizing idea and their reductionist logic. All argue that the existing structure of international trade constrains the success of many LCDs' development efforts while accelerating the ICs', because the power of the ICs determines who trades what at which price.[42] Put differently, the development and underdevelopment are partial, interdependent structures of one global system. The condition of the LICs are closely related with the capitalist expansion of the ICs.

Second, dependency theorists are, in general, agreed that development and underdevelopment are two sides of a unified system. Underdevelopment, therefore, is the outcome of the historical relationship (through trade and colonialism) between the periphery and the core countries. It is the result of the development of capitalism on a world scale at the expense of the periphery. Historically, underdevelopment and development have been simultaneous processes that have been linked in a functional way, that is, they have interacted and conditioned themselves mutually.[43]

Third, the dependency theorists insist that underdevelopment is not a natural and temporary pre-capitalist stage that must be experienced by all nations. Europe was once undeveloped, but not underdeveloped, as are many

LICs in Asia, Africa, and Latin America. Given the power of the ICs and the weak conditions of the LICs, underdevelopment is not seen as a transitional stage, but rather as a persistent condition that will last so long as unequal exchange between the ICs and the LICs continues. The periphery gears its production to export, not primarily because it lacks internal markets, but because the highly developed productivity of the center compels it to be a complementary supplier, usually of agricultural and mineral products for industrial needs. Supranational lending agencies (especially the World Bank and the International Monetary Fund) are seen as partners of the ICs in this exploitative relationship.[44]

Fourth, the dependency theorists also agree that the subordinate relationship of LICs is not confined to external ties. They claim that dependence extends to the internal social structure, ideology and cultural beliefs, and internal decision-making apparatus. That is, metropolitan-satellite relations are found not only in an international context but also in the internal situation. For instance, the internal dependent class structures of LICs are dominated by a small political and economic elite closely tied to foreign interests who may or may not be physically present in the country. Only cash crop production becomes well developed. Yet, while this is an artifact of the colonial past, it is continued by present political elites because of the advantages it continues to provide them. The surplus generated from such economic activities is diverted either overseas, through exported profits, or internally into conspicuous consumption by local elites and a small labor aristocracy, with limited amounts being invested in capital-intensive technologies or import substitution.[45]

Thus, the view that the world capitalist system causes underdevelopment, by generating and reinforcing within LICs an infrastructure of dependency, is more or less accepted by all dependency theorists. This view has been articulated by Wallerstein and Frank with a wealth of historical evidence. They have not restricted their attention to Latin America only; rather they have shown the working of this process everywhere else including Africa.

Since the early 1980s, with the decline of foreign investment and aid, and the increase in the external debt assumed by the LICs, the dependency theorists still hold the same explanations: that foreign exploitation of the periphery by the core is the culprit. In this situation, interest payments to creditors in the ICs take the place of siphoning off surplus from the periphery to the core, thus creating a form of "debt-peonage."[46] In the case of LICs, which have failed in repayment of their debt, it is argued that the conditions set by the IMF (or by the private bank creditors) are such that the "poor" are forced to shoulder the debt burden.

Where the neoclassicals and modernizationists view debt as a way of transferring wealth from the ICs to the LICs, the dependency theorists view it as a means for extracting wealth from the periphery to the core. The corollary of this is that the free flow of capital and commodities in international markets, instead of leading to economic growth as in the neoclassical approach, serves to widen the gap between the core and periphery, developed and underdeveloped, modern and traditional, north and south countries. From this perspective, the current external debt of LICs reflects merely the contemporary form of that group's exploitation by foreign powers.[47]

3. The Orthodox Marxist Paradigm

Whether or not development of the world capitalist system causes underdevelopment in the periphery has also been debated among orthodox Marxist scholars. According to this school, underdevelopment in the periphery can only be understood in terms of the internal structures of the states, i.e., in terms of their mode of production.[48] This and the emergence and evolution of capitalism in the center (European countries) are relatively common grounds among orthodox Marxists.[49] Their emphasis on the mode of production as their point of entry and essence is also common to all. Their commonality, however, ends in their debates about the appropriate way to analyze economic, political and social structures in LICs. Three broad positions have been surveyed by a number of Marxist scholars.[50] I shall concentrate on those aspects of the debate relevant to our discussion.

The debate centers around the issue of the base of society (its economics) and its superstructure (its politics, culture and ideology). The first is a so-called classical position, often referred to pejoratively by critics as "vulgar Marxism," in which economic forces determine everything else.[51] Warren belongs to this school. The second position stands the first on its head: instead of the economy as determinant, the non-economic aspects of society determine the economy.[52] A third holds a middle position by allowing economic and non-economic aspects of life to affect each other, but by affirming in the last instance that the economy determines everything else.[53] All claim to be true to the spirit and writings of Marx, and all cite ample evidence to support their side of the story.[54]

The first position claims that the two economic aspects, the forces of production (read technology) and the relations of production (read class), combine together to form the base. The dialectical relations of the two in turn determine the forms and development of the superstructure (the political elites, the laws that govern society, the kind of curriculum produced to disseminate education, the kind of music produced, the cultural processes, and so on).[55] Thus, the mode of production contains within itself the power to determine those superstructural laws, cultural processes, etc., within society that are necessary for the reproduction of that mode.[56] In short, in this theorizing the non-economic aspects of society are regarded as epiphenomenon. They exist because they serve to reproduce the economic base or mode of production.

There are theoretical disquiets within this school of economic determinants between those who privilege the forces of production, such as Warren, and those who privilege the relations of productions, such as Dobb.[57] Those who espouse the second position (non-economic determinants)[58], such as Poulantzas, Bowles and Gintis, essentialize some aspect(s) of the super-structure as crucial, taking it (them) to be the determinants of the economy. Like the neoclassicists, this group treats power over the individuals and/or property, or human consciousness as the ultimate determinants of class behaviors, technology and culture. Those who focus their attention on power and property claim that the latter ultimately determines the economic, political and social behavior of society.[59] In contrast, those who focus on human consciousness posit the essential position of humans and their human consciousness (of class), and the realization of that position as the basis on which society changes.[60] Both relegate the economy to the secondary level.

Others, such as Hirst and Hindes, who espouse the third position in an attempt to circumvent the criticism leveled at economic determinants, contend that the superstructure and the base interact and affect one another and, at various points in history, even dominate one another.[61] Nevertheless, this group remains committed to the argument that in the last instance the economy determines everything else. The mode of production, therefore, determines whether (and when) the economy and the non-economy dominate one another at a particular historical epoch.[62] For instance, in LICs, politics and religion may dominate the economy (where domination is a function of the particular mode of production present at that moment in history) and facilitate the exploitation of the society.

These particular tendencies in the "mode school" have all adhered to the same essentialist epistemological terrain and the terms of debate. All claim to have captured in theory the true, essential determinants of social reality. In other words, all appeal to either empiricism or rationalism, or both to support their respective positions. All seem to know what determines the nature of society or what constitutes the true knowledge.

Thus, the issue in the field of development, we believe, includes the conflict among different theoretical versions that attempt to explain the same basic phenomena. This makes an appraisal of these theories an urgent task. But because works dealing with theory often evoke cries of "academic concern only" (or worse, produce boredom), we can offer one other justification as to why a theoretical appraisal is necessary. Just as world views are blueprints for understanding society and its practice, so, too, are development paradigms potential blueprints for development planning and development policy. There is a connection between the ideas that we have and the sort of development we advocate. As such, the uncritical use of any of the paradigms discussed is likely to lead LICs to "maldevelopment" rather than to development. This is so because the culture and tradition, on which the dominant paradigms are based, is different from the ones found in the LICs.

4. Tradition and the Dominant Paradigm

Enormous literature on development now exists. However, all three development literatures rest upon a stance that inherently assumes a particular tradition. This assumption has been subject to relatively little attention, especially with regard to Africa. In other words, the analysis of development paradigms has absorbed the unfortunate habit of treating "the tradition" as somehow naturally a given in the "great texts" analysis.

Reference to such a tradition may be justified as mere practical convenience. The story of the development paradigms discussed had to begin somewhere. But it is not always easy to begin at the beginning, if only because identifying of a point of origin depends on where we think we are now and where we think we are going. The practical "convenience" is always liable to turn into a powerful myth of origin. Other points of departure are excluded, closed off or suppressed. There is no African archeology of knowledge from which we can excavate and to which we can turn. It is drowned out (suppressed) by the dominant tradition.

Identifying the tradition of development paradigm has now become especially problematic. We live in a contemporary international order/disorder in which there is a proliferation not only of research paradigms in the academic analysis of development, but, more generally, a proliferation of myths of origin. The Hegelian trek to universality still echoes as "progress," "development," or "modernization."[63] This kind of mindset helps identify those that have "progressed" or "modernized" to be distinguished from those that have not. Under these criteria, it is all too often the ICs that have progressed, modernized and developed, and it is the LICs that have not.

Contemporary claims about intellectual tradition in general are caught between an awareness that the ICs' dominant myths of origin, namely, all those stories of a move from traditional to modern, from passionate to rational, from barbarism to enlightenment, from feudalism to capitalism, and so on, harbor, as R.B.J. Walker put it, embarrassing subtexts, such as ethnocentricism and racism.[64] The realization that these stories still inform the most basic categories through which we understand and act in contemporary order/disorder still remain in racism. As Walker astutely remarked, the term "development," therefore, now demands quotation marks, in order to distance accounts of what is going on in particular societies from the evolutionary teleology with which the term is indelibly associated.[65] If we have learned anything at all from those innumerable debates about "development" and the strategy to achieve it, it is that empirical (or rationalist) theory, or development policy analysis, should not be arbitrarily isolated from the indigenous societies' philosophical assumptions (and traditions). In fact, the indigenous philosophical values are simply drowned out by loud appeals or claims to "objectivity," "reality," "facts," "rationality," or "universality," as we have shown in our discussion of the three paradigms. Often, these appeals are entwined in the legitimizing of domination. Thus, if we are to avoid the permanent exclusion of certain paradigms, by implication also the exclusion hitherto suppressed other voices, then a deconstruction of the dominant paradigms is necessary.

Deconstruction aims its critique against a conception of knowledge and meaning as graspable essences that independently precede or follow expression.[66] In opposition to such essences, deconstruction contemplates knowledge and meaning as representations unavoidably enmeshed in the heterodox and contradictory nature of language and interpretation. Deconstructionists attempt to tackle the pretense that a thing can be known by what it is not.[67] What we do in short here is, deconstruct the self-evident nature of theories (development or otherwise) by showing that they are artificially constructed, a product of numerous histories, institutions, and processes of inscription which cannot be transcended by mere consciousness. Let us look at the three dominant paradigms from a deconstruction perspectives.

The Neoclassical Paradigm

The neoclassical paradigm understands the development processes as the binary struggle between the forces of rationality and irrationality, modernity and tradition, capitalism and socialism, industrialization and nomadic life, and so on.

Thus, the neoclassical school's emphasis on dichotomization of terms like "traditional" and "modern," with a corollary privileging of the former (ignoring the element in between, and individual variations) has become so much a commonplace of intellectual and academic life that it generally passes unquestioned. On closer examination, however, one finds that this taxonomic system, like others, encodes and helps to construct an associative social hierarchy in which one element is privileged and the other suppressed.

Not only that, the preferred term is also heavily weighed over the suppressed term, where it is taken to be a rational and desirable goal. The domains of the repressed term is then known only in terms of its irrational goal and undesirability. Moreover, since the neoclassical paradigm arguments are constituted by setting opposing terms and weighing them differently, as deconstructionists have observed, this creates power differences where the suppressed term is relegated to serving as a signifier of the preferred/privileged term.

Furthermore, in such a logocentric procedure,[68] the opposing terms are arranged hierarchically, thus displacing the suppressed, irrational term beyond the boundary of the significant, rational and desirable term. To be more concrete: modernity is placed at the apex, and tradition at the bottom of the modernity hierarchy, where the latter is urged to emulate the former in order to modernize or develop. The corollary of this is that those labeled variously as traditional, backward, and pre-capitalist societies are thought that they have nothing to contribute, nothing to teach, and nothing to be emulated by the modern societies other than serving as signifiers of modernity. Indeed, they seem to be condemned to permanent suppression, or exclusion.

The Dependency Paradigm

As with neoclassicals the dependency theorists also make such "truth" claims, claims constructed on particular myths of "progress." As explained earlier, they assume that the world is polarized into a powerful (the core), semi-powerful (semi-periphery) and weaker power (periphery). Capitalism is dependent on just such a polarized world order, where the development of the center is the result of the underdevelopment of the periphery. Moreover, surplus value is assumed to be produced in the periphery and transferred into the center. The market is understood as a mechanism for transferring surplus from one fraction of the ruling class to another as well as for extracting the surplus from the workers in the periphery by the capitalists in the center. Here the exploitation, in a Marxist sense, is explained by outlining the essential structural conditions of its possibilities.

The privileged position of the center, once achieved, is said to be self-perpetuating: the more surplus, the more power the center gains; the more surplus siphoned off, the more underdeveloped the periphery becomes. The main class struggle, therefore is between two antagonistic "classes": the center and the periphery or the first two worlds against the third world.

The developed and the underdeveloped are not only set in opposition to each other, they are also differently weighed in a system where the developed have more power than the underdeveloped. The underdeveloped is suppressed; it mainly functions to highlight the significance of the developed and the powerful. The identity and the meaning of the developed is understood in the context of the presence and permanent suppression of the underdeveloped.[69]

These unequal power relations serve as the essence of capitalism and international capitalist economic relations, in the same way that a particular notion of human nature (as innovative) is the ultimate determinant of capitalism in the neoclassical approach. The result of this unequal exercise of power is that the gains from the world accumulation of world wealth are distributed unequally between the two blocs of nations that participate in the capitalist world economy.

Such categorical thinking creates self-sufficient and exclusive categories or types that order the world conceptually as well as normatively. When institutionalized, such categories or types can become the guiding principles of social policy, thereby helping to mold a world in their own image. Thus, in our case, the center will be categorized under the "normal" type, and all the various peripheries and semi-peripheries will be abnormal deviations. Here, plural differences are reduced to a binary opposition, a normative hierarchy of good and bad, which serves as the ideological basis for the rationalization of the development pattern for the peripheries.

The Orthodox Marxist Paradigm

The same argument applies to orthodox Marxists. Marxism in general is seen as a formal model in which the forces and relations of production are given ontological primacy. In other words, orthodox Marxists claim that Marx intended a special role for the economic structure of a society, insofar as the nature of people depends on the material conditions determining their production. According to this school, Marx claimed

> men are the producers of their conceptions, ideas, etc.--real active men, as they are conditioned by a definite development of their productive forces and of the intercourse corresponding to these, up to its furtherest forms. Consciousness can never be anything else than conscious existence, and the existence of men is their life-process.[70]

The "what and how" of production are historical processes that supposedly Marx defined in terms of the relations between a particular industrial stage (where forces of production, or the means of production, consist of tools and machinery, and knowledge,) and its corresponding social stage, or mode of cooperation (the relations of production such as between lords and serfs, masters and slaves, capitalists and workers).[71]   These social structures, defined in terms of their modes of production, constitute the existing world within which people produce and reproduce their existence and thus come to define human existence.

Orthodox Marxist theories, then, be they of development or some other specific social phenomenon, must take the particular economic structure in which that phenomenon occurs as the primary framework for analysis. This is because different economic structures produce different effects, given their different organization of productive relations.   As discussed earlier, the economic structure is thus considered primary to the extent that it is the underlying framework that both unifies the social whole and determines (in a structural sense) how other aspects, such as politics, will function and be reproduced.

To claim, as orthodox Marxists do, that the "economic" is determinant in the "first" or "in the last instance" is to ignore the always already political nature of the so-called "economic." To isolate something called "the economic" in this way, which precedes such relatively autonomous instances as "the political," is to play into the hands of neoclassical ideology, which would also like to conceal the coercive political force inherent in the relations of production, that is, in production itself.[72]   The economic is not an ensemble of productive forces (determinant in the last or first instance), which exist prior to and without productive relations, without the political relations of force between, say, capitalist and laborer.   To claim otherwise is to impose wage labor in the name of "scientific socialism," claiming the necessity of following "objective" economic laws that only party scientists--not mere workers--can know, and of a following bureaucratic politicism that constitutes the party-state as the determinant in the first or last instance.[73]   By making seemingly neutral categorical distinctions (between political force and "objective" economic development), orthodox Marxists legitimate a division of labor that preserves the coercive work form and the enslavement of the working class to wage labor and the law of value.[74]   The recent violent refusal of this paradigm by East European countries is testimony to the inadequacy of this theory.

Some Conclusions
A deconstruction of the dominant paradigms we have been discussing means a rejection of all forms of essentialist claims by them.   In consequence, a door is opened to an unsettling discursive field that few want opened.   It would mean that there be no dominant paradigm, but different paradigms, socially fabricated stories displaying not only distinctive knowledge of social life (ontologies) but also distinctive claims about truth (epistemologies).   The corollary of this is that a democratization of paradigms will follow in which certain suppressed, despised or excluded discursive fields will have an equal opportunity in a democratic discourse.   This opens the possibility of inviting previously suppressed social, political-economic, and sexual-political cultural domains, as opposed to closing them off through the coercive power of a normative transcendental "science" conceived as absolute knowledge.

Deconstruction, therefore, neither disallows change (revolutionary or evolutionary), nor leads to anarchism.   It does offer certain cautions: not to think of truth in absolute, transcendental, ideal terms; and not to act with the assumption that theory controls and subsumes practice, that consciousness can fully account for the unconscious, that cause and effect always coincide. I believe that there is no absolute theory to guide action which is not historical, that is to say, transitional.

The final point in terms of our discussion of development, is that African development planners (or others in other LICs) no longer have to adhere rigidly to one or two paradigms to guide their development path, as many of them seem to have done with disastrous consequences. (A quick glance at the development path of Brazil, Cte d'Ivoire, Tanzania and Kenya, to name a few, attest to this assertion.) Rather, a deconstructed paradigm will allow policy makers in these countries to hold multiple theoretical positions in order to search for workable solutions to their country's particular development problems (themselves complex and dynamic) at that particular moment, within a democratic political environment, and hopefully within an open (democratic) contemporary international political and economic order.

CHAPTER 15

ENDNOTES

1. Osvaldo Sunkel, "The Development of Development Thinking," IDS
Bulletin 8(3, 1977): 6-11; and Cyril E. Black, The Dynamics of Modernization
(New York: Harper Torchbooks, 1966), p.7.

2. Andre G. Frank, "The Development of Underdevelopment," Monthly
Review Press (September, 1966).

3. Stephen Resnick and Richard Wolff, "Rhetorics, Economics and Marxian
Theories," Association for Economic and Social Analysis Discussion Paper
#31 (March, 1986): 16-32.

4. Sustainable development: This concept acknowledges the intrinsic
relationship between economic, social, and ecological imperatives. First of all,
it means growth that is sustainable in that it does not crumble in the face of
the slightest external shock. It means growth with domestic and external
financial stability. It means growth that is dynamic and that creates the
conditions for future expansion by enhancing investment in human capital, in
particular. Sustainable development is concerned with the poor, the weak,
and the vulnerable. Finally, it is growth that does not wreak havoc with the
atmosphere, with the rivers, forests, or oceans, or with any part of mankind's
common heritage. In a word, high-quality growth entails working together to
achieve a complex set of economic and social goals: neglecting any one would
ultimately endanger the others.

5. Osvaldo Sunkel, "The Development of Development Thinking," IDS
Bulletin 8(3, 1977): 6-11; and Cyril E. Black, The Dynamics of Modernization
(New York: Harper Torchbooks, 1966), p.7. For a general discussion, see
Stephen Resnick and Richard Wolff, "Marxist Epistemology: the Critique of
Economic Determinism," Social Text 6 (1982).

6. Ibid.; and Marion J. Levy, Modernization and the Structure of Societies,
vol.2 (Princeton: Princeton University Press, 1966), pp. 35-36.

7. Cyril E. Black, The Dynamics of Modernization (New York: Harper
Torchbooks, 1966), p. 7; William R. Cline, International Debt and the Stability
of the World Economy (Washington, D.C.: Institute for International
Economics, 1983), p. 9.

8. For a general discussion of the neoclassical approach, see Stephen Resnick, John Sinisi, and Richard Wolff, "Class Analysis of International Relations," in W. Ladd Hollist and F. LaMond Tullis, eds., An International Political Economy, International Political Economy Yearbook, vol.1 (Boulder: Westview Press, 1985) pp. 87-123; and D. A. Rustow, A World of Nations: Problem of Modernization (Washington: Brookings Institution, 1967) pp. 275-276.

9. Usually $300-400 GNP per capital. See J. Smelser Niel, "Processes of Social Change" in N. J. Smelser, ed., Sociology (New York:John Wiley and Sons, 1967).

10. See, M. Francis Abraham, Perspectives on Modernization (Washington: University Press of America, 1980), p. 13.

11. A. Inkeles and D. Smith, Becoming Modern (Harvard University Press, 1974).

12. Daniel Lerner, "Comparative Analysis of Process of Modernization," in S. Rokkan, ed., Comparative Research Across Cultures and Nations (Mouton, 1968), p. 386.

13. Wilbert E. Moore, Social Change (New Jersey: Prentice-Hall, 1974), p. 94.

14. Edward Shils, Political Development in the New States, (The Hague: Mouton and Company, 1970), p. 382.

15. Walter W. Rostow, The Stages of Economic Growth (New York: Cambridge University Press, 1960).

16. Ibid.

17. For a general discussion of the neoclassical approach, see Stephen Resnick, John Sinisi, and Richard Wolff, "Class Analysis of International Relations," in W. Ladd Hollist and F. LaMond Tullis, eds., An International Political Economy, International Political Economy Yearbook, vol. 1 (Boulder: Westview Press, 1985), pp. 87-123.

18. Ibid.

19. Samuel P. Huntington, "The Change to Change: Modernization, Development and Politics" in Comparative Politics, 3(3, 1971): 303; and "Political Development and Political Decay" in World Politics, 17(3, April 1965): 393-4.

20. Leelananda de Silva, Development Aid: A Guide to Facts and Issues (Geneva: Third World Forum, 1982?).

21. The model underlays the development plans of a large number of developing countries. The model was based on a capital:output ratio and presupposed that capital investment of a certain quantity would bring about a given increase in output. If the capital:output ratio were 4:1--an average assumption in most developing country plans--four units of capital, say $4, would result in an increase in output of $1. If 20% of a country's GNP were saved and invested this would lead to an increase of 5% of GNP.

22. See Resnick, Sinisi, and Wolff, "Class Analysis of International Relations," pp. 87-123.

23. Leonard Binder, Lucian W. Pye, et al., "Crises and Sequences" in Political Development (Princeton and London: Princeton University Press, 1971), p. 7.

24. Andre G. Frank, "The Development of Underdevelopment," Monthly Review (September 1966).

25. For instance, Amin is not the same as Frank nor Emmanuel can be compared with Immanuel. Each is different in its theoretical approach and its logic of argument.

26. J. A. Hobson, Imperialism: A Study (Ann Arbor: University of Michigan Press, 1965); K. Nkruma, Neo-colonialism: The Last Stage of Imperialism (New York: International Publishing Co., 1965); Paul Baran, The Political Economy of Growth (New York: Monthly Review Press, 1957); Lenin, Imperialism: The Highest Stages of Capitalism; H. Magdoff, The Age of Imperialism (New York: Monthly Review Press, 1969); and Paul Baran and Paul Sweezy, Monopoly Capital: An Essay on the American Social and Economic Order (New York: Monthly Review Press, 1966).

27. Andre G. Frank, "The Development of Underdevelopment," Monthly Review (New York: Monthly Review Press, September 1966); "Sociology of Development and Underdevelopment of Sociology," Catalyst 3(Summer, 1967).

28. Ibid.

29. C. R. Bath and D. D. James, "Dependency Analysis of Latin American," Latin American Research Review 11(3, 1976).

30. Walter Rodney, How Europe Underdeveloped Africa with a postscript by A. M. Babu (Washington: Howard University Press, 1974).

31. Osvaldo Sunkel and Pedro Paz, quoted in The Gap between Rich and Poor: Contending on the Political Economy of Development," ed. by Mitchell A. Seligson (Westview Press, 1984).

32. Arghire Emmanuel, Unequal Exchange: A Study of the Imperialism of Trade (New York: Monthly Review Press, 1972) pp. 378-380.

33. Ibid.

34. Ibid.

35. Ibid.

36. Ibid.

37. Immanuel Wallerstein, The Capitalist World Economy (London: Cambridge University Press, 1979) and "How Accumulation Works" in Contemporary Sociology 10(1, 1979); The Modern World-System: Capitalist Agriculture and the Origins of the European World Economy in the Sixteenth Century (New York: Academic Press, 1974).

38. Ibid.

39. Ibid.

40. Ibid.

41. The neoclassical school argues that conventional economic factors account for this growth, that foreign investment has played a key role in unleashing this potential for growth, and that this growth has brought modernization and greater equity in social and economic relations. In contrast, dependency theorists argue that industrialization in the NICs has simply transformed, rather than eradicated, the specific structures of external dependence and has done little, if anything, to ameliorate internal dependency conditions (Cardoso, 1981 provides a good comparative overview of these contending perspectives).

42. Osvaldo Sunkel, "Transnational Capitalism and National Disintegration in Latin America," Social and Economic Studies Journal 22(1973): 1.

43. See, The studies of both institutions by Cheryl Payer in The Debt Trap: The International Monetary Fund and The Third World (New York: Monthly Review Press, 1974); and The World Bank: A Critical Analysis (New York: Monthly Review Press, 1982).

44. Theotonio Dos Santos, "The Crisis of Development Theory and the Problem of Dependence in Latin America," in H. Bernstein, ed., Underdevelopment and Development (Penguin Press, 1973).

45. See, R. Peter Dweitt and James F. Petras, "Political Economy of International Debt: The Dynamics of Financial Capital," in Jonathan David Aronson, ed., Debt and the Less Developed Countries (Boulder, CO: Westview Press, 1979), pp. 191-215.

46. See, Arthur MacEwan, "The Current Crisis in Latin America," Monthly Review 36(February 1985): 1-18.

47. For instance, Bill Warren, "Imperialism and Capitalist Industrialization," New Left Review 81(September/October 1973): 3; Geofrey Kay, Development and Underdevelopment: A Marxist Analysis (London: Macmillan, 1975), p. x.

48. Anthony Brewer, Marxist Theories of Imperialism: A Critical Survey (London, Boston and Henley: Routledge and Kegan Paul, 1980), ch. 11.

49. Unless otherwise noted this is taken from the works of Resnick and Wolff, in Stephen Resnick and Richard Wolff, "Rhetorics, Economics and Marxian Theories," Association for Economic and Social Analysis Discussion Paper #31 (March, 1986): 16-32.

50. Ibid.

51. Ibid.

52. Ibid.

53. Ibid.

54. Ibid.

55. Ibid.

56. Ibid.; also see, Maurice Dobb, Studies in the Development of Capitalism (New York: International Publishers, 1947).

57. Ibid.

58. E. P. Thompson, The Making of the English Working Class (New York: Vintage/Random House, 1966), pp. 9-13; 424-

59. Stephen Resnick and Richard Wolff, "Rhetorics, Economics and Marxian Theories," Association for Economic and Social Analysis Discussion Paper #31 (March, 1986).

60. Ibid.

61. Ibid.

62. Resnick and Wolff, "Rhetorics, Economics and Marxian Theories."

63. See for example, Richard J. Bernstein, ed., Habermas and Modernity (Cambridge University Press, 1979); Nancy S. Love, Marx, Nietzsche and Modernity (New York: Columbia University Press, 1986); Vincent Descombes, Modern French Philosophy, trans. by L. Scott-Fox and J.M. Harding (Cambridge, England: Cambridge University Press, 1979).

64. R. B. J. Walker, "The Prince and the Pauper: Tradition, Modernity, and Practice in the Theory of International Relations," in James Der Derian and Michael J. Shapiro, eds., International/Intertextual Relations: Postmodern Readings of World Politics (Lexington, MA: Lexington Books, 1989).

65. Ibid.

66. Barbara Johnson, A World of Difference (Baltimore and London: The John Hopkins University Press, 1987).

67. James Der Derian and Michael J. Shapiro, eds, International/Intertextual Relations: Postmodern Readings of World Politics (Lexington, MA: Lexington Books, 1989).

68. This operation, which at once differentiates one term from another, prefers one to the other, and arranges them hierarchically, displacing the

subordinate term beyond the boundary of what is significant and desirable in context. Ibid., p. 16.

69. Simon Dalby, Creating the Second Cold War: The Discourse of Polity (London and New York: Guilford Press, 1990), pp. 6-7.

70. Robert C. Tucker, The Marx-Engels Reader 1st ed. (New York: W. W. Norton and Company, 1972), p. 118.

71. See, for instance, Maurice Dobb, Studies in the Development of Capitalism (New York: International Publishers, 1947), pp. 1-20.

72. See the works of Louis Althusser and, especially, Nikos Poulantzas' Political Power and Social Classes (London, 1975).

73. Karl Marx, "the Class Struggle in France 1848-1850," in David Fernbach, ed., Surveys from Exile (London, 1975), pp. 49-51; and MEW, vol. 17(Berling, 1964), pp. 23-25, p. 39.

74. Ibid., pp. 51-52, 54, 58; also, Basic Works of Marx and Engels (New York, 1959), pp. 25, 27, 31.

Chapter 16

Descent into Sociopolitical Decay:
Legacies of Maldevelopment in Africa

I. Introduction: The New World Order/Disorder

When the old order changes suddenly or unexpectedly as the international political system did in 1989, it creates many problems for all system actors and stake holders. The old system rules are no longer appropriate, hence no longer binding on major actors and hegemonic stake holders. The new rules do not exist yet except in fragmented, embryonic forms. There follows the inevitable period of transition. There is confusion. There are displacements and expectations. Fears and anxieties deepen in some quarters, while hopes may bloom in others. There must be adjustments by all parties. This search for a new equilibrium affects all stake holders unequally.

The **New World Order (NWO)** is not yet fully established. Africans, African scholars, Africanist scholars, and the administrative military-political-economic-bureaucratic leadership complex in African states are all eager to know where and how Africa, African states, and Africans fit or will fit into this new world order.

Everybody wants to know. All want to know the likely possibilities, the gains and losses, the advantages and disadvantages, the short and long term effects of the consequences of the sudden and unexpected revolutionary changes that took place in the structure of the world's political, economic, and ideological arrangements since 1989. It is known that some actors have order and stability. It is also known that some other actors and stake holders have gained increased disorder and instability. Some have a combined measure of both?

There are other more compelling reasons why Africa and the rest of Third World are concerned about the **New World Order.** The idea of a new world order did not originate from President Bush or Mikhail Gorbachev following the 1989 radical and fundamental transformation of the international

337

political system. Gorbachev's speech at the UN in 1987 which called for the extension of his doctrine of "**perestroika and glasnost**" within the Soviet Union to the entire international community of nations was important in creating the switch to the narrow concern for the "**New World Order**" concept. In true fashion, the Third World was the originator of the initial call for a new world order. That was back in the 1970s. By the end of the decade of the 1960s, "the North-South Axis of international politics has become increasingly important and contentious. The LDCS (Less Developed Countries = The Third World) are increasingly asserting that they have a right to share in the world's economic wealth. They have acted on a number of fronts to enhance their own economic situations and to pressure the industrialized countries to redistribute part of their wealth."[1] This was a call for global economic justice in an organized, forceful fashion.

Such "Third World consciousness and assertiveness has led to a series of demands on the industrialized North. These calls for reforms are collectively known as the **New International Economic Order**" (**NIEO**).[2] This declaration was presented to the UN, and was adopted by the UN General Assembly in 1974. It accused the North of dominating global economic structures in such a way that results in the maldistribution of wealth, unjustly favoring the North at the expense of the South-- The Third World. **To remedy such economic injustice and maldistribution, the Third World called specially for five major changes in the operations of international economics and distribution of global wealth: 1) radical trade reforms, 2) significant monetary reforms, 3) technology transfers to enable the Third World to pursue programs of rapid industrialization, 4) assertion of Third World economic sovereignty and domestic economic control and freedom, and finally 5) extension of economic aid by the North to the South equal at least to 0.7 - 1.0 percent of the North's GNP per year.** The North fought tooth and nail to resist these changes. They made only marginal, largely insignificant changes in response to these demands.[3]

This is the background to the momentous changes of 1989-1991 in international politics. By the time President Bush of the United States of America was calling for America's leadership of the **New World Order** in 1990, some fundamental transformation has taken place in the mental and moral conception of things needing to be changed in the structure of relations between the North and the South: The original call of Third World countries for the **NIEO** has suddenly and cleverly been transformed into the **NWO**! The imperative of the call for economic, distributive, and developmental justice contained in the original document of the 1974 **NIEO**, was conspicuously missing in the concerns and formulations of the **NWO**.

That is why African states are worried and anxious about their fate in the newly emerging order of things to come. There is legitimate fear of intensification of Africa's marginalization. There is fear that external western economic and technical aid which was already dwindling would disappear altogether. Western private investments are likely to be redeployed to the newly independent Eastern European countries, Russia, and the newly independent former Soviet Republics. Finally, there is concern that, in the absence of the "superpower rivalries" of the cold war era, the "unipolar superpower status of the United States" as the leader of the world could mean an absolute neglect and abandonment of Africa, and Africa's needs in the emerging order of thing. These fears and anxieties are not unfounded or misplaced. The chronic instability and sociopolitical decay and disorders in Africa by themselves are nearly sufficient to bring such fears and anxieties into disastrous fruition.

II. The African Continental Case

The focus of this paper is on the interaction among three concepts that can theoretically help to explain and understand the likely future position of African states in the emerging world order: The first is political decay. The second is maldevelopment. The third deals with the legacies of the combined processes of accumulating political decay and socioeconomic maldevelopment. As a whole, the continent of Africa has become a major stake holder in, and a significant contributor to the emerging structure of global, international disorders. Africa now contributes the greatest number of violent and destructive crises per subregion facing the international community. Africa's share in the total number of disintegrative and disintegrating nation states is large enough to lead to the tentative conclusion that the continent will become the major focus for international management of chronic human, economic, political, and general civil disorders for the rest of this rather bloody century.

At present nearly fifty percent (50 percent) of Africa's over six hundred million (> 600,000,000) population are encapsulated within states undergoing complete chaos (Angola, Burundi, Chad, Ethiopia, Liberia, Somalia, Sudan, Spanish Sahara, Rwanda); or operating at the precipice of civil war (Algeria, Egypt, Sierra Leane, South Africa, Uganda, Zaire); or coping with chronic political virulence and instability (Benin Republic, Cameroon, Eritrea, Kenya, Malawi, Mozambique, Nigeria, Togo) Several of these states are held in the unrelenting grip of some negative forces of nature like the drought and famine which have plagued held of the continent from the western Sahel, across the Sahara belt to the Horn, East, and Southern Africa, beginning late 1972, and occurring fairly periodically in different areas to the present time.

The African continent is also the subregion of the world with the highest rate of population growth, the slowest rate of economic growth, and the lowest rate of economic productivity increase (see Table One). The average rate of population growth per year in Africa is about 3.2 percent.

The average rate of growth of the African economies is about 1.5 percent according to World Bank, IMF and United Nations figures; in 1987 that rate fell to 0.8 percent. These international agencies state that African economies would need to grow at 6-8 percent a year to maintain a stable, not necessarily increasing standard of living for the population as a whole. These indicators suggest not just economic stagnation, but disturbing rapid economic decline and depression. This phenomenon alone raises a disturbing scenario for Africa's future economic recovery possibilities as well as deepening concern for the likelihood of any chances for long term sustainable increases in African people's overall standard of living.[4]

These are in away merely a catalogue of intractable problems. What need be added are the governance patterns that have evolved in African states since the golden years of the 1960s when all of Africa was full of hope and promise that political independence would bring justice, freedom, democracy, development-- rapid development, as well as the containment, if not the total eradication of poverty.

However, the governance patterns which emerged, and which were relentlessly institutionalized and consolidated have in themselves become the nightmares of African societies and peoples. African governance became the province of autocratic, patrimonial rulers, while the "offices of African states are now treated as if they were the prebends of decentralized patrimonial states ... which could be appropriated and exploited by their occupants to benefit themselves and their sectional constituents".[5]   These patterns of governance, and the *modus operandi sustained during the last three decades*, have become in Goran Hyden's telling phrase "an albatross around Africa's neck".[6]

Taken as a collective whole, the ultimate tragedy of African states is that they are not making much progress toward social justice, political freedom, democracy or development.   On the contrary they have been marching in step from underdevelopment into maldevelopment, from the margins of potential economic viability in the 1960s into the deep abyss of abundant harvests of poverty in the 1990s,[7] from potential nation-building at the dawn of independence into political fragmentation and disillusionment, from the promise of the consolidation of viable nation-states into the entrenchment of disintegrative subnationalisms of tribal, ethnic, regional, or religious exclusivity and separatism,-- and in several places, clan war-lordism-- three decades later.

III. Descent Into Sociopolitical Decay

The reality of political decay in Africa has been with us for sometime. It was Samuel Huntington's seminal book, <u>Political Order in Changing Societies</u>[8] that gave advance warnings to the theorists of modernization of the

1960s that fundamental cultural, social, and political modernization cannot take place without some measure of disorder. Such changes bring with them the inevitable periods of transition-- transition from one social order to the wished - for social state. We now know that such transitions have revealed the fact that when the old rules of the old order are breaking down, the new rules that are to govern the new order are not yet fully formed; and when the new rules are forming, they do not yet acquire the authority and legitimacy of internalized moral or sentimental attachments.

Therefore, the lag between the efficacy of the rules of the old order, and the moral legitimacy of the rules of the new order presents many difficulties. One of such difficulties is that the transitional period brings with it the uncertainties of expected behavior. Such a period also entails the emergence of autonomous legislators, a kind of everyone for himself original state of nature where virtually anything goes, and powerful, dominant individual and/or group actors assume the authority to make the rules up as they go along, usually in their personal or group self-interests, as the social system evolves.

Thus, from Huntington's contribution, it came to be seen that sociopolitical modernization or development entails inevitable disorders. Some win, but some must also lose. Who wins and who loses are determined under the stains of the competition whose rules are not necessarily clear or valid. At the time the theorists of political development and modernization in Africa and in the rest of the Third World of the 1960s and 1970s were detailing the neat " causes and sequences of political development, the aspects of political development, the crises of political development and modernization"[9] and the economic development theorists of the same period were emphasizing the required recipes and ingredients of economic growth and development or the states of economic growth and development",[10] they all grossly underestimated the seriousness of the inevitable disorders that are bound to attend the processes of cultural, economic, social, and political transformations as colonized, underdeveloped societies struggle with the transitions from their original state of foreign repression and domination, colonial autocracy and totalitarianism, to achieve a political independence that ultimately came without economic independence or control. The conditions of neocolonialism that emerged everywhere in colonized, underdeveloped societies struggle with the transitions from their original state of foreign repression and domination, colonial autocracy and totalitarianism, to achieve a political independence that ultimately came without economic independence or control. The conditions of neocolonialism that emerged everywhere in colonized societies, especially in Africa, quickly led to the institutionalization of what Theodore Lowi calls "the politics of disorder".[11]

In the absence of efficacious or legitimate rules during the transitional period, the politics of sociopolitical change is easily transformed into the politics of sociopolitical decay and disorder. This begins with "system overloads", as demands overwhelm the capacity of governance institutions to meet or produce the needs of citizens. This in my view accounts for the appearance of the "discontinuities between sociopolitical and governmental processes"[12] of development in Africa.

In a general form, it is the failure of African rulers, African leaders, African governments, African governance institutions that accounts for the emergence of first, political decay, then sociopolitical instability, followed by societal fragmentation, and finally political disorders in contemporary Africa. The politics of the African post-colonial states evolved largely as the politics of exclusion, a zero-sum game kind of politics, the politics of allocative or distributive injustices. This kind of politics brings system-wide discontent, a sense of deeply rooted grievance, leading to the loss of loyalty and general support, crises of governmental legitimacy and participation. Such large-scale mass discontents show up in forms of ethnic, regional, religious, sectionalism, and virulent tribal subnationalisms in African societies.

The imperative of African governance at independence was to establish a new social order. Above all else, it was to be a search for a deep rooted justice for groups and individuals. This quest for order in the face of the traditional and primordial structures for loyalty, and the inharmonious group identities, and group interests of the composition of the post-colonial state, was in itself a daunting challenge. The African post-colonial state had no "just" original or inherent historical basis for commanding emotional, sentimental, moral loyalty from its component parts.

The generalized loyalty it enjoyed came from a precarious sense of collective humiliation and oppression that all sections of the state felt against the imperial authoritarian abuses of African peoples. But this was not going to be a sufficient basis for sustainable long term consolidation of national unity. In any case this generalized sense of grievance against the imperial insult soon wore out, and attention shifted as it should to the demands processing and delivery capabilities of the new state. This fact is often readily overlooked in the analysis of the predicaments of the neocolonial state in Africa.

The only morally valid way for the new states to secure the new order and with it such national attachment, sustain loyalty, and thus create long term legitimacy of authoritative rule, was for them to practice, sustain, and consolidate the politics of fairness, envision and create regimes of group inclusiveness and participation, and of distributive, economic justice. Political integration was a necessity in the face of the many ethnic, linguistic, cultural, regional, religious, and formative class cleavages that formed the foundation and structure of the new states. But political and economic resource scarcities were also a critically binding constraint on the capacity of the new governments to process the unlimited demands and developmental expectations of 'identific groups' and individuals, unleashed by the promise of independence, especially coming as they did from the exuberance, and exaggeration of the rhetoric of the promises of the nationalist revolutionary leaders: the existence of the colonial governments was said to be the absolute and only cause of all the problems of African peoples struggling for freedom and independence; therefore the mere and simple removal of the colonial oppressors was going to be the necessary and sufficient action to bring about the immediate establishment of modernization and full development heaven on earth! Unfortunately, nothing is ever that simple. The colonial state was more firmly established than that. It was soon to be discovered that volumes of blood and tears-- extreme sacrifices-- will be needed from the people and their governments before the post-colonial state in Africa could salvage any modest political and economic progress, or secure a rudiment of sociopolitical integration.

The crucial point, therefore, is that the African post-colonial state was not natural. It was an artificial construct of the departing colonial metropolitan power, created precisely for the continuation of the interests of the departing foreign sovereign. In this sense, the African post-colonial state began its existence under conditions that guaranteed it no inherent command of loyalty on any ground other than the potential use of its coercive instruments of power and control. This conformed squarely with the inherited patterns of governance under colonial authoritarianism. The post-colonial state invariably chose to use this structure and pattern of coercive power to govern, and to force sociopolitical integration on terms that were unjust in economic allocation, political access, participation, power sharing, or accountability. What was achieved at best in the end was the troubled "precarious balance between state and society in Africa,"[13] and at the worst end, the chaos and disintegration of the fragile state of the Somalian, Liberian or Ethiopian kind.

In nearly all contemporary African states, this precarious balance rested on a tenuous exercise of autocratic, coercive power buttressed by the creation of governance institutions that increasingly subverted the expected or assumed positive purposes of government, development, and social wellbeing. It is the failure of this kind of political approach, among other forces, that began the slow, downward spiral of the African states' descent into political decay, state disintegration, and violent, social crises which increasingly are tending to chaos in a number of African states.

This original post-colonial state was nothing more than a conditional, glorified, utilitarian, expedient state from the point of view of the nature and structure of the centrifugal and centripetal forces arising from the composition of the state at independence. The groups composing it, and the citizens who found themselves within it largely by accident and the fiat of the imperial dictate had no "original or organic" loyalty to the state. They are going to love or hate it, support or oppose it, depending on the state's capacity or ability to deliver to the groups or individuals, their expected shares of the "national cake" in terms of economic, political value allocations on an ongoing conditional, pragmatic, utilitarian basis. To the extent that there emerges a generalized sense of identific group- collective or individual justice and perceived fairness, support and loyalty would flow to the state. To the extent that unfairness or injustice is perceived to be the intrinsic predipostition of the state, to that degree would support and loyalty be withheld or withdrawn from the state. The crucial factors in such "conditional state of affairs" are perception and rudimentary comparative deprivation scores by the various component parts of the state. These are central to the determination of the level of support and loyalty that the state would receive from such groups and individuals in the end.

One of the obvious missteps that arose was the failure of the post-colonial leaders to develop even the smallest degree of sensitivity to **this contingent basis of support and loyalty within the precarious state.** The ethnic diversity, religious divisions, and class formations and cleavages that were original to the state were soon to be declared, and treated as sources and breeders of treason and enmity to the state. Against these, the coercive powers of the intrusive state began to wage unrelenting war in the name of national unity and state security. The states lost the wars; state fragmentation and decline became inevitable.

IV. Sociopolitical Maldevelopment and African Marginalization

According to Whitaker in How Can Africa Survive,[14] most African states are having a hard time; most are failing and failing backwards. They are not developing as they should or could. They are said to be "pre-modern states" struggling to find their place "in a post-modern world"; they are shaky actors, acting on a stage shadowed by western values, interests, controls, manipulations, and dictates, in all aspects of their institutional, public policy, and governance arenas. Whitaker then concludes that the future of Africa is "a future in shadow".[15] Whitaker is not alone. Most Africanist analysts have concluded that most African post-colonial states have either failed, or are failing boldly. Only a few are seen to be making significant progress on any social, economic, or political scale (Libya, Gabon, Botswana, Algeria, Tunisia, Namibia, Congo Republic, Cameroon, Ojibouti, Morocco, Cote d' Ivoire, Senegal, Egypt. Zimbabwe, Mauritania. [See Table One for the per capita profile of African states]. On a scale of domestic repression and violations of human rights, very few of these "progressing states" can be said to be making political progress in full human terms.

Some African states are having difficulties because of the absence of natural endowments, or because they are landlocked states. The resource poor states in Africa (The Gambia, Chad, Burkina Faso, Lesotho, Niger, Mali, Malawi, Swaziland, etc.) may be excused for their precarious existences. But what of the majority of African states which have abundant natural endowments (Angola, Ghana, Guinea, Kenya, Nigeria, Sierra Leone, Uganda, Zaire, Zambia, just to name a few)? Why have these also failed? A significant part of the answer is to be found in the governance processes of maldevelopment.

In his provocative book, The Black Man's Burden: Africa and the Curse of the Nation-State,[16] Basil Davidson provides a persuasive historical tour of the landscape of the failure of the post-colonial state in Africa. The harbingers of this grand failure must first be located in the destructive encounter between Africa and western Europe that took place during the last seven centuries., the last four of which have witnessed the African holocaust of the slavery and slave trade that occupied the better part of more than 250 years of continuous rape of the continent's peoples, "the imperial bulkanization and pacification" of Africa into European spheres of influence of 1884-5 that formed the territorial bases for the 20th century European colonial states of Africa, as well as the territorial boundaries of the contemporary post-colonial states in Africa, colonialism, and the politics of post-colonial neocolonialism. The consequences of Africa's pre-independence European penetration, conquest, exploitation, brutalization, dehumanization, westernization, expropriation, subjugation, dislocation, and final integration into the imperial, global, capitalist, political economy, is what is generally treated in the literature of development as the political economy of underdevelopment of Africa.

It is crucial at this point to suggest that, beginning with the political economy of post-colonial, independent, African states, as well as their characteristic neocolonial political economy, the proper, more informing, analytic conceptualization should be **the political economy of maldevelopment in Africa**. This new explanatory conception normally absorbs the formative, historical experiences traditionally treated under the political economy of underdevelopment in Africa.

The advantage of this newer conception is that it allows for analysis that includes the dramatic failures of African governance institutions after independence; the tragic failures of African leadership in the social, political and economic arenas; the personalization of rulership, the expropriation of societal resources by the kleptocracy of the ruling classes in a patron-clientalist, autocratic, coerclue, and dangerously, intrusive state. In short, this newer formulation imposes on our analysis of the African political and economic problematic, the necessity of accounting for the independent role of Africans in the contemporary marginalization, exploitation, brutalization, disintegration, the economic impoverishment of Africa, and the people of Africa by their rulers and governments.

The traditional concept of the political economy of underdevelopment of Africa puts emphasis as it should on the role and culpability of external, largely western European forces in the accumulation of the harvest of poverty and marginalization of Africa. It focuses analysis on the systematic integration of Africa into the global, western capitalist market economy in a way that shows that African poverty is not separable from western, imperial fortunes and advancements, or advantages. Further it captures the richness of the logic of value dislocations in Africa as an attendant attribute of the European-values penetration of the continent. It lets analysts capture the essence of the many distortions and contradictions arising from the European determined priorities of cultural, economic, political, and societal evaluation in Africa. The inescapable conclusion of that form of underdevelopment is that Africa's patterns of historical evolution were made to serve the interests of the imperial order, not the needs and interests of African peoples or societies.

Of course, in the nature of human institutions, it was impossible for the imperial order to be "good proof". It was impossible to run the imperial enterprise without some benefits accruing to the "natives" whether intended or not. There is however, a significant drawback to this high powered analytic tool: it suppresses, and deflects attention from any reasonable focus on Africans' share of the responsibility, culpability for the emergence of a colossal socioeconomic, and sociopolitical failure of the post-colonial states in Africa. This is the analytic inadequacy that the concept of the political economy of maldevelopment in Africa helps to resolve, so that analysis can explain both the role of imperial as well as indigenous African actors in the grand failure of Africa's post-colonial state.[17]

Back to Davidson's final observations and conclusions. Africa's post-colonial state, he argues, "had become a shackle on (African) progress by the end of the 1980s... The state was not liberating and protective of its citizens, no matter what its propaganda (and propagandists) claimed: on the contrary, its gross effect was constricting and exploitative, or else it simply failed to operate in any social sense at all. Its overall consequences were in any case disastrous. And the prime reason for these consequences... 'can't be the massive corruption though its scale and pervasiveness are truly intolerable; it isn't the subservience to foreign manipulation, degrading as it is; it isn't even this second-class, hand-me-down capitalism, ludicrous and doomed'... But these were the effects. (The cause) lay in the failure of (Africa's) rulers to reestablish vital inner links with the poor and the dispossessed of (Africa), the

African masses.   It was the failure of post-colonial communities to find and insist upon means of living together by strategies less primitive and destructive than rival kingship networks, whether of ethnic clientalism or its camouflage in no less clientalist (single, or) multiparty systems, (or the expansive military dictatorships, life-presidents with their monarchic, imperial imitations and pretensions).[18]

The failure of Africa's post-colonial states is at once primarily and fundamentally the failure of sociopolitical leadership.   It is also the grand failure of Africa's governance institutions, public policy practices, and the palpable immorality of societal collective behavior at all levels, inclusive of the economic, military, bureaucratic, civil political class.   This is an entrenched class interest complex which doles out crumbs of state to their sectional supporters in an autocratic clientalist kelptocracy.   They export abroad the expropriated resources of state, acquired under "legal subterfuge" or brazenly open embezzlements, so that in the end, the state cannot even benefit from the investment profits, dividends, and profitability of the stolen resources.   If such resources were at least invested in the local economy, they would have some potential beneficial effects to ameliorate to a little degree the chronic failures of the domestic economy.   But because of the near total exportation of such resources, the state treasury as well as the local economy is permanently drained of its multiplier effects, and the moral and economic blood lines.   Nigeria and Zaire are gross examples of states so rich in resources that have been expropriated and exported abroad by their rulers that both have fallen almost to the bottom of the chronically impoverished beggar states of the world at present.

There are also some other problems concerning the explanations for these massive failures.   It is that autocratic rule must rely on coercive forces of the state to personalize, expropriate and exploit public offices for the enrichment of African ruling classes.   It is also true that such diversions of public resources do lead to not only domestic distortions in all sectors of the economy, social institutions, and governance structure, but also to their tragic, socialization- through sociopolitical learning by the generality of the population. The growing kleptocratic behavior of the ordinary citizen, and the sociopolitical cynicism of the masses are the readily observable consequences of how the absence of accountability on the part of the ruling classes filters down and percolates into the consciousness of the ordinary masses of the people, thereby compounding the moral failure of the larger society as a whole.

One view of the traditional explanations of these failures argues that these are results of underdevelopment itself.   This may involve the notion that the post-colonial state lacks adequate education, leadership, training in executive capacity, public policy analytic skills, planning skills, required factor endowments, savings culture, capital mobilization capabilities and the like.   In this view, *wastage is treated as the result of factors of inadequacy, mistaken judgements, unintentional and unintended consequences, the cure then becomes more training skills, more rational planning, more executive capacity, more capital and savings mobilization, more institutional building, and more accountability.* The trouble with this frame of analysis is that it is terribly limited; it misses the core character of the political economy of sociopolitical, socioeconomic maldevelopment: the processes and patterns of maldevelopment do not derive from mistaken judgements, and similar litany of inadequacies of the public decision makers. They derive from instead from rational processes, rationally conceived, rationally planned, and rationally executed to serve the personal ends of the ruling classes, the vested interests of the rational decision makers. In fact it would require less rational capabilities to govern rightly than to govern in the patterns of failed African rulers. It requires a high degree of rationality, sophistication of intellect, intelligence and sheer brilliance of sorts to execute so successfully the politics of maldevelopment to the degree that African ruling classes have done in the last three decades. This is the calculus of deliberately and single-mindedly replacing the objectives of positive state development with the calculus of positive personal enrichment at the complete expense of the citizens of the state. Under these conditions, there is justification for the emergent withdrawals of support and loyalty from the state by its identific group and individual members, using the currencies of their ethnic, communal, regional, religious or class identifications as well as combinations or permutations of these factors.

The fundamental logic of African maldevelopment suggests that the failure of state comes not from misunderstood purposes of governance or the incapacity to meet its standards of conduct, but from an intentional conception of the purposes of governance, of politics, of public activity as service primarily for the interests of rulers and the ruling classes. Government offices are to be used primarily for the material, economic, social, and power- controlling interests of the occupants of such public offices. *The salaries paid to such officers to do their duties for and to the people are merely treated by them as the entrance fees to the seats of public expropriation-- sweet icings on the cake of criminal fraud.*

Consider one recent example from Nigeria. The Babangida military administration had secretly allocated choice public lands to its friends in the political class. The land so secretly allocated to private persons in the government legally belonged to one of the member states, as opposed to the federal government. In order to make this decision irrevocable, General Babangida promulgated a decree during his last week in office in August 1993, vesting all such lands extending to twelve miles from any Nigerian coastline inward, in the federal government. Since a federal decree issued in 1975 had vested all land in the state governments and not in the federal government, the August 1993 decree was made retroactive to 1971! The decree also ousted the jurisdiction of all courts of law or any litigations concerning the scope and content of the last decree throughout the entire federation.[19] It requires an extreme kind of genius and rational calculus for any public official to attempt to expropriate public property in this fashion, and also go to such extreme ends to subvert the law, the courts, the judiciary and the constitution of the federal Republic, just to serve personal, criminal and selfish interests.

It is this kind of intentional, rational calculus that informs the actions of rulers and governments in Africa. It has become virtually impossible for any African ruler and African public offices. Thus public offices are intended for, and used mostly to enable their holders become wealthy at the expense of the masses of the state. The poverty of African states is more the product of this calculus than it is the product of the lack of natural endowments, and the other factor scarcities or systemic inadequacies discussed above. Therefore, the political economy of maldevelopment in Africa is the direct product of a rational, systematic process, deliberately and brilliantly engineered to accomplish rationally and sophisticatedly designed objectives that serve the exclusive ambitions and interests of Africa's ruling and political, economic classes.

In such regimes of maldevelopment, large portions of foreign aid, government-to-government loans and transfers, multilateral aids, and even private foreign investments find their way into the pockets of government officials at the highest levels of state. What analysts can and do often observe is that **the public explanations and statements of government officials do conform to the internationally acceptable rationales for such public policies. Things are said to be done in the name of the people for the people; this practice allows the public officers to divert attention from their internal calculus of intended hidden agendas and personal services. Public discourse on public policies do conform on the surface to rational public expectations and explanations for public directed public policy goals and objectives. But the private execution of public policies serves the interests of the policy decision makers, and the personal, vested interests of the ruling classes.**

Again the case of recent practices in Nigeria will illustrate the point being made here. In Nigeria it has become common public knowledge that contractors must may kickbacks as high as 20-50 percent of the face value of public contracts. But the expropriation does not end there. It is common knowledge that a contractor can secure payment for contracts not executed at all, but which are certified by public officials as completed. In such cases, the entire value of the contract is shared among the scheming public officials and the contractor.

Another practice is for the government to advance say, 50 percent of the face value of the cost of a public project to the contractor before any work is done; and then terminate the work of the contractor several months later from non-performance. But the contractor in this case is not compelled to pay back the money already "legally" paid out. The project is then recontracted to another contractor at newly inflated costs far in excess of the original cost estimates. New kickbacks are then paid again. This practice can continue for as many as five times on a single project. Such abuses are further aided by the frequency of changes of governments. When new regimes come into existence through coups d' etats and the like, the new governments promptly terminate several contracts awarded by their predecessors, only to reaward many of the same contracts to their friends at inflated costs so that the flow of the kickbacks can continue indefinitely.[20]

The results are to be seen in the landscape of unfinished, abandoned public projects, non-cumulative development patterns, inferior quality of finished projects, premature breakdown or collapse of completed projects, some before they are put into public use. This rationally and intentionally programmed waste serves the purposes of public officials and political rulers at several points in the system. I will be fool hardy for analysts to continue to assume that these are the products of some "dumb, incompetent bureaucrats", or mistaken administrative failures that could be cured by more training or the addition of more executive capacity."

Maldevelopment has become a way of life, a way of governance in the African post colonial states. That is why Basil Davidson's characterization of the African post-colonial state as "a curse on Africa" is apt. That it is also a "curse" on sustainable African development is quite apparent at present. Disturbing though such characterization may be, the fact remains that African states cannot hope to escape from their present marginalization and economic depression and decline without beginning with the understanding of the true causes of African states' contemporary predicaments. Malpolitical economy is bad governance for African peoples; but it is indeed good, very good, governance instrumentality for African states' ruling classes and their sectional clientele. This is the paradox and duality of contemporary African political economy.

V. Profiles and Progressions of the Legacies of Maldevelopment in Africa

The decade of the 1960s became know in Africa as the decade of freedom. African states stormed the gate of the United Nations seeking admission as sovereign actors, anxious to "rove" that they too belong among the club of free and civilized nations. It was indeed the decade of intoxicating promise, of hopes unbounded. Liberation was at hand. Development was in the air; it was going to come like a hurricane sweeping across the continental landscape. Africa was going to shrink time, so it could catch up with the west. Independence was going to bring progress in huge, giant scoops, so that Africa could and would do for her children in 50 years what it took the imperial west centuries to accomplish. Internally, limitations were either unseen, or if seen, were discounted. Africa was known to have huge natural endowments, the stuff of great nations in the making. Harnessing such nature's bounties is all that is required to catapult this sleeping giant of a continent into the brotherhood of material progress, abundance and prosperity. Africa will beat the western imperial oppressors at their own game. It was only a matter of time.

Externally, the optimism was even more electric. The promise of Africa's natural resources was economically irresistible. What was needed immediately was to ensure the containment of the communists way out in the far East, to be sure they do not go anywhere near this new capitalist paradise-in-waiting. The continent belonged to the "free world", and must be made secure for it at any cost in the great confrontations of the East-West, cold war ideological rivalries. In hindsight, this was the climate that made possible the lending of huge loans to African states by western governments, banks and financial institutions, private corporations and the like.

Whatever the expectations of resources exploitation through such investments and loans, the ultimate result is Africa's crippling contemporary debt burden which stood at about $283 billion in 1990.[21] Now Africa is sinking under the weight of this debt, unable to secure new loans or pay back what it borrowed. The burden is so crippling for development that no African state could easily afford the debt servicing costs without mortgaging as much as half of its external earnings per year. These "wages of altruism", to borrow a phrase from Whitaker, can be seen in more naked terms: "in 1986, some 16 African countries transferred 350 percent more money to the IMF than they received from it in 1985."[22] Even under normal conditions, not much economic development and progress can take place under such unfavorable, and unequal terms of exchange.

The decade of the 1960s also witnessed the launching by African leaders and educational elites, of many abstract ideological and political ideas: Kaunda's political philosophy of humanism; Nyerere's African socialism; Nkrumah's scientific Marxist-Leninism and African personality; Awolowo's democratic socialism; Sekou Toure's radical marxism, Qadaffi's Islamic revolutionary rebirth, Pan-Africanism, Afro-Marxism, African communalism, etc. These were followed by the doctrines of single-party democracy; state capitalism; welfare statim, etc. All of these have now been shown to have failed in all their pretensions. There emerged little correspondence between the ideas postulated by the ruling classes and the actual practices of governance by most of them. The few possible exceptions-- Tanzania, Botswana, Guinea Bissau, and Libya-- only go to prove the failures.

By the end of the decade of independence, political assassinations and military coups d'etat have become the norm of governance is several African states. Ideally, the decade of the 1970s was going to be the decade of African economic development. For the UN, it was Africa's second decade of economic development. But the pattern of governance was beginning to travel a different road from any road that could lead to cumulative, sustained economic development. There had emerged an abyss of dissonance between governance institutions and rulership behaviors, and the planned strategies of economic development. Military, single-party, and even multiparty autocracies mushroomed all over the governance landscape.

The United Nations (UN), the Organization of African Unity (OAU) and the Economic Commission for Africa (ECA) all cooperated to develop the Lagos Plan of Action for the economic development of Africa from 1980 - 2000. That plan put great emphasis on African national and collective self-reliance, and self-sustaining strategies of development for the African states.[23] The plan noted the heart of Africa's development strategies has been more sharply felt in Africa than in other continents of the world. Indeed, rather than result in an improvement in the economic situation of the continent, successive strategies have made it staminate and become more susceptible than other regions to the economic and social crises suffered by the industrialized countries."[24] However, the decade of the 1980s only deepened the political and economic crises of African states. By the end of the decade of the 1980s, the spiral of socioeconomic and political decay has turned into the avalanche of declining standards of living along with increasing large scale civil war casualties, growing repressions, invidious violations and abuses of human rights on large scale across the continent. In most of African states the standards of living of citizens have been declining from the time of the promise of independence in the 1960s to the present time of doom and gloom, of hopelessness and pessimism, of the decade of the 1990s.

The decade of the 1990s has been redesignated once gain by Africa, the UN, the World Bank, the IMF, and the West as the decade of African economic recovery. This assumed that African economies were ever healthy at any time before! But the decline of African economies and Africans' standards for living are yet to reach bottom. The economies of some of the African states are actually enjoying a robust "free fall" at present. There is little prospect of a major upswing on the economic horizon as we approach the halfway mark of the last decade of this century. The year 2000 is around the corner, but no indications of economic revival, especially in those violent and self-destructing states of Africa, are visible as of now.

By adopting a very crude rule of thumb, we could assume that one third of the explanation may be within the scope of external factors. Another third of the explanation may be attributable to unfortunate natural disasters or acts of the gods or God. *But at least the last third of the search for explanations must be located in the deliberate misgoverning of Africa for the rational calculus of self interests of Africa's ruling classes. In the long run no national development, no national progress can result from the continued utilization of the strategies and patterns of intentional socioeconomic, and sociopolitical maldevelopment in African states.*

Table One
Profile of African States' Economic Poverty: 1989

Country	Per Capita $	Population Growth Rate Per Year	Exports $Million OR $B'N	Imports $Million OR $B'N
Algeria	2170	3.0	8.6B	7.7B
Angola	925	2.7	3.8B	1.5B
Benin Pep.	360	2.9	2.50	442
Botswana	2500	2.7	1.8B	1.7B
Burkina Faso	330	2.9	262	619
Burundi	200	3.2	81	197
Cameroon	1040	2.7	2.1B	2.1B
Cape Verdi IS	740	3.0	10.9	107.8
CAR	440	2.6	148	239
Chad	130	2.1	174	264
Congo Rep.	1050	3.0	751	564
Cote d'Ivoire	750	3.5	2.5B	1.4B
Djibouti	1030	2.6	190	311
Egypt	630	3.0	2.6B	7.3B
Eritrea	NA	NA	NA	NA
Ethiopia	130	3.1	429	1.1B
Equat. Guinea	411	2.6	41	57
Gabon	3090	1.4	1.1B	780
The Gambia	230	3.2	122.2	155.2

Country	Per Capita $	Population Growth Rate Per Year	Exports $Million OR $B'N	Imports $Million OR $B'N
Ghana	380	3.1	826	1.2B
Guinea Bissau	160	2.4	14.2	68.9
Guinea Rep.	380	2.8	645	551
Kenya	380	3.6	1.1B	2.4B
Lesotho	240	2.6	66	499
Liberial/prewar	400	3.4	505	394
Libya	5500	2.8	5.6B	5.7B
Madagascar	200	3.2	290	436
Malawi	250	1.8	390	560
Mali	250	2.4	295	513
Mauritania	500	3.1	3.3B	5.4B
Morocco	900	3.1	3.3B	5.4B
Mozambique	110	4.6	90	764
Namibia	1240	3.6	1.02B	864
Niger Rep.	270	3.4	308	386
Nigeria	395	3.0	13.0B	9.5B
Rwanda	310	3.8	117	293
Senegal	615	3.1	801	1.0B
Sierra Leone	325	2.6	130	183
Somalia	210	3.3	58	354
South Africa	2600	2.6	24.0B	18.8B
Sudan	330	3.0	465	1.0B
Swaziland	670	2.7	543	651
Tanzania	240	3.4	340	1.2B
Togo	395	3.6	331	344
Tunisia	1253	3.0	3.5B	5.5B

Country	Per Capita $	Population Growth Rate Per Year	Exports $Million OR $B'N	Imports $Million OR $B'N
Uganda	290	3.7	273	652
W. Sahara	NA	NA	NA	NA
Zaire	180	3.3	2.2B	2.1B
Zambia	580	3.5	1.1B	1.1B
Zimbabwe	540	2.9	1.7B	1.4B

Source: Compiled from country data in Global Studies: Africa, 5th Ed. Dushkin Publishers, 1993.

These are not offered as hard figures. They are indicative of conditions crying out for radical changes. The per capita figures do not tell us much about another disturbing aspect of the problem: the concentration of the wealth of the post colonial African states so exclusively in the hands of the top two percent of the population-- the very top class of the military, political, economic, elite bureaucratic, ruling oligarchies. Seen in these lights, the economic conditions of the average African is far worse that the per capita figures can reveal

Table Two

Profile of Harvest of Poverty & Declining Standard of Living

PER CAPITA INCOME RANGE	NO. OF COUNTRIES IN RANGE
Above $5000	1
$3000-5000	1
$2000-2999	3
$1000-1999	5
$ 500- 999	10
$ 000- 499	30
Total # Countries	50

Source: From Table One.

Table Three

Indicators of a Hurting Continent

Total GNP	Growth Rate	Food Production 1970 / 1989	Population
			Growth
$150 Billion	1.5%	100% / 80%	3.2%
(Same as Belgium's GNP		Pop. 350/ 600	
Pop.= 10 Million)		Million/Million	
(World Refuges= 100%)		Africa's Shre= 50% (> 5 million)*	

Source: Global Studies: Africa, 1993. p.186.

* The number of displaced Africans may be higher than ten million!

There is little doubt that Africa as a whole is hurting badly. Take the case of the renewed war in Angola: The UN was reporting in October 1993 that an estimated 1,000 people were dying per week, while 3 million people were expected to be affected by the threat of starvation and escalating was unless the international community could respond rapidly and decisively to halt the slaughter, and reach isolated regions with massive food relief deliveries. The new government of Eritrea unformatted the UN and the international community in November 1993 that 4 million of its people were in imminent danger of starvation, and called for emergency response to its call for massive assistance. On November 19, 1993 the BBC reported that "Burundi is facing a humanitarian tragedy on the scale of Bosnia and Somalia put together." In the Sudan the protracted civil war and carnage have occupied the better part of that state's nearly 40 years of political independence. While the rest of the world did pay as little attention as possible to Sudan's continual tragedy, the toll of war and starvation there has been higher than that of either the 30 years of slaughter in Ethiopia or the carnage of warlordism and fratricide in Somalia and Liberia put together. Sudan's tragedy has caused more than 3 million displaced persons and 1.5 million refugees alone.

The tale of large scale human and material waste resulting from fratricidal, even genocidal, warfare within several African states since independence defies comprehension on any moral or civilized scale. It will take many more years to restore what has been destroyed in such states than has taken them in the last thirty years to lay waste. There is no cumulative progress possible under such circumstances. There are more mine-bombs per capita in Angola today than were laid in any country of Europe during World War II! The report is that removing these mine-bombs would cost far more than Angola and the world community can afford at present, were the war itself to end today. The leading contributors to such large scale human carnage include Angola, Burundi, Chad, Ethiopia, Liberia, Mozambique, Nigeria (1966-1970), Namibia (war of independence), Rwanda, South Africa, Sudan, Spanish Sahara, Uganda, Zaire, and Zimbabwe (war of liberation from racist domination),[25] These countries combined account for nearly half the total population of the entire continent of Africa. If a bridge built yesterday is destroyed tomorrow; if a factory built today is bombed out of existence next week; if roads, railway lines, schools, houses, hospitals, and other infrastructures are destroyed as fast as they are being built as they have been in many African states plunged into these bondless chaos, then there could be little real hope for tomorrow's accumulation of wealth and progress.

It is not being argued here that all of these tragedies were brought about by the behavior of African leaders and governments alone. The problems are far more complex in their causes than that. But the focus on the analysis of sociopolitical and socioeconomic maldevelopment forces us to account for the portion of the causes attributable to African leaders and governments, and Africans.

These Profiles are indicative of a continent scrambling for survival and existence. The efforts of the West to help restructure African economies through the World Bank/IMF Structural Adjustment Programs (SAP) have only worsened the survival capabilities of African states, economies and peoples. Structural adjustment programs have been designed largely to impose "conditionalities" that would force African states to meet negotiated schedules for the repayment of their debts, and to open up such economies to foreign (western) imports in the promotion of "free trade", and externally controlled programs and policies of economic and political reforms. The negative implications of the programmed combination of "debt, democracy and development" reforms under SAP have been explored in more detail in a recent essay.[26]

There is plenty of pessimism all around; perhaps the bluntest of such pessimism has been captured in the exaggerated conclusions of Lance Morrow: " Africa... has begun to look like an immense illustration of chaos theory, although some hope is forming on the margins. Much of the continent has turned into a battleground of contending dooms: AIDS and overpopulation, poverty, starvation, illiteracy, corruption, social breakdown, vanishing resources, overcrowded cities, drought, war (mostly intra-state civil wars), and the homelessness of war's refugees. Africa has become the basket case of the planet, the 'Third World of the Third World', a vast continent in free fall."[27]

Pessimism or exaggeration notwithstanding, the wages of maldevelopment in Africa correspond more disturbingly to the biblical "*wages of sin*". They are leading to the death, dying, and ravaging of millions of African peoples in the hands of their rulers and their external collaborating forces. Africa's regimes of misrule may therefore, not soon be easily relegated to the dust-heap of history.

But there is some dawning of hope in the new awakenings of intensified struggles for individual and collective self-reliance, freedom, self-determination, democracy, democratization, and the reconstituting of civil societies in Africa. Many of Africa's peoples are beginning to organize in open rebellions and struggles against their ruling authoritarian abusers. In the several organized masses' self-affirmations is to be found one possible gateway to hope and freedom's humanistic renewal in Africa.

CHAPTER 16

ENDNOTES

1. John T. Rourke, International Politics on the World Stage, 4th Edition, The Dushkin Publishing Group, Inc. 1993. p. 503.

2. Rourke, p. 504.

3. Rourke, pp. 503-505.

4. F. Jeffress Ramsay, Editor, Global Studies: Africa, 5th Ed., The Dushkin Publish Group, Inc., 1993. pp. 5-9; 186-191; See also Tables One to Three in the test, pp. 33-37.

5. See The Carter Center Reports: Perestroika without Glasnost in Africa, February 1989; Beyond Autocracy in Africa, February, 1989; African Governance in the 1990s, March, 1990. Emory University, Atlanta, GA.

6. Prestroika without Glasnost in Africa, p.2

7. See Lance Morrow, "Africa: The Scramble for Existence", Global Studies: Africa, 5th Ed., 1993. pp. 186-191.

8. Samuel Huntington, Political Order in Changing Societies, Yale University Press, 1969.

9. See for example Lucian Pye, et al., Causes and Sequences of Political Development, Princeton University Press, 1972.

10. See for example, W. Arthur Lewis, Politics in West Africa, Oxford University Press, 1965.

11. Theodore J. Lowi, The Politics of Disorder, W.W. Norton & Co., Inc., 1971.

12. Lowi, p. viii; See specifically "Prologue: When Institutions Fail", pp. 1x-x1. i.e. (pp. 9-11).

13. Donald Rothchild and Naomi Chazan, Editors, The Precarious Balance, West View Press, 1988.

14. Jennifer Seymour Whitaker, How Can Africa Survive, Council on Foreign Relations Press, 1988.

15. Whitaker, Chapter 8, pp. 218-232.

16. Basil Davidson, The Black Man's Burden: Africa and the Curse of the Nation-State, Times Books, 1992.

17. See Michael Parenti, The Sword and the Dollar: Imperialism, Revolution, and the Arms Race, St. Martin's Press, 1989. pp. 7-36.

18. Basil Davidson, pp. 290-291. The inverted quotations are from Chinua Achebe, Anthills of the Savannah, Anchor Books/Doubleday, pp. 130-131.

19. See Newswatch, November 22, 1993, pp. 24-25.

20. See Newswatch, May, 10, 1993, and October, 25, 1993, for two spectacular accounts of "The N2.1 billion Scandal", and "Massive Fraud at NNPC: N5 billion Swindie. Oil Lifting Bonanza. Oil Concession Racket: respectively, as indicators of such practices in Nigeria.

21. See Susan George, "Uses and Abuses of African Debt", Global Studies: Africa, 5th Ed., 1983. pp. 206-211.

22. Ibid., p. 6.

23. OAU, Lagos Plan of Action for the Economic Development of Africa: 1980 - 2000, Geneva, International Institute for Labor Studies, 1981.

24. Ibid., Preamble, p.1. See also David Fashole Like, and Timothy M. Shaw, Continental Crisis: The Lagos Plan of Action and Africa's Future, University Press of America, 1984.

25. See Current History: A World Affairs Journal, Volume 92. No. 574, May, 1993. This issue was devoted to the coverage of the crises in Angola, Ethiopia, Liberia, Mozambique, Somalia, Sudan and South Africa, the Clinton administration's policy on Africa, and the role of the international relief effort in Somalia.

26. See Ladun Anise, "Triple Imperatives of Contemporary African Governance: Debt, Democracy and Development, A Critical Perspective", in Festus Eribo, Oyeleye Oyediran, Mulatu Wubneh, and Leo Zonn, editors, Center for International Programs, East Carolina University, Greenville, North

Carolina, Publication #1, March 1993, pp. 77-100. See also Susan George, Global Studies: Africa, 5th Ed., 1993, pp. 206-211, cited above.

27. Lance Morrow, "Africa: The Scramble for Existence", Global Studies: Africa, 5th Ed., 1993. p. 186; pp. 186-195. See also the following critical essays in Robert J. Griffiths, Editor, Annual Editions: Third World 94/95, The Dushkin Publishing Group, Inc., 1994, Selections #s 1-6, pp. 2-25; 33-34, pp. 140-150; and 37, pp. 158-160. These focus specifically on African states' current problems.

Chapter 17

Political and Economic Restructuring in Africa:
Constraints and Possibilities for the 1990s.

... the current African crisis is not just a narrow economic crisis but also fundamentally a political crisis. Besides the usual political instability or crisis of legitimacy, this political crisis is reflected in the pervasive lack of democracy, which some perceive as a conflict between state and people's power -- a crisis arising from lack of popular participation in the development process.[1]

In the decades to come Africa is likely to witness frequent and devastating drought and famine, increasingly rapid rates of desertification, epidemics, plagues of locusts and other such calamities. As a result the political climate is likely to become hotter and more difficult for those in power.[2]

The vast majority of nations in sub-Saharan Africa are currently implementing structural adjustment programs. The achievements have been very modest and in most cases tenuous.[3] There is agreement however on the social, political and economic tensions, coalitions and conflicts which structural adjustment programs have generated. In Zaire, Zambia, and Nigeria, to name a few, adjustment programs have accentuated the delegitimization of the state, led to political violence, riots and regime turnover and culminated in severe economic dislocation and deterioration. It is the position of the Organization of African Unity(OAU) that even the efforts of the UN to support the restructuring process through the United Nations Programme of Action for African Economic Recovery and Development(UNPAAERD) "did not witness any significant change for the better in Africa...from all economic indicators, the continent of Africa appeared to have been by-passed by (the) positive developments in the world system."[4] The harsh monetarist prescriptions of the International Monetary Fund(IMF) and the World Bank have not restored investor confidence in African economies and they have not reduced the foreign debt profiles or promoted foreign exchange earnings. On the contrary, African states have dismantled all the political, economic and social gains of the past three decades, accumulated more foreign debts and exposed their respective economies to foreign penetration, domination, and exploitation. There are some very visible impacts and implications of structural adjustment which would no doubt affect the location and role of Africa in the global division of labor; and determine the context of class contradictions and struggles in the 1990s:

1). adjustment has delegitimized the state thus eroding its tenuous hegemony;

2). it has increased the alienation of the people from the agents and agencies of the state;

3). it has intensified class contradictions and struggles, proletarianized the middle classes and further impoverished the lower classes;

4). it has increased the social and eonomic burdens of vulnerable groups-women, youths, children and the unemployed and made life simply difficult for these groups;

5). it has created severe economic dislocations- higher debts, rising debt-servicing ratios, inflation, scarcity of essential goods, unemployment, devalued currencies, and agricultrural stagnation;

6). it has increased the degradation of the environment by forcing the elites into all sorts of extra-legal ways of making money including the importation of toxic wastes and by compelling the poor to abuse their environment in the struggle to make a living by exploiting natural resources without regard for conservation;

7). promoted social deacy, violence, cynicism and uncertainty- petty-crime, prostitution, armed robery, drug-use and trafficking, corruption, currency laundering and the sort;

8). made African economies more vulnerable to foreign penetration, manipulation, domination and exploitation as international finance institutions, donors and Western governments have now taken on the direct and/or indirct responsibility for dictating political and economic policies and models for African states;

9). the intensification of repression, political intolerance, and human rights abuses in the effort to convince investors that the state was "really in charge" and had popular forces under control and in the effort to force orthodox adjustment policies on the people, their organizations and society without mechanisms for equitably redistributing power, resuorces as well as the pains and gains of restructuring; and

10). a massive and unprecedented brain drain to Europe, North America and the Middle East due to unemployment, repression and the need to escape the pains of adjustment. In this regard "Africa has lost a third of its skilled people to Europe" alone according to the UNDP's Human Development Index for 1992.[5]

It is only in the context of these and other consequences of structural adjustment in Africa that we can effectively make projections as to the future of Africa and the future of adjustment in Africa. We would like to point out that our position is not that adjustment of the patterns and structures of politics, power, production, exchange and consumption is not necessary in Africa. On the contrary, it is our view that the World Bank and the IMF have approached the problem from a difficult and impossible angle by denying the political context of the African predicament (until recently for the World Bank) and by expecting decadent, corrupt and repressive regimes and elites to implement such difficult monetarist policies and programs. In the rest of this paper, we look first, at the implications of orthodox structural adjustment for state and society in Africa; second, at why adjustment has failed in Africa; and third at the new global order, adjustment and the future of Africa.

IMPLICATIONS OF ADJUSTMENT FOR STATE AND SOCIETY

There is now, almost unanimous agreement among intellectuals and policy makers in and outside the African continent that orthodox adjustment programs as devised and supervised by the IMF and the World Bank are not working.[6] At a more general level, attention has recently become focused on the negative consequences of adjustment programs which do not pay particular attention to existing socio-economic and political inequalities in underdeveloped social formations. M. de Larosiere, Managing Director of the IMF has equally argued that public support is essential for the success of adjustment programs and that if there are "no pay-offs in terms of growth...while human conditions are deteriorating" it would be impossible to continue the adjustment program. He concluded that "human capital is after all the most important factor of production."[7] This realization did not in any way encourage a fundamental change in the prescriptions of the IMF restructuring processes in underdeveloped countries. The United Nations Development Programme(UNDP)'s Human Development Report 1990 is clear on the fact that "structural adjustment programmes...have increased the burden of poverty of recipient nations and their people."[8] In its two-volume study of the impacts of structural adjustment programs in the third world- Adjustment with a Human Face, the UNICEF drew attention to the need to include "poverty alleviation" programs in adjustment packages if they are not to cause more problems than envisaged by policy makers.[9]

Specifically in the case of Africa, attacks against structural adjustment have arisen not from opposition to the need for change but from a recognition of the negative political, economic and social contradictions and conflicts which the program has tended to accentuate or generate. Carol Lancaster argued in a recent study of adjustment in Sub-Saharan Africa that by 1983 "it had become clear that few of the nearly 20 agreements between the IMF and the African governments had been successful."[10] She also took the position that the IMF adjustment model, "has almost never worked in sub-saharan Africa."[11] In 1988, the United Nations Programme of Action for African Economic Recovery and Development (UNPAAERD) in its continent-wide review of adjustment programs conceded that there were a few gains in "a handful of countries...in certain macroeconomic indicators" such as reduced inflation rates and higher export volumes. It however concluded that "for the majority of African states, there has not been even a hint of recovery."[12] Claude Ake has noted that adjustment programs are being pursued by African states in a "desperate attempt to contain the crisis (of the continent) and save the state." However, he argues that policies of "massive retrenchment of public employees, the withdrawal of government subsidies, and the dismantling of welfare schemes, the privatization of public corporations, the deindigenization of the economy...are replete with contradictions and address the symptoms and not the causes of the problems." It is Ake's contention that adjustment programs will inevitably deepen the crisis of the continent because they do not address the specificities and implications of the historical experiences of African countries as well as the content and character of contemporary politics, political balances and struggles:

> ...the withdrawal of welfare measures, minimal in the first place, in a context where the most elementary needs are lacking only intensifies the contradictions between the rulers and the subordinate classes. And so does the mass retrenchment of workers. Privatization can only deepen the class contradictions for it is bound to mean the cheap sale of public stock to the few who are already well-off; the attempt to make public corporations efficient and profitable cannot work because the political class must continue to use them as a means of

accumulation; deindigenization of the economy entails the strengthening of those exploitative ties and the dependence which underlies underdevelopment. In any case, destatization can only go so far because the objective conditions which produce statism remain as strong as they have always been.[13]

Ake's position was supported by the United Nations Economic Commission for Africa(ECA) when it argued in its Economic Report on Africa 1990 that "policy prescriptions widely adopted during the decade(1980-1990), based on conventional adjustment programmes, have failed to address the fundamental structural issues in Africa's development; hence their failure to arrest the downward trend, less reverse it and bring about a sustainable process of development and transformation."[14] Adebayo Adedeji, as Executive Secretary of the ECA, was quite direct in his opposition to the adjustment program when he noted that "on-going SAPs" have led to "enormous social costs have been imposed on the vulnerable segments of the population; the human resources for transformation are crippled; domestic structural inequalities increase and the marginalization of Africa proceeds apace."[15] Finally, in a surprising though not unexpected move, the World Bank shifted some distance away from the IMF when in its 1989 report on Africa it admitted its own past failures in Africa and embraced the call for protecting vulnerable groups, empowerment of the people, democratization and adjustment with a human face:

> It is not sufficient for African governments merely to consolidate the progress made in their adjustment programs. They need to go beyond the issues of public finance, monetary policy, prices, and markets to address fundamental questions relating to human capacities, institutions, governance, the environment, population growth and distribution, and technology. Changes in perceptions and priorities, as well as in incentives, will be required to bring about improvements. Above all, to channel the energies of the population at large, ordinary people should participate more in designing and implementing development programs.[16]

It is obvious, therefore, that structural adjustment programs forced on African states by mounting problems and deepening socio-economic and political contradictions have not achieved the goals set by the IMF and the World Bank: increased production, investment and growth achieved through the efficient use of resources. More importantly, orthodox adjustment programs have destroyed the social fabric of African societies, promoted a culture of corruption, cynicism and crass individualism; taken corruption and violence to unprecedented levels; and delegitimized the state is a devastating manner.

Why have these adjustment programs, in spite of vitriolic propaganda,[17] failed generally in Africa? In the next section argue that adjustment programs have failed for several reasons: the way in which the African crisis was defined; the arrogance and unshifting orthodoxy of the World Bank and the IMF; lack of attention to structural contradictions; a focus on the symptoms and manifestatioons of dependence and underdevelopment as against the structural causes; the central concerns of the adjustment package; and the character of politics and political power in the continent.

THE FAILURE OF ADJUSTMENT IN AFRICA: OLD WINE IN NEW BOTTLES?

We noted above that adjustment programs have a limited chance of success if they fail to take proper cognizance of existing socio-economic and political power balances and contradictions. The fact remains that ultimately, it is the internal character of power, politics and social relations that determine and influence the ability of the government to implement the often harsh prescriptions of the IMF and the World Bank. African governments and the ECA are agreed that some adjustment is inevitable in the face of the current crisis and further marginalization in the global system. The disagreement is on the content, context, relevance and manageability of the adjustment program.

Eboe Hutchful has provided an outline of issue areas to be considered in the implementation of adjustment programs in view of the "significant implications for the reproductive space and dynamics of political regimes."[18] Though Hutchful concentrates on Ghana, in this section, we shall draw examples from the Nigerian experience with structural adjustment. The first issue area is the depth of the pre-adjustment crisis as well as the "rate and severity of the decline" before adjustment. In the case of Ghana the economy was already in ruins and hardship had become part of the people's reality. The harshness of the IMF and World Bank prescriptions therefore made very little difference to the people. In Nigeria, the reverse was the case. The oil boom had given the impression that the problem was with how to spend the money not with how to generate it. By 1986 when the adjustment package was introduced most Nigerians were of the view that the set-backs were going to be temporary; after all, the country was still in the oil producing business. What this means is that the point at which adjustment is introduced and the severity of the policies must pay due cognizance to the existing preparedness of the people to withstand the pains of restructuring. Hence, in Ghana, opposition was not as violent and persistent as it has been in Zambia and Nigeria. A second critical issue area is the degree of adjustment required for recovery. The lending institutions have tended to impose very harsh conditionalities on African countries- conditionalities which pay very little regard to the structural differences, regime types and opportunities for manoeuvre internally and externally. As Hutchful has rightly noted, "almost all African programs belong in the high conditionality end of the scale" and this situation implies that regimes have less room to set their "own reform agenda and construct the appropriate coalitions."[19] This has been another major source of opposition to structural adjustment in Africa. The package is seen as foreign formulated, foreign inspired and foreign imposed in a grand strategy to recolonize the continent under the supervision of the IMF and the World Bank. Because of the stringency of the conditionalities, African regimes have had very limited room for 'domesticating' their packages and local innovations easily become incorporated into set patterns handed down by the lending bodies. Though the Nigerian military junta started off pretending to incorporate public interests in the process of adjustment, it ended up in succumbing to all the dictates of the Fund and the Bank.

Third, is the external environment which affects the ability to draw international support, resources and technical assistance to mediate the harshness of adjustment in conditions of poverty and underdevelopment. With the changes in Eastern Europe and the apparent redirection of international interest and support away from Africa, this becomes an even more pressing issue. The record of waste, mismanagement, and wide spread corruption in African states have contributed immensely to eroding possible support from the international environment.[20] Thus, we now begin to hear of "aid fatigue" and "compassion fatigue" in the international community. In reality these are mere excuses to justify declining assistance, investments and the redirection of political and economic aid to Eastern Europe and parts of the Middle East.

The fourth issue area is the "nature of national constituencies and socio-political actors, their composition, interests, tolerance thresholds, their 'discourse of resistance', and ability to resist adjustment"[21] which are of utmost importance to the success of adjustment. Unfortunately, the lending agencies have over the years tended to treat these matters, critical as they are, rather lightly. Specifically, this point is about the track-record of the dominant elites, the character of their politics, their ability to reproduce themselves through the careful manipulation of power and ideological discourses, the dominant world-view, their relations to non-bourgeois forces, the character of their relation to foreign interests, the use to which they put the state and their pattern of production and accumulation. In Africa, the dominant elites are mostly responsible for the deepening crisis today through their records of waste, corruption, nepotism and commitment to the reproduction of unequal exchange relations with foreign capital. As well, their tenuous relation to production has contributed significantly to the expansion of the bureaucracy, parastatals and commerce and the stagnation of productive activities. The Nigerian example is of particular relevance. The bourgeoisie has never been known, until relatively recently, to be interested in production. Even then, this is hardly a major preoccupation of the burgeois class. The state has always been a means to capital accumulation. The hegemony of the dominant classes has always been tenuous and it has since political independence relied on the manipulation of religion, ethnicity and region to retain political dominance and win access to the state. The bourgeoisie has always been concentrated in the real estate, service and import-export sectors of the economy as against involvement in agriculture and other productive activities. Finally, its factionalization and fractionalization, inability to build hegemony, its corruption and incapacity to effectively manage society and improve on the living conditions of the majority has alienated the people from the state and its agents and agencies. When such a dominant elite comes up with harsh monetarist policies, it cannot mobilize support for it. Rather, it will ignite opposition, and riots against its programs. Hence, in Nigeria, Zambia and Cote d'Ivoire, adjustment programs have been met with strong opposition from the people as they see them as another attempt by the dominant elites to make life difficult for the poor.

Hutchful introduces another very critical issue area for consideration when he talks of "regime dynamics": the composition and character of ruling coalitions; mechanisms for securing "vertical and horizontal solidarities;" nature of political discourses and the "relationship between technocrats and politicians, and between political and technocratic rationality and decision-making centres in individual regimes, and in particular the autonomy and insulation from political pressures enjoyed by the technocratic staff."[22] Again, lending agencies hardly go beyond the surface in their negotiations with African power elites for adjustment support. Where the bourgeoisie has historically depended on the state for largesse or accumulation, adjustment is unlikely to be palatable to it. Policies which emphasize financial rationality, accountability and discipline are usually resisted by elites who are used to accumulation through inflated contracts, stealing from public coffers, using public positions for accumulation and relying on connections with public officers to get rich. This has been the case in Nigeria. If stabilization makes it more difficult for the elites to accumulate through access to the state, the whole process of corruption can become more desperate and brazen. This only erodes the effectiveness of the adjustment package and reduces the credibility of the political elites who impose harsh policies on the people and turn around to loot public resources without restraint in order to maintain their pre-adjustment life styles. While adjustment packages usually demand devaluation, desubsidization, deregulation, privatization and the general withdrawal of the state from economic activities, such recommendations not only run contrary to the expectations of African peoples but often address the wrong issues. The focus is often on state intervention not on the character and nature of the intervention. Even in the advanced capitalist societies, the state is still very prominent in promoting private accumulation and in protecting the poor and disadvantaged through health subsidies, unemployment insurance, cheap housing, subsidized public transportation and even free primary education with hundreds of thousands of fellowships and scholarships for higher education. This is precisely what African peoples expect of their governments. However, adjustment has meant higher food prices, stagnating incomes, devalued wages and salaries, scarcity of essential goods, inflation, retrenchment of workers, imposition of user-fees on social services, higher cost of education and higher house rents for workers. These policies have tended to generate opposition to the state and adjustment while leading to riots and repression by the state in the effort by its custodians to hold on to state power. Without doubt, the "neoclassical basis of structural adjustment" as outlined above, "contradicts...the tenets of nationalism, statism and welfarism and their embedded notions of entitlements which are central to many African regimes".[23]   National development programs and public statements by African leaders since political independence in the 1960s have focused on the need for mobilization and the responsibility of the state to cater for the needs of the majority in society. This was also one of the cardinal points raised by the nationalists in the struggle for political independence. Under adjustment, African regimes are now compelled to go against all the promises they had made to the people over the years. It becomes very difficult to push through a completely different set of prescriptions which go directly against the tenets of nationalism and welfarism which are still strongly enshrined in African culture and value systems. As well, internal factionalization and fractionalization pose major challenges to the success of adjustment. Bureaucrats tend to support adjustment; they have to implement them any way. Not all factions of the officer corps in the armed forces support adjustment hence it has become one major excuse for coups and counter-coups. In Nigeria, both the Vatsa coup of 1986 and the Orka coup of 1990 were opposed to structural adjustment. While a fraction of the bourgeoisie in league with foreign capital might support adjustment, local investors are often in opposition because floating interest rates and devaluation make it difficult to borrow, lower wages depress the buying power of workers and trade liberalization removes all the protection they previously enjoyed against imports. Politicians are often divided into three groups- those who support adjustment whole heartedly; those who oppose adjustment from a populist angle so as to win the support of non-bourgeois forces in their political objectives and; third, those who oppose adjustment purely from a nationalistic position. Such divisions make it difficult for the government to effectively mediate or contain popular pressures and maintain a steady course on the implementation of adjustment programs. Of course, the fluidities of national solidarities which accompany intensifying intra- and inter-class divisions equally impede the ability of the regime to confront societal crisis in a holistic fashion while responding to the urgent demands of social interests within the limits of available resources.

The "moral and political credibility of the leadership (the perception that the leadership is not personally corrupt and can be relied upon to decide wisely in the national interest)" as well as its ability to play constituency against constituency, juggle accountability to international interests and national constituencies, "create a 'discourse of reform' and effectively exploit political symbolism"[24] and its skill in sharing the costs of adjustment between interest groups can make a major difference to the implementation of adjustment. Lending institutions waste their time when they expect leaders who are generally perceived by their people to be untrustworthy, corrupt, inept and unjust to implement even harsher policies than those which already alienate the people from them. In the case of Ghana, Jerry Rawlings had a good rapport with the left, students and academics (at least initially), he had the legacy of Kwame Nkrumah and the socialist rhetoric of the early days of political independence to rely on, and given the very vibrant intellectual culture of the country, it was easy to get the people to debate and experiment, even at the grassroots level, with ideological positions previously debated in the university campuses. The reverse was the case in Nigeria. Ibrahim Babangida declared a 'war' against trade unions, students and the left. He declared them extremists and barred them from the political process. He proscribed trade unions, rehabilitated disgraced and discredited politicians and military men, and had no patience with ideological discussions. Babangida also lacked any national symbols, he accentuated the retreat into ethnic, regional and religious basis of acquiring and using political power, shielded corrupt public officials from punishment and has himself been accused of corrupt practices. The point therefore was that he was not trusted. The numerous debates he sponsored on housing, foreign policy, political restructuring and so on, were perceived as diversions and his tendency to accumulate excessive powers to himself and office convinced many Nigerians that he could not be trusted or relied upon to lead the country out of its economic predicament.[25] More importantly, the Babangida regime was unable to share the costs of adjustment equally; a few rich have become super rich as contractors, military officers and top bureaucrats and their friends collaborate to enrich themselves while the majority are subjected to retrenchment and other harsh consequences of the adjustment program. His regime found it very difficult to mobilize and retain the support of critical social actors. Under such conditions adjustment can make little progress and often remains bogged down to financial manipulations with the structures not experiencing any adjustment.[26] At the time General Babangida was humiliated out of power in August 1993, he had run down the economy, accetuated political pressures and conflicts and mortgaged the economic future of Nigeria.

The point remains that the more repressive and undemocratic a regime is, the less its chances of effectively implementing adjustment programs. Repression and human rights violation encourage opposition elements to develop concrete political programs to oppose the regime. One way of advancing the interest of the opposition is to discredit and where possible sabotage the policies of the government and adjustment programs are easy targets in this area. A more open and democratic regime- compare Rawlings in Ghana, even now, to Babangida and Abacha in Nigeria- can convince the people to make sacrifices; convince the people that there is hope in the future, and convince external supporters that it is not only in command but has the support of the people in the process of change no matter how painful. Coalitions, conflicts and contradictions are easily managed or mediated and organized interest groups in particular, the labor unions and students as well as peasants and local investors give support and openly defend adjustment policies in the collective effort to find solutions to the deepening crisis. This is possible only where the regime is fairly institutionalized, enjoys some credibility, is not steeped in corruption and is capable of accommodating alternative positions and interpretations of the path to progress and reform.

THE NEW GLOBAL ORDER AND AFRICA: POSSIBILITIES FOR THE 1990s

Monemental changes have taken place in the global system in the last decade or so. From the crumbling of the Berlin Wall and the reunification of Germany, through the disintegration of the Soviet Union as a nation and super power, to the emergence of the United States as the sole super power and the release of Nelson Mandela in South Africa, the world is experiencing a restructuring of global political and economic relations. The Palestinians and Isealis are negotiating peace. A date for democratic, one person one vote elections have been set in South Africa. The UN is involved in trying to restore peace and democracy in Haiti. There are increasing concerns for democracy, gender and environmental issues in the global system. The net implication of these and other changes for Africa is that it is going to be increasingly pressured to adopt market reforms in the context of the triumph of the market all over the world, even in communist China. As well, Africa is being marginalized, investors are divesting from Africa and reinvesting in Eastern Europe, donors are complaining of aid and compassion fatigue; and responses to political conflicts, famine and natural disasters have been left largely to voluntary humanitarian bodies. As Boutros Boutos-Ghali has noted, "When African Governments become tagged as bad debtors or bad prospects, private investment goes elsewhere. Long-term financial   flows into sub-Saharan Africa declined from $10 billion to $4.7 billion between 1982 and 1990. Eighty-four per cent of this reduction can be accounted for by the decline in private flows."[27] In spite of the implementation of very difficult policies aimed at attracting foreign investment, "that investment is not materializing."[28] Though the iron curtain is down, the poverty curtain remains as solid and as high as ever. The debt burden remains a formidable obstacle to recovery and growth in Africa. According to Boutros-Ghali, Africa's external debt is "unsustainable. External debt is a millstone around the nect of Africa."[29]

While these conditions of neglect, disinterest and marginalization might look rather unfavorable to Africa, it does contain possibilities for mapping out an alternative path to growth, development and democracy. In fact, I would go as far as arguing that the current crisis is very good for Africa. This is the opportune moment for Africa to face up to the challenges of the present and plan for the future. The crisis is certainly forcing many Africans to rethink their priorities and reorganize their political positions. It is forcing on Africans a new appreciation for African products and compelling people to save, rationalize spending, and to take more interest in politics and governance. The so-called new world order makes little or no room for Africa, except those nations that are of some importance to centers of imperialism. The new world order contains no economic agenda which Africa needs to recover from its present predicaments. In fact, the new order seems more attuned to destroying the remaining vestiges of communism, incorporating Russia into the orbit of Western capitalism, setting up new trade blocs to shut Africa away from the global market, and reproducing Africa's place as a market for western products and technology. For America and the developed world, there is certainly a new world order. For Africa it is still a world dominated by imperialist interests where the region remains underdeveloped, dependent, poverty-stricken, marginalized, foreign dominated, debt-ridden, and of little consequence in the geo-strategic calculations of the western powers. How has Africa responded to these developments?[30]

In February 1990 the ECA with the support of African governments and UN agencies produced the <u>African Charter for Popular Participation in Development</u> as a document to promote the operationalization of the <u>African</u>

Alternative Framework to Structural Adjustment Programme and the World Bank's recent publication Sub-Saharan Africa- From Crisis to Sustainable Growth.[31] The ECA's alternative framework agreed on the need for adjustment but disagreed on the undue emphasis on financial matters, unrestricted rolling back of the state, blanket privatization, devaluation and liberalization. More importantly, it argued that adjustment programs stood little chances of success with the impoverishment of the people, their marginalization and repression. The World Bank's report moved from its traditional position of focusing purely on economic matters to admitting its own shortcomings as an organization, emphasizing the need for popular participation in decision-making, decentralization of power structures, accountability, some role for the state in the economy, empowerment of popular organizations, the need for "special measures...to alleviate poverty and protect the vulnerable"[32] and the need for structures to enable "ordinary people" to "participate more in designing and implementing development programs."[33]

With these new positions, even if superficial, the ECA came up with the Charter to operationalize the new emphasis on empowerment and democratization. Though the document is still far from perfect and contains some of the usual apologetic and overtly optimistic expectations which fail to take cognizance of entrenched class interests in African states, it represents a new reality in articulating options to the crisis..

The African Charter in asserting the role of popular participation in the economic recovery process stated clearly that the present crisis "is not only an economic crisis but also a human, legal, political and social crisis" which is "unprecedented and unacceptable" because it is manifested "tragically and glaringly in the suffering, hardship and impoverishment of the vast majority of African people." Perhaps this definition of the character of the crisis is the most important contribution of the document. What it does is to call on policy makers in and outside Africa to look at the crisis from a holistic, but especially political dimension rather than just a balance of payments crisis and so on. It is in line with this perspective that the Charter insists that "there must be an opening up of political process to accommodate freedom of opinions, tolerate differences, accept consensus on issues as well as ensure the effective participation of the people and their organizations and associations." It therefore makes specific prescriptions at the levels of the people; students; youths, Non-Governmental Organizations(NGOs) and Voluntary Development Organizations(VDOs); the media; the government; and the international community to ensure the attainment of the goals of empowerment and democratization.

At the level of government for instance, the document insists that as a starting point, African governments must begin to "adopt development strategies, approaches and programmes, the content and parameters of which are in line with the interest and aspirations of the people and which incorporate, rather than alienate, African values and economic, social, cultural, political and environmental realities". In addition, it calls on governments to pursue development objectives with the interests of the people in mind with emphasis on "popular participatory process...which aim at transformation of the African economies to achieve self-reliant and self-sustaining people-centred development based on popular participation and democratic consensus." To achieve these goals, more economic power must be extended to the people through equitable income distribution, support for their productive capacity, enhanced access to land, credit, technology and information; the protection of children; promotion of the role of women; promotion of literacy and skills training; greater participation and consensus building; elimination of laws and bureaucratic obstacles which militate against development and people's participation; increased employment opportunities for the rural and urban poor; strengthening small scale indigenous entrepreneurship and intensifying efforts at promoting effective sub-regional and regional economic cooperation. Of course, nothing like these exist presently in any African country, perhaps on paper in the former socialist inclined countries. If such policies were in place and pursued with some degree of seriousness, the current crisis will not have come about in the first place. With entrenched social divisions and interests, there are certainly fundamental obstacles to getting African leaders and decision-makers who have over the decades monopolized decision-making and the singular rights, along with politicians, to allocate resources and determine the direction of growth and development.

At the international level, the Charter calls for support in Africa's "drive to internalize the development and transformation process." In particular, the IMF, World Bank and other bilateral and multilateral donors are called upon to "accept and support African initiatives to conceptualize, formulate and implement endogenously designed development and transformation programmes." To achieve these goals, technical assistance should be directed at strengthening national capabilities for policy analysis and the design and implementation of economic reform and development programmes;" the decentralization of the development process must be supported in order to foster the democratization of development; the new emphasis on popular empowerment, "active participation of the people and their organizations in the formulation of development strategies and economic reform programmes and open debate and consensus-building process" need to be given full support and the reduction of the stock of Africa's debt and debt servicing obligations should be given urgent attention.

Addressing the place of women in the unfolding political struggles in Africa, the <u>Charter</u> comes out clearly to reinforce the provisions of the 1989 Abuja Declaration on Women and notes that the new partnership required to transform the region "must not only recognize the importance of gender issues but must take action to ensure women's involvement at all levels of decision-making." It specifically calls on all African governments to "set ... specific targets for the appointment of women in senior policy and management posts in all sectors of government."[34] The document calls on women and their organizations to continue to "strive for the attainment of policies and programmes that reflect and recognize women's roles as producers, mothers, active community mobilizers and custodians of culture;" and advocates gender equality at home, at the work place and in society in general.

Specifically on adjustment programs, the <u>Charter</u> is emphatic on the fact that:

> ...the human dimension is central to adjustment programmes which must be compatible with the objectives and aspirations of the African people and with African realities and must be conceived and designed internally by African countries as part and parcel of the long term objectives and framework of development and <u>transformation</u>.[35]

Finally, the international community is called upon to give direct support to grassroots organization, trade unions, women's and youth's organizations, and NGOs in their training, networking and other activities.

In spite of these seemingly attractive pleas and declarations, it will be mistaken not to highlight the obstacles to Africa's recovery. As it stands, the IMF has shifted no ground in its conceptualization and interpretation of the African crisis. Its prescriptions are still the same and it has little room for concern about the human cost of structural adjustment. Its commitment to monetarism remains unshaken. Though the World Bank made significant concessions in 1989 by emphasising political conditionality, empowerment, democratization and accountability, it is yet to demonstrate this new shift in practice. As Robert Browne has noted, "merely because the forces of enlightenment succeeded in obtaining publication of the document does not guarantee that the bureaucracy will be mobilized to implement it- a task which would be Herculean even with the best of intentions."[36]   As well, international banking institutions are yet to demonstrate their recognition of Africa's specificities and peculiarities within the underdeveloped world. It cannot be expected therefore, that the <u>Charter's</u> call on the international community and on African governments will be heeded in the very near future, not at least, until serious internal restructuring take place within the continent to encourage donors, lenders and the international community to take a second look at Africa. Yet, we can conclude that the negative consequences of structural adjustment policies in Africa have helped to significantly encourage challenges to the state and its custodians; and has promoted an unprecedented alliance between popular groups.

The new struggles for empowerment, social justice, human rights, political participation, the decentralization of decision-making; and multi-party politics cannot be stopped. The on-going changes, even in the most hard-core repressive nations like Kenya and Zaire cannot be stopped. Whatever the gains of the on-going struggles, the fact remains that:

> ...the new democratic governments, or those retained after honest elections, will be confronted with the difficult challenge of reviving stagnant economies. In most cases, they will inherit depleted treasuries, high debt repayments, declining earnings from commodity exports, low levels of private investments and increased dependence on international aid and loans...[37]

Beyond structural adjustment, beyond the positions of the IMF and the World Bank, and beyond the changes in the global system, the challenge for popular forces and their organizations in the 1990s will be to survive the pressures in the emerging global system, sustain the drive for a stronger civil society and democracy in the context of deepening systemic crisis. It is now clear, even to the most conservative forces in Africa that there are no alternatives to democratization, empowerment, accountability and the revival of the production systems of African economies. Reliance on the West and the international community will be just a secondary step in the march towards a fundametal structural transformation (rather than adjustment) of African economies. With the current state of deterioration, decay and crisis, there is reason to hope that some good will eventually come from the current state of pain and hopelessness.

CHAPTER 17

ENDNOTES

1. Adebayo Adedeji, "Development and Ethics: Putting Africa on the Road to Self-Reliant and Self-Sustaining Process of Development". Keynote address delivered at the first plenary session of the Thirty-third Annual Meeting of the African Studies Association, Baltimore, Maryland, November 1-4,1990,p.9.

2. Adotey Bing, "Salim A. Salim on the OAU and the African Agenda," Review of African Political Economy (50) (March 1991), p.63.

3. See Adebayo Adedeji,"Economic Progress: What Africa Needs" Transafrica Forum Vol.7 (2) (Summer 1990),pp.11-26.

4. Chu Okongwo, Nigeria's Minster for Budget and Planning speaking on behalf of the OAU at the Review of UNPAAERED, New York, September 3-13, 1992. Reproduced in Africa Recovery Vol. 5 (4) (December 1991).

5. Quoted from "Improved 'global governance' demanded," Africa Recovery (August 1992), p.13.

6. See World Bank,Sub-Saharan Africa: From Crisis to Sustainable Growth(World Bank,1989); Economic Commission for Africa,Economic Report on Africa 1990(Addis Ababa: ECA,1990); and Institute for African Alternatives(IFAA),Alternative Development Strategies for Africa(London: IFAA,1989).

7. M. de Larosiere, Address to ECOSOC, July 4, 1986.

8. West Africa (June 11, 1990),p.968.

9. See Giovanni Andrea Cornia, Richard Jolly, and Frances Stewart(eds.)Adjustment with a Human Face...Volumes I and II op. cit.

10. Carol Lancaster,"Economic Restructuring in Sub-Saharan Africa" Current History Vol.88 (538) (May 1989),p.213.

11. ibid.

12. See E. Harsch,"Recovery or Relapse?" Africa Report Vol.33 (6) (1988),p.57.

13.   Claude Ake,"The Present Crisis in Africa: Economic Crisis or A Crisis of the State?" in Julius O. Ihonvbere(ed.)The Political Economy of Crisis and Underdevelopment in Africa: Selected Works of Claude Ake(Lagos: JAD Publishers,1989),p.48.

14.   Economic Commission for Africa,Economic Report on Africa 1990(Addis Ababa: ECA,1990),p.VII.

15.   Adebayo Adedeji,"Development and Ethics..." op. cit.,p.6.

16.   World Bank,Sub-Saharan Africa: From Crisis to Sustainable Growth op. cit.,p.1.

17.   This sort of propaganda can be found in the World Bank's Accelerated Development in Sub-Saharan Africa: An Agenda for Action(Washington DC: World Bank,1981).

18.   Eboe Hutchful,"Structural Adjustment and Political Regimes in Africa". Mimeo, University of Toronto, 1990,p.1.

19.   ibid,p.2.

20.   See Trevor Parfitt and Stephen P. Riley,The African Debt Crisis (London Routeledge,1989).

21.   ibid

22.   ibid

23.   Eboe Hutchful, "Structural Adjustment..." op. cit.

24.   ibid

25.   See Julius O. Ihonvbere,"Structural Adjustment, the April 1990 Coup and Democratization in Nigeria," Africa Quarterly Volume 29 (3-4) (1990).

26.   See Mokwugo Okoye,"A Time of Sadness" The African Guardian(September 24, 1990) and "Five Years of Strangulation" Newbreed(Lagos) (1 October, 1990).

27.   Boutros Boutros-Ghali, New Concepts for Development Action in Africa, (New York: UN Department of Public Information, March 1993), p.2.

28. ibid

29. ibid

30. We can devote our time to only a few responses here. There are scores of responses from the setting up of the African Economic Community in Abuja in 1991, to the Lagos Plan of Action, the Kampala Declaration and so on, Africa seems to be suffering from a flood of responses to its deepening crisis.

31. See ECA, African Charter for Popular Participation in Development (Addis Ababa: ECA,1990); ECA, African Alternative Framework to Structural Adjustment Programmes (Addis Ababa: ECA,1989) and World Bank,Sub-Saharan Africa: From Crisis to Sustainable Growthop. cit.

32. World Bank, From Crisis to Sustainable Growth...op. cit.,p.XI.

33. ibid, p. 1.

34. ibid, p.21.

35. ECA,African Charter for Popular Participation in Development, op. cit.,p.26.(emphasis added). One significant difference between World Bank and ECA positions is the latter's emphasis on transformation as against adjustment.

36. Robert S. Browne,"The Continuing Debate on African Development," Transafrica Forum Volume 7 (2) (Summer 1990),p.35.

37. Africa Demos Vol. 1 (2) (January 1991), p.1.

Chapter 18
Developing Nations in the New World Order:
Alternative Research Focus for Africa

Introduction

The end of the Second World War led to the division of the world into two diabolically opposed structures that evolved into a Cold-War which lasted for over a generation. At the same time, it also led to the decolonization of various African countries. The new nations became participants in an already established international political and economic structure biased in favor of their former colonial masters.

As a direct consequence of the foregoing, African nations were marginalized within the structure of international political and economic discussions. Although the Berlin Wall (a symbol of the Cold-War) no longer exists, the African state boundaries carved out by the Europeans in the Berlin Conference of 1854-55 remains a symbol of European colonial conquests in Africa. Consequently, the end of the Cold-War which also implies the resurgence of economic issues on the high agenda of international political and economic fora is predicted to also result in the further marginalization of Africa in the new discussions. Thus, "internal" and "ethnic" tensions are unlikely to attract external or extra-continental attention or assistance in Africa except where the "national interest" of the U.S. and/or other western governments are perceived as being in danger. Secondly, given the rapid technological changes around the world, Africa's "colonial" commodities are unlikely to attract effective demand, and as a consequence, "Africa's experiment with democratic forms of government is likely to be short-lived because of the political fallacy of composition: there is an insufficiently developed bourgeoisie for such pluralism to be sustained."[1] For these reasons, the future of Africa is not so certain, at least in terms of orthodox development processes.

Given the above context, this essay will (a) explore a definition of "development" as it applies to Africa using three works that provide insights into African development; (b) examine what appears to be the principal obstacles to development in Africa; and, (c) articulate the framework of Domestic Development Emphasis (DDE) as an alternative research focus for studying and evaluating research and development policies in African countries.

The Concept of Development in Africa

In <u>Development in Theory and Practice</u> (1991), Jan Knippers Black is of the view that the term "development" has become user-friendly depending on who is defining and using the term. According to Black, "If there is a commonality among its many uses, it might be in denoting enhancement; that is, increasing value or desirability; but that leads us once again back to subjectivity."[2] Black argues that the study of international or Third World development is complicated by the diametrically opposed meanings attached to development explanations and strategies and asserts that:

> Development is a standard borne by those who would promote ... the virtues of entrepreneurship and individualism and those who would nurture community and collective concerns; by those who would pursue strategies of top-down initiative and decision-making and those who advocate a bottom-up, or grass-roots, approach; and finally, by those who would exploit and maim Mother Nature for the benefit of either business or labor in today's world, as well as by those who concern themselves with a bountiful and livable environment for future generations.[3]

The foregoing explores most aspects and purposes of "development" and relevant prevailing analytical viewpoints, and implementation strategies over the years. However, relevant to this work's focus of understanding problems in Africa, J. A. Schumpeter's definition of economic development is more instructive. Schumpeter defines economic development as "only such changes in economic life as are not forced upon it from without but arise by its own initiative from within.... Every concrete process of development finally rests upon preceding development."[4] According to Schumpeter, the key motivators of economic development are credit, entrepreneurs, leaders, capital, and the money market. In Schumpeter's definition, leaders fulfill their functions-more by will, intellect, "authority," and "personal weight" than by original ideas.[5]

Four elements of the above definition crucial to understanding development in Africa are: (1) development is not forced from outside but arises from internal initiative; (2) the process of concrete development rests upon preceding development; (3) development is not mere economic growth; and (4) leaders are the key motivators of economic development, especially in a multiethnic state. Also, in his discussion of the applicability of the above elements to the African situation, Ahmed Abubakar argues that although colonization of African countries resulted in the forestalling of any development initiatives from within, African economies were not destroyed and supplanted by modern capitalist economies. The view that economic development is not simply economic growth is a relevant proposition for this work's focus of understanding the chaotic economic situation of Africa from within.   According to Abubakar, elements such as "... attributes of will, intellect, authority, and personal weight"[6] have been mainly used by African leaders to suppress and oppress rather than to foster economic development. While Schumpeter's and Abubakar's definitions of "development" apply to Africa, these definitions can only be considered the "best" definition when expanded to include ideas for improvement in the material condition of the people.

Consequently, a definition of development relevant for Africa would involve one that includes ideas of the progressive evolution of a society towards the attainment of individual and community freedom of thought, economic and social relevance that enhance the productive capacity of Africa. Concepts which are guaranteed by popularly accepted forms of political relationships in many African countries can be institutionalized to ensure that citizens are literate, that employment is guaranteed within a reasonable degree, agricultural and community-based food production encouraged, maintained and rewarded, the development of infrastructure by the state made a pre-condition for industrialization and that citizens' participation in decision-making structures that enhance their self-worth is encouraged. Such institutionalization will result in a renewal of citizens' pride in their places of origin which in turn will result in a need for improved productive capacity for Africa and arguably a decrease in urban migration and its consequences.

Development and Exploitation - A Contrast of three authors

Relevant aspects of the works of Andre Gunder Franks' (1967a), James H. Mittleman's (1988) and Ahmad Abubakar's (1989) on development and underdevelopment are significant to understanding Africa's experiences and situation from within.

For instance, the core of Franks' argument is the idea of underdevelopment. Frank uses "underdevelopment" to reveal conditions that characterize the less-developed countries today. Subsequent analysis by Simon and Ruccio extend Frank's idea showing that these conditions of underdevelopment are not identical with those applicable in discussions of undevelopment in general.[7] Frank asserts that underdevelopment is neither original nor traditional. Maintaining a global perspective, he argues that undevelopment and underdevelopment are different concepts, and that underdevelopment is "... a reflection of the development of the capitalist system on a world scale."[8] Frank's major focus is that the structure of dependency created by international capitalism causes underdevelopment. From this viewpoint, underdevelopment expresses a particular kind of relationship of exploitation by developed, capitalist and industrialized western nations, regions or a group of nations of the underdeveloped, backward and agrarian African countries.

Frank's discussion provides insights for developing a historical framework for understanding Africa's underdevelopment. Equally significant is the relevance of his viewpoint to the explanation of some of the dynamics of Africa's relationship with the west at the end of the Cold-War. Frank's discussion of the strategies of exploitation of one nation by another through trade supports Walter Rodney's (1981) now familiar exposition on trade, unequal exchange and exploitation.[9] And, finally, Frank's argument that the more closely tied a nation is to the metropole the higher the rate of underdevelopment since the end of colonial rule meant the removal of European flags from various African countries, and the need to continue European presence resulted in the raising of European economic logos in various cities. Following Frank's argument, some of the major consequences for Africa was marginalization during the Cold-War and subsequent abandonment at the end of the Cold-War; the later is engendered by technological innovations in various industrial centers of the world. Furthermore, the end of the Cold-War will tend to resemble post World War II in the movement of private investments and foreign aid toward Europe and the former Soviet Union to the disadvantage of Africa and other Third World countries. In light of the above, Frank's work provides useful historical insights for understanding the sources of Africa's development problems.

On the other hand, in <u>Out From Underdevelopment</u>, Mittleman argues that development is blocked by an internal and external constellation of power and privilege. He insists that "development is the increasing capacity to make rational use of natural and human resources for social ends."[10] And given that rational use of human resources has not resulted in any noticeable enhancement of the well-being of the many, Mittleman argues that understanding the cornerstone of all strategies of development requires a good understanding of capital accumulation. For him, capital accumulation is critical to understanding the dynamics of the Third World as the debates in the region do not so much concern "political institutions - as the generation and allocation of capital: how to wrench limited resources from the existing units of production and channel them so as to uplift the national economy."[11] Again, given that accumulation cannot take place in the absence of production of some type, and that for humans to consume, they must produce and without production, consumption and subsequent accumulation decline to a crisis point, it becomes urgent to understand and transcend the dead ends implied by a negative implementation of this cycle for Africa.

Within this discussion of negative implementation, productivity level is equally reflected in an overall low level of education in the continent and a consequent low level of accumulation with the state as the principal agent of accumulation. The state in this monopolistic role is unchallenged largely for two reasons: most African countries have principally two social classes -- the wealthy few in alliance with the state versus the poor peasantry. The majority of the citizens are peasants, largely uneducated and literally powerless with no stakes in the state structure and its maintenance. Secondly, the semi-upwardly mobile cadre made up of mostly educated people who could potentially have a stake in the state with a possibility of mounting claims to participation in decision-making is silenced or exiled. As Mittleman points out, "to the extent that subtle forms of social control fail, outright repression is used. The armed forces are unleashed to enforce 'law and order' and to neutralize dissident groups. In an acute crisis of accumulation, the soldiers are apt to move into politics and topple the civilians who hold the reins of power."[12] Mittleman's work provides insight into Africa's development problems from two main angles. As an outside but interested observer who has lived and studied in Africa, his insight is especially useful for understanding the too often negative perception about Africa and Africans' capacity for development. His work seeks to reduce the gap in the relationship between theory and practice with respect to development in Africa. He writes,

> By now it is commonplace to note that the media and films have traditionally fostered racist images of Third World peoples: Tarzan was the strongest man and Jane had the most voluptuous breasts in the African jungle. Whites portrayed superior beings, while blacks played subordinating roles. The impression of exoticism lingers because it is a simple and convenient technique for imposing intellectual order on an unknown Africa and a veiled Orient."[13]

Given this reality, what kinds of decisions for instance would be made by a young ivy-league graduate who is yet to visit Africa or study the historical and contemporary conditions in Africa but is an employee of the State Department or the World Bank? What influences would he or she draw from? What images would inform the imagination of this young person? These are relevant questions as the development problems in Africa are not solely internal in nature. The external nexus is important especially with respect to foreign aid and debts.

Secondly, Mittleman's work gives insight to understanding the external nexus whose impact and influence on African underdevelopment remains a major confounder of Africanist researchers. To illustrate, Mittleman continues:

> Over the centuries the inherently ethical aspects of the development debate have endured. There is the story of the English administrator serving overseas in the early days of empire. He stumbled upon a 'native' lolling beside a lake and decided to do the chap a good turn. The colonizer gave the local a swift kick to the ribs, awakening him from a deep sleep, and demanded: 'Why are you idling with a dozen or so fish beside you instead of catching more?' The lackadaisical response was: 'I have caught all the fish that my family can eat today.' Unperturbed, the Englishman didactically informed his acquaintance: 'My good man, if you net another string of fish, you can sell it in the market place.' The local repeated his point: 'But we already have enough to eat.' So the English official persisted: 'With the proceeds of your sale, you can employ other fishermen.' By this time, the local was feeling quite dumbfounded. He asked: 'What then?' 'Why,' said the Englishman, 'then you can retire and sleep all day along this lovely waterfront.[14]

According to Mittleman, the situation cited here not only raises the ethical question 'development for what?' but at the same time suggests the background that informs popular and deep-seated socio-economic processes. This background refers to the problems inherent in Africa's participation within already established political and economic systems. The integration of the Third World into the world capitalist economy creates two development problems for Africa. In the first instance, Africans were invited to participate in a structure whose rules and regulations were foreign to them and consequently were often participants in their own underdevelopment. Secondly, because most of the initial discussions were conducted between European governments and later between African governments and officers of multinational corporations, individual Africans especially the peasants were either construed as cannon fodder for capitalist international accumulation or excluded. Consequently, the decolonization of African countries simply replaced one group of foreign elites with a different group of elites without a change in the status of the peasants. Thus, majority of the independent African governments continue to participate in the marginalization of their own citizens. This situation results in a lack of productive capacity and innovative energy necessary for effective development of the continent.

While Mittleman's work provides some understanding of the perception of Africa from extra-continental lenses, Ahmad Abubakar, an African economist in his Africa and the Challenge of Development: Acquiescence and Dependency versus Freedom and Development, argues that "... much of Africa's prevailing predicament can be explained no longer in terms of colonial experience but rather in terms of the wrong way the early African power elite perceived independence and the resulting way in which they managed their economies and societies."[15] Abubakar's premise is that given that colonialism was overthrown more than 25 years ago, the leadership of the various African countries are responsible for mismanaging the continent's development projects and processes. He asserts that,

> Relatively few of the educated Africans at the time of independence were highly educated. Consequently most of the educated succumbed to the psychology of inferiority imposed on the populace by the colonial rulers, with the result that anything European was perceived as superior. This perception led to the effort to ape European culture and consumption patterns, which, combined with many years of schooling, set the elite apart from the people."[16]

According to Abubakar, this psychological separation was the beginning of Africa's crisis. He maintains that development strategies for Africa were urban-biased and never people-oriented.[17] Production and import were outward-looking and catered to the taste of the elite. Thus the African food crises, according to Abubakar, is a direct result of the unreformed colonial economic structure maintained by the colonialists and later, maintained by the African elites to facilitate the production and export of raw materials to the western industrial centers at the expense of food production for Africa, especially for the peasants. Commenting on Schumpeter's definition of economic development, Abubakar maintains,

> "there is the tendency to argue that, after all, African leaders inherited economies whose development bases had been tampered with. Changes were forced from outside, consequently preceding development which would have formed

> a foundation for further development, was distorted. It is true that the two events happened. But I will argue that the disruption of the indigenous economies was not sufficient to hinder development."[18]

Abubakar advances two arguments for the above claim: (a) that the foundation of African economies were virtually intact, though imperialism and colonialism certainly imposed structures on these economies to facilitate the exploitation of labor and raw materials; and, (b) that in spite of the disruptions in the development process of some countries such as North Korea and China and without a basis for internal and concrete development, these countries have nonetheless remained models of self-reliance.

Africa's development problems are further confounded by a glaring confusion on what constitutes development. Abubakar states that,

> In Africa economic development is hardly understood in terms of building productive capacity; it is understood only in terms of material well-being.... economic development is synonymous with structures such as high-rise buildings, stadia, divided highways, expensive hotels, modern airports, teaching or specialist hospitals, ... television, and so on.

Though these things are associated with development, few people pause to ask: Is this type of development rooted in the needs of the populace? ... And where did the productive capacity that builds these structures ... come from? ... We have to import managers, technical experts, and spare parts. Since we lack the capacity to manage and maintain structures built for us, it means that we are engaging in an irrelevant type of development, a type that neither is rooted in the people nor builds productive capacity.[19]

Ahmed Abubakar's work here is useful for comprehending Africa's development problems for a number of reasons. As the views of an indigenous participant with a long-term record of involvement in various development projects, part of Abubakar's argument represent a serious symptom of a larger problem facing African economies -- a general lack engagement with the fundamental issues and the linkages between them and the development/undevelopment problem. Specifically, Abubakar's claim that though colonialism and imperialism were factors in Africa's underdevelopment that these experiences left "...African economies virtually intact,"[20] constitutes a serious misreading of both the history and consequences of Africa's encounter with the West. Although a detailed presentation of the history of that contact is beyond the scope of the present essay, consideration of viewpoint that regards time and therefore history important to development issues enables one to ask questions such as: How will Africa be compensated for her enslaved children who worked the fields and industries of the New World? Will the tons of diamonds and gold hauled out of Mozambique and Ghana respectively be returned to their rightful owners? Questions like these pondered in line with Abubakar's claim will result in the development of research projects from an Africa-based viewpoint.

Secondly, Abubakar's argument that China and North Korea represent models of self-reliance is not grounded on evidence. In the first instance, China does not lack a basis for internal and concrete development as claimed by Abubakar. Also, North Korea's success (though questionable) is hardly a model of self-reliance given that country's economic and military linkages with China and Russia. However, Ahmed Abubakar is right that these countries did something right -- they managed, somewhat successfully, the penetration of foreign economic influences in their societies. But, he seems to misunderstand the bases on which the leaders of these two countries were able to curtail foreign intrusion. Africa was colonized and imperialized while China and North Korea experienced only the later. Significant to this observation of the different strategies of domination is the difference in the processes of domination: that colonization is complete occupation of a territory with the power to dictate the rules by which everyone else participates, while imperialism is capitalist economic exploitation -- in this case of the Third World. Misunderstanding and/or ignoring the foregoing basic difference can only lead to wrong and inadequate policy prescriptions for Africa.

Beyond his discussion of the lack of self-reliance strategies, Abubakar explores Africa's inability to build self-sustained productive capacity. For instance, he praises Japan's successful economic development strategies despite a lack of natural resources. He writes that in Japan,

> Agricultural land is limited and minerals are almost completely absent. Japan imports 100 percent of its uranium, nickel, and bauxite; 97.7 percent of its crude oil; 87 percent of its iron ore; 78.5 percent of its coal; 75.6 percent of its copper; and 04.6 percent of its lead. But Japan ranks among the seven industrial powers of the world, the only non-Western country to enjoy this privilege.[21]

From Abubakar's point of view, Japan's success is a direct result of sheer hard thinking and hard work which combined have led Japan to economic liberation which African countries can and should emulate. This recommendation is contradicted when he later observes that "The struggle between the status quo and change will continue for a long time and will continue to assume a more violent form unless the *privileged part of the world* is ready to make some concessions.... Africa is the weakest of all continents ... [and] the choice before Africa is clear: it is either development or dependency."[22]

I contend here that a conclusion that takes into consideration the dynamic of the international political system to which both Japan and Africa are a part will no doubt offer a more plausible comparison between both regions. Japan's privileged position in the Cold-War bipolar structure and the fact that Japan is a homogenous country with an industrial base dating back to the Tokugawa era suggests a linkage between domestic and external structures as a significant explanation. Thus, comparing Japan's success with Africa's failures without exploring the extent to which both have the freedom to design independent strategies of economic development within the constraints inherent in the international system will, at best, produce inconclusive results.

From the above it seems clear that a more than adequate understanding of the principal obstacles to development in Africa is required if progress is to be made in the 21st Century. Such an approach will result from concerted and sustained efforts by African scholars and nations in their quest to study and/or design implementable strategies of economic development. Thus, understanding the linkages between the international political/economic structures and the extent to which African countries can collectively or individually transcend the international system's constraints becomes urgent.

From the beginning, most leaders of independent African nations have opted for a collective rather than an individual approach to the transcendence of the problems of underdevelopment. According to President Julius Nyerere, for example, "We the countries of the Third World, ... are weak separately, we could have strength if we acted in unity."[23] However, historical trends suggest that the response of independent African nations to united action at the continental level is an indication that basic problems need to be resolved first at the individual countries' levels. For example, the OAU refuses to be involved in internal disputes like civil wars in member nation's territory such that over a million people died in the Nigerian civil war between 1967-1970. The OAU also failed to respond to the famine crisis in Ethiopia that claimed several thousand lives and resulted in the eventual collapse of Emperor Haile Selassie's regime in 1974. The observation here is that the parameters for cooperation remain undefined. Perhaps military/defense issues are more intractable to deal with, but the same lack of vision and action surrounds efforts at economic cooperation. For example, "The Lagos Plan of Action (PLA) for the Economic Development of Africa, 1980-2000 was the first comprehensive, continent-wide effort to formulate an African-led policy strategy for the economic development of the continent. It was the first significant articulation, moreover, of the fundamental need to address African problems via a long-term strategy, based primarily on self-reliant objectives."[24] However, although the Lagos Plan of Action was signed in April 1980 by fifty African Heads of State and Government it has not realized any progress. Instead, Africa in the 1980's and 1990's has slipped further into poverty, disease and political chaos.

What explains the failure of this continent-wide effort by the governments of the various states? Robert J. Cummings, Professor of African Economic History at Howard University, asserts that "External factors such as international terms of trade, debt, externally designed and imposed adjustment programs; and environmental factors such as drought,"[25] offer part explanation for the failure of the LPA. Cummings is of the view that ineffective governmental policies are equally responsible. For example, while many African governments have ignored domestic sources of finance for economic development, they have relied on foreign aid from the same sources that seem to constrain their development. The practice of relying on the developed countries is equally implied in the heads of states' plan to finance the LPA. "The cost of the LPA was estimated at $128.1 billion over 1986-1990 period. The LPA signatories committed their nations to finance $82.5 billion or 64.4 percent of the total cost through the mobilization of domestic resources."[26] The balance was optimistically expected to come from the Northern industrialized countries. And given, that every nation in Africa is indebted to the International Financial Institutions -- a symbol of a lack of domestic resources -- how did these nations intend to raise their share of the cost? One can only speculate on the basis of past and current practice that this portion of the costs would be raised through borrowing from the North which will further depreciate any attempt at enhancing Africa's productive capacity for development. As one critic of the Lagos Plan of Action sees it,

...the Plan envisages a massive transfer of financial resources from these [economic northern] countries, a massive transfer of technology and know-how at the least cost of African states and finally a free access to developed countries' markets for the "industrial products" emanating from Africa. These objectives have so far eluded African states within the EEC-ACP framework and within the bilateral agreements reached between the African states and this group of countries. The expression of such optimism by the African blueprint is, therefore, an exercise in self-deception and grossly exaggerates the factor of "benevolence" within the dominant international mode of production and exchange.[27]

From the above, it can plausibly be concluded that obstacles to African development may indeed reside mostly in Africa -- especially within the leadership that seems to lack the initiative to explore new ways of understanding the problems as a first step to finding relevant solutions. It becomes possible here to revisit the prospects of Mittleman's 'native' fisherman referred to above. It seems plausible to infer, given the current evidence of failed leadership in Africa, the incidental nature of the African/colonial discourse (from the African perspective), resulted in the establishment of an African leadership that was obliged to pursue entrepreneurial manifestations without understanding the base -- note that historically, the English 'gentleman' neither sits down with the 'native' on the river bank nor walks with him to the promised glory of the market place.

On the part of scholars, there is no consensus on how the problem came about or how to transcend it. Some perspectives blame the repressive governments in Africa without offering any viable explanation as to why the state has been and remains an instrument of repression. Still others, join the World Bank and the prophets of the neoclassical school of thought in blaming government intervention in the economies and protectionism as obstacles to development. The critics however, are yet to account for the role of the General Agreement on Trade and Tariff and the Most Favored Nation status agreements among the industrialized countries as government intervention in the economy. Instead, the Newly Industrialized Countries (NICs) are presented as evidence of the success of market economies and enjoin African states to become more integrated as a way out of underdevelopment. Yet another group of researchers blame the Multinational Corporations for capital repatriation as the reason for a lack of capital accumulation in Africa. Revisiting Schumpeter and Abubakar adds another dimension to the problem -- both argue that Africa lacks effective and visionary leadership sufficient to plan, execute and preside over economic and political liberation of the continent. However, while some scholars (Kennedy 1988, Abubakar 1989 and Cummings 1992) have identified leadership as the problem, they have so far failed to present clear analyses of the fundamental reasons underlying African leaders' lack of will to change.

In A Man of the People, Chinua Achebe, a leading African novelist captures an essential aspect of the problem. In his discussion of Chief Nanga's lack of vision within his office as the Minister of Culture, Achebe offers the following insights as possible explanations to the relationships between the problem and the apparent inertia within the leadership:

> We ignore man's basic nature if we say, as some critics do, that
> because a man like Nanga had risen overnight from poverty and

insignificance to his present opulence he could be persuaded without much trouble to give it up again and return to his original state.

A man who has just come in from the rain and dried his body and put on dry clothes is more reluctant to go out again than another who has been indoors all the time. The trouble with our new nation ... was that none of us had been indoors long enough to be able to say 'To hell with it.' We had all been in the rain together until yesterday. Then a handful of us - the smart and the lucky and hardly ever the best - had scrambled for the one shelter our former rulers left, and had taken it over and barricaded themselves in. And from within they sought to persuade the rest through numerous loudspeakers, that the first phase of the struggle had been won and that the next phase - the extension of our house - was even more important and called for new and original tactics; it required that all argument should cease and the whole people speak with one voice and that any more dissent and argument outside the door of the shelter would subvert and bring down the whole house.[28]

Achebe's presentation of Chief Nanga's inability or reluctance to show leadership skills is quoted in detail because it illustrates the misappropriation of power evidenced in the activities of post colonial politicians in Africa who made haste to occupy the offices left by the colonizers. According to Achebe, the masses were important as tools for gaining independence. However, after independence, the new leadership not only abandoned the idea of Africa for Africans, but immediately set out to use the only organized institutions like the military to silence critics.   While, the new leaders learned the consumption patterns of their former colonizers, they failed to learn the capitalist accumulation patterns and the expansionist dynamics of its productive base. Though writing specifically about Nigeria, Achebe is addressing a significant part of the problem in Africa when he asserts that,

The trouble with Nigeria is simply and squarely a failure of leadership. There is nothing basically wrong with the Nigerian character. There is nothing wrong with the Nigerian land or climate or water or air or anything else. The Nigerian problem is the unwillingness or inability of its leaders to rise to the responsibility, to the challenge of personal example which are the hallmarks of true leadership.[29]

Colonial administration, the basis for most African leadership strategies in Africa, can best be described as authoritarian rule by bureaucrats. In conjunction with the problem of leadership, certain aspects of Africa's colonial structure remains a hinderance to any attempt at presenting a viable development alternative. Such structures include but are not limited to the remuneration system which favored bureaucrats over farmers resulting in the shifting of the focus of most Africans from agriculture and farming for consumption to the search for prospects in the public sector, specifically government jobs. Another example involves the exportation of raw materials from Africa and the consequent shifting of Africans' focus to finished and imported goods. This is part of the unarticulated consequence envisaged by Mittleman's 'native' fisherman when he asks the English administrator the question, "What then?" Part of the reason the current problem exists is because African leaders implemented the suggestion to participate in the international market place without exploring the prospects for existing African realities. Thus, a re-orientation in terms of structures which tended to exclude Africa and Africans during and after the colonial period will move the continent in a significant direction to encouraging professional and job diversification.

However, the fundamental problem in Africa which cannot be ignored for much longer is the lack of committed leadership with the will to promote harmony and economic/political development. And, to the extent that the citizens continue to starve in the midst of the opulence and wealth of the few, the general tendency is in the direction of anarchy or at best massive revolutions against autocracy. Although the wind of change in post-colonial Africa seems to have favored those "in the shelter," the heat emanating from the end of the Cold-War seems vented in the opposite direction.

Although the problems of development in Africa are similar to those of other non-western countries, the approaches to solving the problems and the results obtained are significantly influenced by differences in location in relationship to the west, and the historical impact of colonialism. Though resource-rich, Africa is located outside of the technologically funded regions of Asia and Europe. Also, though most leaders of third world countries (especially those in Asia) have encouraged and enhanced the development capacities of their citizens, those in Africa appear to have stifled the same through glaringly nonchalant attitudes to the human condition on the continent. While the Asian regimes have had a long history of political stability, the reverse has been the case for Africa. The question becomes: What form has stability taken on the African continent since colonization? Given the noted instability of African nations' political encounters and projects, what aspect of African experience has made it possible for Africa and Africans to continue participation within international political and economic systems? Thus, the significant task for scholars and policy-makers in Africa is the extent to which development policies in Africa can be refocused from within at the end of the century.

Alternative Development Focus and its Implications for Africa

The end of the Cold War offers an opportunity to re-evaluate the relevance of the various theoretical claims for the successes and failures of development projects in the Third World, especially Africa. My emphasis is on a careful examination of previous research programs and conclusions which seem to have stalled or failed and to compare them with programs that have produced relevant success.

In his Forms of Explanation: Rethinking the Questions in Social Theory (1981), Alan Garfinkel discusses success and its relationship to individual characteristics and societal structure. Nevertheless, the forms of explanations he offers are useful for understanding the development of an alternative research focus/program in Africa's foreign relations and especially African strategies for political and economic development and stability. He shows that in order to arrive at a plausible answer or at least one as close to that as possible, questions need to take existing conditions, such as structural presuppositions, into consideration. Employing the use of generalized counterfactuals he argues that, "... every explanation has presuppositions which serve to limit the alternatives to the phenomenon being explained.... [And that] in some cases the presuppositions take a special form."[30]

The structural presuppositions relevant to the role of the state need to be explored consistent to the African experience. For instance, while Peter Evans (1979), Theda Skocpol et. al. (1985), and others argue that a triumvirate relationship between the state, international capitalists and the local bourgeoises are preconditions to development in Latin America and Asia, the same may not be true for Africa. Consequently, it is necessary to explore the relationship between the internal structure of each African country and how those structures facilitate or constrain political and economic development at the national or continental level. It is necessary to state here that all the discussion here is premised on the re-incorporation of African women as full participants in the development processes from decision-making to implementation of projects. To facilitate the discussion, I will label this approach the Domestic Development Emphasis (DDE). Within this project, the new emphasis for Africanist researchers would be to understand the role of the state relevant to African experience of previous, current and future development projects.

Understanding the role of the state within African nations' political and economic realities is significant here because the state as it currently exists is mostly perceived as a colonial invention. My contention here is that while the state as a concept in international political discourses is perceived as naturally emerging from internal social transformations in Europe, Asia and Latin America, in the case of Africa, it has been seen as an imposition for capitalist expropriation of resources to the metropole.   To that extent, there is no perceived connection between the role of the state and other systems within the African nation.   Thus, even though African countries are now independent, the colonial institutions, especially, the military and the state structures are still carrying out their colonial functions of wealth expropriation -- only this time for the benefit of the ruling class.   Furthermore, while other multi-ethnic countries such as the United States are held together by the state structures and arguably a common language, the state in Africa remains an instrument for disuniting the ethnic groups in African countries and as an agent for private/ethnic wealth accumulation.

Although ethnicity and ethnic groups remain important for examining important issues, at the continental level, Africa is the only regional/continental block that lacks either a common language or religious unity.   Latin American countries with the exception of Brazil are unified by a common language -- Spanish.   In addition, Catholicism forms the central religion of the region.   Similarly, the Middle East is unified by two potent nationalistic factors -- Islam and the Arabic language.   Although, the Asian countries vary from ethnically homogeneous countries like South Korea to pluralistic ones like Malaysia, collectively, the Asian countries were brought under single states due largely to the influence of colonization and benevolent dictatorships.   In contrast, African countries -- especially south of the Sahara are linguistically, ethnically and religiously different.   Language as a *sine qua non* to development in Africa south of the Sahara is an issue that can no longer be ignored.   Development in Africa can be facilitated through the refocusing of research to examine the relevance of adopting specific African languages to serve both as means to mutual understanding and as media for instruction/commerce within and between African countries.   The more Africans can learn each others' languages (which unarguably is the source of epistemological world views in any culture), the less tension and the more likely differences can be resolved and energies focused on development.   For it is inconceivable that after several decades of independence the languages of instruction in schools, diplomacy within the OAU and of cultural exchanges in Africa remain the languages of the colonizers.   Only in Africa are Europeans not required to make any efforts to understand an indigenous language.   It is unlikely that Japan and South Korea will have attained their current economic significance if the Western countries were able to impose English or Dutch as the language of diplomacy and commerce within those countries.

Furthermore, the relationships between economic development and tax structure in African countries need to be explored. Currently, African countries are more vulnerable to external shocks resulting from decline in oil revenues and other raw materials than their European counterparts.[31] A research focus on this issue-area will yield alternative income-generating strategies, especially tax collecting mechanisms that will significantly cushion various African countries against external price shocks. A new basis for generating revenue insulated from external shocks will tend to increase African countries' political bargaining strengths in other issue-areas beyond the control of African countries.

Agricultural production constitutes perhaps the most significant aspect of African development that needs refocusing. It is becoming fashionable in academic circles to note that without Africans working the land, the North America would not have developed so quickly to become the currently powerful United States of America. If Africans had the strength and knowledge first of the African homeland enough to work under stress in other territories, it is plausible to expect contemporary Africans to work the continental homeland from an African initiative.

In light of the foregoing, agricultural production needs to be the basis for everything else in Africa. For if it made America great, the least we can expect from agricultural production in Africa is its ability to feed Africans. This means that Domestic Development Emphasis should be anchored in agricultural production. Given previous attention to Import Substitution Industrialization and Export Led Industrialization, one can plausibly argue that African governments and scholars have viewed agriculture as the least important segment for development and consequently those that are mostly engaged in agriculture -- women have had to be neglected. Refocusing development research in this area means that African women from all areas must be participants at all levels.

In the final analysis, re-thinking development in Africa must reveal the structural presuppositions including the questions asked and the sources of evidence for the answers they provide. Instead of asking why development has failed in Africa, I suggest that an alternative question should be: what would have been the fate of African countries without the western/colonial encounter and interference? This question will allow for a shift in research focus away from prevailing dependency and interdependency analytical frameworks to a systematic evaluation of Africa from an African epistemological perspective.

CHAPTER 18

ENDNOTES

1.   Julius E. Nyang'oro and Timothy M. Shaw, eds. *Beyond Structural Adjustment in Africa: The Political Economy of Sustainable and Democratic Development.* (New York, 1992), pp. 6-7.

2.   Jan Knippers Black, *Development in Theory and Practice.* (Boulder, 1991), pp. 15-16.

3.   Ibid. p. 15.

4.   Cited in Ahmed Abubakar, *Africa and the Challenge of Development: Acquiescence and Dependency versus Freedom and Development.* (New York, 1989), p.6.

5.   Ibid.

6.   Ibid. p. 7.

7.   Lawrence H. Simon and David Ruccio, "A Methodological Analysis of Dependency Theory: Explanation in Andre Gunder Frank," *World Development* Vol. 14 No. 2, (1986), p. 196.

8.   Andre Gunder Frank, "The Development of Underdevelopment," in *Latin America: Underdevelopment or Revolution.* (New York, 1969), p. 3. See also Simon and Ruccio, op. cit. and Ronald Chilcote (1981), pp. 290-291.

9.   Walter Rodney, *How Europe Underdeveloped Africa.* (Washington, 1981), p. 22.

10.   Ibid.

11.   Ibid. p. 71.

12.   Ibid. p. 83.

13.   Ibid. pp. 8-9.

14.   Ibid. p. 21.

15.   Ahmed Abubakar, *Africa and the Challenge of Development.* (New York, 1989), p. 1.

16.   Ibid. p. 2.

17.   Ibid.

18.   Ibid. p. 7.

19.   Ibid. pp. 9-10.

20.   Ibid. p. 7.

21.   Ibid. p. 9.

22.   Ibid. p. 121.

23.   Cited in Ahmed Abubakar (1989), p. 53.

24.   Robert J. Cummings, "A Historical Perspective on the Lagos Plan of Action," in Julius Nyang'oro and Timothy Shaw, eds., *Beyond Structural Adjustment in Africa.* (New York, 1992), pp. 29-47.

25.   Ibid. p. 29.

26.   Ibid. p. 42.

27.   Cited in Julius Nyang'oro and Timothy Shaw (1992), p. 42.

28.   Chinua Achebe, *A Man of the People: A Novel of Political Unrest in a New Nation.* (New York, 1967), pp. 34-35. See also James Mittleman, (1988), pp. 84-85.

29.   Chinua Achebe, *The Trouble with Nigeria.* (London, 1983), p. 1.

30.   Alan Garfinkel, *Forms of Explanation: Rethinking The Questions in Social Theory.* (New Haven, 1981), p. 108.

31.   See for example, Stephen Krasner, *Structural Conflict: The Third World Against Global Liberalism.* (Berkeley: University of California Press, 1985).

CONCLUSION?

This is not a concluding chapter for this edition. I believe any rigorous examination of the fundamental issues of political/economic life in Africa (anywhere for that matter) will always be inconclusive. It is as true for the African political economy as it is for any serious intellectual inquiry that one can never possess the final answers. It is my firm belief that those who think they do are those who do not understand the questions. Of course, one can answer certain questions with certainty, as some authors in this book have attempted to do. But usually such questions are trivial. The most important questions, such as those raised in this edition, are likely to be insoluble.

This must be so for three reasons. First, no one has the absolute wisdom to discover the ultimate answers. Like so many unknown African philosophers, we must confess that because we are not divine, we must search for truth without ever fully possessing it. But the pursuit itself, I believe, is valuable in itself. Although deprived of absolute knowledge, we can still gain some limited understanding of the questions. Through studying the many forgotten greatest books from greatest African minds, we can learn how to weigh the plausibility of competing arguments. I am not thinking of competing arguments in a binary sense, rather as Marimba Ani, in her seminal work, **Yurugu**, reminded us in morphosyosisl sense.

Second, our political, social, cultural and economic knowledge about Africa, I contend, is too complex to be explained in simple formulations. By nature, in general, human beings strive for diverse and conflicting ends. Therefore, we can never arrange political and economic life to fulfill all of Africa's natural needs and capacities. We must rank what often seem to equally worthy ends. In understanding the necessity for such choices, we gain a tragic insight into the current political, economic and social condition in Africa.

We should not become discouraged, however, when we are not certain of difficult questions. By relentlessly posing questions to ourselves and to others, by refusing to settle for easy answers, we must strive to free Africa and Africans from illusions. We must also devote ourselves to questioning in the tradition of great African minds, if we seek the dignity of living without self-deception. Only as long as we are thinking can we be fully awake from our thousands of years of sleep, and thus fully alive, and reclaim our alienated self.

deception. Only as long as we are thinking can we be fully awake from our thousands of years of sleep, and thus fully alive, and reclaim our alienated self.

Of course, a political regime must first secure the material needs of life of its community -- which is what this study is all about. But it must also nurture the mind and the spirit if life is to be worth living. Although any political regime can never satisfy our deepest yearnings for meaning and purpose in our lives, it can at least accommodate our natural need to explore with one another the mystery of what it means to be a human being. Tragically, no present political regime in Africa can honestly claim to at least achieve this minimum requirement. Rather than fostering the pursuit of the good life, it seems, political life in Africa impedes that pursuit.

Third, our knowledge of Africa's history, political economy and traditions are inadequate, since our knowledge of them is linked with the dominant political-economy paradigm. Delinking the African history and tradition from the dominant political and economic paradigms is even more problematic, mainly because we live in a contemporary international political and economic order/disorder in which there is a proliferation not only of research paradigms in the dominant academic analysis of development, but more generally, a proliferation of myths of the origin of development. The Hegelian trek to universality still echoes as "progress," "development," or "modernization." This kind of mindset helps identify those who have "progressed" or "modernized" to be distinguished from those who have not. Under these criteria, it is all too often the industrialized Western countries (IWC) who have progressed, modernized and developed, and it is the non-industrialized, non-Western countries (NINW) who have not.

Contemporary claims about intellectual tradition in general are caught between an awareness that the IWC's dominant myths of origin, namely, all those stories of a move from backward to advanced, from passionate to rational, from barbarism to enlightenment, from feudalism to capitalism, and so on, harbor embarrassing subtexts (such as ethnocentricism and racism), and the realization that these stories still inform the most basic categories through which we understand and act in contemporary order/disorder; development/underdevelopment. Thus, as one scholar astutely remarked, the term "development" now demands quotation marks, in order to distance accounts of what is going on in particular societies from the evolutionary teleology with which the term is indelibly associated. Caught in this way, contemporary African development thought has become embroiled in far-reaching debates about modernity and the promises of enlightenment.

If we have learned anything at all from the various readings offered here, issues about political, economic and social "development" and the strategy to achieve them, it is that empirical (or rationalist) theory, or development policy analysis, should not be arbitrarily isolated from the indigenous societies' philosophical assumptions (and traditions). In study after study on Africa, including this one, the indigenous philosophical values are simply drowned out by loud appeals or claims to "objectivity," or "reality," or "facts," or "rationality," or "universality," Often, these appeals are entwined in the legitimizing of the legacy of colonialism manifested in the domination of the dominant development paradigms. This is precisely why I called, in my piece, for a deconstruction of the dominant paradigms.

The new colonialism knows no limits. Expendable populations will be expended. National sacrifice areas will be sacrificed. There is no sanctuary. The new colonialism is like nuclear radiation; what it does can never be undone. Left to its own dynamics, to run its course, it will spread across the planet like the cancer it is. The place to end it is where it has taken root, on the African land where it has divulged its inner nature.

And the time to end it is now.

Mulugeta Agonafer

BIOGRAPHY

Mulugeta Agonafer, Ph.D., is currently an Assistant Professor of Human Services at Springfield College, Springfield, Massachusetts.

Dr. Agonafer received his early education from Tafari Makonnen High School in Addis Ababa, Ethiopia. He immigrated to the Untied States in 1973 and attended Indiana University, Indiana, where he earned his B.A. in Political Science and his second Bachelor's degree in Electrical Engineering Technology from Purdue University, Indiana.

He earned his Master's degree in Political Science from Western Washington university, Bellingham, Washington, and a doctorate in International Relations, Comparative Government and Political Economy from the University of Massachusetts, Amherst.

Dr. Agonafer has been a full-time instructor at Penn State University for four years before relocating to Alexandria, Virginia, where he continued to teach at Strayer College while he was working on his book, "Contending Theories of Development..." at the Library of Congress. Prior to his teaching experiences, he had been a trainer to a developmentally challenged clientele at what was then called Fort Wayne State School in Fort Wayne, Indiana. His background prior to immigrating to the United States included serving as a department head while teaching full-time at a comprehensive high school in Jimma, Keffa Province, Ethiopia. In addition, he had also been training Peace Corps in the Ethiopian language, culture, and teaching methods with scarce resources during summer seasons in Ethiopia.

Dr. Agonafer has published articles on Africa and has made numerous presentations at academic conferences in various parts of the United States. He had also conducted numerous workshops which included African-Americans and Multinational Corporations, African-Americans in International Politics, African Women and International Organizations, African and African-American Economic Development, and Africans and African-Americans in the Contemporary International Order/Disorder.

INDEX